W9-DFN-758

AT THE END
OF THE CENTURY

ONE HUNDRED YEARS OF ARCHITECTURE

Hiroshi Sugimoto, Church of the Light, Ibaraki, Osaka, 1997 (Architect: Tadao Ando, 1989)

AT THE END OF THE CENTURY

ONE HUNDRED YEARS OF ARCHITECTURE

Organized by
Richard Koshalek and Elizabeth A. T. Smith

Edited by Russell Ferguson

with essays by
Zeynep Çelik
Jean-Louis Cohen
Beatriz Colomina
Jorge Francisco Liernur
Elizabeth A.T. Smith
Anthony Vidler
Hajime Yatsuka

The Museum of Contemporary Art, Los Angeles
Harry N. Abrams, Inc., Publishers

This publication accompanies the exhibition "At the End of the Century: One Hundred Years of Architecture," organized by Richard Koshalek and Elizabeth A.T. Smith for The Museum of Contemporary Art, Los Angeles.

"At the End of the Century: One Hundred Years of Architecture" has been made possible by Ford Motor Company.

Significant additional support has been provided by The Ralph M. Parsons Foundation; The Ron Burkle Endowment for Architecture and Design Programs; The Japan Foundation; Peter B. Lewis; Lenore S. and Bernard A. Greenberg; Maeda Corporation; Mori Building Company, Ltd.; and the Graham Foundation for Advanced Studies in the Fine Arts.

Taisei Corporation, Kajima Corporation, Obayashi Corporation, Takenaka Corporation, Shimizu Corporation, and Dentsu Inc. have also generously contributed to the exhibition.

EXHIBITION TOUR
Museum of Contemporary Art, Tokyo; Colegio de San Ildefonso, Mexico City; Ludwig Museum / Josef-Haubrich-Kunsthalle, Cologne; Fundacão Bienal de São Paulo, Brazil; The Geffen Contemporary at MOCA, Los Angeles; Solomon R. Guggenheim Museum, New York.

Editor: Russell Ferguson
Assistant Editor: Stephanie Emerson
Editorial Assistant: Jane Hyun
Photo research: Dana Hutt
Designer: Catherine Lorenz
Printed and bound by Toppan, Japan

250 South Grand Avenue, Los Angeles, California 90012
Clothbound edition published in 1998 by Harry N. Abrams, Incorporated, New York

Library of Congress Cataloging-in-Publication Data
Richard Koshalek and Elizabeth A.T. Smith.
At the end of the century: one hundred years of architecture / Richard Koshalek and Elizabeth A.T. Smith; with essays by Zeynep Çelik, Jean-Louis Cohen, Beatriz Colomina, Jorge Francisco Liernur, Elizabeth A. T. Smith, Anthony Vidler, Hajime Yatsuka.
p. cm.
Exhibition presented at The Museum of Contemporary Art, Los Angeles, 27 February - 25 June 2000.
Includes bibliographical references.
ISBN 0-914357-55-7 (MOCA pbk. : alk. paper)/ISBN 0-8109-1986-9 (Abrams cloth)
1. --Exhibitions. 2. I.
II. Museum of Contemporary Art (Los Angeles, Calif.) III. Title.
N 2000

CONTENTS

Luis Barragán, Barragán House,
Tacubaya, Mexico City, 1947.
Photo by Alberto Moreno

SPONSOR'S FOREWORD

Alex Trotman
Chairman and Chief Executive Officer
Ford Motor Company

"At the End of the Century: One Hundred Years of Architecture" offers audiences an opportunity to reflect on the role architecture and urban planning play in our world. It weaves the viewpoints of international scholars and historians across the decades, so that viewers will have a clearer appreciation of the past and a deeper understanding of the future.

As Ford Motor Company approaches its own centennial, it is our hope that this worldwide exhibition of the most outstanding architectural works, ideas, and directions of our century will stimulate a new dialogue for the future.

Through research and development of innovative technologies, Ford is committed to the creation of automotive products which meet all the technical and environmental challenges of the twenty-first century.

We hope you enjoy the exhibition.

Charles and Ray Eames, Eames House, Pacific Palisades, California, 1945-49. Photo by Julius Shulman

FOREWORD

Richard Koshalek

"At the End of the Century: One Hundred Years of Architecture" is the latest in a series of singular architecture exhibitions organized by MOCA that have garnered national and international acclaim. Beginning with our commissioning of the museum's two buildings by Frank O. Gehry and Arata Isozaki, MOCA has developed its own unparalleled program of exhibitions during the course of the past decade. These include major exhibitions such as "Blueprints for Modern Living: History and Legacy of the Case Study Houses", "Arata Isozaki", "The Architecture of Louis I. Kahn", and "Urban Revisions: Current Projects for the Public Realm", the latter two of which toured internationally to cities in Europe, Asia, and North America. To date, MOCA has also organized several smaller but no less significant individual projects with architects Frank Israel— "Out of Order: Franklin D. Israel"—Wolf D. Prix—"Paradise Cage: Kiki Smith and Coop Himmelb(l)au"—and Frank Gehry—"The Architecture of Disney Hall". In addition to highlighting architecture as a contemporary artistic discipline, these projects—and in particular, the Case Study and Disney Hall exhibitions—have underscored MOCA's commitment to architectural excellence in our community.

Surveying the global terrain of twentieth-century architecture and urbanism from the vantage point of the turn into the next millennium, "At the End of the Century: One Hundred Years of Architecture" clearly surpasses MOCA's previous efforts in terms of scope and ambition. It also has posed an enormous challenge in terms of structuring the conceptual framework for such a vast and far-reaching body of material to which widely differing points of view can be brought to bear. Of utmost value has been the long-term collaboration between our museum's curatorial team and the scholar/advisors whose contributions throughout the research and organizational process have shaped the project's structure and content. This ongoing relationship has enabled us to incorporate the highest standards of scholarship within a presentation that is not only of compelling interest to the academic and professional communities, but most importantly, enlightening to and engaging for the non-specialist visitor.

Keeping architecture and design at the forefront of public awareness is of crucial significance to the health and vitality of our civic realm. One of the aims of this exhibition, which is oriented to the general public in different contexts and cultures, is to provide a basis for increased awareness of some of the major architectural works that are being created in our own time and recognition of the enhancement that such works bring to the social, cultural, and economic life of diverse peoples and places.

Another of the foremost aims of the project, organized by a contemporary art institution, is to underscore the vitality and significance of architecture as a contemporary art form. Consistently exploratory, both in terms of formal and technical innovation and as a reflection of important cultural and social tendencies, architecture can embody—or challenge—our most deep-seated values and aspirations. Its physicality and functionality enhance, rather than diminish, architecture's capacity to communicate ideas that can be discerned by a broad public. In the hands of the most talented architects, whether they are formal innovators (such as Le Corbusier in the early and middle years of the century) or skilled interpreters of political and social agendas (such as Albert Speer and his grandiose monuments for Hitler in the 1930s), a broad variety of ideas with powerful cultural implications are given palpable form, often with dramatic impact.

"At the End of the Century: One Hundred Years of Architecuture" posits a history through which such developments can be traced and understood. Yet despite the size and scope of the exhibition, it is not exhaustive, nor does it encompass all the canonical works of architecture that might be expected in a more conventional survey. Instead, it offers a way to consider the present by examining key developments of the past, and suggests implications for the future in terms of the power of architecture and urbanism to shape and reflect our cultures and ways of life.

In Los Angeles, key figures have helped shape MOCA's identity as a leading presenter of architecture and design programming, and as a staunch advocate for the role of architecture in the civic life of the city. MOCA Trustee Ronald W. Burkle's establishment in 1997 of an endowment for architecture and design has ensured the ongoing presence of this programming at MOCA, and the further growth of the museum's reputation in this regard. Burkle's vision represents a sustained commitment to architecture and design at MOCA, and for this we are extremely grateful.

MOCA's former Chairman, Frederick M. Nicholas, has consistently championed and supported our efforts, not only in architecture, but in numerous other exhibitions and aspects of our institution's functioning and growth. His inspired leadership and generosity of spirit continue to be of inestimable importance to MOCA's position in the worlds of contemporary art and architecture, as well as its presence in the sphere of Los Angeles' cultural institutions. Of special note as well is Nicholas's early leadership in the Walt Disney Concert Hall project. His tireless efforts to enable Frank Gehry's innovative concept to be realized laid the groundwork for a major cultural and architectural landmark for Los Angeles.

To celebrate and honor his matchless commitment to MOCA, the discipline of architecture, and this exhibition, therefore, it gives me the greatest pleasure to dedicate "At the End of the Century: One Hundred Years of Architecture" and the accompanying publication to Frederick M. Nicholas.

Adolf Loos, Moller House, Vienna, 1928. Graphische Sammlung Albertina, Vienna

Lewis Hine, Empire State Building under Construction, c. 1929 Museum of the City of New York

ACKNOWLEDGMENTS

Richard Koshalek and Elizabeth A.T. Smith

A project of this scope and scale could not have been accomplished without the participation of many individuals who have played key roles in its realization over the course of more than five years. MOCA colleagues and project staff, advisors, consultants in an array of areas including research, exhibition design, media and technology, modelmaking, and translation, as well as lenders, funders, volunteers, and numerous others who have contributed advice, direction, and concrete assistance deserve our deepest gratitude for helping to bring this exhibition and book to fruition.

We extend our foremost thanks to MOCA's Board of Trustees, our colleagues, and the team of project staff that has assiduously worked to execute the project's myriad and challenging components. Kathleen S. Bartels, Assistant Director, expertly coordinated the complex tour arrangements and led the extensive press and media relations for the exhibition, while providing gracious and generous direction throughout the organizational process, particularly during its final stages. Erica Clark, Director of Development, spearheaded the numerous long-range efforts necessary to receive funding for the exhibition, and helped secure key loans from France. John Bowsher, Exhibitions Production Manager, assisted by Zazu Faure, Exhibitions Production Assistant, and the MOCA exhibition technicians, thoughtfully and carefully directed the physical presentation and technical requirements of the exhibition, coordinating with the exhibition designer and many consultants to customize the installation to the vastly differing spaces of each of the host venues. Robert Hollister, Registrar, assisted by Rosanna Hemerick, Registrarial Associate, creatively met the challenges of managing complex requirements for transportation and care of an unprecedented number of objects with the highest standards of professionalism as well as a welcome spirit of adventure and good humor. Russell Ferguson, Editor and Associate Curator, and Stephanie Emerson, Editor, assisted by Jane Hyun, Editorial Secretary, directed the realization of this publication to reflect both groundbreaking scholarship and the highest quality of design. As a member of the project team from the beginning, Ferguson also made numerous insightful contributions to the exhibition's curatorial focus and content, ranging from identifying advisors to selecting objects for the exhibition checklist to commissioning new photography for the book and exhibition.

To the project staff for the exhibition, we extend our deepest appreciation and recognition for the extent and quality of their work, without which it would have been impossible to realize such a major, far-reaching effort. Cara Mullio served as the project's chief researcher and coordinator of loans, willingly taking on these and numerous essential administrative tasks that exceeded our requirements and expectations in her passage from volunteer to research assistant to curatorial associate. Dana Hutt contributed extensively to the research phase of the project, undertaking this work with thoroughness and insight and applying the same high standards of precision and care to her subsequent role as coordinator of photographs for this publication. Shoko Takada provided invaluable assistance to the loan coordination process and executed myriad other administrative and organizational matters with diligence as well as infectious enthusiasm. We also extend our deep thanks to Michael Darling for his insightful contributions to the exhibition's interpretive components and for his skillful assistance in other aspects of the project.

Many additional MOCA staff and project personnel played important roles throughout various phases of the exhibition's development. We deeply appreciate the guidance of Alma Ruiz, Assistant Curator, with identifying and securing loans from Latin America and in particular, Mexico, as well as her expert coordination of aspects of the exhibition's tour. Colette Dartnall, Curatorial Associate, was a crucial provider of assistance at key points throughout the exhibition's development, especially with skillful coordination of visual art loans and gracious facilitation of communication in French. Dawn Setzer, former Assistant Director of Communications, Media Relations, oversaw the complexities of the show's media relations process with her usual consummate professionalism. Kathleen Johnson, Grants Officer, wrote many of the proposals that helped fund the project. David Bradshaw, Media Arts Technical Manager, provided expertise in identifying and coordinating technical requirements for the exhibition. Danny Yee, Designer, and Brent Riggs, Preparator, capably assisted with graphics throughout many phases of the project. Marisela Norte, Facilities and Operations Secretary, graciously assisted with communication in Spanish, as did Tony Santos, Shipping/Receiving Clerk, with communication in Portuguese. Former MOCA staff Bonnie Born and Stanley Tom also made significant contributions during the research and organizational phase of the project in the areas of administration and technology, respectively. In addition, the essential assistance offered by volunteers and interns has been deeply important to the successful realization of the exhibition. Joyce Dever, Henriette Fremont, Jacquelyn Fung, and Nathan Marsak are among those to whom we are profoundly grateful for the varied and necessary help they have given to the project that has encompassed research assistance, translation, drafting, and organization of information and materials.We also extend special thanks to Debra Cohen and Thomas Stahl for their extensive help with matters pertaining to German loans.

A distinguished group of specialists in their fields has collaborated with us, some for a period of more than five years, to shape the direction and outcome of this exhibition and book. First and foremost we praise the singular collaboration with Frank O. Gehry that has resulted not only in the extraordinarily innovative design for this exhibition (in which he was assisted by Edwin Chan, Randy Jefferson, and Keith Mendenhall), but that previously created the literal environment in which the show is housed in Los Angeles — The Geffen Contemporary at MOCA. Since 1980, when MOCA was at its beginning, Frank has been a friend without peer, and was among the first people to encourage MOCA's commitment to the discipline of architecture — as well as this exhibition.

We express great appreciation to the advisors — Zeynep Çelik, Jean-Louis Cohen, Beatriz Colomina, Margaret Crawford, Jorge Francisco Liernur, Anthony Vidler, and Hajime Yatsuka—whose essential scholarly contributions to the development of the exhibition's conceptual underpinnings and identification of its content are articulated in the groundbreaking texts included in this publication. Catherine Lorenz, designer of this publication, brilliantly crafted a visual identity for the book that carries over into the exhibition's graphics. Our gratitude goes also to Paul Gottlieb, Eric Himmel, Toula Ballas, and Ray Hooper at Harry N. Abrams, our partner in this publication. Catherine Gudis, research consultant, conducted crucial primary research early in the life of the project and curated the video component of the exhibition in collaboration with Peter Kirby, media consultant, who expertly edited and produced it and advised us on a host of related technical and conceptual issues. Takehiko Nagakura, assistant professor of design and computation at Massachusetts Institute of Technology, and Kent Larson, architect, co-leaders of the "UNBUILT" project of three-dimensional computer-based animations, collaborated with us to present several innovative renditions of unrealized works in the exhibition. Roy Thurston, assisted by Adam Finkel, built scale models of skyscrapers that form the centerpiece of the exhibition's section on this important twentieth-century building type. Wladimir Teixeira de Souza Rosa built the impressive model of Brasilia, and Jari Jetsonen and Adam Wheeler assisted with additional model needs. David Leclerc, Margarita Nieto, and Marianne Wada provided translations of texts included in this publication. Hiroshi Sugimoto eloquently interpreted facets of this century's architecture in the new photographs that he generously allowed us to use in the exhibition and book.

Lenders from throughout the world, to whom we are deeply grateful, have graciously provided long-term loans of objects to the exhibition. These include the following institutions: Academie d'Architecture, Paris; Ad Art/ Electronic Sign Corporation, Stockton; Josef and Anni Albers Foundation, Connecticut; Archigram Archives, London; Archives municipales de Lyon; Archives of American Art, Washington, D.C.; Archives of the Municipal Engineer, Municipality of Tel Aviv; Archivio Centrale dello Stato, Rome; Archivio del Debbio, Rome; Archivio Lingeri, Milan; Archivo Williams, Buenos Aires; Art Institute of Chicago; Avery Architectural and Fine Arts Library, Columbia University, New York; Bank of America Art Program, San Francisco; Barragán Foundation, Birsfelden, Switzerland; Bauhaus-Archiv, Berlin; Bel Geddes Collection, Hoblitzelle Theatre Arts Library, The University of Texas, Austin; Berlinische Galerie, Berlin; Bibliothèque Municipale de Lyon; Busch-Reisinger Museum, Harvard University, Cambridge; Canadian Centre for Architecture, Montréal; Centraal Museum Utrecht; Central State Archives of Literature and Art, Moscow; Centro Studi Fondazione Terragni, Como; Chicago Historical Society; Colegio de Arquitectos de la Ciudad de Mexico; Colegio de Ingenieros de Caminos, Canales, y Puerto, Madrid; Rare Books and Manuscripts, Clarence Stein Papers, Cornell University, Ithaca, New York; Deutsches Architektur Museum, Frankfurt; Domino's Pizza, Inc., Ann Arbor; Dresden Stadtarchiv; Escuela Tecnica Superior de Arquitectura, Madrid; F.R.A.C. Centre, Orléans; Fondation Le Corbusier, Paris; First Garden City Heritage Museum, Letchworth; The Buckminster Fuller Institute, Santa Barbara; Getty Research Institute, Research Library and Special Collections and Visual Resources, Los Angeles; Marian Goodman Gallery,

New York; Graphische Sammlung Albertina, Vienna; Solomon R. Guggenheim Museum, New York; Henry Art Gallery, University of Washington, Seattle; Henry Ford Museum and Greenfield Village, Dearborn, Michigan; Hertfordshire County Archives, Hertford, England; Hirshhorn Museum and Sculpture Garden, Washington, D.C.; Historisches Museum der Stadt Wien; Archives of Sutemi Horiguchi, Meiji University, Kawasaki, Japan; Huntington Library, San Marino, California; Incontri Internazionale d'Arte, Rome; Instituto de Ciencias de la Construccion Eduardo Torroja, Madrid; Instituto de Pesquisa e Planejamento Urbano de Curitiba; Instituto Lina Bo e P.M. Bardi, São Paulo; Instituto Nacional de Bellas Artes, Mexico City; Junta Constructora del Templo de la Sagrada Familia, Barcelona; Kunstsammlung zu Weimar; Faculty of Engineering, Kyoto University; Landesarchiv Berlin; Landesbildstelle Berlin; The John Lautner Foundation, Los Angeles; Library of Congress, Prints and Photographs Division, Washington, D.C.; Los Angeles County Museum of Art; Magistrat der Stadt Wien; Musée des Beaux Arts, Lyon; Musei Civici, Como; Museum für Angewandte Kunst, Vienna; Museum of Contemporary Art, Chicago; The Museum of Modern Art, New York; The Museum of the City of New York; Nassau County Museum Collection; National Building Museum, Washington, D.C.; National Gallery of Art, Washington, D.C.; National Museum of American History, Washington, D.C.; New York Historical Society; The Oakland Museum; Office of the EUR, Rome; Oriental and India Office Collections, The British Library, London; Paride Accetti Collection, Milan; Facultad de Arquitectura y Bellas Artes, Pontificia Universidad Catolica de Chile, Santiago; Queens Museum of Art; Regional Plan Association, New York; Rockefeller Center, New York; Rodchenko-Stepanova Archive, Moscow; Royal Institute of British Architects, London; Russian State Library, Moscow; Saatchi Collection, London; Sainsbury Centre for Visual Art, University of East Anglia, Norwich; San Francisco Museum of Modern Art; August Sander Archiv, Cologne; Howard Schickler Fine Art Photography, New York; Shchusev Museum, Moscow; Stadtmuseum Berlin; Stiftung Archiv der Akademie der Künste, Berlin; Department of Special Collections, Syracuse University Library, Syracuse, New York; Technische Universität, Berlin; Technische Universität, Graz; Technische Universiteit Delft; Tretjakov Gallery, Moscow; Università degli Studi di Pisa; Università di Parma; College of Environmental Design, University of California, Berkeley; Special Collections, University of California, Los Angeles; University Art Museum, University of California, Santa Barbara; Architecture Archive, University of Pennsylvania, Philadelphia; Villanueva Foundation, Caracas; Vitra Design Museum, Weil am Rhein; The Walt Disney Company, Burbank; Welwyn Garden City Central Library, Osborn Collection; Wiener Stadt-und-Landesarchiv; and The Frank Lloyd Wright Foundation, Scottsdale.

We also wish to express deep thanks to the many individuals and architects' offices who have also generously lent objects to our exhibition or provided essential information to us regarding loans. These include: Tadao Ando; Yuri Avvakumov; Atelier Zo/Team Zoo; Steve Baer; Geoffrey Bawa; Behnisch & Partners; Felix Candela; Prunella Clough; Eileen and Michael Cohen; Coop Himmelb(l)au; Charles Correa; Lucio Costa Office; Kamran Diba; Eladio Dieste; Gunther Domenig; B.V. Doshi; Peter Eisenman; Frank Escher; Norman Foster Associates; Frank O. Gehry & Associates; Nicholas Grimshaw & Partners; Mario Schjetnan/Grupo de Diseño Urbano; Zaha Hadid; T.R. Hamzah & Yeang; Itsuko Hasegawa; Hodgetts + Fung; Steven Holl; Arata Isozaki and Associates; Toyo Ito Architect & Associates; The Jerde Partnership International; Elaine K. Sewell Jones; Lee Kaplan; Kikutake Architects; Pierre Koenig; Kohn Pederson Fox Associates PC;

Leon Krier; Kisho Kurokawa; Charles I. Larson and Dr. Magli Sarfatti Larson; Legorreta Arquitectos; Jeffrey Leifer; Mary Lutyens; Kunio Maekawa Associates, Architects & Engineers; Roberto Magris Studio; Maki and Associates, Architecture and Planning; Richard Meier & Partners; Enric Miralles Arquitectos; Morphosis; Eric Owen Moss; Helga and Hans Jurgen Muller; Oscar Niemeyer Foundation; Jean Nouvel; Pei-Cobb-Freed and Partners; Cesar Pelli & Associates, Inc.; Renzo Piano Building Workshop; Raili Pietilä; Max Protetch; Pedro Ramirez Vasquez; Jean Rasenberger; Andre Ravereau; Stuart Regen and Shaun Caley; Raj Rewal; Kevin Roche, John Dinkeloo & Associates; Richard Rogers; A. G. Rosen; Seizo Sakakura Associates, Architects and Engineers; Margarete Schütte-Lihotzky; Kazuo Shinohara; Julius Shulman; Skidmore, Owings and Merrill; Anthony Slayter-Ralph; Paolo Soleri Office; Joshua Soren; Peter Smithson; James Steele; Kenzo Tange Associates Urbanists-Architects; TEN Arquitectos; Clorindo Testa; Jørn Utzon; Venturi, Scott Brown and Associates, Inc.; Paulina Villanueva; Judith Wachsmann; and Michael Webb. In addition, our extensive research and loan process could not have been realized so fruitfully without the crucial assistance and advice of the following individuals, including Ric Abramson; Berenice Aguilar Prieto; Svetlana Artamanova; Kim Bradley; Tim Bruinsma; Orly Erel; Tom and Jeri Ferris; Donatella Manzan; Mina Marefat; William Menking; Dion Neutra; Philip Nobis; Janet Sager; Juliette Salzmann; Peter Wittmann; Sergio Zeballos; and Christina Zwingl.

Our colleagues at institutions hosting the exhibition are deserving of our thanks for their interest in and enthusiasm for this project and their willingness to work with us to present it to their audiences. Special appreciation is extended to Yasuo Kamon, Director, Kunio Yaguchi and Junichi Shioda, Chief Curators, Osamu Fukunaga, Curator, and Chika Mori, Assistant Curator, of the Museum of Contemporary Art, Tokyo, as well as Yoshiteru Kaneko and Junichi Uenohata of Delphi Inc.; Dolores Béistegui, Coordinadora Ejecutiva at the Antiguo Colegio de San Ildefonso, Mexico City, as well as to its overseers Francisco Barnés de Castro, Rector, and José de Santiago, Coordinator of Difusión Cultural at the Universidad Nacional Autónoma de México, Rafael Tovar y de Teresa, Presidente, and Eduardo Amerena, Secretario Técnico, at the Consejo Nacional para la Cultura y las Artes, and Cuauhtémoc Cárdenas Solórzano, Jefe, and Clara Jusidman, Secretaria de Educación, Salud y Desarrollo, at the Gobierno del Distrito Federal; Milu Villela, President, Tadeu Chiarelli, Chief Curator, Rejane Cintrao, Assistant Curator, and Ricardo Resende, Exhibition Designer, of the Museu de Arte Moderna de São Paulo, and Julio Landman, President, and Romao Pereira, Manager, of the Fundacao Bienal de São Paulo and the IAB-Instituto de Arquitetos do Brasil; Winfried Fischer, Museen der Stadt Köln; Dr. Kathinka Dittrich Van Weringh, Kulturdezernat der Stadt Köln; Jochen Poetter, Director, Bernd Dudek, Executive Manager, and Ralf Hofenbitzer, Exhibition Technician, of the Ludwig Museum, Cologne; and Thomas Krens, Director, and Lisa Dennison, Deputy Director and Chief Curator, of the Solomon R. Guggenheim Museum, New York City.

Finally, we wish to express our deepest gratitude to the sponsors of "At the End of the Century" — Ford Motor Company, The Ralph M. Parsons Foundation; The Ron Burkle Endowment for Architecture and Design Programs; Peter B. Lewis; Lenore S. and Bernard A. Greenberg; Maeda Corporation; Mori Building Company, Ltd.; and the Graham Foundation for Advanced Studies in the Fine Arts. Key individuals at these organizations provided leadership to galvanize support for our project, and we would particularly like to acknowledge Mabel H.

Cabot, Director, Corporate Programming, and Jack Telnack, former Vice President of Design, at Ford; Joseph Hurley and Christine Sisley at The Parsons Foundation; and Richard Solomon at the Graham Foundation.

We also express our enduring appreciation to the many wonderful friends and colleagues in Japan who steadfastly supported this project throughout its development. Mr. Minoru Mori, President, Mori Building Company, Ltd., made an extraordinary personal commitment as well as facilitating critical support from Taisei Corporation, Kajima Corporation, Obayashi Corporation, Takenaka Corporation, and Shimizu Corporation. Dr. Matabee Kenji Maeda, Chairman, and Mr. Yasuji Maeda, President, Maeda Corporation, made one of the first strong commitments which gave a signal of confidence that allowed us to further pursue the project in Tokyo (following their earlier deep commitment to our Louis I. Kahn exhibition). Profound thanks are also due to former Ambassador and Mrs. Walter Mondale (longtime friends of the museum and the arts in America); and additionally to Ambassador and Mrs. Thomas Foley; Mr. Shin'ichiro Asao, President of the Japan Foundation; and Jon Jerde and Eddie Wang of The Jerde Partnership International. In a project of this scope and complexity, friendship and loyalty provide the strength to keep everything moving forward in the most positive manner. Everyone named above has demonstrated this amply, but special note must also be made of two people who have gone above and beyond the "normal" definition of friendship: Arata Isozaki and Aiko Miyawaki. For nearly twenty years we have had the extraordinary privilege of collaboration with them on numerous projects, each more rewarding than the last. We look forward to new opportunities to continue this marvelous relationship, and express our abiding thanks to them.

The support of these individuals and institutions, enabling this distinctive view of our century's architecture and urbanism to be shared with a broad worldwide audience, bespeaks a passionate, enlightened commitment to the role of the arts and arts institutions as a vital element in the life of our society.

Andreas Gursky, *Hong Kong Island*, 1994. Monika Sprüth Galerie, Cologne

RE-EXAMINING ARCHITECTURE AND ITS HISTORY AT THE END OF THE CENTURY

Elizabeth A.T. Smith

Twentieth-century architecture is generally considered in terms of the singular works it has produced within the framework of modernism. Such buildings as Frank Lloyd Wright's Fallingwater and Guggenheim Museum; Le Corbusier's Ronchamp and Villa Savoye; Louis I. Kahn's Salk Institute for Biological Studies; Ludwig Mies van der Rohe's Barcelona Pavilion; and Robert Venturi's Vanna Venturi House have achieved canonical status within the field of architecture, viewed as pivotal and highly original works both within their creators' individual development and in the subsequent course of architectural history. Yet despite their iconic status for architects, many of these buildings are not widely familiar outside the profession and its related arenas of practice and discourse. From throughout the twentieth century, however, a variety of significant buildings can be identified that are well known and recognizable to a broad public worldwide. These range from New York City's Empire State Building and Chrysler Building to the Sydney Opera House to the Centre Georges Pompidou in Paris to the fantastic themed environments of Las Vegas and Disneyland. The notoriety of these works rests not so much upon the technological innovations they embody and certainly not on their authorship, but rather depends on their distinctive identities as images that have become inextricably intertwined with their civic presence.

"At the End of the Century: One Hundred Years of Architecture" aims to present such landmarks as emblematic of larger tendencies, movements, and directions that have shaped the twentieth century's architectural culture. Rather than foregrounding a series of singular architectural achievements, it positions them within a context of related works — built and unbuilt — and ideas, many of which are considerably lesser known even to the architecture community. In so doing, the project seeks to consider the historical frameworks within which such works were conceived and to emphasize their cultural, social, political, and economic underpinnings as well as their formal and technological ones. While the geographic range of "At the End of the Century" is global and its temporal expanse vast, the project does not purport to be exhaustive nor does it include documentation of all of the canonical works or "masterpieces" that might be expected in such an expansive survey. Instead, it posits a chronologically-organized sequence of episodes, movements, and thematic developments that from our vantage point at the end of this century are of compelling significance and interest.

Robert Venturi, Vanna Venturi House, Chestnut Hill, Philadelphia, 1964, with Mrs.Venturi. Photo by Rollin R. La France

Frank Lloyd Wright, Fallingwater,
Bear Run, Pennsylvania, 1936.
Photo by Ezra Stoller

Hiroshi Sugimoto, Chrysler Building, New York City (Architect: William van Alen, 1930), 1997

Hiroshi Sugimoto, Guggenheim Museum, New York City (Architect: Frank Lloyd Wright, 1942-60), 1997

Due to the scope of material covered, the project deliberately offers a broad range of ideas and themes rather than a single dominant narrative or focus. Yet throughout the exhibition, certain consistent motives can be discerned that resonate to a greater or lesser degree within each of the sections into which it is organized. These include the defining role of tradition (as well as the more-noted innovation) in giving shape to much of the century's architecture and urban forms; the crucial significance of technology in the past one hundred years not only to the making of buildings but also to ways of living throughout the world; the importance of expanding our assessment of architecture to include an informed view of work created in non-Western and/or "third world" contexts; and a keen interest in both the macrocosm and the microcosm — the city plan, or large-scale urban vision, as well as the intimate environment of the domestic sphere.

The structural and conceptual basis of this project has emerged from a long-term collaborative process between its curators and a group of distinguished scholar/advisors. In his or her individual scholarly work, each of the contributors has advanced groundbreaking ideas about various facets of the century's history, yet from markedly different points of view and areas of expertise. Collectively, their knowledge and attitudes about what should be included in such an exhibition has ranged widely, at times complementing and at times conflicting with each other's ideas and sparking extended debate. The outcome of this large and admittedly unwieldy attempt to assess the vast terrain of the past one-hundred years' architecture thus represents a consensus about certain overarching themes of crucial importance, but also manifests the eccentricities of each contributor's particular vision; like all histories, it is subjective, inflected by surrounding circumstances and passions.

In constructing "At the End of the Century's" interpretive framework, we have distilled and selected from approaches to meaning in architecture that view it, variously, as the shaping of space, the articulation of signs, the assertion of economic, political, or cultural hegemony, the result of tectonic developments, or the establishment of various forms of social order and control. We have aimed to avoid a polarized treatment of elements that many earlier historians and polemicists have positioned as antithetical — for instance, the traditional and the modern, the regional and the international, the organic and the rational, as well as high and low (avant-garde and populist) forms of architectural practice — in favor of an emphasis on discursive dimensions of overlap, cross-pollination, and hybridization. This synthetic impulse, informed strongly by recent intellectual developments including postcolonialist and feminist theories, represents our collective view of the most valid, appropriate, and vital way in which to consider and reconsider both the canonical and the lesser-studied aspects of one hundred years of architecture at this moment at the century's end.

The team that has shaped this project has drawn on a voluminous literature on twentieth-century architecture ranging from comprehensive overviews to highly specialized studies focusing on single architectural works or closely related groupings of works and ideas. During the period of conceptualization and research, and while reflecting on our own role as chroniclers of history, we have read and re-read numerous essential texts by authors including Reyner Banham, Charles Correa, Le Corbusier, Hassan Fathy, Sigfried Giedion, Henry-Russell Hitchcock, Jane Jacobs, Rem Koolhaas, Adolf Loos, Lewis Mumford, Colin Rowe, Antonio Sant'Elia, Vincent Scully, Manfredo Tafuri, Robert Venturi and Denise Scott

Berenice Abbott, *The Night View*, c. 1936. Museum of the City of New York. Gift of Todd Watts

Brown, and others — many of whose books are included as objects of display in the exhibition to emphasize the importance of history and theory to so much of the century's practice. We have also relied heavily on the recent scholarship of historians including Catherine Cooke, William Curtis, Kenneth Frampton, Diane Ghirardo, Dolores Hayden, Spiro Kostof, Mary McLeod, Roberto Segre, Lawrence Vale, and others, in addition to the more direct contributions of our project's advisors — Zeynep Çelik, Jean-Louis Cohen, Beatriz Colomina, Margaret Crawford, Jorge Francisco Liernur, Anthony Vidler, and Hajime Yatsuka — each of whom has made substantive contributions to the study of twentieth-century architecture from a highly specialized and unique perspective.

Antonin Raymond, Architect's Summer Residence, near Karuizawa, Japan, 1933. The Architectural Archives of the University of Pennsylvania

In developing the exhibition's concept and outlining its content, we have profited immensely from the extensive and penetrating studies of recent years that have deepened our understanding of such early twentieth-century movements as German Expressionism, the Russian avant-garde, the Bauhaus, and Italian Rationalism, as well as the City Beautiful movement and the architecture and urbanism of colonialism. Additionally, a growing body of literature on the works of both well-known and more obscure figures ranging from Le Corbusier, Eileen Gray, Edwin Lutyens, Oscar Niemeyer, Kenzo Tange, and Frank Lloyd Wright, to Geoffrey Bawa, Felix Candela, Bertram Goodhue, Sutemi Horiguchi, Antonin Raymond, Margarete Schütte-Lihotzky, and Konrad Wachsmann, has immeasurably aided and broadened our research process. The amplitude of the existing scholarship has allowed us to present a more balanced picture of the movements, tendencies, and directions of the first part of the century in that the contributions of "major" and "minor" figures are interwoven around the main points that each of the exhibition's thematic sections articulate. A fresh approach to this well-trodden terrain necessitated an intermingling of the iconic and the less widely known, in order to highlight the extra-architectural dimensions — political, social, economic, demographic — of the subjects presented and to give greater prominence to the currents of tradition that have co-existed with those of modernism throughout the century.

Our treatment of developments in the second half of the century has been a much more problematic and difficult undertaking. The extent of scholarship on the work of the post-World War II period and of our own time is considerably less than that which exists on early modernism and, as with any foray into the contemporary era, the act of assessing significance is a more highly charged and speculative endeavor. Adherence to a multi-thematic framework has enabled our selection of mid- and late-twentieth century works and ideas to be positioned in relationship to those examined in the first part of the exhibition — for instance, the house as a locus for innovation, the application of grand planning schemes, and recurrent manifestations of colonialism — and for a context for their evolutionary development to be provided. Not surprisingly, the final sections of the exhibition are our most tentative because as subjects they remain still-unfolding dramas.

Throughout the history of twentieth-century architecture, instances of ideological polarization and contradictory assessments abound that, when viewed as polemical constructions, provide a glimpse into the shifting, cyclical nature of meaning and historical interpretation. Some of the examples that have informed our thinking and sharpened our awareness of the problematics of constructing such analyses include the opposing positions that have been articulated by proponents of both innovation (modernism, internationalism) and tradition (historicism, the vernacular, the localized) in a variety of contexts and points in time.

Reconsidering Opposing Viewpoints: The Rational and the Expressive

Writings produced during the formative years of the modern movement, for instance, those of the historian Nikolaus Pevsner — *Pioneers of Modern Design from William Morris to Walter Gropius* (1936) and *An Outline of European Architecture* (1945) — place rational and functional concerns at the forefront of this nascent tendency in architecture so as to more clearly frame it as a radical break with the currents of the past. Pevsner's writings advocate functionalism, denigrating expressionistic impulses and associational values in architecture. Such a neatly oppositional stance between rationalism and organicism, however, has been significantly eroded by subsequent developments in modernism, and complicated by a more recent generation of historians and interpreters whose studies of such figures as Le Corbusier and Mies van der Rohe have subjected their work to a more extensive and problematized analysis.

Aldo Rossi, Centro Direzionale, 1977. Collection Centre Canadien d'Architecture/Canadian Centre for Architecture, Montréal

Similarly, in the later part of the century, key anti-modern polemicists, including Robert Venturi and Denise Scott Brown, Leon Krier, and Aldo Rossi, staked out oppositional positions to the work and ideas of a previous orthodoxy to establish the radical terms of their own discourse. A generation later, however, revisionist scholarship points to a more complex series of influences and trajectories between modernism and postmodernism. A foremost example is the case of Alison and Peter Smithson's deeply significant contributions to the development of a postmodern urbanism and their anticipation of tendencies that later assumed paramount importance in anti-modernist debates. Through their extensive writings and development of theories based on a sociological interest in the "as found" and their city planning projects for sites including London and Berlin in the 1950s, the Smithsons alone and as part of the group Team X posed fundamental challenges to the principles of modernist planning, while at the same time continuing to espouse a Corbusian architectural vocabulary dubbed the "New Brutalism."[1]

Many writers and theorists of our own time have sought to reconsider and rehabilitate modernism, again in reaction to the apparent hegemony of a

1 For an illuminating discussion of the Smithsons' work and ideas of the 1950s and their contribution to ensuing debates and directions, see David Robbins, ed., *The Independent Group: Postwar Britain and the Aesthetics of Plenty* (Cambridge, Mass. and London: The MIT Press, 1990), 242-245.

Ludwig Mies van der Rohe, Friedrichstrasse Skyscraper, 1921. The Mies van der Rohe Archive, The Museum of Modern Art, New York. Gift of the architect.

previous generation's discourse. For instance, in a 1984 essay, the architect and theorist Rem Koolhaas considers the contextual bases of two of early modernism's signature works, both designed for sites in Berlin — Ludwig Hilberseimer's proposal for a housing project in nine city blocks (1920-24), and Mies van der Rohe's proposed Friedrichstrasse Office Building (1921) — both of which had come to be considered emblematic of modernism's brutal effrontery to a preexisting urban context. Examining the contextual studies of Hilberseimer's project and the siting of Mies's Glass Tower, Koolhaas emphasized these architects' concern with urbanism in terms of the dialogic relationship between old and new that their works catalyzed. In his further analysis of the urbanistic strategies of such buildings as Harvey Corbett and Raymond Hood's Rockefeller Center in New York City and Ivan

Leonidov's project for the Ministry of Heavy Industry in Moscow, he maintains the position that "the early modern architects had more awareness of and concern for the architectural environment and the occupants of their buildings than do the postmodern architects of the 1980s."[2] While clearly shaped by the polemical concerns central to Koolhaas's own critical practice, this assessment amplifies our understanding of the nuances of modernist urbanism in terms of intended relationships between building and site. Koolhaas's penetrating examination of Leonidov's project probes its programmatic significance as a complex response to the richness and importance of its site on Moscow's Red Square as well as to its own thematic and symbolic character in relationship to context and history, going so far as to position these concerns as the primary focal points of Leonidov's design.

Other reassessments of the ahistoricism of modernism have proliferated in recent years. "The more one scrutinizes the Modern Movement today, the more the exceptions seem to overwhelm the rule, the less valid seems the unified vision so unmistakable in books and magazines of the 1930s. Scratch the surface and the illusion of consistency disappears," Peter Blundell Jones wrote in 1988.[3] A champion of the organic tradition, Jones has argued vigorously and persuasively for the reconstruction and expansion of the scope of modernism to position the expressionistic, regionally inflected work of such architects as Alvar Aalto, Gunnar Asplund, Ralph Erskine, Hugo Häring, and Hans Scharoun centrally within modernism and to overturn the peripheral status their work (with the exception of Aalto's) has generally occupied. Highlighting these architects' deployments of a "perspectival" spatial order as deriving from a basis in their neo-classical training and a profound understanding of the principles of axial planning and traditional ordering, Jones intriguingly complicates the view of how influences are transmitted and vocabularies developed across supposedly irreconcilable boundaries. Additional recent scholarship has positioned aspects of classicism and modernism in close alignment, both in the formalism of the work of Mies van der Rohe and also in socio-political terms as in the numerous civic buildings sponsored by the government of Fascist Italy from the late twenties into the early forties.

Postcard of R.C.A. Building, Rockefeller Center, New York City, 1931-34. Photo by Gottscho

Likewise, as its oppositional relationship to modernism is reassessed and refined, definitions of postmodernism continue to shift. One of the more provocative, put forth by Hajime Yatsuka in 1986, concerns the avoidance of a hierarchical order, or what could also be called the "privileged center," in a work of architecture. This definition involves the use of a dispersed compositional and spatial focus and stresses the importance of fragmentation and irresolution as symbolic gestures.[4] Yatsuka's argument surrounding the condition of postmodernism and its application within architecture revolves around the notion of a complex, consistent system of

[2] Rem Koolhaas, "A Foundation of Amnesia," *DQ*, no. 125 (February 1984): 6.

[3] Peter Blundell Jones, "From the Neo-Classical Axis to Aperspective Space," *Architectural Review* 183 (March 1988): 18.

[4] Hajime Yatsuka, "Post-modernism and Beyond . . . ", *The Japan Architect* 61 (February 1986): 62.

hybridized elements that he describes as the "acceleration and co-vibrancy" of images and meaning drawn from modernism as well as from other historical sources. Such an assessment extends and complicates the ideas found in earlier efforts to articulate an emergent set of tenets for postmodernism, including Venturi's famous take-off on Mies van der Rohe's "Less is more" of modernism to "Less is a bore."

The Regional and the International: Complexities and Contradictions

The extreme difficulty of facile categorization also emerges when considering the relationships manifested in the architecture and urbanism of non-Western contexts between a universalizing, international idiom and a variety of localized conventions and conditions. From the applications of political and cultural colonialism which were imposed within numerous such contexts including Istanbul,

Sutemi Horiguchi, Meteorological Station, Oshima Island, Shizuoka Prefecture, Japan, 1938. Photo by Giichi Kimura

New Delhi and Algiers prior to and throughout the first part of the century, to the persistence of a form of cultural and economic colonialism surrounding the impulse toward internationalism, many individual buildings, urban designs, and city plans have been produced by both Western and non-Western architects that seem to represent a pure application of the International style or other, earlier Western models. At the same time, a corpus of work exists that seeks to steadfastly reject such principles, embodying a resistance to the all-pervasive values of westernization and internationalism.

During the second half of the century, however, hybridization and cross-fertilization among differing vocabularies have increasingly emerged as paramount operative elements within a broad spectrum of architectural works. In both Western and non-Western contexts, these phenomena reflect the transmission and interweaving of forms, ideas, and influences in the cultural, social, political and economic spheres. Enhanced recognition of the validity of diverse approaches to the making of architecture in both the periphery and the center have de-emphasized purely stylistic concepts of originality and derivation, wherein non-Western work was characteristically judged in relationship to its Western source of influence, to a more illuminating consideration of how issues of content, context, and social organization meld within an expanded sphere of technological and aesthetic reference.

Exploring the nature of the dialogue between localized and universalized elements in architecture forms a significant part of this project. In the case of Japan, where relatively little scholarship is yet available to non-Japanese-speaking scholars about developments earlier in the century, we have considered as one of a group of case studies some aspects of architecture in the 1930s. During this decade, a number of important buildings were designed by architects including Junzo Sakakura, Kunio Maekawa, Sutemi Horiguchi, and others that manifest localized elements within a framework of Westernized standards of forms and building technology. Jonathan M. Reynolds has shown that, while in major public buildings of the 1930s the influence of ultranationalism mandated, to some extent, the incorporation of traditional Japanese motifs, a much less oppositional relationship between nationalism and modernism existed in Japan. In this culture modernism lacked the overtly political associations of its application in Europe; architects who employed the modernist idiom were at the same time largely enthusiastic for and deferential about aspects of Japanese tradition.[5]

In the case of Latin American architecture, where there has also been a paucity of scholarly material available outside the region, some recent literature has emerged to supplement the bulk of the primarily formal and tectonic studies of the fifties and sixties. The nature of regionalism and the complex interactions between the architecture of the center and the periphery in Latin America has been eloquently analyzed by several scholars who have particularly focused their re-evaluations on the work of the mid-century. The essay included in this volume by Jorge Francisco Liernur on the evolution of architecture in Latin America keenly examines the cross-fertilization between this region's architectural culture and that of Europe and North America. At the same time, he traces Latin American architecture and urbanism as a distinct set of regionalisms that derive from specific historical, geographic, economic and political, as well as cultural and intellectual, circumstances, helping to erode still widely-held assumptions about the characteristics of this region's architecture as cohesive and unified. Treating a broad panorama of work in Latin America from the early part of the century to the present, Liernur's study makes a substantial contribution to our understanding of the position it occupies within a larger architectural history.

Changing Modes of Historical Analysis

During the past decades, the efforts of many writers and historians, ranging from J.B. Jackson and Venturi and Scott Brown to Dolores Hayden and Margaret Crawford, to reexamine the relationship between "high" and "low" forms of architecture have also contributed to the shaping of this project. At its outset, one of our team's debates revolved around the issue of whether its focus should be

[5] Jonathan M. Reynolds, "The Tokyo Imperial Household Museum Competition: Nationalism and Modernism in Japanese Architecture," *The Japan Architect* 62 (August 1987): 6-7.

Thomas Struth, *Marunouchi (Over the Roofs), Tokyo*, 1986

"architecture" (unique works the authorship of which is known and that are generally recognized as works of quality) or "the built environment" (the larger framework of the urban landscape, vernacular or commercially-oriented structures the authorship of which may be unknown, and buildings of social or economic rather than purely architectural significance). Our resolution of this issue emerged from a consensus that it would be most interesting and appropriate to examine the century from the perspective of how these elements have intertwined, both by attempting to look closely at the contexts in which works of architecture have been made and to determine how successfully they have related to these contexts, and also to be inclusive of built works that reflect the wider scope of cultural studies — motorway and roadway systems; mass produced yet traditionally styled housing; environments oriented to tourism and entertainment; and structures indicating the jarring demographic and economic juxtapositions within the contemporary city.

To reiterate the premises stated above, our project does not purport to survey the complete scope of twentieth-century architecture, but instead presents significant moments in the century's history as "clusters" of analysis intended to bring certain issues into sharper focus. The physical organization of the exhibition is, by necessity, arranged chronologically, allowing these issues to be positioned in a framework of temporal identification and relevance. Therefore, our treatment of historical movements such as the Russian avant-garde and the Bauhaus, for instance, positions them following a section on "Manifestoes for a New World," linking them temporally and conceptually to a climate of radical innovation in the teens and twenties. On the other hand, our view of broader tectonic and typological developments locates them late in the exhibition's chronology, enfolding examples from a wide temporal time span within a "cluster" positioned as a hallmark of the mid- and late twentieth century's technological and economic efflorescence.

Grand Planning at the Turn of the Century: Mapping a World Order

"At the End of the Century" begins with a consideration of "grand planning" at the outset of the present century and reprises the theme at selected junctures later in the exhibition. This unifying vision of urban order can be examined in three distinct turn-of-the-century contexts — in Chicago, with Daniel Burnham and Edward Bennett's grandiose plan to classicize this youthful, industrial city; in Istanbul, with Joseph Antoine Bouvard's designs for recasting certain key quarters of the city as up-to-date with western European standards; and in Vienna, with Otto Wagner's extensive replanning of the city and designs for civic buildings that, while rooted in the Beaux Arts, begin to articulate a nascent modernism. Paradigmatic of a tendency that looks back to the nineteenth century, such grandiose schemes for recasting the urban fabric represent an urge toward the application of a civic order and coherence associated with classical tradition.

Otto Wagner, Donaukanal Ferdinandsbrucke, Vienna, Austria, 1905. Museen der Stadt Wien

A significant manifestation of this impulse was the influential 1893 World's Columbian Exposition held in Chicago, masterminded by Burnham and Bennett and prefacing their 1909 publication of the Beaux Arts-inspired Plan for Chicago. Celebrating the cultural, economic, and technological achievements of the United States and positioning them in relationship to the esteemed classical traditions of the European past, this event galvanized an entire generation of American planners whose designs were applied in contexts ranging from San Francisco to Detroit to Manila in the first decade of the century. The ideal of imposing coherence upon and aggrandizing non-European urban fabrics in the image of Western tradition was also widely manifested during this period in Latin American cities.

Tony Garnier, La cité industrielle, 1901, Quartier d'habitation. Musée des Beaux-Arts, Lyon

In contrast to these applications of an idealized vision stemming from the Beaux-Arts tradition, Tony Garnier's replanning of the French city of Lyon demonstrates the goal of organizing and rationalizing an urban context as a city oriented to the worker based on socialist principles. In many respects Garnier's example anticipates and was directly influential on Le Corbusier's development in the 1920s of a set of urbanistic principles based on zoning the modern city into areas of distinct function. These were ideas that Le Corbusier and his followers applied widely in schemes for other European, American, and non-Western contexts. Later in the century, this tendency emerged repeatedly in realized works and in the creation of new capital cities, manifested as an ethos of internationalism and modernization and often closely linked to the development of automobile-oriented transportation in the post-World War II period.

Colonialism in the Early Twentieth Century

Examined through the lens of colonialism, the theme of the "dual city" — in which Western architects' visions for non-Western contexts contrast sharply with their existing morphologies — emerges as a salient development in architecture of the early and middle years of the century. The planning and architecture — built and unbuilt — of such colonial contexts as New Delhi, Canberra, and Algiers highlights the relationship of architecture to politics as well as the problematics of articulating regional identity in the presence of cultural colonialism, the latter a recurrent theme that has not only persisted but even escalated to dizzying proportions within the present-day context of global communications, transportation, and the mass media.

In formal terms, a marked contrast exists between the traditionalism of Edwin Lutyens's 1921-31 plan for New Delhi and his design of numerous governmental buildings in this new colonial capital, and Le Corbusier's modernist Plan Obus for Algiers, an unrealized study undertaken between 1930-33. Both, however, can be viewed from the vantage point of applying ideas inextricably linked

Sir Edwin Lutyens, Viceroy's Palace, New Delhi, 1912-31. Photo by Arthur Gill. British Architectural Library, RIBA, London

to the position of dominance of the colonizer within contexts wherein local tradition was de-valued and/or exoticized. The individual approach of each architect to the grafting of a distinct vocabulary onto such contexts differed. Lutyens, who studied examples of earlier Indian architecture and sought to integrate certain features into his designs for New Delhi, produced a somewhat hybridized architecture in which references to regional traditions and usage of local materials were fused, yet largely subsumed, within a primarily Victorian architectural vocabulary and planned according to Western notions of symmetry and grandeur. Le Corbusier, on the other

Erich Mendelsohn, Einstein Tower, Potsdam, 1920. Photo by Dana Hutt

Erich Mendelsohn, Einstein Tower, Potsdam, 1920. Photo by Dietmar Katz. Kunstbibliothek, Staatliche Museum zu Berlin

hand, rejected any references to traditional or localized elements in his plan and design of buildings for Algiers, yet he produced extensive sketches of local scenes during his travels that are highly exoticized interpretations of its culture.

The plan of Lutyens's New Delhi can be linked to that of several other related works produced under the aegis of colonial patronage of the same period, including Walter Burley Griffin and Marion Mahony Griffin's Plan for Canberra (1911-12); Henri Prost's Plan for Casablanca (1914); and Ernest Hébrard's Plan for Hanoi (1923). These are also characterized by the importation of an architectural and urbanistic vocabulary associated with the image of the power of the colonizer. Le Corbusier's search for a modernist monumentality in his studies for Algiers and also for the replanning of Buenos Aires (1929) and Rio de Janeiro (1936) was not to be actualized until some years later, when in mid-century the building of new capitals, primarily by Western architects applying the modern idiom in non-Western contexts, represented a new ethos of economic and cultural dominance.

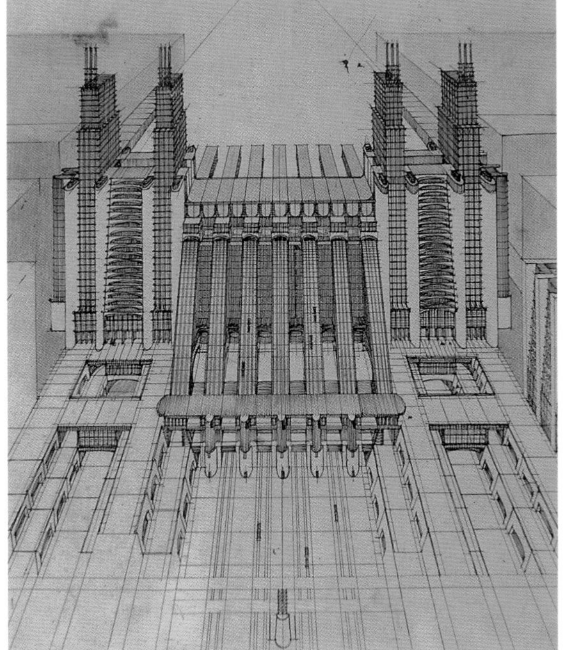

Antonio Sant'Elia, *Stazione d'aeroplani e treni ferroviari, con funicolari e ascensori su tre piani stradali*, 1914. Musei Civici di Como

Manifestoes for a New World

In counterpoint to the hegemony of a persistent traditionalism during the early decades of the century, a series of radical reworkings of attitudes toward architecture and its relationship to changing ways of life emerged during the same period. The polemical, utopian designs of such architects as Italian Futurists Antonio Sant'Elia and Mario Chiattone and German Expressionists Bruno Taut, Hans Scharoun, and Hans Poelzig are among the earliest and most powerful articulations of a visionary sensibility that pointedly rejected tradition in favor of a heady embrace of the possibilities of modernism. Their largely unbuilt

Hans Poelzig, Concert Hall, Dresden, 1918. Deutsches Architektur Museum Archiv, Frankfurt

works evolved in tandem with their development of numerous theories and manifestoes in which ideas about architecture for a new age, inspired by the forms and materials of technology and liberated from the constraints of the past, were put forth with an often fiery rhetoric. Disseminated through books, pamphlets, journals and newspapers including *Wendigen*, *Frülicht*, and *Der Sturm*, these include such influential early pronouncements as Adolf Loos's essay "Ornament und Verbrechen" (Ornament and Crime), published in the *Neue Freie Presse* and the journal *Trotzdem* in 1908, and the Futurist Manifesto, first published in the newspaper *Le Figaro* in 1909. The 1919 *Programm des Staatlichen Bauhauses in Weimar* — the first publication of the Bauhaus with its utopian proclamation about architecture as the "cathedral of socialism" — also counts among the most influential statements about a heroic new modernist vision. It is contemporaneous with related journals in other contexts such as *De Stijl*, *Pasmo*, *L'Esprit Nouveau*, and the Manifesto of the Japanese Secession movement (1924) that also served as important vehicles for the dissemination of radical works and ideas among architects in those contexts. The articulation of a theoretical stance was to become an important underpinning of twentieth-century avant-garde movements seeking to define themselves in fundamental reaction to earlier movements or directions.

Lyonel Feininger, Kathedrale (Cathedrale) from the brochure *Programm des Staatlichen Bauhauses in Weimar*, April 1919. Los Angeles County Museum of Art, The Robert Gore Rifkind Center, purchased with funds provided by Anna Bing Arnold, Museum Associates Acquisition Fund, and deaccession funds.

Visions of a New Order: The Russian Avant-garde

In the aftermath of the Russian Revolution, the activity of avant-garde architects whose goal was to craft a new identity for architecture in the service of a nascent proletariat culture, foregrounds the social dimension of architecture in this distinct historical moment and place. Rather than surveying the complete scope of the Russian avant-garde's work from the late 1910s to the end of the twenties, however, this chronotopic approach focuses on a selection of civic projects conceived as generators of collective spirit. Some of the earliest examples are experimental designs by Alexander Rodchenko, Gustav Klucis, and others for functional structures to be used in public spaces for the display and transmission of visual and aural propaganda. These include Rodchenko's 1919 *Project for a Street Kiosk* and Klucis' numerous designs for small towers including loudspeakers and other devices to broadcast propagandistic messages to the masses.

As the momentum of revolutionary society developed and the government consolidated its power, a series of major architectural projects were undertaken by a variety of avant-garde architects. These designs include Vladimir Tatlin's Monument to the Third International (1920), which existed only as a large mock-up but was envisioned to tower over the city of Leningrad as an embodiment of the aspirations and achievements of the Revolution; competition projects for the

Palace of Labor (1924) and the Pravda Building (1924), for which the Vesnin Brothers, Ilya Golosov, and Konstantin Melnikov developed the most noteworthy radical designs; and Ivan Leonidov's Project for the Lenin Institute (1927-8). The forms of these unrealized designs were inspired by those of engineering, heavy industry and other technologically-based construction elements which seemed to embody the promise of an intrepid new age and way of life.

Alongside these monumental projects which remain among the best-known examples of early modernism despite their unbuilt status, works on a smaller scale yet with an equal or even more profound measure of social impulse were realized, primarily in the 1920s. These include collective housing and workers' clubs of which Golosov's Zuev Workers' Club (1926) and Melnikov's Kauchuk Club (1927) and Rusakov Club (1927-28), all in Moscow, are foremost examples. While experimental in their architecture, these and other built workers' clubs, which served as important social and educational centers in their urban neighborhoods, did not, however, involve equally progressive interior elements such as those

Vladimir Tatlin, Monument to the Third International (1920), computer rendering by Team Unbuilt, 1998

Alexander Rodchenko, Workers' Club at 1925 Paris Exposition. Rodchenko-Stepanova Archive

Gustav Klucis, Maquette for Radio Announcer, 1922. The Museum of Modern Art, New York. Sidney and Harriet Janis Collection

envisioned by Alexander Rodchenko in his designs for constructivist furnishings for a prototype Workers' Club presented in the Russian Pavilion of the 1925 "*Exposition des arts décoratifs*" in Paris.

The utopian yearning of this period toward a radically transformed society further manifested itself in the vigorous graphic designs of Rodchenko, Klucis, El Lissitzky, and others. Their advertising or exhortatory street posters were often closely linked to architecture and incorporated images of powerful, heroically-scaled human figures alongside imagery drawn from industry or technology. The breakdown of boundaries among the disciplines of design, engineering, and art stands as one of the hallmarks of this period during which the avant-garde dedicated itself to the service of revolutionary ideology — an extraordinary commingling of architecture and politics. Later, in the thirties and early forties, in the Soviet Union and elsewhere, the marriage of architecture with the ideology of the state would take on markedly different forms of expression inflected by the ideology of totalitarianism. Furthermore, in the post-World War II period, the dominance of International-style modernism as an idiom of Westernization would also permeate numerous instances of state patronage of important civic architecture.

Alexander Deineka, *Let's transform Moscow into a model socialist city of the proletarian state*, 1931, poster. Photo by Jim Frank. Courtesy of Merrill C. Berman Collection

Modern Learning and Living at the Bauhaus

The Bauhaus occupies a place of unquestioned significance as a vital springboard for a host of new and sometimes conflicting ideas about the relationship between art, design, architecture and modern life. While best known for its impact on the emergence of an "International Style" of functional, efficient design, the Bauhaus was in fact an extraordinarily diverse institution in which a variety of aesthetic attitudes were espoused from its beginnings in 1919 to its closure in 1931. The character of work produced during the early, formative years of the Bauhaus — its initial period in a Henry van de Velde-designed building in Weimar — reveals a link to expressionism and to the Arts and Crafts Movement and reflects the hybrid, transitional character of this moment in the formation of the institution's sensibility. Walter Gropius, the first director of the Bauhaus, stated his vision for the school at its outset in the following rhetorical terms that evoke an almost medievalizing ideal of unifying the arts under the aegis of architecture: "Architects, sculptors, painters, we must all return to handwork! . . . Let us, therefore, establish a new guild of craftsmen, free of that class-dividing arrogance which seeks to erect a haughty barrier between craftsmen and artists! Let us desire, conceive, and create together the new building of the future, which will embrace everything — architecture, sculpture, and painting — in one entity, and which will mount toward heaven from the hands of a million craftsmen as the crystal symbol of a new and coming faith."[6]

Our examination of this lesser studied phase of the Bauhaus, alongside that of the period following its move to the Walter Gropius-designed Dessau Bauhaus in 1925 — stems from a desire to consider its contributions from a

[6] Gropius's proclamation of the ideals behind the founding of the Bauhaus and its program was published in a four-page brochure dated April 1919 and has been extensively reprinted in later literature on the Bauhaus. See, for example, Howard Dearstyne, *Inside the Bauhaus* (New York: Rizzoli, 1986), 38-39.

Walter Gropius, Bauhaus Dessau, 1925. Bauhaus-Archiv, Berlin

broader standpoint. The highly experimental character of its program of studies and the investigations pursued by its students and faculty in a wide variety of media — weaving, metalwork, furniture design, photography, stage design, painting and sculpture, as well as architecture — merits renewed consideration from the viewpoint of the diverse aesthetic impulses that cohered among these many pursuits. Examples of experimental photography in which the architecture of the Bauhaus building itself serves as the framework for dynamic images of students and faculty bespeak the vitality of the institution. These range from the quasi-documentary to the evocative, as in Lotte Beese's *Portrait of Otti Berger and studio house*, 1930, and Lux Feininger's *Two girls on the roof of the Bauhaus*, 1927, to the energetic stylization of Gunta Stölzl's 1928 collage *W*, taking the weaving workshop as its subject as well as Iwao Yamawaki's collage *The Attack on the Bauhaus* that was published in a Japanese journal in 1932.

The legacy of the Bauhaus persisted not only in terms of the work of its faculty and former students in diverse sites around the world including

Director's Office, Bauhaus Weimar, 1923. Bauhaus-Archiv, Berlin

Lotte Beese, *Portrait of Otti Berger and studio house*, 1930. Bauhaus Archiv, Berlin

England, Israel, and Latin America, but also in its strong impact on the future of architectural and design education. As a pedagogical institution, the Bauhaus shaped the thinking of a generation of architects, designers, and artists toward the creation of work intended for mass production and for social utility. The transplantation of many key figures associated with the Bauhaus, such as the architects Gropius, Mies van der Rohe, and Marcel Breuer; the artists Laszlo Moholy-Nagy, Gyorgy Kepes, and Josef Albers; and the weaver Anni Albers to the United States had a considerable impact in transmitting formal and pedagogical emphases. Their influence was crucial to the formation of such American institutions as the New Bauhaus and the Illinois Institute of Technology in Chicago and Black Mountain College in North Carolina as well as the incorporation of a Bauhaus-inspired emphasis in the Graduate School of Design at Harvard University under Gropius.

The Rational Kitchen

Following World War I the innovative design of kitchens minimized the time, space, and effort required of domestic labor. The Frankfurt Kitchen prototype, designed by the Viennese architect Margarete Schütte-Lihotzky in 1925 for Ernst May's "minimumexistenz" apartment-house developments in Frankfurt, was scaled to the size of galleys in railroad restaurants and implemented in thirty different versions. In addition, Schütte-Lihotzky designed a "school kitchen" in which young women could be trained in the proper utilization of this efficient new domestic environment.

Margarete Schütte-Lihotzky, Frankfurt Kitchen, detail of sink and counter area, 1927. Archiv Margarete Schütte-Lihotzky

Concurrent with the development of Schütte-Lihotzky's pivotal prototype were related attempts by various architects including Gerrit Rietveld, J.J.P. Oud, and Moisei Ginzburg to design rational, modern kitchens for use in cooperative housing developments, community kitchens and the single-family home. These were often closely linked to theories of scientific domestic management and studies on hygiene and the efficiency of movement from a body of literature emergent since the late nineteenth century by American and European writers such as Charlotte Perkins Gilman in *Women and Economics*, 1898, and *The Home*, 1903; Frederick Winslow Taylor in *Principles of Scientific Management*, 1911; Christine Frederick in *The New Housekeeping: Efficiency Studies in Home Management*, 1913, and *Household Engineering: Scientific Management in the Home*, 1919, translated into German in 1922; and Erna Meyer in *Der neue Haushalt* of 1926. Yet most plans for the rational kitchen, however, persistently maintained the sexual division of labor, with women as unpaid domestic laborers and consumers and the nuclear family as the model social unit.

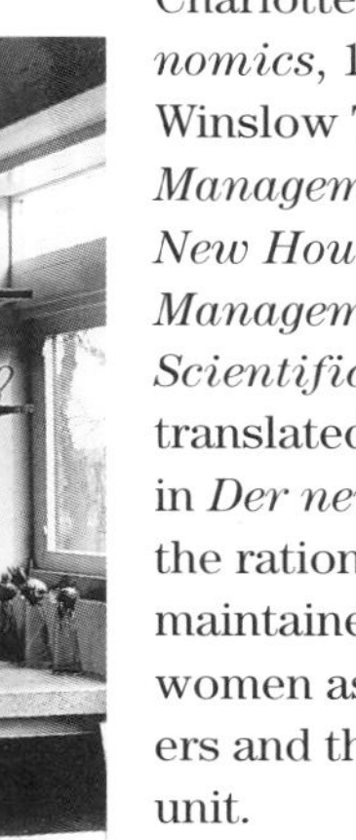

Gerrit Th. Rietveld, kitchen in Rietveld- Schröder House, Utrecht, 1924. Centraal Museum Utrecht/ Rietveld Schröder Archive

Gerrit Th. Rietveld (with T. Schröder-Schrader), Rietveld-Schröder House, Utrecht, 1924. Centraal Museum Utrecht/Rietveld Schröder Archive

Ludwig Mies van der Rohe, Houses 1-4, Weissenhofsiedlung, Stuttgart 1927. Photo by Dana Hutt

Minimum vs. Maximum Houses:
Mass Housing and Villas in the 1920s and 1930s

Throughout the twentieth century, the architecture of the house has been a locus for experimentation with ideas about forms, materials, social goals and patterns of living, and individual expression. At several junctures during this expansive period, experimental impulses and the urge to innovate have been most pronounced. The twenties and thirties witnessed an efflorescence of the standardized minimal dwelling unit intended for mass housing alongside a corpus of single-

Frank Lloyd Wright, Jacobs House, Madison, Wisconsin, 1936-37. Photo by Pedro E. Guerrero

family houses designed as architectural manifestoes and/or as luxury dwellings for an élite clientele. Frequently, both types were designed by the same architect. Mies van der Rohe's housing at the Weissenhofsiedlung in Stuttgart (1927) and his minimal Ground Floor House presented at the 1931 Berlin exhibition on "The Dwelling in our Time" contrast with his luxurious, elegant single-family Tugendhat House in Brno (1930) in terms of scale, materials, and finishes, yet also present basic similarities in their open plans, concern with hygiene (light and air), and overall modern disposition.

Likewise, a number of related examples of the same period illustrate the similarities between mass housing and private villas as well as their functional, economic, and aesthetic differences. Among these are Le Corbusier's design for high-rise mass housing in the Immeubles-Villas project (1922) and his dwelling unit presented in the Pavilion de l'Esprit Nouveau (1925), which contrasted with his houses for individual wealthy clients such as the Villa Stein-de-Monzie in Garches (1927) and the Villa Savoye in Poissy (1929-31), and Frank Lloyd Wright's

Le Corbusier, Villa Stein-De-Monzie, Garches, 1927. Fondation Le Corbusier

Karl Ehn, Karl-Marx-Hof, Vienna, 1927. Magistrat der Stadt Wien

sumptuous Fallingwater in Bear Run, Pennsylvania (1936), realized in the same year as the Jacobs house, a design for a low-cost dwelling in Madison, Wisconsin.

Other singular examples of mass housing built during this period include Karl Ehn's Karl-Marx-Hof in Vienna (1927), Bruno Taut and Martin Wagner's Berlin-Britz Siedlung in Berlin (1925-31), Moisei Ginzburg's Narkomfin Communal House, Moscow (1928), and Juan Legarrata's workers' housing in the Balbuena district, Mexico City (1932). Later in the century, a widespread urge toward mass housing would be repeated in the immediate post-World War II period not only in response to the housing shortages of the depression and war years but also as an outgrowth of the application of technologies developed during the war to peacetime.

During the twenties and thirties additional noteworthy examples of single-family houses abound. These include R.M. Schindler's Schindler-Chace House in Los Angeles (1921), designed for two families sharing a communal kitchen; Eileen Gray's E-1027 House, Roquebrune (1926-27); Konstantin Melnikov's Melnikov House, Moscow (1930); Sutemi Horiguchi's Okada House in Tokyo (1934); and Juan O'Gorman's House for Diego Rivera and Frida Kahlo in Mexico City (1934) and his own house in El Pedregal (1953-56). Conceived for progressive, wealthy clients, or in many instances, as the homes of the architects themselves, these buildings evince a plethora of experimental and innovative qualities in the intimate environment of the domestic sphere — a typology that in the past few decades has resurfaced with astonishing vigor and diversity of expression.

R.M. Schindler, Schindler-Chace House, Los Angeles, 1921. Photo by Grant Mudford

The Garden City and The New Town: Experiments in Europe, America, and the Middle East

The Garden City as a new town-planning type encompasses several distinct but related directions during the first few decades of the century. Foremost among these is the English garden city — the earliest and perhaps most significant contribution to rethinking patterns of collective living in a context removed from the city center. Influenced by the writings of Ebenezer Howard in *To-morrow: A Peaceful Path to Real Reform*, 1898, re-issued as *Garden Cities of To-morrow* in 1902, Raymond Unwin and Barry Parker's First Garden City of Letchworth (1904) was organized with the aim of metropolitan decentralization to address social concerns of health and hygiene as a corrective to the crowded, unhealthful conditions of the late nineteenth-century industrial city.

In Germany, the influence of Howard's ideas about Garden City planning resulted in the establishment of an organization, the Deutsche Gartenstadtgesellschaft, to promote its principles as early as 1902.[7] Linked also to the efforts of the Dresdener Werkstatten für Handwerkskunst (Dresden Arts and Crafts Workshops), which had been founded in 1898 in the spirit of the English Arts and Crafts movement, the Gardenstadt Hellerau was conceived in 1906 and built from 19010-13.[8] Planned by Richard Riemerschmid with Theodor Fischer, Hermann Muthesius, Heinrich Tessenow, and Baillie Scott, the architecture of the Gartenstadt Hellerau demonstrated a significantly greater emphasis on the use of traditional housing styles as a folkish, anti-industrial statement.

7 Peter G. Rowe, *Modernity and Housing* (Cambridge, Mass. and London: The MIT Press, 1993), 96.

8 John Zukowsky, ed., *The Many Faces of Modern Architecture: Building in Germany Between the World Wars* (Munich and New York: Prestel Verlag, 1994), 238.

Konstantin Melnikov, Melnikov House, Moscow, 1930. Collection Centre Canadien d'Architecture/ Canadian Centre for Architecture, Montréal

Konstantin Melnikov, Melnikov House, Moscow, 1930

Thinking surrounding the Garden City planning type extended into the next decades with the work and ideas of Scottish planner Patrick Geddes, among whose contributions are a Garden City-oriented plan for Tel Aviv in the mid-1920s. The application of this plan provided a distinctive urban environment for the International Style buildings that proliferated in Tel Aviv in the 1930s, resulting in one of the few contexts in the world where modern architecture is conjoined with a finely grained, low-rise urban organization. Historian Spiro Kostof points out that, "The popularity of the Garden City as a principle of planning was its extreme flexibility, its relatively easy ensconcement into any ideology. The concept might travel along with that English form of 'medieval' street flanked by cottages that Unwin and Parker popularized, or it could be separated from that form altogether and wedded rather to medium- and high-rise apartment buildings, and even to more regular layouts."[9]

"Letchworth, the First Garden City: Health of the Country—Comforts of the Town," 1925, poster, First Garden City Heritage Museum

In the United States, two major garden-city plans on the English model were realized in the 1920s — Sunnyside Gardens, Queens, New York (1924), planned by Clarence Stein and the Regional Plan Association of America; and the town of Radburn, New Jersey (1929), planned by Stein and Henry Wright. These American examples exercised a strong influence on later new town and suburban developments, primarily in terms of land-use issues stemming from the growing presence of the automobile and manifested in the application of greenbelts and zoned roadways. Most recently, they have also served in part as inspiration for the movement toward a "new urbanism" which emphasizes traditional planning forms in order to create and enhance community and in pronounced reaction to the modern planning and urban renewal that proliferated in the sixties and seventies.

An unrealized, experimental project that departs from aspects of the Garden City type but remains rooted in the idea of a decentralized, suburban vision is Frank Lloyd Wright's design for Broadacre City (1930-35). A critique of urban congestion and of modern city plans, Wright based his project on the ideals of providing an acre of land to every family, zoning for small-scale farming and industry in close

[9] Spiro Kostof, *The City Shaped: Urban Patterns and Meaning Throughout History* (Boston: Little, Brown and Company, 1991), 77.

Dizengoff Circle, Tel Aviv, 1930. Air Photo Archives, The Department of Geography, The Hebrew University of Jerusalem, Israel

Frank Lloyd Wright, Living City, 1958; Wright's later version of Broadacre City. Frank Lloyd Wright Foundation, Scottsdale, Arizona

proximity to residential areas, and interrelating multiple modes of transportation, including the private automobile. First published in Wright's 1932 book *The Disappearing City* and later exhibited to the public in the form of detailed scale models in 1935, Broadacre City anticipated in many respects the suburban developments that were to become commonplace throughout North America following World War II. It represents yet another manifestation of the far-reaching investigations into changing patterns of life, work, and recreation that abounded in the first third of the century as a response to sweeping societal changes and the often poor living conditions characterizing both urban and rural settings.

The Politics of Monumentality in 1930s Architecture

During the volatile decade of the 1930s, monumentality in architecture was widely employed not only in neoclassical, rationalist formal terms, but also as a deliberate statement about power and authority. The most extreme ideological linkages between architecture and the state to emerge in this period can be discerned in three European contexts — Italy, Germany, and the Soviet Union — but can also be seen in examples of patronage by non-totalitarian governments in locations including France and the United States.

In Italy, an authoritarian architecture of monumentality received its strongest expression primarily during the ten-year period from the 1932 Mostra della Revoluzione Fascista to the 1942 Esposizione Universale di Roma. A stark, stripped-down classicism, together with abundant symbolic references to Italy's glorious past, characterized the structures, pavilions, and plans developed for these two major expositions, as well as individual architectural works including Giuseppe Terragni's more modestly scaled Casa del Fascio, Como (1932-36) and Pietro Lingeri and Terragni's unrealized Danteum project (1938). These characteristics were anticipated in such works of the late 1920s as Enrico del Debbio's imposing Foro Mussolini (1927-28) and Accademia di Educazione Fisica (1928), both in Rome. In Germany during approximately the same ten-year period but escalating in the later 1930s with the consolidation of Adolf Hitler's power, Albert Speer's grandiose designs for a new imperial Berlin to be called "Germania" exploited colossal scale and used bombastic Egyptian, Babylonian, and classical motifs in a vocabulary of regimental repetition.

Gunther Forg, *E.U.R. Palazzo della Civiltà* Rome, 1983/89 (Architects: Giovanni Guerrini, Ernesto La Padula, and Mario Romano, 1937-42). Museum of Contemporary Art, Chicago, Gerald S. Elliott Collection

Monumental architecture was also abundant in the Soviet Union in the 1930s, as communicator of the ideology of the Stalinist era. Unlike the visionary, technologically inspired designs of the avant-garde architects of the late teens and twenties, the built works of the thirties were characterized not only by overwhelming scale but also by such devices as classicizing forms, symmetrical organization and the use of massive, enduring materials. Many unrealized designs of this period also utilized a similar vocabulary, including the project for a Palace of the Soviets, envisioned as the state's supreme monument, for which architects were instructed by the Committee for the Construction of the Palace to make use of "both new designs and the best designs of classical architecture."[10] A

Giuseppe Terragni, Casa del Fascio, Como, 1932-36. Photo by Richard Abramson

Enrico del Debbio, Foro Mussolini, Rome, 1927-28, in 1937. Courtesy of Prints and Photographs Division, Library of Congress

competition for the project was won by a design by Boris Iofan, V.A. Shchuko, and V.G. Gel'freikh, on which the architects labored from 1931-39, producing numerous variations of the design for a towering building topped by a massive statue of Lenin. The architecture of the Moscow Metro, begun in the mid-thirties and continuing into the forties, embodies some intriguing applications of a monumental and generally classicizing idiom, in that the stations were designed by a variety of different architects to convey an aura of grandeur, power, and stability. With a dual emphasis on the technological sophistication of the new Metro as a transportation system and the symbolic implications of classical forms, large scale, and ornate materials, the Soviet state sought to foster public confidence at a time of economic crisis and coming war.

Albert Speer, Vogelschauperspektive auf die Nord-Süd-Achse, steel engraving by Alexander Friedrich, 1941. Londesarchiv Berlin

John Russell Pope and Otto R. Eggers, *National Gallery of Art*, 1937. The National Gallery of Art, Washington, D.C. Acquired from Eggers and Higgins, Architects.

The exaggeratedly scaled buildings and city plans cited above were overt expressions of state-sponsored totalitarian ideologies. In the United States and elsewhere in Europe, a corpus of related public buildings and works realized under the aegis of state patronage also employed classicizing and/or monumental idioms. American examples range from the neo-classical National Gallery of Art in Washington, D.C., designed by John Russell Pope from 1929-36, to the massive infra-structural works of the 1930s embodying the imagery of production and industrial might such as the Boulder, Hoover, and Fort Peck Dams built under the Works Progress Administration of Franklin D. Roosevelt's New Deal. While less overtly linked to an authoritarian political ideology, these remain indelible demonstrations of the machinations and strength of government during a time of economic crisis and social upheaval.

Charles Sheeler, *View of Boulder Dam*, 1939. The Lane Collection, Museum of Fine Arts, Boston. Architect: Gordon Kaufmann, Hoover Dam, Boulder City, Nevada, 1931-36

[10] Igor A. Kazus, "The Great Illusion," in *Art and Power: Europe Under the Dictators 1930-1945* (London: Hayward Gallery, 1995), 190.

Hugh Ferriss, *Hoover Dam*, 1941. Avery Architectural and Fine Arts Library, Columbia University in the City of New York. Architect Gordon Kaufmann, Hoover Dam, Boulder City, Nevada, 1931-36

"World of Tomorrow": The Future of Transportation

As with earlier expositions, world's fairs and international events such as the Olympic Games, the New York World's Fair of 1939 served as a staging ground for visionary design. The futuristic, consumerist orientation of exhibits at the Fair, in particular General Motors' "Futurama" and Ford Motor Company's "Road of Tomorrow" and "Cycle of Production," captivated the imagination of the American public with the possibilities of technology and the ideal of progress embodied in

New York World's Fair, 1939, Ford Motor Company Pavilion, "Road of Tomorrow," view of roof. Henry Ford Museum and Greenfield Village Research Center

August Sander, Reichsautobahnbrücke Neandertal, c. 1936. August Sander Archiv/SK Stiftung Kultur; VG Bild-Kunst, Bonn

the latest examples of industrial design. Norman Bel Geddes's and Walter Dorwin Teague's designs for the General Motors and Ford pavilions, respectively, offered dazzlingly stylized environments for the communication of information about the companies' products, in part by means of elaborate and novel multi-media, participatory displays.

The motto of the fair — "Building the World of Tomorrow" — frames a view of the rhetoric behind the development of American highways and automobile-based transportation systems that have subsequently transformed the twentieth-century landscape, revealing how these concepts shaped and were shaped by related ideas about urban planning that would not be fully implemented until the post-World War II era. These American developments contrast with the German Autobahn network of the 1930s — a related automobile transportation system that was similarly a product of state patronage, but a much clearer political statement about industrial might and technical prowess to serve the ideology of nationalism.

Shell Oil advertisement, "Through the City of Tomorrow Without a Stop," 1937. Norman Bel Geddes Collection, Theatre Arts Collection, Harry Ransom Humanities Research Center, The University of Texas at Austin. By permission of Edith Lutyens Bel Geddes, Executrix

Devastation and Reconstruction: The Rebuilding of Cities

By examining the effects of war and massive urban destruction in Europe and Asia on the rebuilding efforts of the 1950s and beyond, the tendencies of planners and architects to view such catastrophic events as opportunities for the imposition of radically altered urban fabrics can be foregrounded. Le Corbusier's large-scale urban plans of the 1920s — the Contemporary City for Three Million Inhabitants of 1922 and the Plan Voisin of 1925 — stand as the progenitors of many of the city plans, urban designs, and buildings that continue to be imposed in settings around the world. In the immediate post-World War II period and in subsequent decades, the most extensive, sweeping planning and building efforts according to a Corbusian model took place in contexts deeply devastated by war such as London, Berlin, Rotterdam, and Hiroshima. Additionally, massive urban revisions

Rotterdam, 1940. Courtesy of Prints and Photographs Division, Library of Congress

Rotterdam, 1946. Courtesy of Prints and Photographs Division, Library of Congress

and extensions occurred under the aegis of urban renewal programs in the United States, or according to the mandates of modernization in Latin America and many non-Western contexts.

A case study of Berlin and aspects of its rebuilding offers a view of a variety of different approaches at mid-century to the theory and practice of urbanism. The competition for the redesign of Berlin Hauptstadt, won by the team of Friedrich Spengelin, Fritz Eggeling, and Gerd Pempelfort in 1958, was implemented as a fairly straightforward modern plan. Yet the most innovative approach to the problem of reconfiguring this important center was represented in the design of the British architects Alison and Peter Smithson, who won third place in the competition. Their project approaches Berlin's replanning from a perspective of integration of the distinct scales of building, street, district, and city, interrelating rather than separating automobile and pedestrian traffic patterns. Refining ideas that they had first explored in designs of the early and mid-1950s for London's Golden Lane Housing and in later CIAM conferences as Team X, with a group of like-minded colleagues, they sought to articulate an alternative to Corbusian planning strategies. Although not realized in this context, the Smithsons' proposal for Berlin Hauptstadt elaborated a significant new vision of the particular and the organic that introduced crucial challenges to the orthodoxy of modernist planning principles.

Mass-produced Housing and Industry after World War II

A widespread urge toward the application of war technology and new materials to housing, primarily in the United States, occurred in the aftermath of World War II. Wartime housing and defense projects as well as the impact of war production on construction preface the creation of the American suburban community Levittown, in which mass-production techniques were used to create the largest

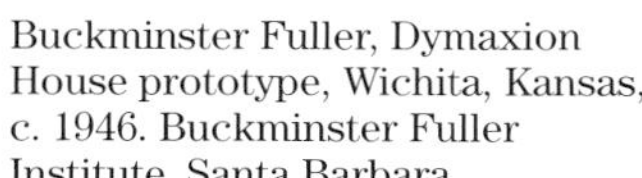

Buckminster Fuller, Dymaxion House prototype, Wichita, Kansas, c. 1946. Buckminster Fuller Institute, Santa Barbara

private housing development ever realized by a single builder, and a variety of concurrent avant-garde experiments.

Modern architects interested in mass, low-cost housing eagerly embraced the possibilities offered by prefabrication techniques developed during wartime and looked to examples such as William Wurster's 1941 Carquinez Heights defense housing in Vallejo, California, as works the efficient construction of which could be emulated and applied on a widespread scale in peacetime. Stemming also from the influence of R. Buckminster Fuller's investigations into technologically based construction systems as early as the 1920s, and the example of his Dymaxion House prototype that was realized as a full-scale built version in 1946 in Wichita, Kansas, under the aegis of the Beech Aircraft Company, their efforts to rationalize housing construction include Konrad Wachsmann and Walter Gropius's General Panel Houses system, begun in 1942, and the modern housing prototypes of the Los Angeles Case Study House program, epitomized by Pierre Koenig's Case Study House #22 (1959-60) and A. Quincy Jones and Frederick Emmons's unbuilt Case Study House #24 (1961). Among the numerous high-rise/low-rise housing efforts realized through the application of prefabrication techniques throughout the world beginning in the later 1940s and 1950s, these examples reveal the mutual aspirations of both avant-garde architects and mass-oriented builders to revolutionize the creation of housing utilizing new technologies and production techniques, albeit with decidedly different results and images, in the American context of nascent suburbanization and postwar social transformation.

Creation of New Capitals in the Second Half of the Century

Three major new capitol complexes by renowned architects realized in the fifties and sixties — Le Corbusier's plan and design for Chandigarh, India (1951-65); Lucio Costa's Pilot Plan for Brasilia, Brazil (1957) together with Oscar Niemeyer's designs for Brasilia's civic buildings; and Louis I. Kahn's Capitol Complex in Dhaka, Bangladesh (1962-71), embody the foremost examples of the modern idiom used to shape emerging national identities. Their planning and architecture make clear statements about the imagery and symbolism sought by governments outside of the political center — an idiom of technological and cultural progress, allied with modernization and westernization — that in some cases led to the hiring of well-known American and European architects to design these important civic buildings and places in non-Western nations.

Chandigarh, established as a new capital for the Punjab state, was envisioned as a symbol of independent, postcolonial India. Le Corbusier's plan and design of major buildings in Chandigarh situated the capitol complex at some distance from the rest of the city and elevated it to underscore its position as the "head" of the city, visible and accessible by means of a large axial thoroughfare. Conceiving a grouping of major buildings within this citadel-like organization — the Secretariat, the Assembly Building, the High Court, and the Governor's Palace, which was not realized — Le Corbusier designated a series of political as well as compositional relationships.

Louis I. Kahn's design for Sher-e-Bangla Nagar, the National Assembly Building on the outskirts of the city of Dhaka, Bangladesh, was begun in 1962 as the legislative capital of East Pakistan. Having visited Chandigarh, Kahn

Le Corbusier, Mill-owners' Association building from across the Sabarmati River, Ahmedabad, India, 1960. Fondation Le Corbusier

Louis I. Kahn, National Assembly Building, Dhaka, Bangladesh, 1963. Photo by Rena Gunay. Aga Khan Trust for Culture

acknowledged its importance and the beauty of its architecture but developed his own design for Dhaka in a different direction. He conjoined the buildings as a single, interconnected composition rather than as a series of discrete elements in response to the failings he perceived in Corbusier's grouping.[11] Seeking to develop a clarity and cohesion among its parts, Kahn elaborated the design to include schools, libraries, housing, and various elements surrounding the centrally-linked assembly building and mosque. The meaning and purpose behind these buildings' functions was for Kahn of consummate importance. In the case of the Assembly, the act of coming together for legislative purposes was viewed as an enlightened and almost transcendent activity, which Kahn sought to address in his architecture. He commented, "What I'm trying to do is establish a belief out of a philosophy I can turn over to Pakistan so that whatever they do is always answerable to that."[12]

The creation of the city of Brasilia, spearheaded by President Juscelino Kubitschek to initiate rapid development and more widespread modernization in Brazil and to help instigate a national identity, represents an important instance where foreign architects were not commissioned to produce such an important site. Instead, the plan of the city was configured by Lucio Costa, winner of a national competition in 1957, and its buildings designed by Oscar Niemeyer. Costa's cruciform-shaped plan evoked an image of flight that symbolized the idea of rapid forward progress. Its monumental scale, positioning different sectors at large distances from each other, was organized around an automobile-oriented transportation system, which also represented an urge toward mechanization and ideas about technological progress. As in Chandigarh, the residential groupings were sited away from the city's central focus, but were even more distinctly separated from it, intended by Brasilia's architects and planners to foster a non-hierarchical social organization encompassing upper, middle, and lower echelon bureaucrats in residences identical in form and layout.[13] As in Corbusier's Chandigarh, Oscar Niemeyer's designs for the buildings of the Capitol Complex, which are also sited around a vast open plaza, provide the focal point for Brasilia, representing not only a clear architectural hierarchy but also the symbolic presence of government dominating the landscape. The insistent modernism of Niemeyer's sleek, curvilinear designs crystallized Kubitschek's national aspirations toward progress and mechanization in a relatively unindustrialized country, giving form to his vision of Brasilia as "the dawn of a new day for Brazil."[14]

Geoffrey Bawa, New Parliamentary Complex, Sri Jayawordenepura, Kotte, Sri Lanka, 1982. Photo by Richard Bryant

Analysis of these major civic buildings and complexes reveals the way in which they represent their creators' application of *a priori* ideas about planning and architecture, regardless of local traditions and contexts, and the way in which these systems of urban organization and buildings function in relation to

[11] David B. Brownlee and David G. De Long, *Louis I. Kahn: In the Realm of Architecture* (New York: Universe Publishing, 1997), 111.

[12] Ibid., 110.

[13] Lawrence Vale analyzes the subsequent failure of this attempt at social engineering in *Architecture, Power, and National Identity*, (New Haven: Yale University Press, 1992) 119-21.

[14] Ibid., 125.

patterns of living in the region. As a counterpoint to the heroism of these plans for monumentally scaled, International Style modern buildings and cities, the New Parliamentary Complex of Sri Jayawordenepura, Kotte, Sri Lanka (1982), designed by Geoffrey Bawa, offers a more locally inflected engagement with such issues as appropriateness of design to climate, regional architectural idioms versus international or "signature" styles, and the realities of urbanistic function.

The "Center" and the "Periphery": Interactions and Hybridizations

During the course of this century, as modernism has emerged as a global phenomenon extending from Europe and the United States to Latin America, Asia, the Middle East, and Africa, its interaction with regionalist modes has produced complex and intriguing forms of architectural hybridization. In the crucial transformative decades of mid-century, instances of national expressions in international contexts at the world's fairs of the late 1930s in Paris and New York offer compelling examples of variations in the ethos of internationalism. At these fairs the architecture of national pavilions was of consummate importance to the identity of the sponsoring nation in the continuously shifting arena of international political, economic, and cultural relations. In the cases of nations seeking to assert their identities alongside those of the major world powers, these prominent commissions often fell to leading architects who were also considered "advanced" such as Alvar Aalto, who created a groundbreaking modern design for the Finnish pavilion at the 1939 New York World's Fair, the significance of which is also in part attributable to the regional inflection of the forms and materials employed in the pavilion's interior. In contrast, Junko Sakakura's pavilion for Japan at the 1937 Paris World Exposition pointedly rejected all localized or otherwise traditional architectural features in favor of International-Style modernism.

Steven Holl, Museum of Contemporary Art, Helsinki, 1993-98

Extending this theme further in the context of their own locales throughout the century's middle period from the 1920s through the 1960s, significant works by such architects as Reima Pietilä in Finland, Sutemi Horiguchi, Kunio Maekawa, and Kenzo Tange in Japan, and Juan O'Gorman, Carlos Raúl Villanueva, and Lina Bo Bardi in Mexico, Venezuela, and Brazil, respectively, represent various responses to and adaptations of modernism. The work of these architects has contributed substantially to distinctive revitalizations and extensions of the International-Style idiom. In subsequent decades, a wide variety of architects ranging from Charles Correa and Ricardo Legorreta to Jean Nouvel and Steven Holl have built upon the legacy of their forerunners to develop major works that are significant carriers of regional identity, inflected with cultural and/or contextual references, yet remain firmly within the vocabulary of modernism. Within an increasingly globalized architectural culture, the ideological position of the

Alvar Aalto, Finnish Pavilion, New York World's Fair, 1939. Photo by Ezra Stoller

architect working in non-Western or other contexts considered peripheral rather than central can be cast into relief, and the phenomenon of regionalism as a climactic, economic, political, social, and cultural expression can be examined.

The Architecture of Ecology

Ecology in architecture takes on a plethora of forms and can be defined as a responsiveness to climactic and topographical concerns as well as social ones and a desire for energy efficiency in the making and maintaining of buildings. In the mid-1940s Richard Neutra realized a number of designs for schools and community centers in Puerto Rico in which he applied ideas about open planning, indoor/outdoor living, and simple, industrial materials developed for

Kenzo Tange, Town Hall, Kurashiki, Japan, 1958-60

Hassan Fathy, Village square and mosque, New Gourna, Egypt, 1948. Aga Khan Trust for Culture. Photo by C. Avedissian

ADAUA (Association for the Development of Traditional African Urbanism and Architecture), Extension to Kaedi Regional Hospital, Mauritania, 1989. Aga Khan Trust for Culture. Photo by Kamkan Adle

markedly different settings to the tropical climate of this context. Unlike Neutra's approach to the application of a standardized system, Hassan Fathy's late 1940s design of the new town of New Gourna, Egypt, was predicated on a rejection of modernism and an embrace of local construction techniques, regional typologies, vernacular forms and images, and existing social patterns. In many respects the attitude of the Western-educated Fathy was as much a political statement as an architectural one, reflecting his strong opposition to a generic internationalism.

Concerns related to those espoused by Fathy can also be seen in other designs for efficient, site responsive housing in India by such architects as Charles Correa and Balkrishna Doshi of the sixties, seventies, and eighties, albeit within a more stridently modern and hybridized vocabulary. Other significant examples in non-Western contexts include Fabrizio Caròla of the Association for the Development of Traditional African Urbanism and Architecture's extension to Kaedi Regional Hospital in Mauritania, and Shushtar New Town in Iran, designed and partially completed from 1974-80 by DAZ Architects. The planning of the new town emphasizes horizontal rather than vertical organization, in part as a way to incorporate traditional patterns of living and circulation in opposition to the imposed Western idiom of the high-rise.

The countercultural experiments of American architects of the sixties and early seventies, including Paolo Soleri, Steve Baer, Sim van der Ryn, and Peter Calthorpe, reveal a strong desire for energy efficiency and a predilection for ad hoc living and working environments. The spirit behind Soleri's Arcosanti, an ecologically-based community in the Arizona desert, is echoed in the Ciudad Abierta, an urban and architectural experiment by Alberto Cruz and the Cooperative Amereida begun in 1970 near Valparaiso, Chile.

Throughout the second half of the century, issues of energy efficiency have increasingly emerged as important to a wide spectrum of architects, including those who are most recently exploring its application within the framework of "High Tech." These range from Norman Foster and Renzo Piano in Europe, to Hamzah and Yeang, Itsuko Hasegawa, and Team Zoo in Asia, to the Grupo de Diseño Urbano of Mexico City and the planners and leaders of the city of Curitiba, Brazil. Their concern demonstrates the increasing awareness, not only within the architectural profession but also among the public in general, of the world's limited resources in the face of burgeoning population, advancing technology and global economics.

Steve Baer, Baer House, near Corrales, New Mexico, 1975. Photo by Julius Shulman

Charles Correa, Kanchenjunga Apartments, Bombay, 1983

Structural Expressionism

The twentieth century has witnessed enormous technological leaps that have radically and fundamentally altered ways of life during the past one hundred years. Likewise, the development of new technologies and materials associated with building (folded slab construction, structural prefabrication, tensile structures, concrete shell construction, radial glazing systems, etc.) have profoundly impacted form-making throughout the century.

Encompassing stadia, opera houses, churches, airports, train stations, industrial complexes and cultural facilities, a diverse range of technologically inspired building types spans the 1930s to the present. Centering on works in which structure has been taken to the point of developing its own rhetoric, becoming the foremost defining element of building, the enormous reach of technology and the way in which it has impacted architecture through engineering comes into sharp focus. Once a primary focus of the study of modern architecture, this tectonic approach can be reconsidered and updated by examining works that are recognized

Eero Saarinen, TWA Terminal, Idlewild Airport, Queens, New York, 1962. Photo by Ezra Stoller

Eduardo Torroja, Grandstand at Zarzuela Racetrack, Madrid, 1935. Instituto de Ciencias de la Construccion Eduardo Torroja, Madrid

James Stirling and James Gowan, Leicester Engineering Building, Leicester, England, 1960. Deutsches Architektur-Museum Archiv

as classic examples of structurally expressive modernism from the turn-of-the century experiments with relationships between organic form, geometry, and structure of Antoni Gaudi, to the mid-century designs of engineers Eduardo Torroja, Pier Luigi Nervi, and Felix Candela, and architects Jørn Utzon, James Stirling, and Eero Saarinen. In addition, less familiar examples of structural inventiveness can be found in the work of Eladio Dieste, who focused on the construction techniques associated with brick as a major defining element of buildings such as the Church at Atlantida, Uruguay (1959) and Raj Rewal, who

Renzo Piano and Richard Rogers, Centre Georges Pompidou, Paris, 1972-77. Photo by Michel Denance

Kazuo Shinohara, Tokyo Institute of Technology, Centennial Hall, Tokyo, 1987. Photo by Masao Arai

designed and built major structural complexes in India including the Permanent Exhibition Complex in New Delhi (1972). Related uses of structure as a primary determinant of form have emerged in a diversity of more recent buildings by architects including Nicholas Grimshaw, Richard Rogers, Renzo Piano, Kazuo Shinohara, Zaha Hadid, Enrique Norten, and Frank Gehry, in a variety of international contexts during the past quarter century.

Nicholas Grimshaw, International Terminal at Waterloo Station, London, 1993. Photo by Peter Cook

Zaha Hadid, Vitra Fire Station, Weil-am-Rhein, Germany, 1994. Photo by Paul Warchol

The Edge of Utopia: Megastructures and Infrastructures

A selection of utopian and visionary experiments of the late fifties and sixties, including works of the Archigram group in England and the Metabolists in Japan, offer a counterpoint to the type of structural experimentation applied in built works during the same period. These unrealized projects demonstrate often fantastic ways in which architects have gravitated towards the ideas and forms of technology and concepts of service encompassing modular units, interchangeable parts, plug-in components, etc., as purely investigatory devices.

Visionary urban projects such as Kenzo Tange's Tokyo Bay Plan (1960), Kisho Kurokawa's Helix City (1961), and Arata Isozaki's Clusters in the Air (1962), together with projects including Ron Herron's Walking City (1964), Archizoom's No Stop City (1970), and Superstudio's radically reinvented urban fragments of the late sixties reveal various approaches to and contexts for the application of these ideas. Related designs for single buildings including Cedric Price's Fun Palace (1961), Michael Webb's Drive-In House (1963-66), and Coop Himmelb(l)au's Cloud Project (1968-72) probe the notion of the megastructure at the service of the utopian, and illuminate the roots of these ideas in the buoyant sense

Arata Isozaki, Clusters in the Air, 1962. Centre Canadien d' Architecture/Canadian Centre for Architecture, Montréal

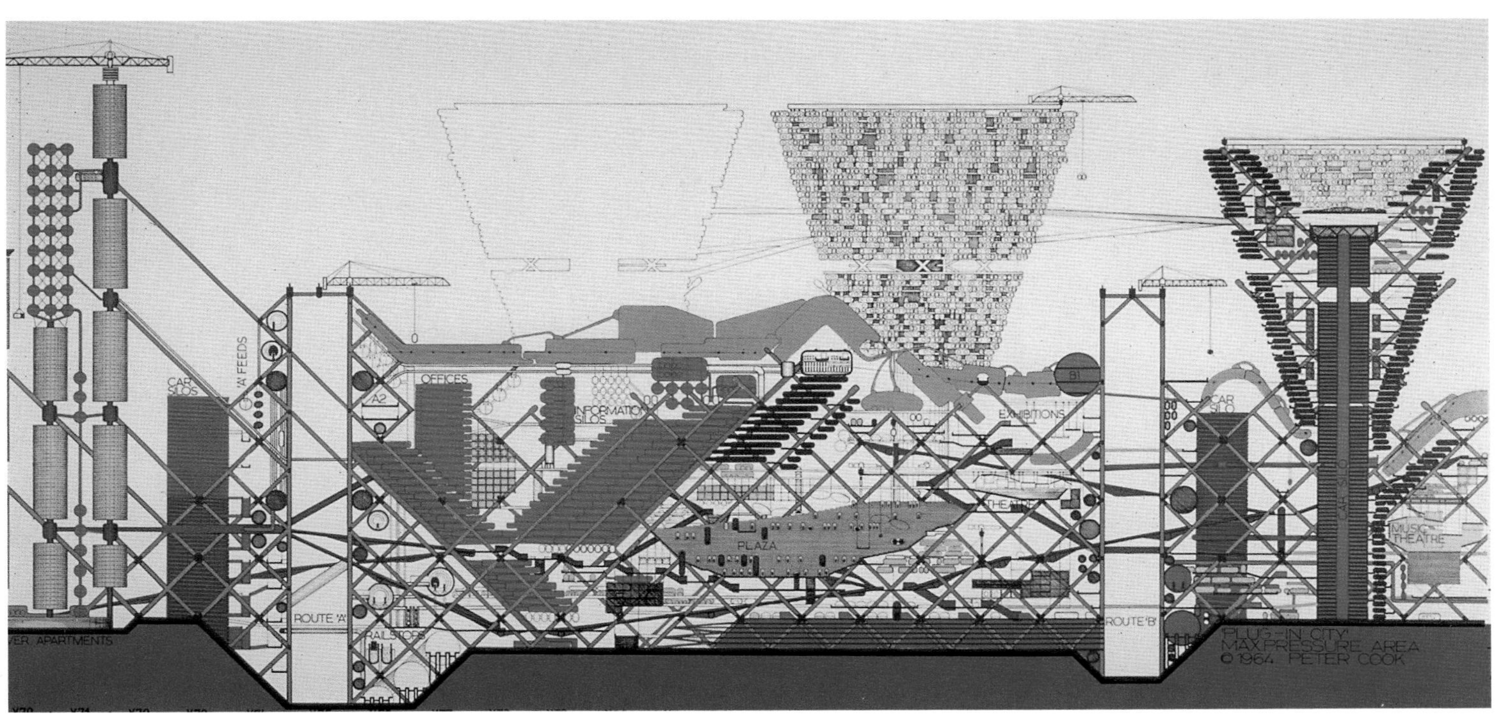

Peter Cook (Archigram), Plug-In City, 1964. Centre Georges Pompidou

Kenzo Tange, Expo '70, Osaka

Kenzo Tange and URTEC, Tokyo Bay Plan, 1960

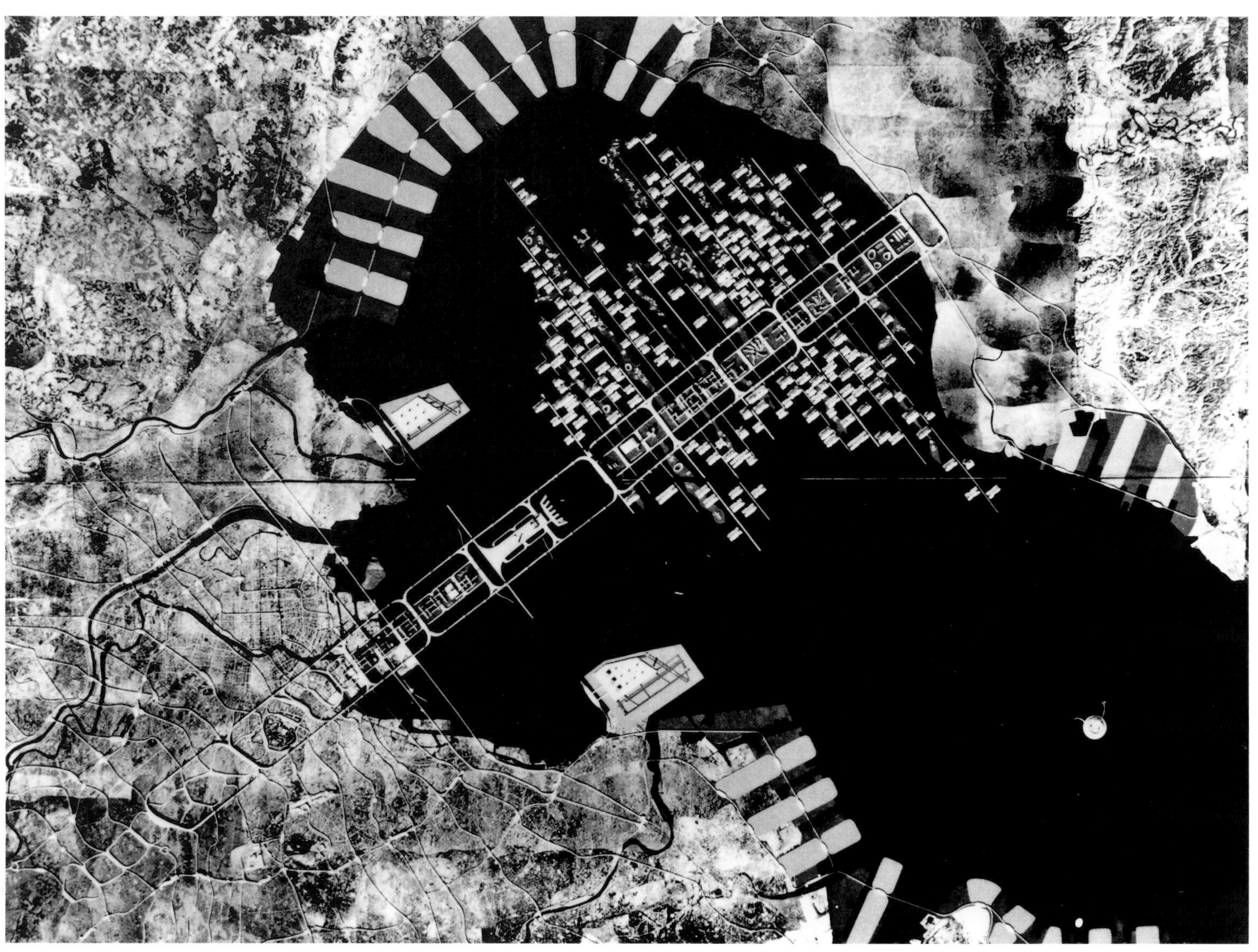

of possibility and experimentation that characterized the 1960s. At Expo '70 in Osaka, Japan, designed by a team of architects headed by Tange, wildly inventive concepts about megastructure and infrastructure were realized and presented to the public in the context of new communication, information, and transportation technologies.

The Rise of Theory in the 1960s and 1970s

Theory surfaced as a powerful force in architecture during the sixties and seventies, a transitional period in which architects sought to establish an oppositional framework to the hegemony of modernism and to explore new directions in the making of form. Many of the theoretical impulses disseminated through publications, journals, and other texts during this period have continued to play a major role in the transmission and shaping of recent architectural discourse.

Searching for an alternative to the modern movement, which had become widely institutionalized and seemed formulaic and banal to a younger generation, architects turned to areas of inquiry that had been suppressed or overlooked under modernism to find new sources of inspiration. This youthful avant-garde began to demonstrate renewed interest in historical and vernacular modes of architecture and in traditional patterns of city organization. Among the most influential texts of this period are Kevin Lynch's *The Image of the City* (1960), Robert Venturi's *Complexity and Contradiction in Architecture* (1962), Aldo Rossi's *L'architecttura della città* (1966), Reyner Banham's *Los Angeles: The Architecture of Four Ecologies* (1971), and Christopher Alexander's *Timeless Way of Building* (1979), all of which, with differing emphases, extolled the traditional, the popular, and/or the sociological as newly fresh and vital modes of reference.

Banham also played an instrumental role as a historian of modernism by reviving interest in some of its earlier utopian manifestations, including Italian futurism and the Russian avant-garde. Architects and historians were largely

Office for Metropolitan Architecture, The City of the Captive Globe, 1972. Deutsches Architektur-Museum Archiv

reintroduced to this body of work and ideas through Banham's pioneering 1960 study *Theory and Design in the First Machine Age*. The theories put forth in *Delirious New York* (1978) by Rem Koolhaas, who sought to reinterpret aspects of earlier modernism and to incorporate the sensibility of spatial dynamism and the utopianism of technology into his own work, can be understood in some respects as prefigured by Banham's scholarly contributions and the eclectic range of his architectural interests. Other architect/theoreticians looked to such extra-architectural disciplines as philosophy, literary theory, and linguistics as fields of inquiry with intriguing implications for architectural analysis. In addition, the writings of Peter Eisenman, Jose Rafael Moneo, Diana Agrest and Mario Gandelsonas, and others published in the journal *Oppositions* edited by Eisenman and Kenneth Frampton in the mid-1970s broke new ground in the development of typological and semiotic issues as bases for architectural theory. The fertility of this period as a testing ground for new ideas and directions which in many instances were not tested or applied in the architects' built works until years later corresponds to the vitality and urgency of theoretical investigation that occurred in the early years of the century within modernism.

Walt Disney introduces Disneyland on television, 1954

Culture of Spectacle: Cities of Fantasy, Tourism, and Entertainment

"Disneyfication" has emerged as a major phenomenon of the late twentieth century, in which ideas about innovation and tradition merge and in which futuristic and fantastic impulses collide with exoticism and kitsch. Walt Disney's initial concepts of the 1960s for EPCOT (Experimental Prototype Community of Tomorrow) emphasized the planned environment of the future as a utopian, yet populist and entertainment-oriented, ideal community that would encompass a residential sector alongside a series of recreational and commercial attractions, linked by a high-tech transportation system. Its embodiment of futuristic impulses was realized in the resort of EPCOT Center in Orlando, Florida, yet Disney's vision of a living environment as a significant planning component of EPCOT remained on the drawing boards until its recent manifestation in the Disney-sponsored residential community of Celebration, Florida, in which a complex combination of tradition and innovation is invoked.

While Disney theme parks have proliferated in sites around the world and have even encroached upon urban centers, as in New York City's newly redeveloped Times Square, the city of Las Vegas offers a related but divergent example of a constructed setting oriented to mass entertainment. In the constantly shifting urban landscape of the Las Vegas strip, the spectacular, touristic, and fantastic appear in an exaggerated form, controlled by the dictates of the market and by the public's appetite for ever-increasing forms of novelty and stimulation. Juxtaposing highly staged evocations of ancient Egypt, Manhattan, Monte Carlo, and the Roman empire, the architecture of Las Vegas' hotels and attractions fulfills a scenographic function that collapses time and space in a dizzying variety of historical and urban references.

New York-New York Hotel and Casino, Las Vegas, 1996. Photo by Jack Dempsey

The House as an Aesthetic Laboratory

A selection of pivotal residential designs from the second half of the century are key examples of experimentation with ideas about form, space, materials, technology, and personal expression. Reiterating many of the concerns found earlier in the century during the efflorescence of house architecture in the twenties and thirties, they also offer distinct differences that reflect the scope of developments in architectural culture and tectonics over the past fifty years.

Many of these works have served as laboratory-like settings wherein their architects have tested a variety of unorthodox theories or approaches on the intimate scale of the house. A broad range of aesthetic sensibilities is demonstrated within these innovative house designs by architects ranging from Luis Barragan, Juan O'Gorman, Charles and Ray Eames, Bruce Goff, Kiyonori Kikutake,

Juan O'Gorman, House in El Pedregal, Mexico, 1953-56. Photo by Esther McCoy. Esther McCoy Papers, The Archives of American Art, Smithsonian Institution

Bruce Goff, Bavinger House, Norman, Oklahoma, 1957. Photo by William P. Bruder

Charles and Ray Eames, Eames House, Santa Monica, California, 1945-49. Photo by Julius Shulman

Oscar Niemeyer, and Mies van der Rohe in the forties and fifties; Frank Gehry, John Lautner, Ricardo Legorreta, Richard Meier, Kazuo Shinohara, and Robert Venturi in the sixties and seventies, and Tadao Ando, Elizabeth Diller and Ricardo Scofidio, Gunther Domenig, Toyo Ito, Enric Miralles, and Morphosis in the eighties and nineties. Some (like designs by Frederick Kiesler of 1959 and John Hejduk of 1978-79) were envisioned from the outset as investigatory paper projects. In all instances these houses, often designed as residences for the architects themselves, are highly experimental, unique environments, representing touchstones in the development of recent and current discourse.

John Lautner, Malin "Chemosphere" House, Los Angeles, 1960. Photo by Julius Shulman

Enric Miralles, Casa Garau-Agusti, Belaterra, Barcelona, 1988-93

Kiyonori Kikutake, Skyhouse, Bunkyo Ward, Tokyo, 1958. Photo by Yukio Futagawa

Richard Meier, Smith House, Darien, Connecticut, 1965-67. Photo by Scott Frances

Toyo Ito, Silver Hut, Tokyo, 1984. Photo by Tomio Ohashi

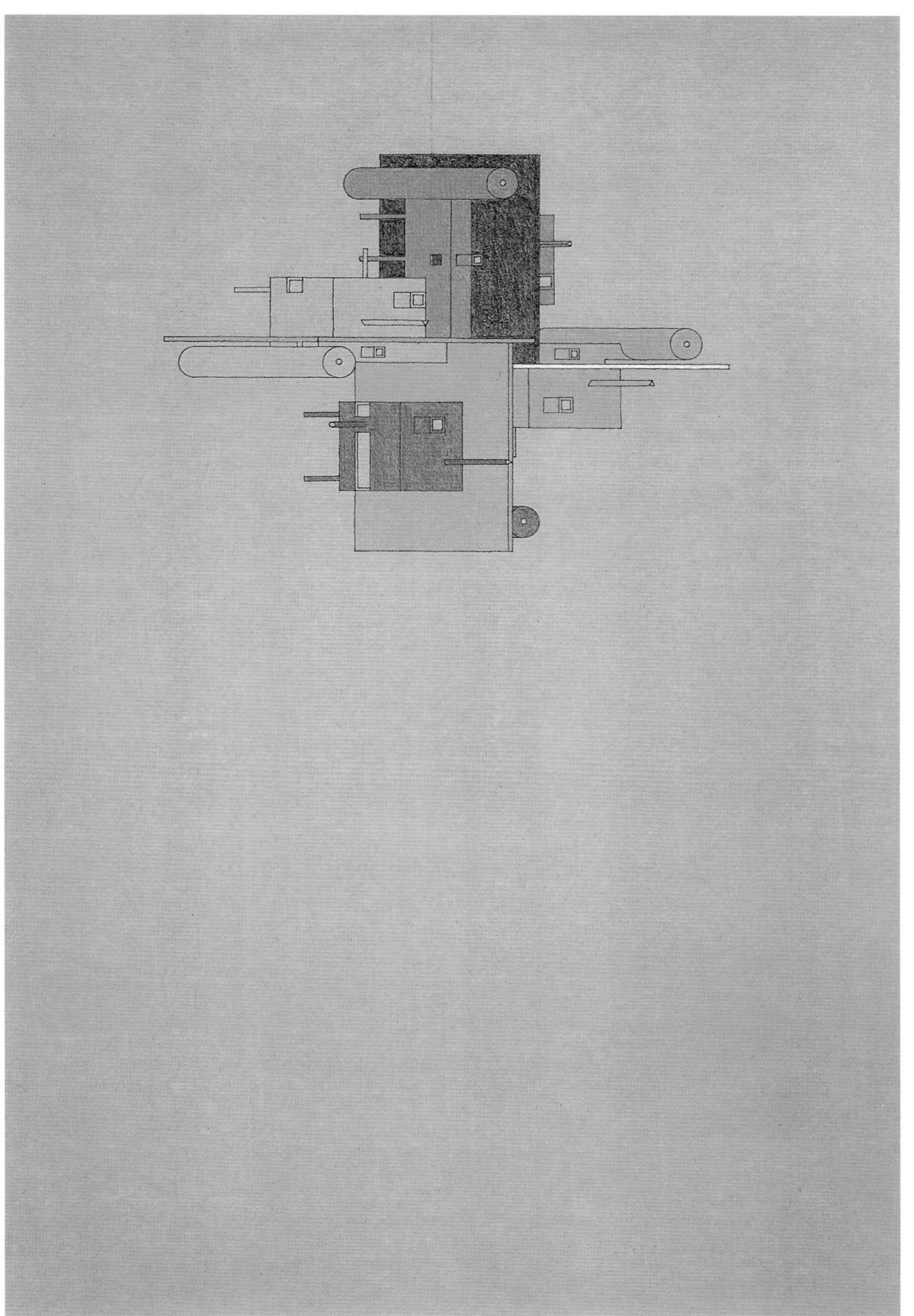

John Hejduk, Axonometric projection seen from the South of the North East South West House, c. 1978-79. Collection Centre Canadien d'Architecture/Canadian Centre for Architecture, Montreal

Edward J. Steichen, *The Flatiron*, 1909 print from 1904 negative. The Metropolitan Museum of Art, New York, Alfred Stieglitz Collection, 1933. Architect: Daniel Burnham, Flatiron Building, New York, 1902

The Skyscraper: A Twentieth-century Building Type

The skyscraper constitutes the quintessential building type of the twentieth century, from its most significant early developments in American cities including Chicago and New York to recent projects in Asia that underscore the changing social, political, and economic landscapes at the end of this century. In the literature on skyscrapers, the economic and political matrix that informs much

Cass Gilbert, Woolworth Building, New York, 1913, view from the northeast. Collection of The New York Historical Society

Kenzo Tange, Tokyo City Hall, 1994. Photo by Osamu Murai

Frank Lloyd Wright, Mile-High Skyscraper, 1956. Frank Lloyd Wright Foundation, Scottsdale, Arizona

current architectural analysis is deeply evident. Instead of a concentration on matters of form or technology, numerous recent writers have pointed to zoning and other governmental regulations, the bottom-line mentality of real estate markets and construction costs versus profit margins, and the vagaries of corporate identity and personal ego as factors that have all played a major role in the genesis of the skyscraper during the course of this century. Patrons' commitment to design quality not for its own sake but because of a belief in its profitability further bespeaks the economic underpinning of developments in this building type, especially during the past fifty years. At the same time, the technological motivation behind the skyscraper — its hallmark at the outset of the century — has continued to evolve with increasingly lighter and more economical frameworks. Whether structure is exploited, as in the vocabulary of High Tech, or masked with heavy cladding reflecting historicizing impulses, the push toward creating ever-greater height records seems to continue unabated, especially in designs for cities such as Shanghai and Kuala Lumpur that are at present key sites for the evolving economic crucible of the turn into the next century.

Richard Rogers, Lloyds of London, London, 1978-86. Photo by Richard Bryant

Kenzo Tange, Shizuoka Press Administration Building, Tokyo, 1965-70. Photo by Osamu Murai

Hiroshi Sugimoto, Shizuoka Press Administration Building (Kenzo Tange 1965-70). 1997

left: Norman Foster, Hong Kong Shanghai Bank, 1986. right: I.M. Pei, Bank of China, Hong Kong, 1990. Photo by Paul Warchol

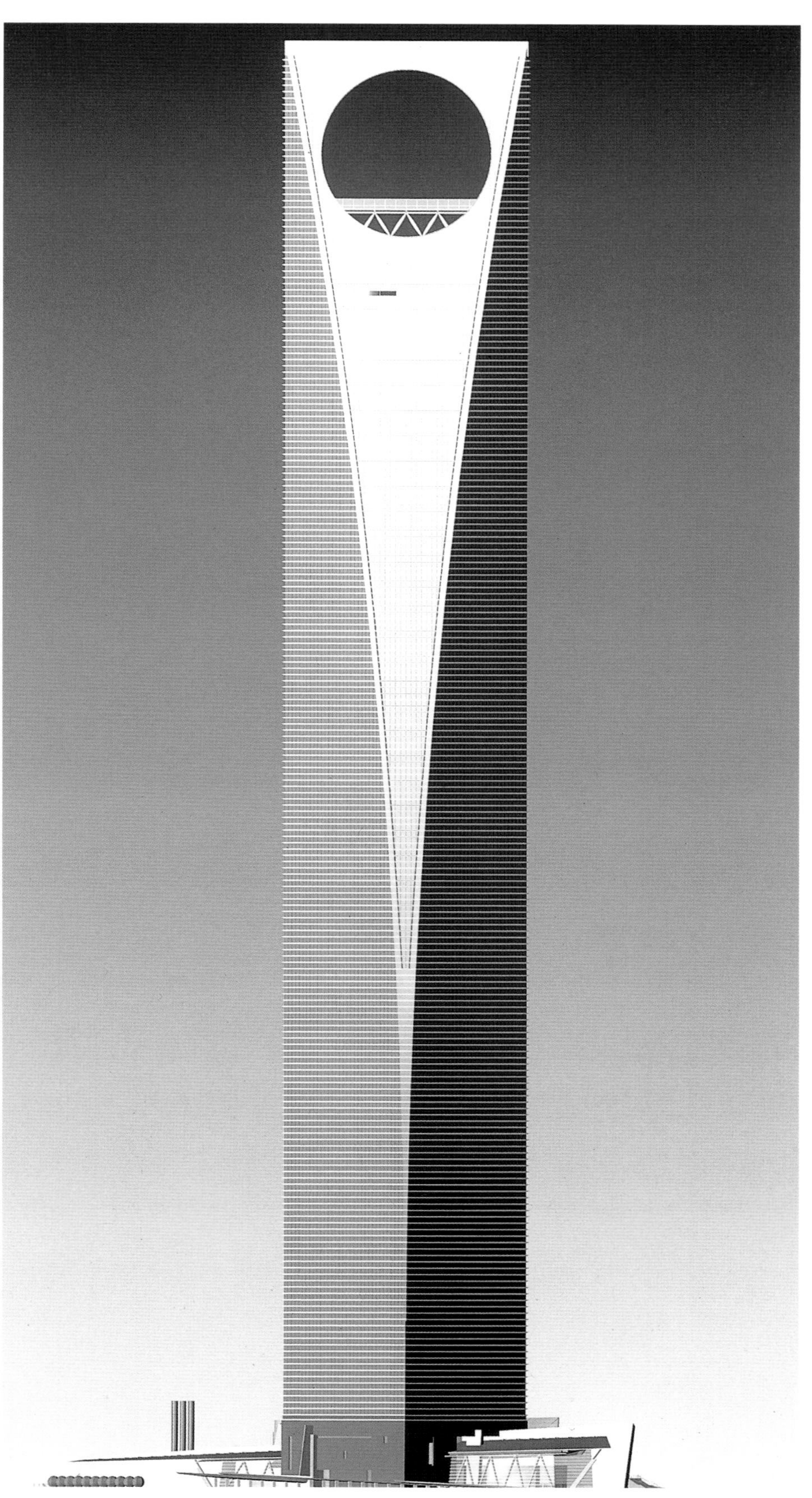

Kohn Pedersen Fox Associates, Shanghai World Financial Center, Shanghai, completion date: 2002

Frank Gehry, Guggenheim Museum, Bilbao, 1997. Photo by Jeff Goldberg

SPACE, TIME, AND MOVEMENT

Anthony Vidler

In the context of an exhibition that attempts to survey twentieth-century architecture and urbanism on a world scale, representing more than a century of buildings, cities, projects, and theories, it is useful for a moment to step back from the heterogeneous collection of diverse movements and styles in order to identify some underlying common themes. Such themes might be less concerned with claims of avant-garde "newness," "breaks" with the past, or stylistic similarities, and more with attitudes toward "modernity" in general. Interrelated questions such as the "nature of Modernism," the "question of technology," the "idea of history," the "problem of form," the social theory of "metropolis," and many others come to mind. But even as the conventional history of modern architecture has tended to reproduce the history fabricated by the avant-gardes themselves, in a historical justification of self-justification, so to speak, so too, a history of more general themes takes the risk of falling into an opposite error: that of imposing a unifying narrative from outside architecture, an approach that has been largely discredited. We have learned to be skeptical of grand theses about the progress, rise, and fall of architecture and society drawn from the application of Darwinist and other theories to the social sciences. Even today, claims are made for the "end of architecture" neatly tied to the "end of history" and coinciding with the "end of the century." And yet some critical and thematic history of our own period, one that does not fall into the trap of an unthinking repetition of historical sources and art-historical commonplaces, while also avoiding the pitfalls of "world-view" history, is obviously necessary, if only as a starting point for interpretation.

Among the possible candidates for such an overriding theme, the idea of space, and of modern space in particular, has engaged not only historians and theorists, but also architects themselves throughout the century; since, that is, the inception of this idea in architectural thought as it gradually supplanted late-nineteenth-century visions of time and history. By the First World War, indeed, the notion of space had emerged as *the* single idea that characterized modernist, avant-garde architecture throughout Europe and the United States. Such an idea, in its many different incarnations, and with multiple and often opposing ascriptions, has continued to be a preoccupation throughout the century.

From Time to Style

It is a commonplace of architectural history to state that at some time quite early in the nineteenth century, perhaps even at the end of the eighteenth, architectural thinkers and writers joined their counterparts in other disciplines — philosophy, literature, painting, and so on — in a common interest in, if not obsession with, *time and temporality*. This increasing awareness of history, of the historical styles, led inevitably to the general sense that historical narrative formed the basis for architectural design.

Thus the historical and critical interpretation of architecture in the eighteenth and nineteenth centuries was largely dominated by concepts of "style" and "genre" similar to those operative in the domain of painting. Marked by nineteenth-century debates over the relative merits of historical revivals — "Gothic" versus "Classic" — and by the emergence of new functional demands in industrial society, architectural history was generally cast in the form of a narrative tracing the succession of major or minor stylistic periods. From James Ferguson in the early nineteenth century to Nikolaus Pevsner in the mid-twentieth, some version of this narrative of the styles has remained constant.

This basis in a temporal narrative, more often than not a narrative of progress, seemed to offer the reassuring authority of a law of historical development to an architecture deprived of religious and quasi-universal symbolic value by secularization and the Enlightenment, an authority that gained even more significance when joined to the emerging science of evolution after Darwin. A work might thus be constituted as representative of another era, bringing that era's principles, morals, ethics, and cultural values into play in the present. The medievalizing theories and designs of Augustus Northmore Welby Pugin, John Ruskin, and William Morris were based on this premise. Alternatively, according to the historicist principle that each epoch in the past seemed to have its own manner of speaking, its own language, authentic to its society and no other, an architectural theory might call for a language appropriate to modern times, one that future historians could signal out as being distinctively modern: the Viennese architect Otto Wagner set out this position comprehensively in his *Moderne Architektur* of 1896. In each case the architectural work was seen as deeply founded on and in history, with a strong sense of its place with respect to the past, present and future.

Formed in this way under the aegis of nationalist romantic ideals that sought a unity between aesthetic character and architectural style, stressing the moral virtue of a "natural" language expressing the culture of an entire "people," this version of architectural history was, paradoxically enough, equally easily assimilated as the armature for a more ahistorical and formalist analysis, such as that developed in the late nineteenth century by Heinrich Wölfflin and his followers. The crude but satisfying periodization embedded in Hegelian historicism was an easy way to give chronology and sequence to the appearance of formal qualities, such as "linear," "planar," and "massive" form, in a rough historical order, a way of endowing pictorial attributes with historicity. After Wölfflin, while scholars have attempted to complicate periodization, disturb previous "crude" stylistic divisions, and introduce new styles like "late Roman," "Mannerism," and "Rococo" into the canonical roster of "Classic," "Gothic," and "Renaissance," they have done little to subvert these fundamental outlines. The invention of terms such as "Postmodern," "Late Modern," "Deconstructivist," and the like to categorize contemporary architecture has demonstrated the staying-power of this approach, that seeks to identify a nucleus of specific stylistic attributes in order to measure normalization, deformation, and transformation in relation to temporal "periods."

From Style to Space

At some time towards the end of the nineteenth century, however, and fast gaining ground in the first years of this century, this sense of historical authority was challenged, first in philosophy and psychology, then in the arts in general. History and temporality were subjected to a critique that attempted, in general terms, to relieve the present of the "burden" of the past. We might take Nietzsche's essay, "Of the Advantage and Disadvantage of History for Every Day Life," as paradigmatic of this movement, an attempt to counter the overpowering force of history by a modernity that sought to avoid the trap of time.

Out of this critique of history a new paradigm gradually emerged for architecture, around the idea of something that was loosely understood as *space*, a universal flux that would have the potential of finally escaping from history and of installing a new world of action and life in place of the old.

The new preoccupation with space was founded on the understanding that the relationship between a viewer and a work of art was based on a shifting "point of view" determined by a moving body, a theory worked out in late nineteenth-century psychological aesthetics by Robert Vischer and Theodor Lipps, and popularized in art criticism by Adolf Hildebrand; the spatial dimension rapidly became a central preoccupation for those interested in understanding the special conditions of architecture, an art that, while perceived visually, was experienced in space. In architectural history, similarly, the notion of architectural space as having a historical specificity was used to give new life to the historicist paradigm: the history of styles was gradually dissolved into, or replaced by, the history of spaces.[1] Given historical specificity as a product of culturally determined vision by pioneers of formal analysis like Alois Riegl, "space" became central to the architectural histories of August Schmarsow and Paul Frankl. Thus, in his thesis of 1913-14, *Die Entwicklungsphasen der neueren Baukunst*, translated as *Principles of Architectural History*, Frankl grafted a spatial history of architecture since the Renaissance on to the time-honored periodization of historicism. His four categories, "spatial form," "corporeal form," "visible form," and "purposive intention," were explored in the context of four periods or phases, with the intent of reformulating the question of style according to spatio-formal criteria that acted together to form a total building:

> The visual impression, the *image* produced by differences of light and color, is primary in our perception of a building. We empirically reinterpret this image into a conception of *corporeality*, and this defines the form of the *space within*, whether we read it from outside or stand in the interior. But optical appearances, corporeality, and space, do not alone make a building. . . . Once we have interpreted the optical image into a conception of space, enclosed by mass, we read its *purpose* from the spatial form.[2]

Linked in this way to corporeal and social function, space, for many avant-garde architects after 1900, became the primary instrument of urban and

1 See Paul Zucker, "The Paradox of Architectural Theory at the Beginning of the 'Modern Movement'", *Journal of the Society of Architectural Historians* 10, no. 3 (October 1951): 8-14; see also the useful compilation by H.F. Mallgrave and E. Ikonomou, *Empathy, Form, and Space: Problems in German Aesthetics, 1873-1893* (Santa Monica: The Getty Center for the History of Art and the Humanities, 1994).

2 Paul Frankl, *Principles of Architectural History. The Four Phases of Architectural Style, 1420-1900.* Translated and edited by James F. O'Gorman (Cambridge: The MIT Press, 1968), 1.

architectural reform. Its apparent ability to supersede "style" and the "styles," its abstraction and universalism, its capacity to be conceived in terms of modern activities and modern movement — speed and communication — and its ability to accommodate the new, healthy body of modern citizens, all of these assumed virtues and more were adopted rapidly as the premises of design and the polemical manifestoes of modernism.

The subsequent history of modern architecture, indeed, might be, and often has been, written as a history of competing ideas of space. Thus, to cite only a very few examples, the Dutch architect Hendrick Berlage wrote on "Raumkunst und Architektur" in 1907; August Endell, who had followed the lectures of Theodor Lipps in Munich, joined spatial theory to empathy theory in his *Die Schönheit des grossen Stadt* of 1908; both authors have been seen as influential on the spatial ideas of Mies van der Rohe.[3] The Dutch architects and painters in the de Stijl group, including Theo van Doesburg and Piet Mondrian, advanced their revolutionary concepts of "neo-plastic" space in their own journal. In the United States, Frank Lloyd Wright took on the entire space of the continent in his vision of a "prairie" space, fit for democratic individualists. His Viennese assistant, Rudolph Schindler, dubbed this "space architecture" in a brief homage to what he called this "new medium," published in 1934.

Space and Time

Ideas of space, however, were not easily detached from their origins in historicist thought; the relationship of new spatial ideas to history, and their emergence from and within historical discourse was ambiguous, and perhaps has never been absolutely resolved. "Time," after all, was still a property of activity in space and, as heralded in Filippo Tommaso Marinetti's Futurist Manifesto published in the Paris *Figaro*, February 20, 1909, movement and speed were never quite able to disassociate themselves from temporality and historicity. The compromise position, a collapsing of time into space, or vice versa, emerging long before the popularization of Einstein's formula of "space-time," was equally difficult to withdraw from history, or from the progressive narrative of historicism. To take a well-known example: that of the "search for lost time" conducted by the narrator of Marcel Proust's novel *A la recherche du temps perdu* (In Search of Lost Time) (1913), a novel that despite the misleading overtones of Edwardian nostalgia in its English translation as *Remembrance of Things Past*, was concerned as much with the spatialization of time as with the persistence of memory. As Julia Kristeva in her recent study of Proust has noted:

> When faced with two inexorable forms of temporality — death . . . and change . . . — and with the illusory rebirth of youth, the novel goes beyond the vagaries of linear time and recovers a sort of temporal anteriority. Hence, by avoiding time's two implacable imperatives — death and change, which are also imperatives of desire, be it the desire to love or the desire to dominate — what we might call a "timeless time" locates a series of sensations on the margins of time, that is, in space. The recollection-sensation does away with time and replaces it with an eternity — the spatial eternity of a literary work that Proust compares to a cathedral.[4]

3 See the excellent discussion of Mies's spatial antecedents in Fritz Neumeyer, *The Artless Word: Mies van der Rohe on the Building Art* (Cambridge: The MIT Press, 1991), 171-193.

4 Julia Kristeva, *Time and Sense: Proust and the Experience of Literature* (New York: Columbia University Press, 1996), 89.

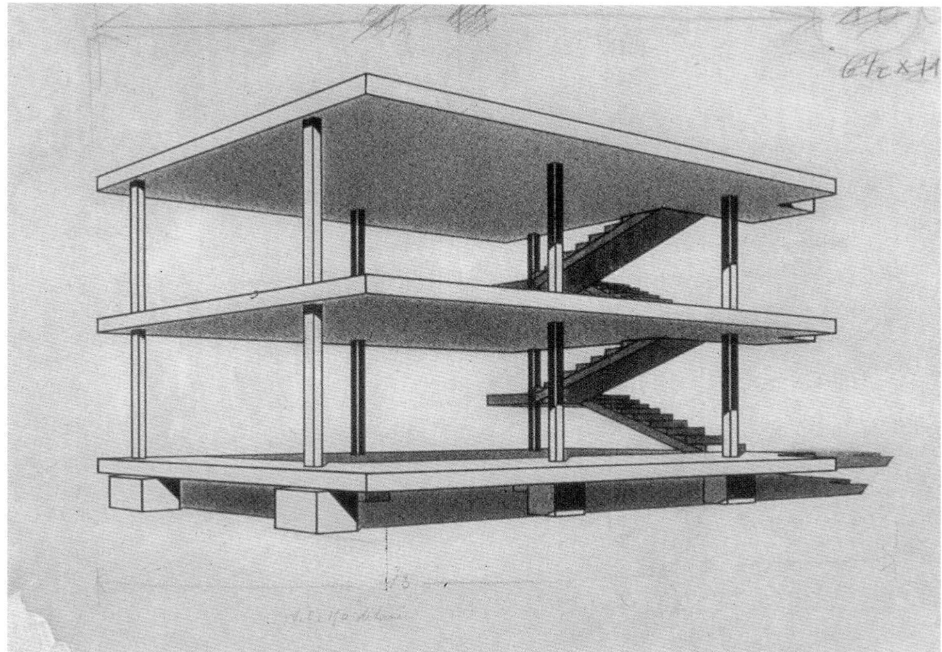

Le Corbusier, Dom-ino House skeleton, 1914. Fondation Le Corbusier

Between Proust's idealized image of the cathedral, and the experiments of the avant-garde after the First World War, there existed this common denominator: that space was seen to represent a terminus, or envelopment for time, and that time was conceived as the inevitable, and often discomforting, disruption of spatial continuity. Indeed, the very ambiguities and tensions between (historical) narrative and (spatial) memory were the material for many avant-garde explorations of time/space relations — Le Corbusier's attempt to reconcile the notion of the architectural promenade (narrative) and geometrical purism (space) in the model of the Dom-ino House (1914) is only the most well known of such experiments.

It is a logical result of these ambiguities that, of the many characteristics that have been identified as specific to architectural form, that of "space" has proved to be the most elusive. After all, "style," "structure," "function," and "composition" are, if not tangible, at least knowable through one representational means or another — physical description, analytical drawing, three-dimensional model. "Space" however is essentially intangible; it escapes representation. The "space" of a building or urban area is neither physically evident nor subject to easy depiction. Its qualities, indeed, can only be characterized through a study of what is not represented — the white ground of a plan, the implied sense of visual and bodily projection in perspective views — or at best through its transformation into something which it is not — a figure-ground reversal, a solid model of the voids in a building. Space, as Proust discovered, eludes verbal precision. The effects of a single space might shift in nature according to subjective and individual states of mind, take on differing social, gender, and sexual roles, alternate between claustrophobia and agoraphobia, inspire dread with what Pascal termed its "eternal silence," and at the same time create the image of comfort through associations with "place" and "home." Thus a consistent refrain throughout the century will be the essential indefinability of space as a category of analysis and synthesis, and the corresponding interpretative anxiety it has aroused. It is my argument that this very ambiguity, boundary-breaking and limit-crossing, continues to make the idea of space especially useful in confronting contemporary questions of site, situation, and place, as well as opening up the possibility of interpreting a range of newly emerging architectural positions regarding the *informe*, or "non-form," that have so far resisted traditional concepts of formal analysis.

Warped Space

In architecture, the most radical of the initial attempts to join time, space, and psychological experience was that of Expressionism between 1910 and 1918. Paul Scheerbart's manifestos and Bruno Taut's drawings of 1914-18 deliberately construed space as reflecting the tormented psychological states of modern alienation. As Ernst Bloch noted, this resulted in the desire to construct an entirely

Bruno Taut, *Schnee Gletscher Glas*, Plate 10 in *Alpine Architecture*, 1919. Collection Centre Canadien d'Architecture/Canadian Center for Architecture, Montréal

new, "non-Euclidian" kind of space, what El Lissitzky termed "pan-geometrical." Whether or not such a space was ever attainable, the formal results were clear: "Expressionism experimented with it by generating stereometric figures through rotating or swinging bodies, which at least have nothing in common with the perspective visual space (*Sehraum*); an architecture of the abstract, which wants to be quasi-meta-cubic, sometimes seeks structures appearing to be similarly remote, not organic any more, nor even meso-cosmical."[5] Such a space, as we know it from Taut's drawings, was dynamic, crystalline, and potentially infinite.

The very notion of a "non-Euclidian space," one that might escape the bounds of limited perspectival vision and thence, like Alice's mirror, act as a means of stepping into the new world, was, however, tantamount to an admission of utopian "impossibility." For, in any event, as Bloch recognized, the old Euclidian world was entirely necessary for any non-Euclidian hypothesis to have an effect: "Of course the space of these bodies of rotation remains as Euclidian as any other, and the so-called un-Euclidian pan-geometry provides positive ways for architecture also in the symbolic illusions." Panofsky, to whom Bloch refers as his authority, was equally skeptical in his discussion of El Lissitzky's idea of "pan-geometry." "In fact," he noted, "the space of [Lissitzky's] 'imaginary' rotating bodies is no less 'Euclidian' than any other empirical space."[6] This is no doubt why the Expressionist spatial medium *par excellence*, and precisely the medium in which Expressionist architecture found its fullest development, was, in fact, not architecture *per se*, but film. At the moment when Expressionism attempted to assert a world of purity in glass, the real foundation of such crystalline utopias was revealed, in the sets of *The Cabinet of Dr. Caligari* (1919) as much in the wastelands of Alfred Kubin's *Die andere seite*, to lie in the uncanny eruption of the uneasy psyche. The destiny of Taut's "alpine architecture" was in the end to reside in Ernst Junger's *Auf den Marmorklippen* (1939). Standing between a nostalgic dreamland of fairy-tale happiness and the broad and ever-expanding domain of the terrifying Chief Ranger, Junger's marble cliffs transformed the alpine landscape of Taut's dreams into the sinister lookout that pointed towards, and was in some way complicit with, Fascism, in what George Steiner has characterized as its alienated coldness.

Robert Wiene, *The Cabinet of Dr. Caligari*, 1919. Courtesy of The Academy of Motion Picture Arts and Sciences

In France, the reflections of Henri Bergson on time, movement, and space were quickly picked up by architects and artists, incorporated into the popular writings of Elie Faure, and were taken up by the painter Ozenfant and the architect Le Corbusier, later to be elaborated into the latter's poetic evocation of a modernist *espace indicible* or "ineffable space." It was hardly coincidental, then, that historians of the Modern Movement like Sigfried Giedion, armed with the same spatial concepts in their own discipline, were able to find a neat correspondence between "space" and the "modernity" of the century. This type of developmental history of space was to be canonized, so to speak, within the modernist tradition by the publication of Sigfried Giedion's *Space, Time and Architecture* in 1941.[7] For Giedion, as for most modernist architects, the invention of a "new" conception of space was the leitmotiv of modernity itself, supported by the avant-garde call for an escape from history, that affirmed the importance of space both for architectural

5 Ernst Bloch, "Building in Empty Spaces" ["Die Bebauung des Hohlraums," in *Das Prinzip Hoffnung* (Frankfurt am Main: Suhrkamp, 1959)], in *The Utopian Function of Art and Literature. Selected Essays*, translated by Jack Zipes and Frank Mecklenburg (Cambridge: The MIT Press, 1988), 196.

6 Ibid.

7 Sigfried Giedion, *Space, Time and Architecture: The Growth of a New Tradition* (Cambridge: Harvard University Press, 1941).

form and for modern life as a whole. The idea of space held the double promise of dissolving rigid, stylistic characterization into fundamental three-dimensional organizations and of providing the essential material, so to speak, for the development of a truly modern architecture. Giedion celebrated just these qualities as proto-modernist exhibitions of the will to overcome all structural and spatial limitations in the service of a new architecture.

Giedion took his starting point from an interpretation of Baroque architecture that saw its undulating walls and complicated spatial and physical structures as the predecessors of modernity, in the process formulating an image of the Baroque that was both triumphant and prospective. For him, the Baroque and its complex questioning of Renaissance-perspective stability and realist representation, its combination of perspectival multiplicity and illusion, found in its most developed form in the work of Borromini and Guarini, seemed, in retrospect, to prefigure Cubism. When joined to the spatial interpenetration exhibited in the engineering structures of the late nineteenth century, the potential of the Baroque was turned into constructive possibility: "This possibility was latent in the skeleton system of construction, but the skeleton had to be used as Le Corbusier uses it," concluded Giedion, "in the service of a new conception of space."[8] In this model of spatial history, the role played by structure became pivotal; Giedion's pairing of Borromini's lantern of Sant'Ivo and Tatlin's project for a monument to the Third International has itself become a commonplace, as has his analysis of Guarini's cupola of San Lorenzo, where "the impression of unlimited space has been achieved not through the employment of perspective illusions or of a painted sky but through exclusively architectural means" that go "to the very end of constructional resources." It remained only for modern construction methods to overcome these limits, and for modern architects to imagine modern space, and the equation *spatial imagination+structural invention=progress* would be confirmed.

Space, Time, and Metropolis

From Expressionism to high Modernism, the dominant notions of space/time were all, as the film sets of Fritz Lang emphasized, tied to the experience of the modern metropolis. As described in the opening pages of Robert Musil's *Man Without Qualities*, this seemed like

> a kind of super-American city where everyone rushes about, or stands still, with a stopwatch in his hand. . . . Overhead trains, overground trains, underground trains, pneumatic express mails carrying consignments of human beings, chains of motor vehicles all racing along horizontally, express lifts vertically pumping crowds from one traffic level to another.[9]

Recording the tempo of this city was Musil's "hero," Ulrich, standing before his window with a stopwatch in his hand. Time was, in the metropolis, an almost tangible phenomenon, marked in the daily rhythms of transport and the productive and commercial needs of capital. Thus the German sociologist Georg Simmel contrasted "the tempo and multiplicity of economic, occupational and social life" of the city with "the slower, more habitual, more smoothly flowing rhythm" of small-town existence. In his now celebrated essay, *"Die Groszstadt und das Geistesleben,"* translated as "The Metropolis and Mental Life" (1903),[10] Simmel argued that it was this difference that formed the fundamentally *intellectual*

8 Ibid., 416.

9 Robert Musil, *The Man Without Qualities* (New York: Alfred Knopf, 1995).

qualities of urbanity, as opposed to the emotional and deeply rooted sociability of the small town or countryside existence. Thence, too, the close relations between this intellectual spirit of metropolitan life developed as a defense against too-quickly changing stimuli and the money economy itself; the symbiotic relationship between the necessary quantification of relations of production and consumption, and the mental activity most suited to the city.

This universal calculation of mind and money, pervasively bred in the metropolis, was illustrated most powerfully for Simmel, as for Musil's Ulrich, by the entirely modern phenomenon of "the general distribution of pocket watches," the democratization of clock-time; this was so integral to the life of the city that, "if all the watches in Berlin suddenly went wrong in different ways even only as much as an hour, its entire economic and commercial life would be derailed for some time." "The technique of metropolitan life," he concluded, "is unimaginable without the most punctual integration of all activities and mutual relations into a stable and impersonal time schedule." And it would be such a schedule, operative in the

Fritz Lang, *Metropolis*, 1926. The Museum of Modern Art Film Stills Archive, New York

networks of public transportation, that would overcome the "long distances" of the sprawling city and prevent the waiting and broken appointments that would otherwise result in "an ill-afforded waste of time."[11] Time, in this respect, was the essential motor of metropolitan life; it was the agent of economic transactions and the indispensable metronome of social life; it measured the new tempos and rhythms of the city, calculated their intersections, and ensured their dominance.

[10] Georg Simmel, "Die Grosstadt und das Geistesleben," *Die Grosstadt. Jahrbuch der Gehe-Stiftung* 9 (1903), translated by Edward A. Shils, in *Georg Simmel in Individuality and Social Forms*, edited by Donald N. Levine (Chicago: Chicago University Press, 1971), 324-339.

[11] Ibid., 328.

Fernand Léger, *Ballet Mécanique*, 1924. The Museum of Modern Art Film Stills Archive, New York

It is, of course, a commonplace of cultural history to trace this sensibility of a new urban temporality to the studies of time and motion made possible by the development of photography: the experiments of the French physiologist, Etienne-Jules Marey, into the recording of movement, are especially celebrated.[12] A parallel reading of Giedion's two complementary books, *Space, Time and Architecture* (1941) and *Mechanization Takes Command* (1948), is enough to make the point: time and motion studies, filmic processes, new industrial production methods like the assembly line, all contributed to an ethos of "new temporality" joined to a sense of a "new spatiality."[13] In Walter Benjamin's evocative formulation:

> Our taverns and our metropolitan streets, our offices and furnished rooms, our railroad stations and our factories appeared to have us locked up hopelessly. Then came the film and burst this prison-world asunder by the dynamite of the tenth of a second, so that now, in the midst of its far flung ruins and debris we calmly and adventurously go traveling.[14]

The self-conscious exploitation of filmic techniques and machine rhythms in a film such as Fernand Léger's *Ballet Mécanique* of 1924 was only the most obvious of such "explosions."[15]

Space, Time, and Motion

The relation of these ideas of time and motion to architecture was, after 1900, made direct and instrumental by their introduction into the organization of the modern workplace by figures such as Frederick Winslow Taylor and Henry Ford. A number of historians, notably Charles Maier[16] and Judith Merkle[17], have described the wide-ranging influence of Taylor, Ford, and their followers, not so much on the factory floor, although there too it was pervasive, but in the sense of a generalized ideology that in Europe went by the name of scientific management or, as Gramsci termed it, "Americanismo."[18] This ideology, originating before the First World War but gaining ground with the social and economic demands of reconstruction after 1918,

12 Etienne-Jules Marey, *Du mouvement dans les fonctions de la vie*, Paris, 1868; *La méthode graphique dans les sciences expérimentales*, Paris, 1885. Marey invented the Spymograph for recording the human pulse; the Myograph, for recording the reactions of a frog's muscular system to electrical stimulation; a photo-gun to capture the movement of a bird in flight; and, a method of registering the movements of a walking figure, named *chronophotographie*. See Sigfried Giedion, *Mechanization Takes Command* (New York: Oxford University Press, 1948), 17-24.

13 See, for the best description of this turn-of-the-century culture, S. Kern, *The Culture of Time and Space, 1880-1918* (Cambridge: Harvard University Press, 1983).

14 Walter Benjamin, "The Work of Art in the Age of Mechanical Reproduction," in *Illuminations* (New York: Shocken Books, 1969), 236.

15 For *Ballet Mécanique*, see Judi Freeman, "Bridging Purism and Surrealism: The Origins and Production of Fernand Léger's *Ballet Mécanique*," in Rudolf E. Kuenzli, ed., *Dada and Surrealist Film* (New York: Willis, Locker & Owens, 1987), 28-45.

16 Charles S. Maier, "Between Taylorism and Technocracy: European Ideologies and the Vision of Industrial Productivity in the 1920s," *Journal of Contemporary History* 5, no. 2 (1970): 27-61.

17 Judith A. Merkle, *Management and Ideology: The Legacy of the International Scientific Management Movement* (Berkeley: University of California Press, 1980).

18 Antonio Gramsci, *Selections from the Prison Notebooks of Antonio Gramsci*, translated and edited by Q. Hoare and G.N. Smith (London: Lawrence & Wishart, 1971), 285-318.

offered, or so its proponents claimed, a series of systematically connected solutions to crises of management, production, economics, and thence politics. As Taylor himself emphasized, "The great revolution that takes place in the mental attitude of the two parties [labor and management] under scientific management is that both sides take their eyes off the division of the surplus. . . . and together turn their attention toward increasing the size of the surplus."[19] From the factory to society to the state, the advocates of scientific management envisaged a non-political new order controlled by engineers and technocrats according to the precise and unarguable principles of science. Labor disputes would vanish, wages and profits increase, and the machine civilization triumph. When allied to the social and productive innovations of Ford, with his moving assembly line, standardization and expansion of the mass market, the ideological package "Americanism" held broad appeal for a wide political spectrum. In Germany it appealed to reformers in the *Werkbund* as well as conservative technocrats and later fascists; in Italy it formed the basis of Futurism's radical espousal of the machine, as well as of Mussolini's productivism and Gramsci's Fordism; in France, neo-Saint-Simonians on the left and right, syndicalists and socialists, joined a host of Taylorist associations; in Russia, Lenin advised the new Soviet to take a close look at this "last word of capitalism," "a combination of the subtle brutality of bourgeois exploitation and a number of its greatest scientific achievements."[20] As we shall see, a number of modernist architects, including most prominently Le Corbusier, pledged their faith in this seemingly universal panacea.

But what exactly was Taylorism? And what might have been the basis of its wide appeal, not only to managers, but also to politicians, planners and architects? Taylor's method, by his own account,[21] was the result of his attempt as a gang boss to break his workers' habits of "systematic soldiering." By means of coercion and threat, systematic training, layoffs, and pay cuts he demonstrated that it was possible to persuade workers to accomplish a "fair day's work" — i.e. one defined by his estimate of potential productivity on the job. First worked out in practice in the context of the Bethlehem Steel Works, where he described his success in encouraging a worker called "Schmidt" to increase the amount of pig-iron handled from twelve to forty-seven tons per man per day,[22] the "method" was then extended by Taylor to more complex processes in machine shops. The principles were simple enough: they consisted of a combination of analysis of the work process into easily understood and rationally sequential steps, their application to "scientifically selected" workers with knowledge of the extent of their physical capacity, and incentives in the form of incremental increases in pay.

These principles were developed by Taylor's followers and rivals: the contracting engineer, Frank B. Gilbreth, with his wife, the psychologist Lillian M. Gilbreth, elaborated the visual representation of work processes by the use of photography. The "chronocyclograph" was developed in order to trace the path of a movement, whence a three-dimensional model was constructed. These representations were then calibrated with time — "time study," noted Gilbreth, was "the art of recording, analyzing, synthesizing the time of the elements of every operation"[23] — in order, as Giedion demonstrated, to constitute a perfect fusion of space-time relations.

These were further developed into time and motion studies that were undertaken with an eye to the limiting factor of all work — fatigue. The Gilbreth's jointly written work, *Fatigue Study*, published in 1916, was subtitled "the

[19] Frederick W. Taylor, *Testimony of Frederick W. Taylor at Hearings Before a Special Committee of the House of Representatives, January, 1912* (New York: Taylor Society, 1926), quoted in Maier, 32.

[20] Quoted in Maier.

[21] See Frederick W. Taylor, *Shop Management* (New York and London: Harper & Bros., 1903), and *The Principles of Scientific Management* (New York and London: Harper & Bros., 1911).

[22] This account is analyzed in Harry Braverman, *Labor and Monopoly Capital: The Degradation of Work in the Twentieth Century* (New York: Monthly Review Press, 1974), 102-112.

[23] Frank B. Gilbreth, *Primer of Scientific Management* (New York: Van Nostrand, 1914), 7.

From Frank B. and Lillian M. Gilbreth, *Fatigue Study*, 1916

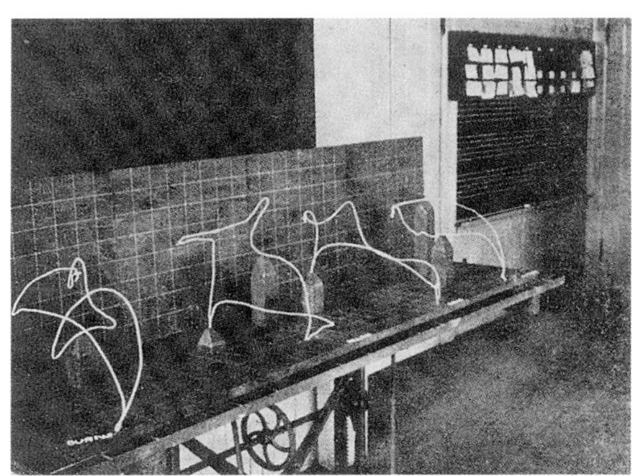

elimination of humanity's greatest unnecessary waste. A first step in motion study," and was directly related to the war production effort. They advocated the systematic education of the worker in his leisure hours; the provision of properly designed chairs and equipment; the study of adequate lighting, heating, and ventilating conditions; economic physical movements for repetitive motions; and safety and fire protection. Their studies, indeed, encompassed the entire space of work, on and off the job, and they developed numerous techniques for the measurement of motion towards the aim of standardizing work procedures with the least inbuilt fatigue. Their "Fatigue Museums," set up in proximity to plants, acted as propaganda for their chair and workbench designs as well as for their always improved measuring devices.

Such early time and motion studies, of course, form the first point of contact with architectural functionalism: the design of the workshop and later the work-station, first applied to the factory, then to the office and finally to the home (especially in rooms, like the kitchen, where work processes were measurable). Diagrams of efficient movements in space became, in the twenties, a commonplace of the "new objectivity." If we add to this concern for time and motion, the potential of the mass-production assembly line for the standardization of furniture, and, of course, the elements of construction, if not entire units dry-fabricated and transported for erection on site, then we have more or less summarized what the notion "Taylorism/ Fordism" signified most directly for architects in the first quarter of the century.

The Taylorization of Space

Here I will give only a few examples of this sensibility. Pervasive after the First World War, it has been dealt with adequately elsewhere. The work of Jean-Louis Cohen and Mary McLeod in particular has clarified the relationship of Le Corbusier to the Taylorization movement.[24] Introduced through Henry Le Chatelier's translations between 1908 and 1911, Taylorism had already found proponents before World War II: Le Chatelier's own articles elaborated the system, joining it to European movements for rational production and engineering theory.[25] By 1914, too, American attempts to apply Taylorism to social life in general were being publicized in France. Le Chatelier, concluding his review of Taylor's system, cited approvingly Christine Frederick's essay on *The New Housekeeping*[26] that had called for a Taylorist revolution in domestic work: this "young and enthusiastic mistress of the American house," wrote Le Chatelier, had described a rationalized domestic system within which a new generation would find its technical education: "Children raised by readers of this domestic manual will later certainly become engineers, better prepared than the present generation for the use of the new industrial methods."[27] Two years later Le Chatelier published a volume of extracts from Frederick's book, *La tenue scientifique de la maison*, to which he contributed an introduction outlining the principles of scientific management, now conceived as extensions of the dwelling. Point by point, from organization to science and labor, Le Chatelier extrapolates from the economics of housework to that of industry, repeating his belief that children brought up with "the scales and the clock" in the kitchen will develop into natural candidates for industrial management.[28]

Le Corbusier first used the word "Taylorisme" in a letter of 1917, where he speaks of Taylorism as "the horrible and ineluctable life of tomorrow."[29] But by the next year, when he joined with the painter Amédée Ozenfant to publish *Après le cubisme* (1918), he is more optimistic. Here "Taylorism" is seen as "no more than a question of intelligently exploiting scientific discoveries;" it is the very expression of *L'esprit moderne* as based on the "rigorous program of the modern factory" — *taylorisme*.[30] The end of the war and the immediate needs of reconstruction seem to have resolved Le Corbusier's doubts, as he echoes Futurist sentiments on the purifying agency of modern conflict:

> The war has ended; all is organized; all is clear and purified; factories are built; nothing is like it was before the War; the great Struggle tested everything, it destroyed senile methods and replaced them with those which the battle proved best.[31]

Jeanneret and Ozenfant herald the birth of the "new spirit" in a narrative that traces a path from the pre-War "epoch of strikes and revindications where art itself was only an art of protest" — the "destructive" and contentious avant-garde — to a new postwar order of scientific rationalization. The path ends in a *retour à l'ordre* and the final supra-political re-organization of society.

Wartime production had indeed furnished models that might be applied to the first need of reconstruction, housing. In the second number of *L'Esprit Nouveau*, Le Corbusier admiringly describes the experiment in mass-produced housing conducted by the Voisin aircraft corporation: the Maisons Voisin. Perfect examples of Fordism in the housing domain, Le Corbusier celebrated the rationalism that had led to a production method that had, in turn, revolutionized architecture itself:

> The enunciation of the problem has by itself provided the means of realization, and, unwittingly, here strongly affirms the immense revolution undergone by architecture: when the manner of building is modified to such an extent, automatically the aesthetic of construction finds itself overturned.[32]

The imperatives of reconstruction had demanded "houses [that] emerged totally formed, made with machine-tools, in the factory, fabricated like Ford assembles the pieces of his automobiles on his rolling carpets."[33] The aircraft industry had pioneered the process; and, after all, "an aircraft is a small house that flies and resists the storms." "Soldier-architects" were by these means enabled to construct complete houses in three days and, transported by road, the dwellings were habitable three hours after being sited.

24 See Jean-Louis Cohen, *Le Corbusier and the Mystique of the USSR*. Translated by Kenneth Hylton (Princeton: Princeton University Press, 1992); Mary McLeod, "'Architecture or Revolution': Taylorism, Technocracy and Social Change," *Art Journal* (Fall 1983): 132-147.

25 Henry Le Chatelier, "Le système Taylor," *Bulletin de la société d'encouragement pour l'industrie nationale* (March 1914); "Le principe de l'organisation," *La Nature* (December 1915).

26 Christine Frederick, *The New Housekeeping. Efficiency Studies in Home Management* (New York: Doubleday, Page, 1913).

27 Le Chatelier, *Le Taylorisme*, Paris (1928): 99.

28 Le Chatelier, *Le Taylorisme*, 27-38.

29 Charles-Edouard Jeanneret, *Journal* (29 December 1917). William Ritter Nachlass, cited by Francesco Passanti, "The Skyscrapers of the Ville Contemporaine," *Assemblage* 4 (October 1987): 64.

30 Charles-Edouard Jeanneret and A. Ozenfant, *Après le cubisme* (Paris: Éditions des Commentaires, 1918), 26.

31 Ibid., 11.

32 Le Corbusier, "Les Maisons Voisin," *L'Esprit Nouveau*, no. 2 (November 1920): 213.

33 Ibid., 214.

The *Maisons Voisin*, mass produced like cars or airplanes, were harbingers of a new order: "to inhabit such houses, one must have the spirit of a sage and be animated with the new spirit. A generation is born that will know how to inhabit the Voisin houses."[34] It was not by coincidence, as we shall see, that this article appeared in a number that also included the translation of Adolf Loos's essay "Ornament and Crime," a study of the modern dance theories of Jacques Dalcroze by Albert Jeanneret entitled "*La Rythmique*," and the second part of Le Corbusier's study of modern factory building dedicated to the repetitively modulated and serial surface of American factories.

If Fordism could produce entire houses, the "revolution" in their aesthetic was to be advanced by a minute Taylorization of every aspect of their interior planning. Beginning with the twentieth issue of *L'Esprit Nouveau*, Le Corbusier provided rhapsodic annotations to advertisements for the domestic furnishing firm Innovation, as if it were the agent that might Taylorize the entirety of life, from the *armoire* to the house itself. An advertisement for built-in closets begins, in Le Corbusier's words, with the message: "*La guerre a secoué les torpeurs; on a parlé de taylorisme; on en a fait . . .*" (The war has shaken off our stupor; one spoke of Taylorism; it was accomplished),[35] a statement that is repeated virtually word for word in *Vers une architecture*.[36]

Taylorism in these terms will revolutionize, not only the mentalities of workers and managers, but their entire domestic environment. Innovation introduces pivoting and expanding racks for economic storage in wardrobes, tie-hangers like cog-wheels, built-in closets that generate a new philosophy of the wall, and, for the industrial nomad, traveling trunks that fold out into complex storage closets. From the object that acts as an extension of the human limbs — "objects which are our tools, objects like the extension of our limbs"[37] — to spatial layouts and new methods of construction, Innovation will Taylorise the world:

> The war has shaken off our stupor; one spoke of Taylorism — it was accomplished. The contractors have bought ingenious machines, patient

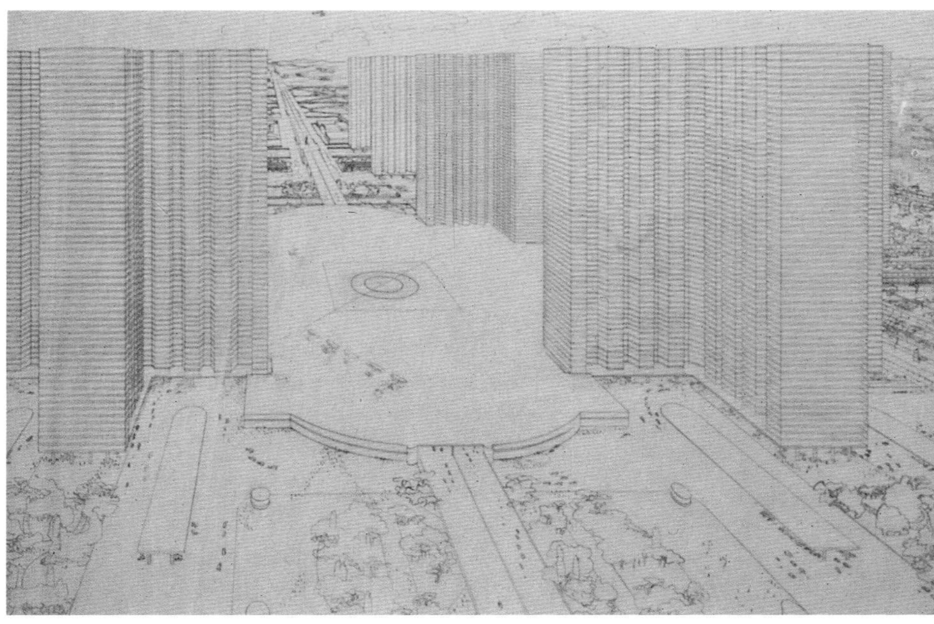

Le Corbusier, *Le Plan Voisin*, 1925. Fondation Le Corbusier, Paris

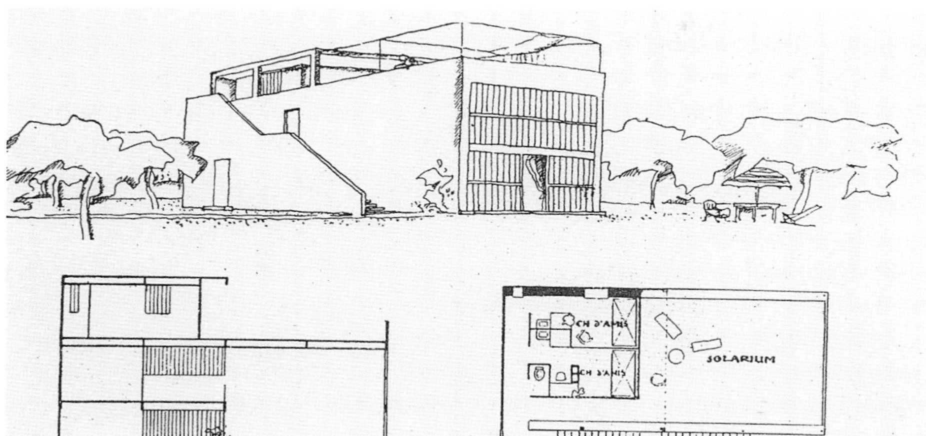

Le Corbusier, Maison Citrohan, 1920. Fondation Le Corbusier, Paris

> and agile. Will the building-sites soon become factories?. . . The house will no longer be that enormous thing cut up by fortress-walls pretending to defy the centuries; it will become a rigorous tool, in the same way as a precise automobile becomes a tool of work. Benefitting from a century of science, of calculation and industry, it will open itself, in its smooth and nervous resistance, to the infinite combinations required by infinitely more refined and precise needs, the consequence of an overwhelming revolution led for the last half-century by the Law of Economy.[38]

Mary McLeod has written the history of Le Corbusier's subsequent attempts to instill a spirit of mass production in the housing market. Inspired by the promise, not fulfilled until 1928, of a law promoting the construction of low-cost housing proposed by Louis Loucheur in 1922, Le Corbusier called on firms like Le Creusot, Citroën, and Renault to concern themselves with mass produced houses.[39] His own house-types, including one named evocatively the "Citrohan" house, provided models; equally hopefully, he dubbed his plan for Paris of 1925 the *Plan Voisin*. Other experiments, as at Pessac for Henri Frugès, were illustrated in the quasi-Taylorist bulletin of Ernest Mercier's *Redressement Français* under the title, *"Pour bâtir: Standardiser et Tayloriser."*[40]

In the text of *La Ville radieuse*, published in 1933, Le Corbusier synthesized his aspirations for the triumph of Taylorism through design. A technocratic elite, led by the engineers and architects, would save the world from war and revolution alike:

> At the request of M. Loucheur, Minister of Labor, we drew up plans for totally industrialized houses, made with the most costly materials and executed in the most meticulous way. We extrapolated the house, so to speak, from clay and quarry and mortar; we transported it to the industrialist's factory, the Taylorization belt.[41]

Here neo-Saint-Simonianism joined with Taylorism to extend the promise of technology to the whole earth; Le Corbusier diagrams the expansion of rationalism through linear metropolises, planned like production belts, joining the great central cities.

[34] Ibid., 215.

[35] *L'Esprit Nouveau*, no. 20.

[36] Le Corbusier, *Vers une architecture* (Paris, 1923), 193.

[37] *L'Esprit Nouveau*, no. 24.

[38] *L'Esprit Nouveau*, no. 20, advertisement for Innovation.

[39] Le Corbusier, "Maisons en série," *L'Esprit Nouveau*, no. 13 (December 1921).

[40] See McLeod, "Architecture or Revolution."

[41] Le Corbusier, *The Radiant City: Elements of a Doctrine of Urbanism to be Used as the Basis of Our Machine-Age Civilization* (New York: Orion Press, 1967), 32.

The full history of twenties Taylorism in architecture has yet to be written; it would no doubt include a host of examples from Germany, where Walter Rathenau elaborated a quasi-mystical vision of industrial progress, and where the Deutsche Werkbund served as a center for debates over building rationalization and standardization; from Italy, where the building programs of Fiat in Turin and Olivetti in the Po valley were infused with modern managerial wisdom drawn directly from America; and from the Soviet Union, where Lenin had called for a study of the application of Taylorism to the pressing problems of Soviet production.

In this last context, architects were eager to apply time and motion studies to the planning of factories and housing. One of the most striking examples, developed by the Typological Section of the Committee for Construction, led by Moisei Ginzburg, involved the planning of the typical kitchen. "The housewife's work in the kitchen," writes Selim Khan-Magomedov, "was subjected to close time-and-motion analysis and a planned arrangement of the equipment involved made it possible to save space."[42] These close studies of movement in the kitchen were tied to Lenin's earlier call for women to be relieved of the "crush of domestic work," the breaking of woman's "domestic slavery" and "menial domesticity."[43] In this way, Taylorism in architecture, for the most part, had its first effects not in the planning of the work-place as such, but in the procedures of architectural design and production of housing, that aspect of architecture most susceptible to Fordism in mass-production and Taylorism in interior planning and furnishing. The "house as a machine for living in," became, so to speak, envisaged as a small factory floor, with its equipment seen as machine tools, extensions of the human body.

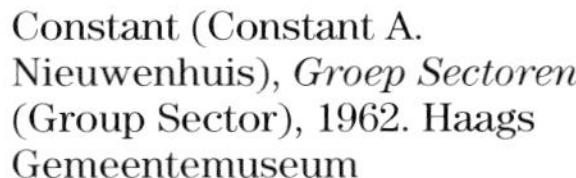

Constant (Constant A. Nieuwenhuis), *Groep Sectoren* (Group Sector), 1962. Haags Gemeentemuseum

Space and the Subject

Taken up after World War II by, among many others, the historians Bruno Zevi, Rex Martienssen, and Renato de Fusco, the idea of a modern space, propaedeutic and distinctive, gradually shed the instrumental overtones of Taylorism in order to respond to new psychologies of the subject on a political, psychological, and sociological level.[44] Thus the political and social characteristics of space, theorized in political geography and sociology since Theodor Herzl, Georg Simmel, and Maurice Halbwachs, were also increasingly seen as keys to the understanding of architecture and urbanism, informing studies as diverse as that of Chombart de Lauwe on Paris and the Situationists' critiques of urbanism in *Internationale situationniste* (1958-69). Psychological and existential theories of space based on the theories of Eugène Minkowski, Jean Piaget, and of course, Martin Heidegger and Jean-Paul Sartre, were equally influential on the interpretation of architecture's "poetics" (Gaston Bachelard's *La poétique de l'espace* was first published in 1957). Architectural "functionalists" were comforted by the empirical experiments of Edward T. Hall (*The Hidden Dimension*, 1969) and Robert Sommer (*Personal Space: The Behavioral Basis of Design*, 1969) at the same time being helped in different ways by the manuals of spatial organization by Christopher Alexander and Kevin Lynch. In the late 1960s, Marxist (Henri Lefebvre) and poststructuralist (Michel Foucault) analyses reinvigorated the idea of space by relating it to power and institutionalized systems of order: prisons, asylums, and schools became the privileged objects of study for historians concerned to locate and resist the sources of power within the professional discourse of architecture itself.

Postmodern Space

Perhaps the most radical destabilization of modernist spatial concepts was the "relativism" introduced by many postmodernist architects and theorists, a relativism that simultaneously endowed space with all the characteristics of a projected subjectivity, and denied it any functional or instrumental role. Thus many recent projects by architects as diverse as Coop Himmelb(l)au, Bernard Tschumi, Peter Eisenman, and Frank Gehry have construed space in a way that ostensibly draws on its "constructivist" and modernist legacies but that in reality denies all the utopian and humanist program of the early modernists.

In the exhibition installation for "Expressionist Utopias" at the Los Angeles County Museum of Art in 1994, for example, the Viennese architectural group Coop Himmelb(l)au invented a spatial language that drew heavily on the motifs of German Expressionism. But, despite overall similarities, the canted planes, intersecting angles, pyramids of light, shifting floors, and tilted walls were not merely imitations of some Expressionist stage set. They derived their force from a continued tradition of disquiet and unease, estrangement and distance from the insistent world of the modern "real." Counter-domestic from the beginning, Himmelb(l)au's work has been equally alive to the psychic forces of projection and introjection that collapse Euclidian space and transform it into what we have called earlier in this essay, "warped space." As Himmelb(l)au announced as early as 1968: "Our architecture has no physical plan, but a psychic plan."

[42] Selim O. Khan-Magomedov, *Pioneers of Soviet Architecture* (New York: Rizzoli, 1987), 348.

[43] Lenin at the First All-Russian Congress of Working and Peasant Women, 1918, cited in Khan-Magomedov, 341.

[44] Bruno Zevi, *Saper vedere l'architettura; saggi sull'interpretazione spaziale dell'architettura* (Turin: G. Einaudi, 1948), translated as *Architecture as Space; How to Look at Architecture* (New York: Horizon Press, 1974); Rex Distin Martienssen, *The Idea of Space in Greek Architecture, with Special Reference to the Doric Temple and its Setting* (Johannesburg: Witwatersrand University Press, 1956); Renato de Fusco, *Segni, storia e projetto dell'architettura* (Rome: Laterza, 1973). See Cornelius van de Ven, *Space in Architecture: The Evolution of a New Idea in the Theory of the Modern Movement* (Assen/Maastricht: Van Gorum, 1978).

Coop Himmelb(l)au, Rooftop remodeling, Falkestrasse, Vienna, 1984-89

In the LACMA installation, such a "psychic plan" was doubled in a tantalizing way. It is at once an archaeological reference to an imaginary scene long buried — that of Expressionist utopia before World War I — and a contemporary scene of deliberate distortion and displacement. Freud once remarked that it would be impossible to conceive of the same space containing two different contents at the same time — he was speaking of the series of monumental constructions over the centuries built one on top of the other in Rome. Only in the mind, he argued, was the retention of two "places" in the same space possible. But it is a peculiar property of some architecture to resonate with double meaning, in such a way as to approxi-

Coop Himmelb(l)au's installation of "Expressionist Utopias" at the Los Angeles County Museum of Art, 1994

mate the imaginary of Freud, and in Himmelb(l)au's "after-image" of Expressionism, such a double exposure there is. Nowhere is this more evident than in the most dramatic event of the installation, in that thick slice of light cut at an angle from one side to the other. Constructed out of real material, it is true, the light is captured between sheets of plexiglass; but as light, it is as if a negative fault line had cracked open the solid fabric of the interior, displaying its inner substance. Earlier projects of Himmelb(l)au had played with the metaphor of skin, peeled back to reveal the flayed flesh of building beneath; now the building has overcome its organic attachment to the human body, and is revealed as pure desire. In a kind of Rosicrucian metaphor of "light from within," this crack of luminosity lures at the same time as it closes itself from accessibility.

Bruno Taut, Glass Pavilion at the Werkbund Exhibition, 1914. Stiftung Archiv der Akademie der Künste

In the LACMA project the light is in a real sense captured, sliced as if between the two glass slides of a microscopic specimen: light that no longer serves its function of lighting, as for example in Bruno Taut's glass pavilion of 1914, but now deprived of all function, simply to be looked at as an exhibit in a museum. Fetishized light then, and cut uncomfortably close to our own bodies as we move carefully through these uncertain spaces. Where previously Himmelb(l)au's images of desire were figured in the many semi-angelic wings that hovered, soared and blazed through the space of projects such as

Bruno Taut, Glass Pavilion at the Werkbund Exhibition, 1914 (interior view). Stiftung Archiv der Akademie der Künste

Coop Himmelb(l)au, The Red Angel, Vienna, 1981. Photo by Gerald Zugmann

The Red Angel Bar in Vienna, in the slice of light any material reference to structure is abandoned. The "angel" is dissolved, as if in the navel of the dream, into an umbilicum of searing nothingness that hurts our eyes. Commentary on Expressionist dreams, and fabrication of our own, this installation fittingly ends up displaying them in the museum as if to offer a cabinet of curiosities dedicated to the exploration of our own spatial warpings. No longer can we be satisfied with the comforting distance that separates us as spectators from the implications of Dr. Caligari's cabinet; we are literally entered into a scene populated by our doubles, and constructed like our psyche. And, inevitably, the moment we feel we are arriving at the center of this strangely comforting experience, we are suddenly and cruelly cut off from any access to what we want most; that trapped light. Perhaps this is, after all, what "utopia" is all about; not so much the happy dream of wish-fulfillment, but the anxious dream of blocked desire.

Spatial Movement

Frank Gehry, Gehry House, Santa Monica, 1978. Photo by Tim Street-Porter

While the "movement" of Himmelb(l)au's forms emulates the psychic plan of a troubled postmodern utopianism, the apparently similar "movements" in form and space exhibited consistently in the work of Frank Gehry, from his initial experiments in perspectival distortion in the Ron Davis studio in Malibu to the recently completed Guggenheim Museum in Bilbao, are more calculated to represent the successive transformations in the very idea of visual and bodily movement over the last twenty years. Thus in his work movement takes many forms: there is the movement of an apparently incomplete construction — "buildings under construction look nicer than buildings finished"; there is the movement of shifting masses — collapsing solids, flying stairs, juxtaposed and twisted volumes — as in the Gehry House (Santa Monica 1978); there is the movement stimulated by intersecting, penetrating and colliding systems, whether constructionally or volumetrically differentiated, most evident in the 1978 projects for the Familian House; there is the movement of shifted or inflected axes, as in the placement of the Loyola Law School pavilions; there is the implied movement of the always dancing inhabitant; and, finally, there is the movement of vision itself, represented in the innumerable plays with perspectival foreshortening. Even the most static of parts will inevitably be disrupted by a deliberate ignoring of the symmetry, a blatant disregard for the rules so deliberately established that, in turn, sets up the conditions for implied or literal movement.

Critics have compared such an architecture of movement to the Dadaist, Constructivist, and Expressionist experiments of the early twentieth century. Kurt Schwitters's *Merzbau* projects have often been evoked, their implications of urban bricolage seeming to authorize Gehry's own scavenging forays along the Venice beach. Certainly his collaborations with contemporary artists and dancers have endowed his architecture with an artistic aura that its assemblage-like qualities have confirmed. Somewhere between architecture and sculpture, construction and collage, ready-made and not-yet-made, his work seems to evade the criteria generally applicable to conventional buildings.

Frank Gehry, Guggenheim Museum, Bilbao, 1997. Photo by Jeff Goldberg

And yet on another level Gehry's projects remain stubbornly within the field of architecture, transforming the tradition in precise and calculated ways. His apparently intuitive and casual working method and deceptively "disordered" formal systems are, indeed, the result of a deeply worked relationship to the canonical problems of modern architecture. This relationship may be transformational, oppositional, ironic or playful; it may imply a shift of focus, a broadening of scope, or a borrowing from another art form; but it is from this reliance on the architectural tradition, and not in the first instance from importations from the other arts, that Gehry's "movement" derives its peculiar force.

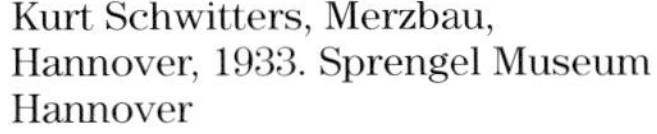

Kurt Schwitters, Merzbau, Hannover, 1933. Sprengel Museum Hannover

Indeed, Gehry's experiments seem to re-enact, but in subtly transformed ways, all forms of implied and analogical movement in architecture. Thus, as if returning to the anamorphism of the Baroque, and extending its criticism of the Albertian picture frame a step further, Gehry, in the Ron Davis House, establishes a condition where a segment of the visual cone is literally captured by the wedge shape of the house itself and where, in a complex doubling of two in three dimensions, one of Davis's own painterly perspective studies was built within the wedge, following the logic of the implied twisting, flattening and foreshortening. Similarly, in the project for the Wagner House, the intersection of the sloped order of the site and the fictive horizontals and verticals of the house produces a series of perspectival distortions that are then built into the house. Perspective, in both cases, is no longer simply a representational technique for describing an already made form, but rather a generative device for the production of spaces that, in themselves, work on the observer who is caught between the insistence of a preconceived order and the evident reality of a perceived distortion. Movement is here engendered both phenomenally, in the uncertainty of the eye, and literally in the twisting of formerly stable spatial constructs.

Similarly, Gehry's response to the visual clues provided by the site of the Davis House or to the sloping site of the Wagner House echo the Romantic picturesque tradition, revived by modernism under the guise of the *promenade architecturale,* or the empiricism of functional differentiation. But more radically, and following the implications of the "building-as-landscape," Gehry has worked to incorporate all the qualities of the random, the apparently incidental, the seemingly oppositional and even the impossible juxtaposition in the architecture itself. Responding both to natural sites and to heterogeneous and unplanned urban

Konstantin Melnikov, Russian pavilion at the "Exposition des arts décoratifs," Paris, 1925. Centre Canadien d'Architecture/Canadian Center for Architecture, Montréal

contexts, they construct themselves as worlds within worlds, manufactured out of the bricolage of their surroundings. In these projects movement is not only implied by the combination of discrete elements and their geometrical displacements, but also generated by intricate promenades through and over the volumes, as if traversing a rocky landscape. Labyrinths within labyrinths give the impression of interiors *en abyme.*

Gehry's own house was selected as a primary example of what the curators called "Deconstructivist Architecture" in the exhibition mounted by The Museum of Modern Art, New York, in 1988. But while Gehry no doubt draws from the *imagery* of Constructivism, his critical distance from the radical projects of the twenties allows for a re-reading that in fact refuses the most radical of modernist *compositional* implications. For where, say in the Melnikov pavilion at the 1925

Frank Gehry, Loyola Law School, Los Angeles, 1981-84. Photo by Grant Mudford

"Exposition des arts décoratifs" in Paris, Constructivism attempted to break entirely with the conventional frameworks of architecture — notably with frontality and institutional typicality — Gehry works to reinstate both.

Firstly, each project, however twisted and distorted the elements, maintains a powerful reference to frontality, generally in the form of a residual facade. This strategy is even more evident in the public projects: the literally free-standing facades of the World Savings Bank (North Hollywood, 1980) thus anticipate the broken facade of the Burns Building on the Loyola Law School campus. Other projects, without conventional facades, nevertheless stress the counterpoint of frontality and twisting movement in their total massing: the twin volumes, one cubic, the other splayed, of the California Aerospace Museum (1985), for example.

Secondly, and in relation to this insistence on the frontal referent, Gehry is dedicated to the subtle re-inscription of typology in the urban context, preferring to transform an existing type — found on the site or nearby — or to combine several types into one to form a new composite, rather than to invent *ex novo* objects that bear no relation to their context. This is so for the domestic projects — the Indiana Avenue Houses (Venice, 1981), the tract house projects of a year later, the Wosk Residence of 1982-84 in Beverly Hills — as for public institutions — the Hollywood Public Library, the Loyola Law School.

In a project for the Herman Miller Western Regional Manufacturing and Distribution Facility, Rocklin, California, the question of urban movement,

Frank Gehry, Herman Miller Western Region Manufacturing and Distribution Facility, Rocklin, California, 1989. Courtesy of Herman Miller, Inc.

raised at the Loyola Law School, is taken further and institutionalized. In the "private" realm of the Herman Miller factory, a public domain is engendered by the splitting apart of the two front buildings to create an enclave that is then populated by separate pavilions containing meeting, lunch, and wash rooms. The "entrance" to this internal acropolis is gained by a ramp, itself angled to the main grid of the assembly and warehouse structures. The entire composition is thereby refocused on the public nature of a private corporation, and urbanity introduced to a rural context.

The animation of function in movement, the almost autonomous play of functionalised forms, points to a final difference between Gehry's architecture and that of the Modern Movement, one that returns us to our introduction of Gehry as working to articulate the problematics of architectural tradition. For in a sense that was implicit in the first tilted roof of the O'Neill Hay Barn (San Juan, California, 1968), and progressively explored in the Ron Davis, Wagner, and Gehry houses, Gehry has been exploring not simply the idea of movement in architecture but more precisely the place of the *subject* in movement in architecture. This subject, situated by the classical tradition as central, the primary observer, the origin of vision and the framer of views, to which all architecture was subservient and whose perspective all architecture imitated, was of course subjected to enormous deformations by modernism. Rendered introspective by the Romantics, and expressively aerobic by the Modernists, this subject was inherited by Gehry as a strangely ambiguous creature, half traditional, half modern. His response has often been seen as a simple reflection of the subject's post-modern fragmentation, emulating in architecture the morselization and cutting of the body predicated by post-structuralist thought.

But another interpretation, founded on the careful experimentation with vision and movement that we have traced, would understand Gehry as trying to determine the appropriate limits of his subject with respect to architecture.

No longer content to be mirrored in, or confirmed by, its environment, this subject would be self-conscious of the illusion of projection, of the psychological and visual displacements of the mind; it would be a subject that refused to be formed or rendered healthy, as the Modern Movement dreamed, but that preferred to establish itself in a complex web of relationships, conceptual, perceptual, literal and phenomenal. Architecture, in this sense, would become both the stage and the stimulation for this self-enactment, at once permitting and testing, focusing and disseminating. For this, architecture would have to become somewhat autonomous in itself, engendering its own life, one analogous to but not imitative of the subject. As we have seen, Gehry's exploration of movement in its different states works to constitute this inner life of architecture. Yet it is a life not entirely cut off from the subject; its autonomy is provisional, and works simply as a mode of generation. Once inhabited, its own distortions work with those of the subject in a form of conversation, one no longer dedicated to reinstating the subject in centralized glory, but to exploring all of the dimensions of the subject's spatial dissemination.

Conclusion: Space and Identity

Recently, theories of identity, gender, post-colonialism, and regionalism have sought to appropriate spatial analysis for their own interests. The spatial interpretation of architecture and urbanism has followed these tendencies, and redefined its ideas of space and its analytical approaches at each juncture. Supporters of discourses based on gender, sexuality, and ethnicity have explored the potentiality of spatial analysis for the assertion of specific values and sites that might confirm and sustain subjects and societies more differentiated in nature and construction than the imaginary "universal subject" of modernism. Sociologists and urban geographers have rewritten Marxism to include the spatial and the territorial in their considerations of class and ethnic struggle; gender theorists have interrogated the "space of sexuality," attempting to identify what might be the dimensions of feminist, gay, lesbian, or "queer" space; post-colonial thinkers have stressed the "liminal" conditions of exilic subjects in space.

In its unsettling ability to join the infinite to the tangible, the sublime to the real, modern space has retained the double dimensions of utopia and melancholy present in its initial theorization. Both these dimensions have been, indeed, fully exploited by contemporary identity theorists; in, for example, the double condition of "liminality" and the "uncanny" experienced by the postcolonial subject characterized by Homi Bhabha, or the space of affirmation and mourning affirmed by theorists of "queer space." Finally, the capacities of the spatial metaphor to both confirm and undermine the places and sites of gender difference have been most significantly mustered on behalf of gender theory by the feminist philosopher Luce Irigaray in her radical rereading of the Heideggerian "space of being." In this way, the theorization of modern space has been brought back to its starting point, so to speak, but with an entirely new instrumentality and on behalf of a new politics of identity and gender. First formulated as a way of understanding and controlling the pathological and psychological states of bodies and minds in movement, now at the end of a century of interpretative experience, psychoanalytical, political, and philosophical, the concept of space seems to maintain its critical force as a measure of the place of differentiated subjects and their desires in the world, even as it provides a link between the abstract contemplation of architectural objects and the act of their construction.

Richard Neutra, Desert House for Edgar Kaufmann, Palm Springs, 1946. Photo by Julius Shulman

THE EXHIBITIONIST HOUSE

Beatriz Colomina

Adolf Loos, Moller House, Vienna, 1928. Graphische Sammlung Albertina, Vienna

In the Renaissance, between the idea sketchily stated and the commission for the permanent real place, came the stage-architecture for the Court Masque, the architecture settings and decorations for the birthday of a favourite prince or the wedding of a ducal daughter; these events were used by the architects of the Renaissance as opportunities for the realisation of the new style. . . . The real before the real, enjoyably consumed and creating the taste for more of the same. . . . Modern architecture follows this old tradition.[1]

How to traverse the enormous field of this exhibition, the architecture of this century? Two routes seem immediately appealing: One is the media, the way in which the architecture of this century is produced in the space of photographs, publications, exhibitions, congresses, fairs, magazines, newspapers, museums, art galleries, international competitions, advertising, computers, etc. The other is the house, understood not simply as one type among others, but as the most important vehicle for the investigation of architectural ideas in this century.

Perhaps no one thing distinguishes twentieth-century architecture more than the central role played by the house. If the nineteenth century can never be imagined without its public buildings — the theater, the opera, the stock market, and the museum — the twentieth century has been from the beginning, and still is as it closes, obsessed with the house. In fact, can one think about an architect without immediately thinking about a house? From Frank Lloyd Wright and Adolf Loos to Peter Eisenman and Frank Gehry, virtually all architects of this century have elaborated their most important architectural ideas through the design of houses.[2] They have become known through their houses, whether built or not: the house is the best advertisement for architecture.

1 Peter Smithson, "The Masque and the Exhibition: Stages toward the Real," *ILAUD Yearbook*, 1981.

2 Victor Horta, Antonio Gaudi, Otto Wagner, Gunnar Asplund, Charles and Henry Greene, Heinrich Tessenow, Bruno Taut, Max Taut, Eileen Gray, Lilly Reich, Walter Gropius, Konrad Wachsmann, J. J. P. Oud, Gerrit Rietveld, Theo van Doesburg, Cornelius van Eesteren, Mart Stam, Hans Scharoun, Charlotte Perriand, Frederick Kiesler, Konstantin Melnikov, Kasimir Malevich, El Lissitzky, Moisei Ginzburg, Pierre Chareau, Bernard Bijvoet, Rob Mallet-Stevens, R. M. Schindler, Richard Neutra, Buckminster Fuller, Paul Nelson, Jean Prouvé, Giuseppi Terragni, Adalberto Libera, Alvar Aalto, Marcel Breuer, Paul Rudolph, Ray and Charles Eames, Craig Ellwood, Paolo Soleri, John Lautner, Arne Jacobsen, John Johansen, William Wurster, Alison and Peter Smithson, Archigram, Oscar Niemeyer, Philip Johnson, Louis Kahn, J. A. Coderch, Bruce Goff, Robert Venturi and Denise Scott Brown, Luis Barragán, Peter Eisenman, Richard Meier, Steven Holl, Alvaro Siza, Tadao Ando, Toyo Ito, OMA, Coop Himmelb(l)au, Frank Israel, Morphosis, Diller + Scofidio, Ben van Berkel . . . and on and on.

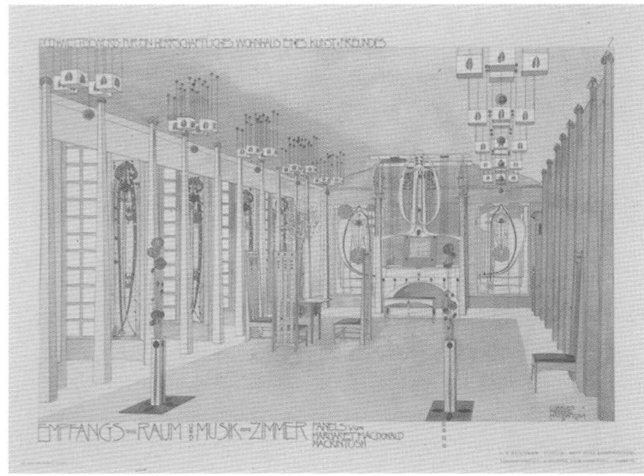

Charles Rennie Mackintosh and Margaret McDonald, perspective of the reception and music room, House for An Art-Lover competition entry, 1901. Hunterian Art Gallery, University of Glasgow

For architects the house has the appeal of the experiment. In smaller, more compact and controlled situations, it becomes possible to speculate. The house becomes a laboratory for ideas. And for that reason, it may be the only possible site of art production left to architecture — the rest is decorated infrastructure. Not by chance is the typical client of the architect-house an art collector or publisher. It has been this way for some time. Charles Rennie Mackintosh and Margaret McDonald's most influential house design was a disqualified entry for the 1901 "House for an Art-Lover" competition. Raoul La Roche, the client of Le Corbusier's 1923 house in Auteil, was an art collector and patron, as were Charles and Marie-Laure de Noailles, who commissioned a villa at Hyères from Rob Mallet-Stevens in 1924, and Charles de Beistegui, who commissioned Le Corbusier to do a memorable penthouse apartment in the Champs Elysées in 1930. Diller + Scofidio's 1989 Slow House on Long Island was also commissioned by an art collector, and the fact that the house was not realized is attributed to the crash of the art market. Publishers have played a similar role as architectural patrons. Jean Badovici, editor of *L'Architecture vivante*, was the client for Eileen Gray's E.1027 in Cap-Martin (1926-27); John Entenza, editor of *Arts & Architecture*, commissioned a house in Santa Monica from Eero Saarinen and Charles Eames in 1945; and OMA's Villa dall'Ava in St. Cloud, Paris, completed in 1991, is the house of the editor of *Le Moniteur*, one of the most important architec-

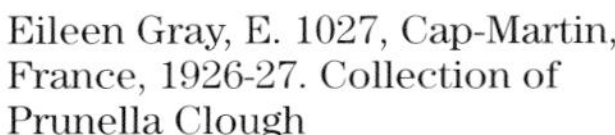
Eileen Gray, E. 1027, Cap-Martin, France, 1926-27. Collection of Prunella Clough

Office for Metropolitan Architecture, Villa dall'Ava, St. Cloud, Paris, 1991. Photo by Hans Werlemann

tural publishers in France. Unsurprisingly, collaborations between architects and publishers have also produced some of the most extraordinary publications of houses, such as the 1929 issue of *L'Architecture Vivante*, "E.1027: Maison en bord de mer," with its hand-colored photographs and drawings of the house and a dialogue between Badovici and Gray on what is architecture. Or the presentation of Villa dall'Ava in an issue of *Le Moniteur, AMC* complete with photographs of a giraffe in the garden. The "House for an Art-Lover" competition was sponsored by publisher Alexander Koch and announced in his journal *Zeitschrift für Innendekoration*. Koch published a special portfolio of Mackintosh and McDonald's entry as an art book with new water-colored perspectives and an introduction by Herman Muthesius.[3]

In fact, many of the most significant houses of this century did not have a conventional client. They were produced for exhibitions, publications, fairs, competitions, and journals, rather than for traditional building sites. Even those

3 *Meister der Innen-Kunst 2: Charles Rennie Mackintosh, Glasgow, Haus eines Kunst-Freundes* (Darmstadt: Verlag Alexander Koch, 1902).

4 For example, the entire issue of *The Sunday Times Magazine* (London), 15 June 1997, entitled "Fastforward: Totally Wired, Waking Up to a New Technology in Your Home," was dedicated to the potential of new technologies to alter the way we live.

houses that were built for actual clients derived their main impact from their publication, before and after construction. In this sense, it can be said that they are all exhibition houses. Images of them have circulated in all forms of media, making a series of polemical propositions about the reorganization of domestic space in the twentieth century. These propositions were then usually extended to other forms of building, and the debate about houses typically became one about architecture per se. Every aspect of architecture, even the city itself, has been rethought in this century through the house and the media.

The city can never be separated from domestic space. What goes on in the public square shapes the domestic space that seems to be detached from it, and vice versa. But in the twentieth century, the two realms — private and public — are completely intermingled. This intermingling itself has a long history. Electricity, appliances, new technologies and building materials, and new forms of communication have radically transformed the house. From the telephone to radio, television, computers, fax machines, and e-mail, the house has been continuously assaulted,

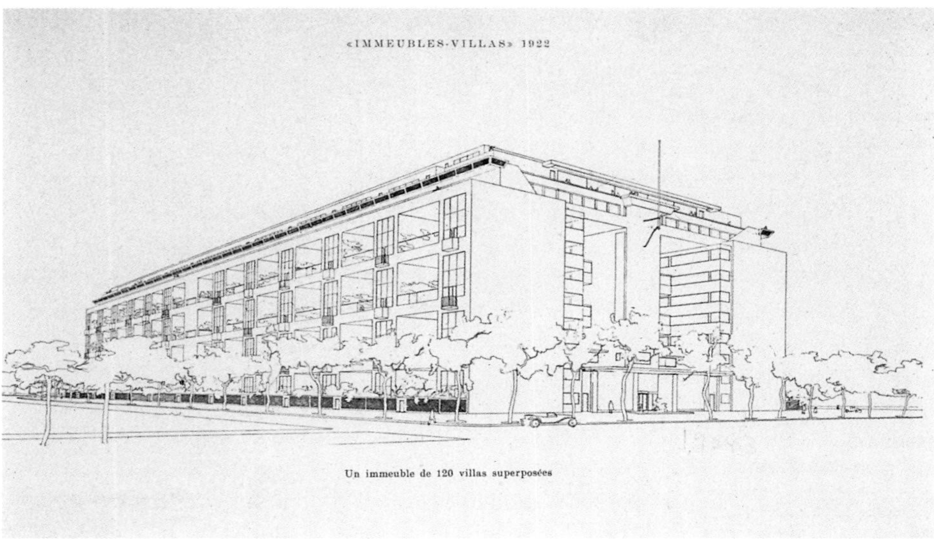

Le Corbusier, Immeubles-Villas, 1922. Fondation Le Corbusier

with what is public and what is private endlessly renegotiated. The house has been turned inside out. Newspapers and magazines at the beginning of the century offered images of the new sense of space established by the telephone. In 1915 AT&T showed houses linked by wires to distant metropolitan and industrial centers. Today the same company presents images of the transformation of the house into office. We are told (even if there are no official numbers yet) that an increasing number of people work out of their homes and commute to an office as little as once a week, or not at all.[4] The house, once again, becomes a factory, a shop, a laboratory, a site of production, as it was in preindustrial times. This electronic cottage is increasingly in the city, so even the commute is unnecessary. The meaning of the house is changing. Advertisements from banks, telephone companies, and computer manufacturers bombard us daily with images of new forms of domesticity: working, banking, telecommuting from home or the beach or a mountainside, surrounded by children and pets. On the other hand, these same advertisements have us performing truly domestic acts — such as tucking a child in bed — from a videophone on the highway. Home is not where it used to be.

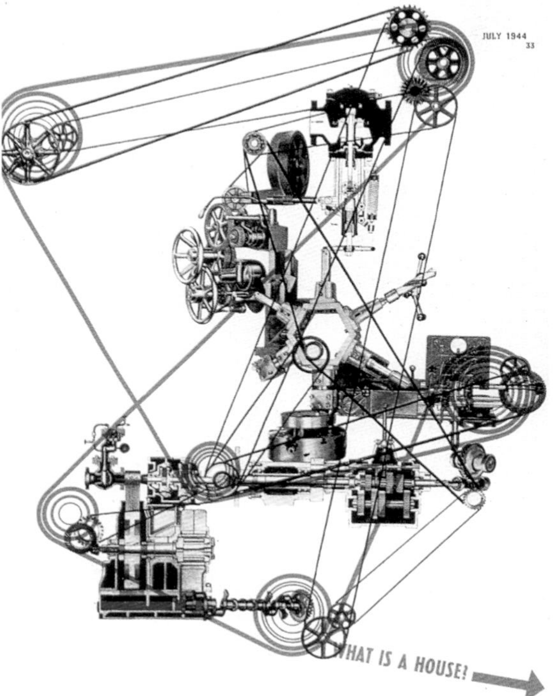

Charles Eames, "What is a House?" in *Arts & Architecture*, July 1944

Since the first decades of the century architects have been completely obsessed with the relationship between the media and the house. Their architecture is unthinkable without it. They have actively engaged the media and used it to transform the house itself. Or more precisely, they have responded to an ongoing transformation, a process that continues today, when it has become a commonplace to point out that the contemporary house, with its televisions, computer networks, fax machines, and other electronic devices, has become a much more public space than the street.

So "what is a house?", to borrow the question that the magazine *Arts & Architecture* asked itself in 1944 as the editors prepared to launch the Case Study program of exhibition houses in Los Angeles. In the twentieth century, we are faced with two striking phenomena (and the Case Study program is paradigmatic of this): the house is in the media and the media is in the house. Here we can start to see a way to think about the architecture of this century without reducing it to a series of masterpieces. Rather than a comprehensive survey, it is like a family photograph album, a small selection from thousands of snapshots which attempts to capture the different media in which architects have built their houses and the effect that those media have had on the architecture.

Houses on Display

Many of the influential houses of the twentieth century were produced for exhibitions. Think, for example, of Mies van der Rohe's Concrete and Brick Country Houses in the Berlin Art Exhibitions of 1923 and 1924. These were the projects that established his reputation as one of the leaders of modern architecture. The houses he was building at the time were very conservative, but the exhibition provided an opportunity for an experimental architecture that would eventually be built.

Exhibitions still play the same crucial role today; if anything, this role has grown. Consider, for example, the 1980 exhibition "Houses for Sale" at the Leo Castelli Gallery in New York. Reversing the traditional process whereby the client commissions an architect to design a house, an international group of eight architects was invited to put their visions of the modern house on "sale." The catalogue clarifies that "drawings may be purchased separately from the commission of the project." While this exhibition can be read as a purely postmodern phenomenon, one of many instances signaling the entrance of architecture into the art market, the seeds for such an event had been planted long before.

Exhibitions of houses are either the display of models and drawings or the display of full-scale buildings in order to communicate to a wider public.

Le Corbusier, Pavillon de l'Esprit Nouveau, Paris, 1925. Fondation Le Corbusier

An example of the first type is the extraordinarily influential 1923 De Stijl exhibition at the Galerie L'Effort Moderne in Paris, where van Doesburg and van Eesteren's innovative models of houses were shown, models whose influence are still evident today. An example of the second is Le Corbusier's Pavillon de l'Esprit Nouveau, a unit of his proposed Immeubles-Villas built for the "Exposition des arts décoratifs" in Paris in 1925. The first exhibition took place in an art gallery, with an audience of cognoscenti; the second was presented to a mass audience at a huge public fair.

With the Pavillon de l'Esprit Nouveau, the house itself became an exhibit: the space of the exhibition and the exhibit became the same thing. The apartment, which was meant to be suspended way up in the air overlooking a new,

Weissenhofsiedlung, Stuttgart, 1927, view in 1932

J. J. P. Oud, Houses 5-9, Weissenhofsiedlung, Stuttgart, 1927. Photo by Dana Hutt

modernized Paris, was placed on the ground in the middle of a park, like some kind of spaceship from the future. The exhibition organizers were so worried about this house that they built a twenty-foot-high fence to hide it. Le Corbusier had filled the house with all the furnishings and art works he considered appropriate for modern life, and visitors could walk through it, imagining the new lifestyle, separated from the fantasy only by thin ropes. Le Corbusier even exhibited his plans for the city within the structure of the pavilion: the domestic house became the site for his whole architectural philosophy.

Perhaps the most significant exhibition of built houses was the "1927 Weissenhofsiedlung," a small suburb of houses on the outskirts of Stuttgart designed by many of the most progressive international architects of the day, complete with streets, lighting, landscaping and furnishings.[5] It was part of the even larger exhibition "Die Wohnung" (The Dwelling), organized by the German Werkbund, which embraced every aspect of the house from kitchen equipment to construction techniques and materials. Despite the large scale of the overall exhibition, it was the built *Siedlung* itself that had such a dramatic influence on popular and professional debates. Model houses always attract an enormous audience. In speculating about the house, architects participate in a culture-wide debate.

Berlin Building Exposition of 1931.

At the Berlin Building Exposition of 1931, whose theme was "The Dwelling in Our Time," full-scale models of houses and apartments were built within

5 Richard Pommer and Christian F. Otto, *Weissenhof 1927 and the Modern Movement in Architecture* (Chicago: The University of Chicago Press, 1991). Karin Kirsch, *The Weissenhofsiedlung: Experimental Housing Built for the Deutscher Werkbund, Stuttgart, 1927* (New York: Rizzoli, 1989).

Mies van der Rohe, Barcelona Pavilion, Barcelona, 1929

another building. Upon entering the large exhibition hall, visitors encountered houses by Hugo Häring, the Luckhardt brothers, Lilly Reich, and Mies van der Rohe occupying the center of the space. All around the periphery was a continuous strip of model apartments and rooms by Marcel Breuer, Walter Gropius, Otto Haesler, Ludwig Hilberseimer, Wassily Kandinsky, and Karl Voelker. A materials exhibition designed by Lilly Reich was installed on the balcony that ringed the space.

Mies van der Rohe and Lilly Reich are particularly good examples of architects who used exhibitions to produce experimental work. At the Berlin Building Exhibition, they both constructed houses in the main hall which were tied together by a wall extended from the heart of Mies's house into the heart of Reich's. (Reminiscent of the walls sliding out into infinity in the Brick Country House, this umbilical cord may be a clue about the enigmatic partnership of Mies and Reich.) Once again Mies was able to achieve one of his most radical spaces in the context of an exhibition, and Lilly Reich was able to build a house for the first and only time in her career. Reich's house was very stark: she used sensuous fabrics, textures, and colors to define spaces, continuing the experimentation of her earlier exhibition designs.[6]

In fact, both Mies and Reich repeatedly stretched the concept of exhibition into that of the house. When the German glass industry commissioned a display of their products for the "Die Wohnung" exhibition in Stuttgart, the designers turned their "Glass Hall" display into a house, a flowing space subdivided into dining room, living room, and workroom by freestanding glass walls. The illusion of ceiling was produced by strips of stretched fabric; the floors were covered with white, grey and black linoleum areas that produced a sense of movement by not quite coinciding with the rooms; the walls were of etched, clear, and grey opaque glass; the chairs were covered in white chamois and black cowhide; and the bench table was rosewood.[7] A sense of the outside was produced by placing plants and a sculpture of a woman on the other side of one of the glass walls. This strategy anticipates the Barcelona Pavilion, Mies's most famous project.

6 For Lilly Reich's work see Matilda McQuaid, *Lilly Reich: Designer and Architect* (New York: The Museum of Modern Art, 1996), and Sonja Günther, *Lilly Reich 1885-1947: Innenarchitektin, Designerin, Ausstellungsgestalterin* (Stuttgart: Deutsche Verlags-Anstalt, 1988).

7 Franz Schulze, *Mies van der Rohe: A Critical Biography* (Chicago: The University of Chicago Press, 1985), 141-42. McQuaid, *Lilly Reich*, 25.

8 Julius Posener, "Los primeros años: De Schinkel a De Stijl," *Mies van der Rohe, A&V: Monografías de Arquitectura y Vivienda* 6 (1986): 33.

9 Rem Koolhaas, *S, M, L, XL: Office for Metropolitan Architecture, Rem Koolhaas and Bruce Mau* (New York: Monacelli Press, 1995), 49.

When commissioned to build the German pavilion for the International Exhibition of Barcelona in 1929, Mies asked the Ministry of Foreign Affairs what was to be exhibited. "Nothing will be exhibited," he was told, "the pavilion itself will be the exhibit."[8] In the absence of a traditional client or program, Mies was able to take his work to new limits, and one of the most influential buildings of the century emerged. Once again Mies and Reich (who collaborated on the project) took the opportunity to make a house: its flowing space, defined by the strategic placement of sensuous materials, continued the investigations of the Brick Country House, the "Velvet and Silk Cafe" of the Mode der Dame exhibition of 1927, and the Glass Hall exhibit at Stuttgart. Mies's house in the Berlin exhibition develops the Barcelona pavilion for specific domestic use and intimates his unrealized court houses of the 1930s. Experimental exhibition techniques become experimental houses.

Eventually the experiment would fall into different hands: for the 1986 Milan Triennale, the Office for Metropolitan Architecture (OMA) constructed its Body Building House, a Barcelona pavilion "bent" to fit the curve of an allotted site within the exhibition building:

> By then phobic about the duty to reveal, we decide to embody our resistance in an exhibit about exhibition. At the time, a clone of Mies's pavilion was being built in Barcelona. How fundamentally did it differ from Disney? In the name of higher authenticity, we researched the true history of the pavilion after the closing of the 1929 World's Fair and collected whatever archeological remnants it had left across Europe on its return journey. Like a Pompeian villa, these fragments were reassembled as far as possible to suggest the former whole, but with one inevitable inaccuracy; since our "site" was curved, the pavilion had to be "bent."[9]

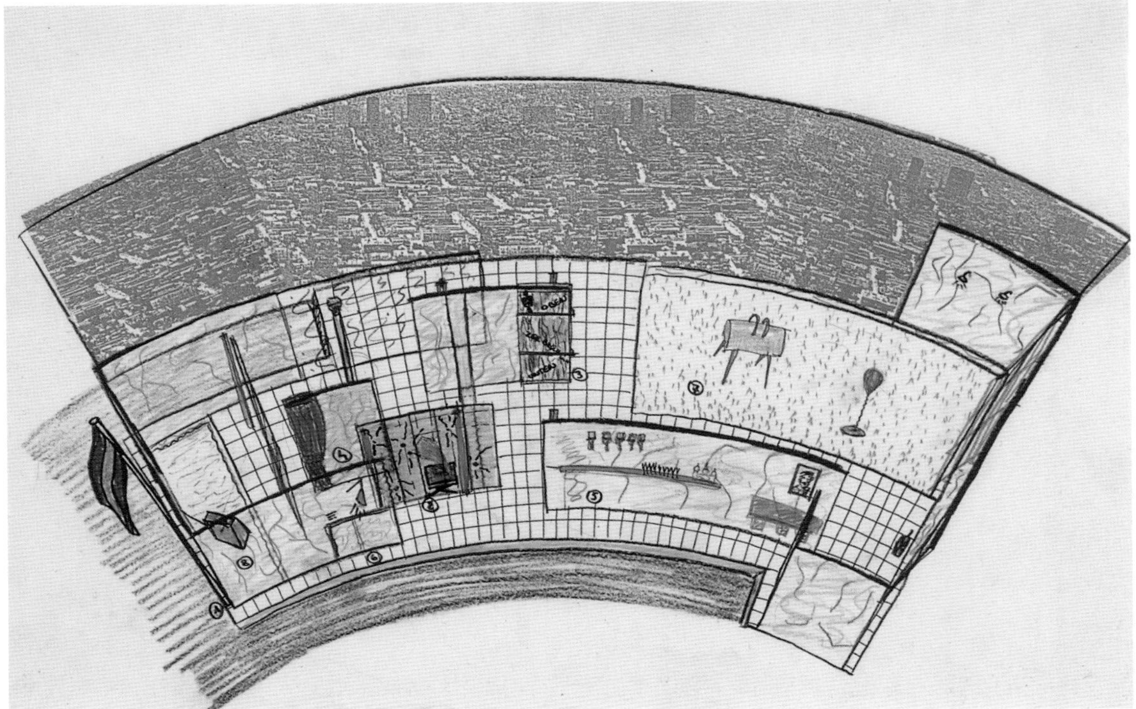

Office for Metropolitan Architecture, La Casa Palestra/ Body Building House, 1986 Milan Triennale

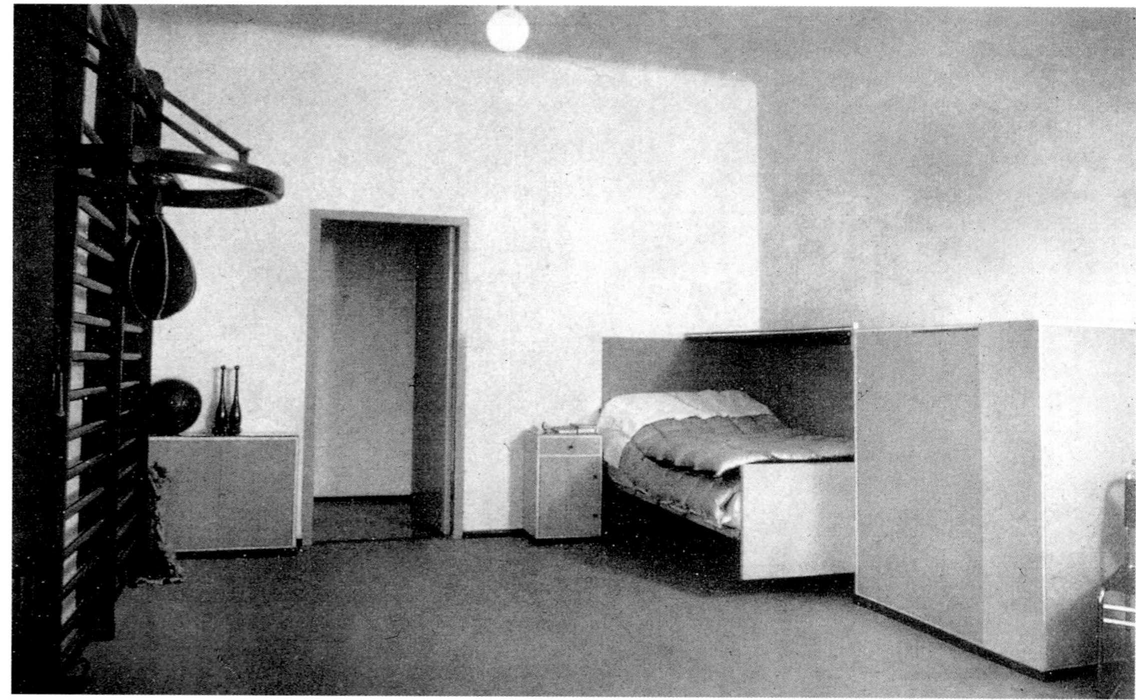

Marcel Breuer, view of man's bedroom, Piscator Apartment, Berlin, 1927

OMA's "true history" of the pavilion is actually a fantasy intended as a homage to the pavilion and to modern architecture, under attack at the time as being "lifeless, empty and puritanical": "It has always been our conviction that modern architecture is a hedonistic movement, that its abstraction, rigour and severity are in fact plots to create the most provocative settings for the experiment that is modern life."[10]

In the Body Building House, the Barcelona pavilion is inhabited by gymnasts, bodybuilders and exercise equipment, in a suprematist explosion of projected images, lighting effects, and lasers.[11] Mies's minimalist statement becomes engorged with activities, and the references multiply. The project alludes to the tradition of body building in modern architecture: Marcel Breuer's room for Piscator in Berlin; Gropius's gym in his Berlin Exhibition apartment; Richard Döcker's gym on the roof at the Weissenhof; the 1,000-meter track that Le Corbusier proposed for the roof of his Immeubles-villas; Richard Neutra's Lovell House; and even the transformation of Mies's Tugendhat house in Brno into a children's gym by communist bureaucrats in the 1960s.

OMA takes modern architecture's dream of a healthy body to a new level. Experimentation in exhibitions always becomes collective in the end, as other architects pick up ideas, work on them, and then themselves generate responses by other architects in different exhibitions. Such is the nature of architectural discourse.

The rebuilding of the Barcelona pavilion is itself an important part of the story of the exhibition house. While many of Mies's buildings have been destroyed, the temporary exhibition building had become such a central monument in architectural culture that it was reconstructed in 1987 on the original exhibition site as a kind of simulacrum. The same thing happened to Le Corbusier's L'Esprit

10 OMA: Office for Metropolitan Architecture, "La Casa Palestra," *AA Files* (London) 13 (Winter 1989): 8.

11 Mg del Carmen Grandas, Imma Julián, and Josep Quetgles, "Mies van der Rohe, 1928-1986," *On* 73 (1986): 21.

12 Peter Smithson, *ILAUD Yearbook* (Urbino, 1981).

Mies van der Rohe, Tugendhat House, Brno, Czechoslovakia, 1930. Photo by Fritz Tugendhat, c. 1930-40. Centre Canadien d'Architecture/ Canadian Centre for Architecture, Montréal

Mies van der Rohe, Tugendhat House. View of the house in the 1960s transformed into a children's gym

Richard Neutra, Lovell Health House, Los Angeles, 1927-29. Photo by Julius Shulman

Nouveau pavilion: since 1977 a replica has sat in a park in Bologna, exemplifying fifty-year-old principles. As Peter Smithson wrote, "To visit it is to be reminded that an architect always needs to have his pots and pans and his view of nature ready in case he is asked."[12] To some extent, reconstructions interfere with the discourse. Many exhibition experiments gain their force precisely by physically disappearing while inhabiting the spaces of publication, of memory, of fantasy. The lack of a specific client or site gives them a permanent role: since they are not pinned down, they remain open to speculation. Reconstruction fixes them, if not finishes them.

Exhibition houses meant to be permanent tend to blend into their environments with time. For example, with the Case Study House program in Los Angeles (begun in 1945 and sponsored by *Arts & Architecture* under John Entenza), the exhibition of houses was no longer enclosed inside a building, as in Berlin, or confined to a suburb, as in Stuttgart, but instead was scattered throughout the city.[13] The houses, which were completely furnished and equipped through an agreement with various manufacturers, were open to the public for six to eight weeks and then occupied. They include some classics — Pierre Koenig's house, Craig Ellwood's

Gregory Ain, Exhibition House in the garden of The Museum of Modern Art, New York, 1950

house, and the Eames house — which have become pilgrimage sites for architects, who try hard to go through them like eager visitors to a fair but can usually be found outside, taking photographs over a fence. Like all the canonical houses of the century, their primary life remains in their publication. The owners of OMA's Villa dall'Ava said that "on a Saturday morning they counted thirty people outside, looking in,"[14] but how many thousands, perhaps hundreds of thousands, have gone through the house via publications?

Museums

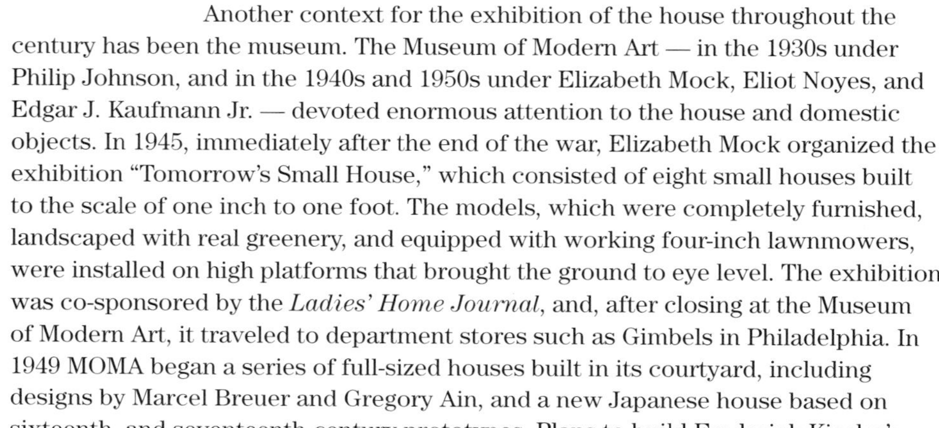

Another context for the exhibition of the house throughout the century has been the museum. The Museum of Modern Art — in the 1930s under Philip Johnson, and in the 1940s and 1950s under Elizabeth Mock, Eliot Noyes, and Edgar J. Kaufmann Jr. — devoted enormous attention to the house and domestic objects. In 1945, immediately after the end of the war, Elizabeth Mock organized the exhibition "Tomorrow's Small House," which consisted of eight small houses built to the scale of one inch to one foot. The models, which were completely furnished, landscaped with real greenery, and equipped with working four-inch lawnmowers, were installed on high platforms that brought the ground to eye level. The exhibition was co-sponsored by the *Ladies' Home Journal*, and, after closing at the Museum of Modern Art, it traveled to department stores such as Gimbels in Philadelphia. In 1949 MOMA began a series of full-sized houses built in its courtyard, including designs by Marcel Breuer and Gregory Ain, and a new Japanese house based on sixteenth- and seventeenth-century prototypes. Plans to build Frederick Kiesler's Endless House in the garden were derailed by construction in the museum but the house was exhibited as a model in the 1952 exhibition "Two Houses: New Ways to Build," alongside Buckminster Fuller's model of a geodesic dome. A large model of Kiesler's house was also included in the 1960 exhibition "Visionary Architects," together with projects by Le Corbusier, Fuller, Bruno Taut, and Frank Lloyd Wright. MOMA was not alone in its interest in the house. The Walker Art Center in Minneapolis built an Idea House behind the museum in 1941 and a second Idea House in 1947. In the 1950s the Guggenheim built one of Wright's Usonian Houses on the site of the future museum.

Frederick Kiesler with model of the Endless House, 1959

Frank Lloyd Wright, Usonian exhibition house at the Guggenheim Museum, 1953. Photo by Pedro E. Guerrero

Despite the involvement of museums, this interest in houses was not just a high-art phenomenon. The blueprints of Breuer's and Ain's houses at MOMA were made available, and the museum went as far as obtaining construction estimates from builders in several suburbs of New York where replicas of the house were actually built. The houses at MOMA were fully furnished, down to the cutlery and hangers in the closets. The manufacturers of all these objects participated in the

13 About the Case Study House program, see Elizabeth A.T. Smith, *Blueprints for Modern Living: History and Legacy of the Case Study Houses* (Los Angeles: The Museum of Contemporary Art; Cambridge: The MIT Press, 1989).

14 Koolhaas, *S, M, L, XL*, 175.

15 See Terence Riley, *The International Style: Exhibition 15 and The Museum of Modern Art*, Columbia Books of Architecture, no.2 (New York: Rizzoli, 1992). And see the chapter "Museum" in Beatriz Colomina, *Privacy and Publicity: Modern Architecture as Mass Media* (Cambridge, Mass.: MIT Press, 1994).

Buckminster Fuller, Wichita House, *Fortune* 33, 1946, 21.

Buckminster Fuller with model of Dymaxion House, as published in *Fortune*, 1946. Buckminster Fuller Institute, Santa Barbara

project and benefited from the publicity. The Walker Art Center launched the magazine *Everyday Art Quarterly* in 1946 to coincide with the establishment of its design department; the intent was to market well-designed objects for the home. In a special issue of the magazine dedicated to the "Idea House II," advertisements extolled the virtues of the equipment and materials being used. In 1949 Kaufmann initiated the "Good Design" program at MOMA in collaboration with the Merchandise Mart of Chicago. Subtitled "A Joint Program to Stimulate the Best Modern Design of Home Furnishing," the shows coincided with the winter and summer housewares markets at the Mart. MOMA also produced many publications that popularized the modern house and its interior, including Elizabeth Mock's 1946 *If You Want to Build a House* and Kaufmann's own 1953 *What is Modern Interior Design?*

Even the so-called "International Style" exhibition with which MOMA inaugurated its department of architecture in 1932 was primarily an exhibition of houses. This was programmatic: as Philip Johnson indicated in an internal memo during the show's preparation, "The most interesting exhibit [for the public] is still that of the private house." He singled out the private house as the best vehicle for the popularization of "the style" and offered more space in the exhibition to those architects who presented houses.[15] In the end, the exhibition was made up almost entirely of domestic architecture.

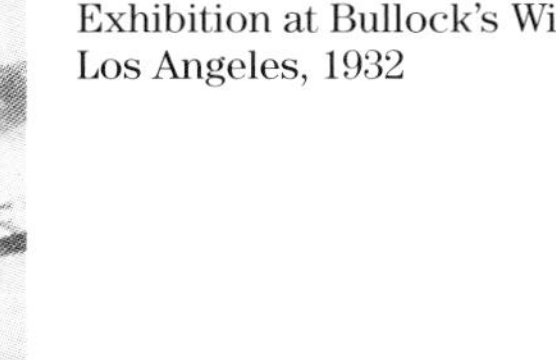

Modern Architecture International Exhibition at Bullock's Wilshire, Los Angeles, 1932

Department Stores

What is not well known about the famous "International Style" exhibition, which traveled the country, is that it was installed not only at other art institutions but also in department stores such as Sears, Roebuck & Co. in Chicago, and Bullock's Wilshire in Los Angeles. (In fact, according to Johnson, attendance at Sears was higher than at MOMA.) The modern house was presented as a product to be sold like any other. Those who could not afford the house itself were offered small fragments, tokens of modern domestic life — furniture, fabrics, lamps, and other fittings — produced by collaborations between designers and manufacturers.

The department store became an ongoing site for the exhibition and promotion of the modern house. Johnson and his co-curator Henry-Russell Hitchcock even presented a series of lectures in department stores. This was not unprecedented. In 1929 the Marshall Fields department store in Chicago imported a collection of modern furniture from France. To attract attention to the furniture during such a bad year for the economy, the store management asked Buckminster Fuller to set up and demonstrate a model of a house he had designed for mass production in 1927 — it was the first public presentation of the Dymaxion House. Fuller gave a continuous series of lectures (at the rate of six a day for two weeks) about the house, stressing its technical merits. The house was "erectable in one day, complete in every detail, with every living appliance known to mankind, built in," and was "absolutely proof against earthquake, flood, fire, gas attack, dirt, pestilence and cyclone." The "transport unit," an amphibious auto-airplane, was stored beneath the house.

Even manufacturers transformed their showrooms into galleries for the exhibition of houses. Prior to the exhibition of the Endless House at MOMA, Kiesler had exhibited a full-scale model of his Space House in 1933 in the showrooms of the Modern Age Furniture Co. in New York. Commissioned to generate publicity for the furniture, the Space House became a popular New York attraction. Once again, modern architecture was called on to play the role of advertising, a lure to direct attention to something other than itself. For Kiesler it was an opportunity to continue his investigations with the eggshell shape, of which he said: "The egg shell is the perfect example of a structure in which walls, floors and ceilings are self-supporting in an architectural sense." The shell of the house was intended for die-cast construction in a factory, but Kiesler's dream of mass production remained just that. The Space House was never more than an advertisement for modern furniture.[16]

In the United States modern architecture is inextricably linked to the department store. Robert McLaughlin, a graduate of Princeton and the founder of American Houses, Inc., introduced a prefabricated house called the "Motohome" at Wanamaker's department store in New York on April 1, 1935. The house was all wrapped in cellophane and tied up with a huge red ribbon, which was cut by Sara Delano Roosevelt, the president's mother. New Yorkers filed through the single-story, five-room house at the rate of eight hundred per hour, and Wanamaker's was forced to stop advertising the house "to keep the crowds from becoming riots."[17] The company offered fifteen models of Motohomes, ranging from a four-room cottage to a two-story, nine-room house with three bathrooms and a two-car garage. Customers could choose their houses by playing with parts of little house models — including trees and shrubs — which could be rearranged to suit their needs.

[16] Beatriz Colomina, "La Space House et la psyché de la construction," in *Frederick Kiesler: Artiste-architecte* (Paris: Centre national d'art et culture Georges Pompidou, 1996), 66-76.

[17] "Sectional Motohome Makes Debut in Cellophane," *Newsweek* 5 (April 13, 1935), 28. See also Brian Horrigan "The Home of Tomorrow, 1927-1945," in *Imagining Tomorrow: History, Technology and the American Future*, ed. Joseph J. Corn (Cambridge, Mass.: The MIT Press, 1986), 150.

The house owed its name to the "motor unit," which contained "all the plumbing, heating, cooking, lighting, and air-conditioning devices."[18] It came fully equipped with heating, air-conditioning, and every possible appliance; it also included a supply of toilet articles, enough food to last three days,[19] and manuals on every domestic issue from home maintenance and decoration to cooking, etiquette, and child-rearing.[20] The unassembled prefabricated house would be delivered to the site in a truck whose sides announced "This Truck Contains One American Home." The magazine *Woman's Home Companion* reported:

> The packaged house is here. . . . Imagine being able to buy your home as you would buy a package of cereals or face powder — a home complete in every minute detail, that you can actually see, touch, examine and discuss before you buy it and above all know exactly what it is going to cost, down to the last penny, before you move in.[21]

Fairs

Experimental houses have often been constructed within fairs — the exhibition house reaches a mass audience. Take George Fred Keck's House of Tomorrow built at the Century of Progress International Exposition in Chicago in 1933. The fair was intended to depict the effects of science and technology on industry and everyday life, but the most popular attraction was a series of thirteen model homes built along the Lake Michigan waterfront. Financed by trade organizations, the houses were intended to show the "impact of modern technology on residential architecture." Keck, who recognized the exposition as a great opportunity to promote modern architecture, built two. The House of Tomorrow, sponsored by General Electric and Goodyear Tire, was a three-story, twelve-sided house with glass walls and an airplane hangar on the ground floor. Pierce Arrow supplied a Silver Arrow automobile, which was kept in the garage alongside the "sport biplane" supplied by Curtiss Wright. Keck's technologically more sophisticated Crystal House was built for the reopening of the fair in 1934, and its garage housed Buckminster Fuller's prototype Dymaxion car. Keck now felt the need to offer a house that "lends itself to prefabrication in order that it may be within the reach of the masses."[22] A less spectacular — but perhaps more radical — proposal was the exhibit featuring "General Houses, Inc.," a Chicago-based manufacturer of prefabricated houses, whose name was modeled on "General Motors." The company was founded by architect Howard Fisher, who had been a student at Harvard in 1929 and was inspired by Fuller's ideas. It aimed at carrying the methods of the automobile industry into the building of houses, or in a slogan of the day, to make "houses like Fords."[23] General Houses intended to act, like many car manufacturers, as an "assembler of parts rather than a primary producer."[24] The company offered eighteen variations of the house that was exhibited at the fair; each was coded with a formula such as "House K_3H4D," which indicated a particular combination of parts from the catalogue.[25]

Likewise, the New York World's Fair of 1939-40 presented several visions of the home.[26] "Town of Tomorrow" consisted of fifteen model homes in a suburban setting, including a plywood house, a glass house, a celotex house, and a Motor Home.[27] With a two-car garage occupying the facade of the Motor Home and the living room facing the rear garden, the automobile had turned the house around. A small entry is squeezed between the two huge garage doors. The Motor Home

18 "The House that Runs Itself," *Popular Mechanics* 63 (June 1935): 805-06.

19 "Sectional Motohome Makes Debut in Cellophane," *Newsweek*: 30.

20 Horrigan, "The Home of Tomorrow," 150.

21 Katherine M. Bissell, "The New American House: An Interview with Robert W. McLaughlin, Jr., Architect," *Woman's Home Companion* 62 (March 1935): 60.

22 Quoted in Thomas M. Slade's "The 'Crystal House' of 1934," *Journal of the Society of Architectural Historians* 29 (1970): 350.

23 Douglas Haskell, "Houses Like Fords," *Harper's Magazine* 168 (February 1934): 286-97.

24 Horrigan, "The Home of Tomorrow," 150.

25 Douglas Haskell, "Houses Like Fords," 289.

26 "To fair planners, a home was not just a house. It was a demonstration of the impact of technology on the most mundane aspects of human behavior; it contributed to the definition of a new American culture adapted to the machine world. . . . The fair's perception of the home and its various physical components was linked to its view of the family as a consumer unit." Joseph P. Cusker, "The World of Tomorrow: Science, Culture and Community at the New York World's Fair," in *Dawn of a New Day: The New York World's Fair, 1939/40* (Flushing, N.Y.: Queens Museum, and New York: New York University Press, 1980), 13.

27 Stanley Appelbaum, *The New York World's Fair: 1939/1940 in 155 Photographs* (New York: Dover, 1977), 91.

George Fred Keck, House of Tomorrow with airplane garage, at "Century of Progress International Exhibition," Chicago, 1933

Spectators viewing the General Motors "Futurama" model at the 1939 New York World's Fair. Norman Bel Geddes Collection, Theatre Arts Collection, Harry Ransom Humanities Research Center, The University of Texas at Austin. By permission of Edith Lutyens Bel Geddes, Executrix. Photo by Margaret Bourke-White

brochure explains: "The main entrance is provided with a normal door for the convenience of callers who do not drive in."[28]

But the hit of the fair was no longer the built houses — it was the Futurama ride in the Norman Bel Geddes-designed General Motors exhibit. Six hundred chairs with individual loudspeakers moved visitors over the imagined world of 1960: seven-lane roads with permissible speed of 100-MPH, experimental homes, farms, industrial plants, dams, bridges, and a model metropolis. Gerald Wendt, science director of the fair, remarked in his opening address on the significance of the automobile for Americans:

> Americans live in their cars. Here they attain temporary privacy, an isolation from pressing neighbors. Here they enjoy the sensation of motion, of action and progress, even though it be vicarious and futile. Here they feel

[28] Rosemarie Haag Bletter, "The World of Tomorrow: The Future with a Past," in *Remembering the Future: The New York World's Fair from 1939-1964* (New York: Rizzoli, 1989), 84.

> too the sense of power and of control over their course and destiny which is otherwise lost in their dependence on society. Here they escape from monotony and often from squalor. Thus the American nation has become mobile, optimistic, and occupied with external change of scene rather than with stability and the improvement of their permanent conditions of living.[29]

The fair announced that the car was the new home for Americans. Strapped into individual seats, visitors to Futurama experienced the world of tomorrow in isolation, as if riding alone in a car.

The car had always been the prototype of the modern house. It inspired Le Corbusier's Maison Citrohan (1920), the idea of the minimum house, the standardization and Fordization of house production, and so on. Architects often photographed their houses alongside the latest car or drew the car in their renderings, and almost every architect — Le Corbusier, Fuller, Gropius, Loos, Mies, Neutra, Wright, etc. — designed a car.

Perhaps the most spectacular manifestation of architects' fascination with the car is the experiments of Archigram in the 1960s, which extended the house out of the car itself. With Michael Webb's futurist "Drive-In House," a project that has evolved over decades, the car plugs right into the house; in fact, it literally turns into a house as the automobile body is turned inside out and occupied. The car, which Webb describes as that "most luxuriously appointed component of vita domestica which, however, wasteful and sad, sits in the driveway unused for most of the day" is here recycled, dissected, and separated into parts — the stereo system, the seats, the windows, the television, the cocktail cabinet, the air-conditioning, the telephone — which are recombined into a new form of domestic space.[30]

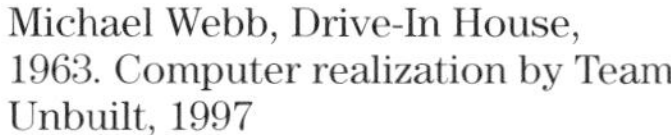

Michael Webb, Drive-In House, 1963. Computer realization by Team Unbuilt, 1997

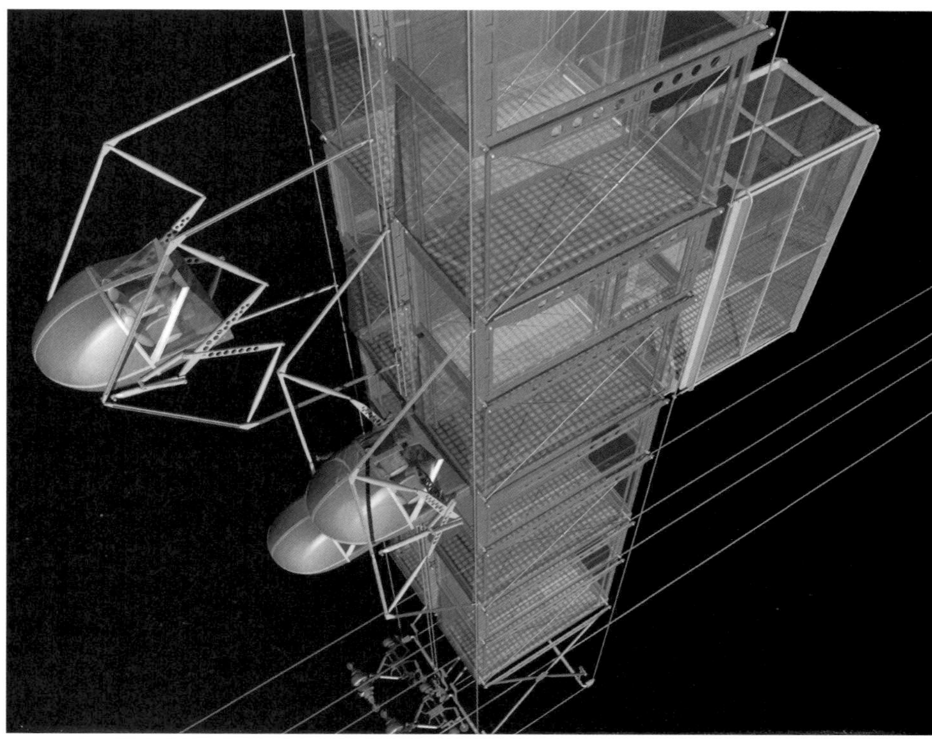

There was another Futurama at the New York World's Fair of 1964. But while in 1939 it was still possible to imagine a metropolis of tomorrow — a modernist proposal of steel and glass towers — by 1964 there was no longer such an image. Instead of a unified urban idea, Futurama 2 offered a collection of isolated houses in improbable places where people would live in the future: on the moon, in the jungle, below ice, under the sea, and in the desert. The house had left its traditional site behind.

The fair also offered an Underground Home, a traditional suburban ranch-style house buried to offer protection from the new threat of nuclear fallout.[31] The house was the project of Jay Swayze, a Texas military instructor-turned-building-contractor of luxury houses who, during the Cuban Missile Crisis in 1962, was commissioned to build a demonstration fallout shelter to specifications provided by the Department of Civil Defense. Swayze turned this military project into a project for a family house: "It seemed more logical to make the home and its surroundings a safe harbor where the family would be protected in comfortable, familiar surroundings."[32] The house offered a controlled environment where one could create one's own climate by "dialing" temperature and humidity settings: "The breeze of a mountain top, the exhilarating high pressure feeling of a Spring day can be created at will."[33] Traditional windows were superimposed on "dial-a-view" murals — every room in the house looked out on a panoramic "landscape" that could be changed at will; likewise, the time of day or night could be "dialed" to fit any mood or occasion. The sponsor of this house was General Electric, which also commissioned Walt Disney to produce the Carousel of Progress, a series of theatrical sets that traced the history of the domestic interior from 1880 to 1964 and its progressive transformation by electricity (it is still on display at Disney's Epcot Center in Florida). In the General Electric pavilion there was a demonstration of thermonuclear fusion every fifteen minutes. Nuclear power, a by-product of military technology, was offered as both mass spectacle and as a transformation of the house.

Propaganda

The house sometimes became the vehicle for the exhibition of national power, as in the 1946 "Exposition des techniques américaines de l'habitation et de l'urbanisme, 1939-1946," in Paris.[34] Directed by Paul Nelson, the exhibition was organized by the French Ministry of Reconstruction and Urbanism, with the National Housing Agency and Office of War Information of the Department of State in Washington; Charles and Ray Eames, along with Richard Neutra, Louis Kahn, and Eero Saarinen were part of the organizing committee. The exposition's theme was the "economic house," and mass-production proposals were emphasized over high-art designs. On display were the new techniques of construction developed in the United States during the war, and four plain, factory-built houses were featured as prototypes of prefabrication. One of the four houses was half cut away to expose the construction technique. Visitors to the exhibition, which was inside the Grand Palais, could only see the houses after passing through an extended labyrinthine tour displaying statistics, charts, new housing types by designers like Buckminster Fuller and William Wurster, construction methods, home appliances and a model kitchen. The experience concluded with a series of films showing completed projects in the United States.

[29] Address by Gerald Wendt, July 5, 1939. (NYWF Archives PR 1.41). Quoted in Joseph P. Cusker, "The World of Tomorrow," 13-14.

[30] Michael Webb, *A & U* 249 (1991): 4-19.

[31] For more about the Underground House, see Rosemarie Haag Bletter, "The 'Laissez-Fair,' Good Taste, and Money Trees: Architecture at the Fair," in *Remembering the Future: The New York World's Fair from 1939-1964* (New York: Rizzoli, 1989), 105-35. And see Beatriz Colomina, "Domesticity at War," *Discourse* 14, no. 1 (Winter 1991-92): 3-22.

[32] Jay Swayze, *Underground Gardens and Homes: The Best of Two Worlds--Above and Below* (Hereford, Tex.: Geobuilding Systems, 1980), 20.

[33] "The Underground Home: New York World's Fair 1964-1965" (Underground World Home Corporation publicity brochure).

[34] *Techniques Américaines de l'habitation et de l'urbanisme, 1939-46* (exhibition catalogue, Grand Palais, Paris, 14 June - 21 July 1946), ed. *L'Architecture d'aujourd'hui* (1946). The exhibition was also covered in *L'Architecture d'aujourd'hui* 6 (May-June 1946): 84-89.

Margarete Schütte-Lihotzky, Frankfurt Kitchen, central view, 1927. Archiv Margarete Schütte-Lihotzky

Model kitchens have played a critical role in the campaigns of politicians and women's movements to rationalize the house. For many progressive architects of the 1920s, the kitchen was a crucial element in the design of the house.[35] It was an important issue in the Weissenhofsiedlung, for example.[36] The organizers provided each architect with design guidelines for the kitchen and utility areas which had been prepared by both the Stuttgart Housewives Association and Dr. Erna Meyer, who had the year before published *The New Household: A Guide to Scientific Housekeeping*. J. J. P. Oud took these recommendations very seriously: he was proud of his Weissenhof kitchen, which he presented as the new ideal of the efficient kitchen. Dr. Meyer, in turn, praised it extensively in her lectures and articles as well as in later editions of her book. Oud's kitchen was often compared to

[35] Nicholas Bullock, "First the Kitchen -- then the Façade," *AA Files* (London) 6 (Winter 1986).

[36] Pommer and Otto, *Weissenhof 1927 and the Modern Movement in Architecture*, 116-22.

[37] *Das neue Frankfurt*, no. 5 (1926-27).

[38] Hall 1 included some model kitchens and Halls 2 and 3 were dedicated entirely to model kitchens. The "Frankfurt Kitchen" was displayed in the mezzanine of Hall 1.

[39] Jean-Louis Cohen, *Scenes of the World to Come: European Architecture and the American Challenge 1893-1960* (Paris: Flammarion, and Montréal: Canadien Centre for Architecture, 1995), 76. Paulette Bernège, *Si les femmes faisaient les maisons* (Paris: Mon Cher Moi, 1928).

[40] McQuaid, *Lilly Reich*, 29.

Margarete Schütte-Lihotzky's *Frankfurter Küche* of 1926, a model kitchen for the low-income housing estates designed by Ernst May, and considered to be the first European realization of the efficient Taylorized kitchen.[37] It followed research by the American social engineer Lillian Gilbreth, and such publications as Christine Frederick's *Household Engineering: Scientific Management in the Home* (1915), which had been translated into German in 1921. The "Frankfurt Kitchen" was one of a significant number of model kitchens on display in the exhibition; a dining-car kitchen from the Mitropa company, whose design had inspired Lihotzky, was also included.[38] Oud's kitchen was larger than the Frankfurt kitchen and had space available for dining, for Meyer believed that the small kitchen was suitable only for servants, whereas the middle-class housewife needed space to cook and supervise her children.

The century is full of model kitchens. Bruno Taut, in his 1924 book *Die neue Wohnung* (The New Dwelling), presented a drawing of a Taylorized kitchen following Christine Frederick's theories. In France, Paulette Bernège was the leading propagandist for domestic management. She contributed to many magazines and in 1928 published the pamphlet *Si les femmes faisaient les maisons*, and was invited to the 1929 CIAM in Frankfurt, which was on the theme of *Existenzminimum* (minimal housing).[39] In her Apartment for a Single Person at the 1931 Berlin Exhibition Lilly Reich introduced a cooking cabinet that when closed appeared to be an ordinary armoire. Opened, it revealed a sink, shelves, two burners, drawers, counter space, a water heater, and a hook on which to hang a teakettle.[40] Closer to today, Viennese architects Coop-Himmelb(l)au designed the compact kitchen X-Time (1990), a metal furniture piece in the deconstructivist idiom. It consists of a sink, three burners, counter space, drawers, and cabinets with twisted planes and doors: a pivoting axis generates alternative positions.

J. J. P. Oud, kitchen in Weissenhofsiedlung House, Stuttgart, 1927

Coop Himmelb(l)au, X-TIME, a kitchen designed for EWE Kitchen Manufacturing company, 1990. Photo by Josef Hoflehner

Vice President Richard Nixon confers with Soviet Premier Nikita Khrushchev in front of kitchen display at an exhibition in Moscow, 24 July 1959. AP/Wide World Photos

The kitchen is the most popular site for modernization of the house. People renew their kitchens almost as often as they change their cars. During World War II the most popular house of the future was not a house, but a high-tech kitchen:[41] full-size models of the "Day After Tomorrow's Kitchen" by the Libbey-Owens-Ford company circulated to department stores all over the country in 1944 and 1945. More than 1.6 million people, including Sigfried Giedion, saw the kitchen. Giedion recalled his experience in *Mechanization Takes Command*: "When we went to see to visit this 'dream kitchen' in one of the large New York department stores, we heard the young ladies' explanation amid spectators five and six rows deep."[42]

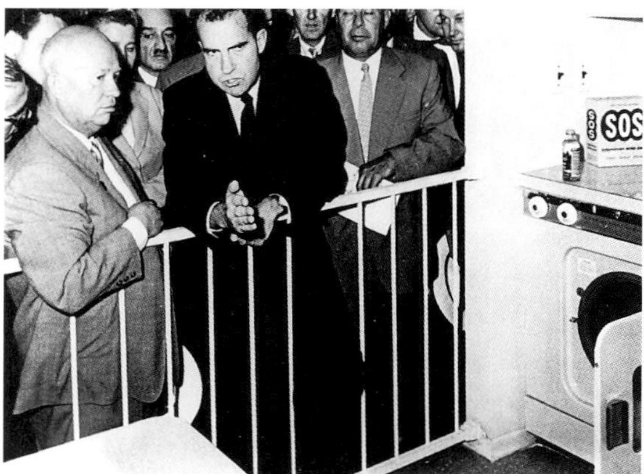

The kitchen has had a symbolic value even for politicians. In 1959, at the peak of the Cold War, Richard Nixon, then vice-president, engaged in the famous "Kitchen Debates" with Nikita Khrushchev in Moscow. What is remarkable about this political exchange, which has been analyzed by Elaine Tyler May, is the focus: "The two leaders did not discuss missiles, bombs, or even modes of government. Rather, they argued over the relative merits of American and Soviet washing machines, televisions, and electric ranges."[43] For Nixon, superiority rested on the ideal of the suburban home, complete with modern appliances and distinct gender roles. He proclaimed that this "model" suburban home represented nothing less than American freedom: "To us, diversity, the right to choose, is the most important thing. . . . We have many different manufacturers and many different kinds of washing machines so that the housewife has a choice."[44]

Nixon was in Moscow to open the American National Exhibition, a showcase of American consumer goods; the main attraction was a full-scale model house, cut in half to show off the building techniques, which was constructed by a Long Island builder and furnished by Macy's. It was in the kitchen of this $14,000, six-room, ranch-style house filled with appliances that the "Kitchen Debates" began with an argument over automatic washers. Appliances had become weapons: America's identity and superiority rested on its kitchens.

Advertisements

Manufacturers have played a crucial role in promoting modern architecture throughout the century: the discourse around the modern house is fundamentally linked to a commercialization of domestic life. In the end, all the different forms of exhibition were really advertisements. The most literal form of exhibition, of course, is actual advertisements, like those for the companies that provided construction materials for the Pavillon de l'Esprit Nouveau. Likewise, the German Werkbund was founded as an alliance of designers and manufacturers, and the Case Study Houses were subsidized by the manufacturers whose materials would be publicized.

Le Corbusier's Weissenhofsiedlung House in a Mercedes Benz advertisement, August 1938

An interesting reversal occurs when architecture offers itself as the stage for advertisements, as when several houses in the Weissenhofsiedlung served as the backdrop for a Mercedes-Benz promotion, or when Neutra's 1932 VDL Research House in Los Angeles was used as background for a 1936 Oldsmobile advertisement. While the car conspicuously placed in Le Corbusier's photographs of his houses provided the context for an "advertisement" of the contemporary good life he wanted associated with his architecture, his houses at Stuttgart became the context for an advertisement of luxury cars. In the history of modern architecture there is a long tradition of fashions shot against the background of modern houses: after the war *Vogue*, *Look*, and *Life* magazine, among others, did spreads featuring Buckminster Fuller's Dymaxion Deployment Unit, exhibited in the garden of MOMA in 1941; Breuer's house in the garden of the museum; Philip Johnson's Glass House in New Canaan, Connecticut; and the Eames House in Pacific Palisades. The exhibition house thus became the ideal site for exhibiting something else.

This commercialization of the modern house becomes evident in the dissemination of modern architecture in popular magazines. All of the century's architectural developments were sooner or later represented there, and some of them were presented there first. It was *Life* magazine, for example, which first published Julius Shulman's famous photographs of Neutra's Kaufmann (Desert) House in Palm Springs, and *Life* extensively covered Frank Lloyd Wright's Usonian

[41] Horrigan, "The Home of Tomorrow," 157.

[42] Sigfried Giedion, *Mechanization Takes Command: A Contribution to Anonymous History* (Oxford, U.K.: Oxford University Press, 1948, reprint New York: Norton, 1969), 617-18.

[43] Elaine Tyler May, *Homeward Bound: American Families in the Cold War Era* (New York: Basic Books, 1988), 16. See also Karal Ann Marling, *As Seen on TV: The Visual Culture of Everyday Life in the 1950s* (Cambridge, Mass.: Harvard University Press, 1994).

[44] Quoted by May in *Homeward Bound*, 17. For transcripts of the debate see "The Two Worlds: A Day-Long Debate," *New York Times*, 25 July 1959, 1-3; "When Nixon Took on Khrushchev," a report of the meeting, and the text of Nixon's address at the opening of the American National Exhibition in Moscow on July 24, 1959, printed in "Setting Russia Straight on Facts about U.S.," *U.S. News and World Report*, 3 August 1959, 36-39, 70-72; "Encounter," *Newsweek*, 3 August 1959, 15-19; and "Better to See Once," *Time*, 3 August 1959, 12-14.

California fashion photographed at the Eames House, 1954

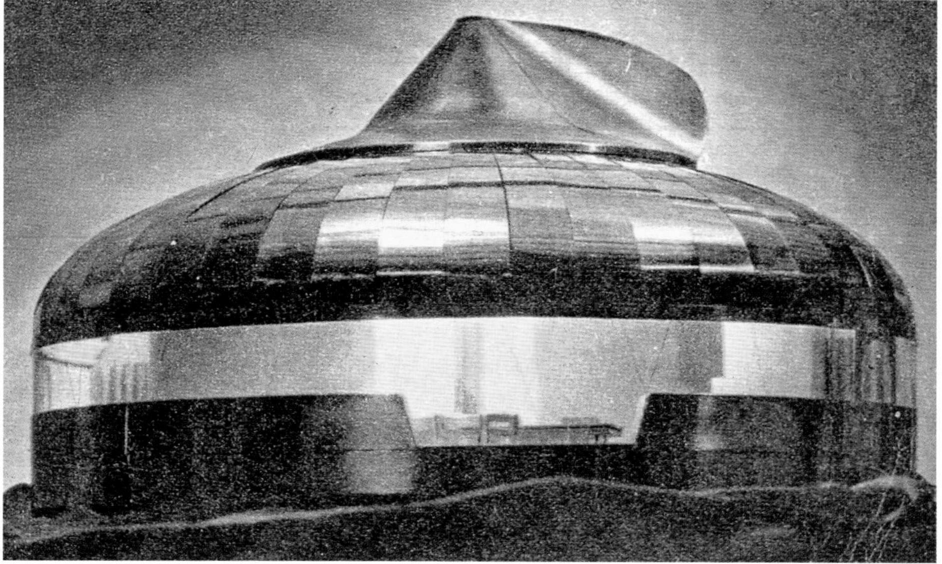

Buckminster Fuller, Wichita House, *Fortune* 33, 1946

Houses; Fuller's Dymaxion House first appeared in *Fortune* magazine. The organizers of the 1946 "Techniques Americaines" exhibition pointed to the importance of popular magazines like *House & Garden*, *House Beautiful*, *Ladies' Home Journal*, and *Sunset* in disseminating new ideas about the house. Often magazines initiated ideas rather than simply representing them. *Ladies' Home Journal* sponsored architectural competitions for the modern house, and it was in this context that Frank Lloyd Wright's Prairie Houses were first published in 1901.

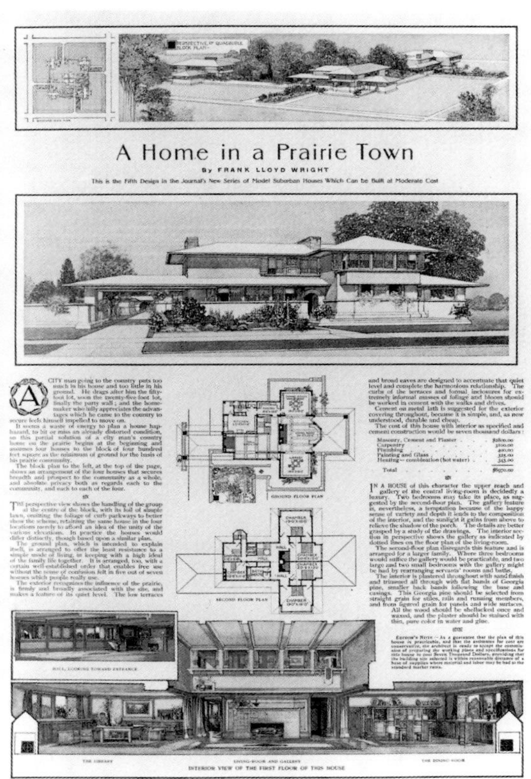

A Home in a Prairie Town

By FRANK LLOYD WRIGHT

This is the Fifth Design in the Journal's New Series of Model Suburban Houses Which Can be Built at Moderate Cost

Frank Lloyd Wright, "A Home in a Prairie Town," published in *Ladies' Home Journal*, February 1901. Frank Lloyd Wright Foundation, Scottsdale, Arizona

Popular magazines were also leaders on the issue of prefabrication. The first symposium on the subject was sponsored not by a professional journal or school of architecture, but by *House & Garden* in 1935; it included "leading prefabricators" such as Robert McLaughlin and Howard Fisher. A photograph of Le Corbusier was included in the magazine with the proceedings of the symposium. The caption reads: "Le Corbusier, prophet of modernism in France and influential throughout the entire architectural world, arrived in America too late to attend our symposium. He has read the findings however, and pronounced them 'très significatifs de l'incomparable force américaine.'"[45] The symposium raised the issue of the unique modern house designed by a signature architect versus the mass-produced house. Fisher and McLaughlin agreed that "modern architecture, to be good, has to be designed by a competent architect thoroughly versed in contemporary methods and materials. Prefabrication will make such skilled professional services available to a great mass of people who could not otherwise afford them."[46] The year before, Douglas Haskell had raised the

[45] "House & Garden Presents: A Symposium on Prefabrication," *House & Garden* 68 (December 1935): 72.

[46] Ibid., 70.

Konrad Wachsmann and Walter Gropius, General Panel House under construction, 1946. Konrad Wachsmann Collection at The Huntington Library, San Marino, California

same issue in *Harper's Magazine*. He argued that if the prefabricated house looked "modern" it was because modern architects like Gropius had already designed their one-off houses to look "as if" they were the prefabricated results of mass-production techniques. Lewis Mumford disagreed with Haskell's defense of "Houses Like Fords," insisting that the very idea of detached houses was inappropriate.[47] But many "high art" architects were committed to the mass production of their designs, as when Gropius collaborated with Konrad Wachsmann on the prefabricated "Packaged House" (later known as the General Panel House) of 1942. Richard Neutra had a continuing interest in the small, low-cost house. From the late 1920s he designed schemes for what he called the "Diatom House," to be built with seashell-aggregate panels; while the Diatom House was never realized, the experiments found their way into Neutra's designs for the Bildcost House series sponsored by *Better Homes and Gardens* in 1938 and the 1939 National Small House Competition of the *Ladies' Home Journal*. Complete building plans of the latter were available for a dollar, and buyers could do with them what they wished. Like Wright, Neutra liked the idea of hundreds of variations of his magazine houses built across the country.[48] In 1938 *Life* magazine presented a feature entitled "Eight Houses Especially Designed by Famous American Architects." The magazine selected clients with different incomes and commissioned one modern and one traditional house for each income bracket, with construction costs ranging from $2,000 to $12,000. Readers could send away for a cardboard model of the house of their choice. Popular magazines also collaborated with manufacturers and art institutions: *Ladies' Home Journal* cosponsored "Tomorrow's Small House" at MOMA, and *Woman's Home Companion* cosponsored Gregory Ain's 1950 house in the garden of the museum.

Straddling the line between high art and mass production, all these houses have had a double life, circulating through popular magazines differently than they do through professional, museum, and art publications — indeed, each medium produces a different house.

[47] Lewis Mumford, "The Flaw in the Mechanical House," *The New Republic* 67 (June 1931),: 65-66. Mumford was responding to D. Haskell, "The House of the Future, " *The New Republic* 66 (1931), 344-45.

[48] Thomas S. Hines, *Richard Neutra and the Search for Modern Architecture: A Biography and History* (Berkeley and Los Angeles: University of California Press, 1994), 128.

Pierre Koenig, Case Study House #22, Los Angeles, 1959-60. Photo by Julius Shulman

Moving Images

Le Corbusier thought that film was the ideal medium to represent modern architecture. In 1929 he made a film with Pierre Chenal called *L'Architecture d'aujourd'hui* (The Architecture of Today), in which he moves from his villas of the 1920s to his plans for the city. Yet again, the house is the vehicle for launching his whole architectural and urban project.

Many modern architects from Rob Mallet-Stevens to Paul Nelson to Charles Eames have designed sets for movies. This would, in turn, suggest a reexamination of the use of the modern house as a stage for a film, as when Abel Gance uses Le Corbusier's Villa Stein as backdrop for the horror movie *La Fin du monde* (The End of the World) (1931), or when Godard uses Villa Malaparte in *Contempt* (1963).

Mallet-Stevens also saw film as the most effective medium for promoting architecture. He argued that it could reach more people than an exhibi-

Jean-Luc Godard, *Contempt*, 1963

tion or a journal: "It permits new forms . . . to reach the most distant corners of the earth. Modern architecture will no longer amaze, it will be understood by everyone; the new furniture will no longer seem eccentric but normal."[49] For a long time Mallet-Stevens only did set designs, architecture as set design, such as the singer's villa and the engineer's house in Marcel L'Herbier's film *L'Inhumaine* (1923). The film was praised by Adolf Loos in a 1924 review for the *Neue Freie Presse* in Vienna. Loos, who had only been in Paris fourteen days when he saw the film, was impressed not by the argument (which he found "puerile"), but by the filmic technique, and the modern cars, the modern architecture, the modern tuxedos, the jazz: "The

Rob Mallet-Stevens, Villa Noailles, Hyères, France, in Man Ray's *Les Mystères du Château du Dé*, 1929

architect: the most modern one in France, Mallet-Stevens, presents in this film images that take your breath away. . . . Visual effects close to those of music, and Tristan Tzara's cry becomes reality: 'I hear the light?'"[50] Other critics were negative, calling Mallet-Stevens's architecture "one of the plagues of French cinema" and comparing its effects to the actual houses built in rue Mallet-Stevens, a whole set of houses designed by the architect in 1927 in a cul-de-sac at Auteil, Paris. Inaugurated by a minister in front of the most distinguished individuals of Parisian arts and letters, this project become a manifesto of modern architecture, a kind of built exhibition. For the critics, cinema is more public than buildings, and for some this is where modern architecture's real damage occurs:

> Fortunately, [rue Mallet-Stevens] is a very small, concealed, private street, where no-one is in fact forced to pass through, and where the people who thoughtlessly asked him to build are probably rich enough not to be obliged to live there. But on the screen, Mallet-Stevens' misdeeds have been numerous and made public. For some years now, there has been hardly a slightly fashionable film which has not been spoiled by his gigantic halls and living rooms, in a simplistic but affected geometry: absolutely out of proportion with the house's exterior and in a style that moreover clashes with the facade.[51]

When Mallet-Stevens finally managed to build a house — Villa Noailles at Hyères (1923-33) — the clients, Charles and Marie-Laure de Noailles, commissioned Man Ray to film *Les Mystères du Château du Dé* (The Mysteries of the Château du Dé) (1929), using the house as the set and guests as actors.[52] Mallet-Stevens sought the collaboration of other architects in this house: Pierre Chareau did an open-air bedroom with a suspended bed; Theo van Doesburg created a small flower-arranging room; the "cubist" garden was by Gabriel Guévrékian. It may have been the Noailles's collecting instincts that led to these contributions, but the resulting design of this house can be said to be more scenographic than architec-

[49] Robert Mallet-Stevens, "Le Cinéma et les Arts. L'architecture," *Les Cahiers du Mois* (Paris), no. 16-17 (1925). Text published in Marcel L'Herbier, *Intelligence du Cinématographe* (Paris: Ed. d'Aujourd'hui, 1977). Cited in Michel Louis, "Mallet-Stevens and the Cinema: 1919-1929," in *Rob Mallet-Stevens, Architecte* (Brussels: Archives d'Architecture Moderne, 1980), 143.

[50] Adolf Loos, *Neue Freie Presse*, Vienna, July 29, 1924.

[51] Jacques Brunius, *En Marge du Cinéma français* (Paris: Eds. Arcanes, 1954), 83. Cited in *Rob Mallet-Stevens: Architecte*, 154-55.

[52] De Noailles also commissioned L'Herbier to do a documentary of the villa, which Jacques Manuel directed. Cécile Briolle and Jacques Repiquet, "Villa de Noailles, Hyères, 1924-33," in *Rob Mallet-Stevens: Architecture, Furniture, Interior Design*, ed. by Jean-François Pinchon (Cambridge: The MIT Press, 1990), 19.

tural, with rooms treated as set designs for everyday life, which is understood as a kind of movie. But the influence went both ways. As Mallet-Stevens wrote: "It is undeniable that film has a marked influence on modern architecture; on the other hand, modern architecture contributes its artistic share to film."[53]

One can repeatedly see a shift through the century, from the representation of modern architecture in the media to its use as a prop for the media. After the famous Shulman photographs of the Pierre Koenig Case Study House #22 (1959-60) presented an ideal image of modern domestic life, the house became a set for more than one hundred movies; the owner reports that the house is still producing a steady income today. The house is both a product to be consumed and a source of income.

Similar arguments can be made about television, including TV series about architecture, and the use of the modern house as a set for domestic dramas. The Museum of Modern Art took a particular interest in television: in conjunction with the "Good Design" program, Edgar Kaufmann Jr. appeared daily on Margaret Arlen's *Morning Show* for two weeks in early 1954. Furthermore, the museum, with the help of a production company, planned a game show entitled "Good Design at the Table." Philip Johnson was a regular guest on television programs until recently, and the center of his discussions was often the house — he even predicted in one program that the house as we have known it in this century will disappear.

Media in the House

The way the house occupies the media is directly related to the way the media occupies the house. On one level, twentieth-century architecture has been transformed by the media in which it has been exhibited; on another level, the design of the house concerns the media itself. It is not by chance that Peter Blake describes his 1954 pinwheel house as a camera:

> Most vacation houses are designed to work roughly like a camera: a box glazed on one side, with the glass wall pointed at the view. The designer felt that he could make the project more interesting if he could find a way to open the house to a variety of views with a possibility of shutting out a view occasionally. . . . Because this house can be adjusted to any orientation and any view or combination of views, it is a universal vacation house for almost any site.

The idea can already be found in Le Corbusier, who equated the window with the camera and argued that, as you would a camera, you can take your house anywhere. Le Corbusier's camera turns out to be cinematographic: The "promenade architecturale" that he choreographed through each house in a succession of ramps and interconnected spaces is cinematic. Furthermore, specific details like the horizontal window are unthinkable outside of cinema. Some projects, like the Beistegui apartment, are organized around a periscope-camera obscura and cinema projector.[54]

A strong relationship is set up between the media equipment installed in the modern house and the house itself. After a while, the architecture absorbs the qualities of the media. Projects are utterly conditioned by the new technologies, even when those technologies are not installed in the house; this pattern is established with each new medium.

For instance, television. In 1929 Buckminster Fuller stated that his Dymaxion House was equipped with the latest media technology (telephone, radio, television, phonograph, dictaphone, loudspeakers, microphone, etc.), even though television was not widely introduced in the United States until after the war. (DuMont and RCA offered their first sets to the public in 1946, and between 1948 and 1955 nearly two-thirds of American families bought a television set.[55]) But in 1927, the year Fuller designed the house, the first public demonstration of television took place. The popular media speculated on the new machine throughout the 1930s and 1940s. In the "Land of Tomorrow" exhibition at the 1939 New York World's Fair, visitors marveled at the images transmitted to the new RCA television receiver. The opening of the fair was, in fact, the first news event ever covered by television in the United States; ten days later, at the Fair's opening ceremonies, Franklin D. Roosevelt become the first American president to make a televised speech. In 1950 the most famous mass-produced suburb, Levittown on Long Island, offered "built-in" TV sets embedded in the walls of its prefabricated Cape Cod houses. Television had become part of the architecture of the American house.

The introduction of this new medium into the house generated an enormous amount of literature and debate in the popular press about the reorganization of a home's space. Home magazines gave endless advice on where to place the set and how to transform the house into a "family theater."[56] A common issue seemed to be the relationship between the fireplace, the television, and the picture window — three "windows" competing with each other. The television had replaced the fireplace as the focus of attention, and it was in conflict with the picture window. It was recommended that TVs be placed away from picture windows to avoid glare on the screen and to ensure privacy (whether one was watching television or not and one's choice of programs, were seen as matters of utmost privacy). The notion of transforming the house into a theater was one way to deal with the initial anxiety and confusion, expressed in popular magazines and movies, over the boundaries between televisual space and the space of the house.[57] The theatricalization of the house established a new kind of line between public and private, the space of television and that of the house.

The popular press constantly associated television with modern architecture. Home magazines displayed unadorned sets in so-called "contemporary" houses while camouflaging the TV in more traditional houses, where it blended with the furniture or was hidden entirely from view. Professional architectural magazines, on the other hand, practically banned television sets from their photographs; rarely do we see a TV in photographs of interiors in the 1950s, a time when ninety percent of Americans owned one.

Architects and artists have addressed the issues raised by the insertion of television into everyday life. In describing Ron Herron's 1974 "Suburban Sets, Royal Pets" project, Reyner Banham argued that while architects tend to think that:

> the function of the picture window is to see out; suburbanites (and Ron Herron) know, contrariwise that the function of picture windows is to be

53 Rob Mallet-Stevens, "Le Cinéma et les Arts. L'Architecture," *Les Cahiers du Mois* (Paris), no. 16-17, 1925. Cit. in Luc Wouters, "Cinema and Architecture," in *Rob Mallet-Stevens: Architecture, Furniture, Interior Design*, 91, n.1.

54 See Beatriz Colomina, "Window," in *Privacy and Publicity.*

55 Lynn Spigel, *Make Room for TV: Television and the Family Ideal in Postwar America* (Chicago and London: The University of Chicago Press, 1992).

56 Ibid.

57 Lynn Spigel, "The Suburban Home Companion: Television and the Neighborhood Ideal in Postwar America," in *Sexuality & Space*, ed. by Beatriz Colomina (New York: Princeton Architectural Press, 1992).

> seen. By the neighbors. That is why picture windows have to be on the front of the house, where people can see them, even if the view they might command is at the back. . . . If you've got it why not flaunt it, says the wisdom of two Fords in every front garden.[58]

In 1978 Dan Graham's *Video Projection Outside Home* proposed a suburban house with a big billboard outside that presents to the street the TV programs being watched in the home: if the television brings the public realm into the private, here the private — the choice of TV show — is publicized.

Contemporary architects are still engaged with television and its offspring, video. Think, for example, of the apartment designed by Donna Robertson and Robert McAnulty for the 1987 exhibition "Room in the City" at City Gallery, New York. In this project the *flâneur*'s perception of the nineteenth-century city is understood to have been replaced by an aimless cruising through television channels, and the television is a window through which the spectacle of the city can be seen by a viewer in a state of distraction. But this window is not only about receiving a view: the antenna alongside the satellite dish allows the intimacy of the house to be broadcast to the outside. The home video is no longer the video seen in the home but the video of the home seen in public. Television not only brings the public indoors, it also sends the private into the public domain.

A number of architects are rethinking the house and its function as part of an ongoing attempt to rethink modern technologies. In the Slow House (1989), Diller + Scofidio explore the relationship between the windshield of the car, the picture window, and the television screen. Three frames define the spatial condition of the beach house: the car windshield and the TV screen are both twentieth-century apertures, as is the picture window. But unlike the first two, the picture window is generally understood as unproblematically architectural. In the Slow House the architects have blurred distinction between architecture and systems of communication. The house serves as a spatial transition between the car and the view. The road leading up to the house is transformed into that of the garage, so one does not have to leave the line of the road and enter a traditional enclosure; rather, the windshield is telescoped into the picture window, where the view of the ocean is juxtaposed with its electronic representation on a TV monitor. The status of the view, and therefore the house that produces it, is problematized by new technologies.

More recently the house has been reconfigured by and around the computer, as a new generation of architects emerges for whom computers are as commonplace as televisions, their work is often exhibited on CD-ROM or encountered in virtual-reality installations. The plans of Thomas Leeser's Twin House (1991-92), for example, began as traditional drawings that were then digitized. Now seen in reverse, the three-dimensional images have become transformed, between a model and a computer image. Having been digitized, the house comes to life within the computer. Even though the house is to be built on a particular site for particular clients, it already occupies digital space, and will carry the traces of that occupation when it is finally constructed.

Other houses, like Ben van Berkel's Möbius House (1993-97), start to reflect the particular geometry facilitated by available design software. The seamless movements of the computer animations with which the houses are

Dan Graham, *Video Projection Outside Home*, 1978. Courtesy of Marian Goodman Gallery, New York

Diller + Scofidio, Slow House, 1989

Diller + Scofidio, Slow House, 1989

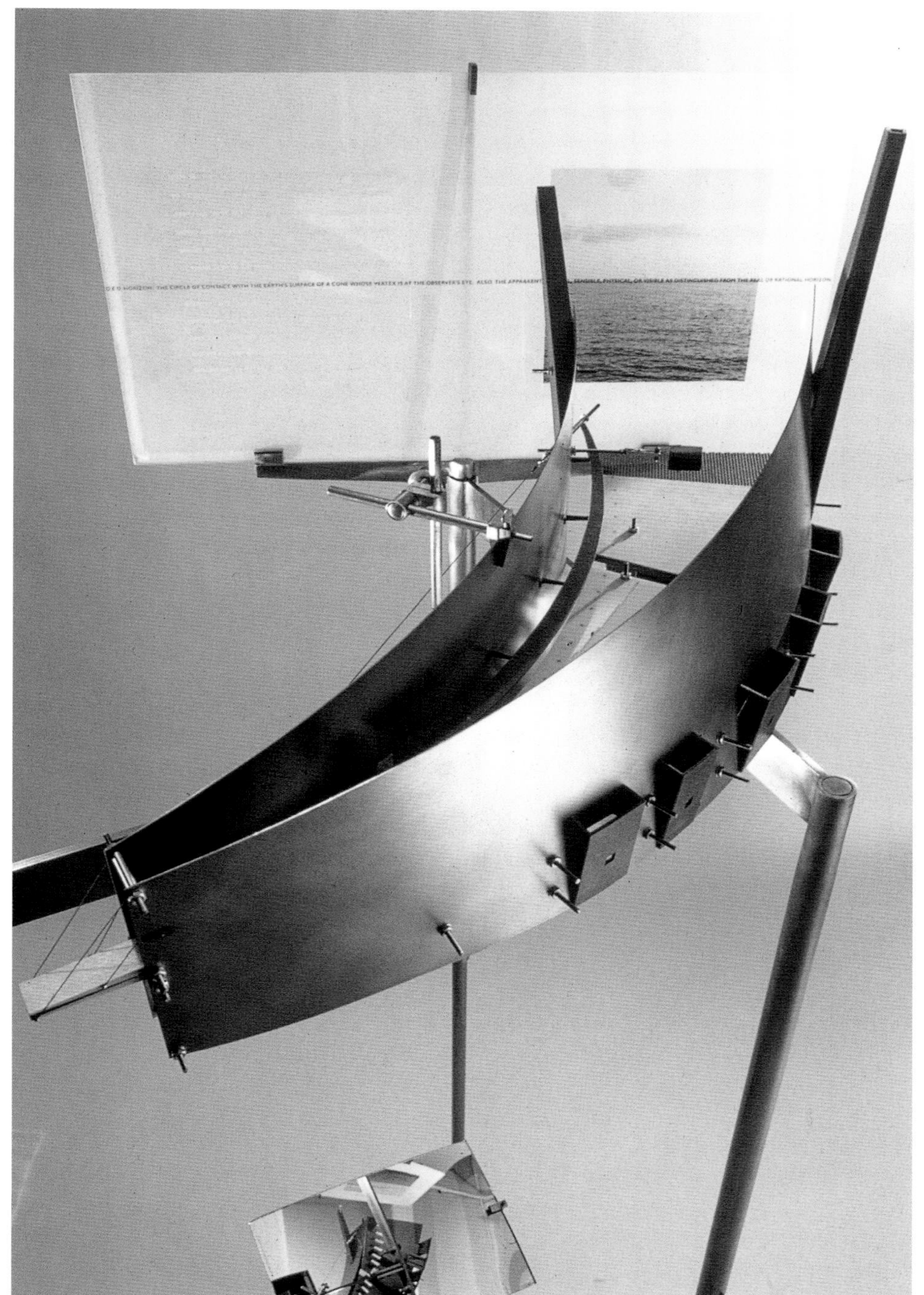

presented foster an architecture of continuous topological surfaces in the same way that cinematic montage fostered the juxtaposed volumes of the modern house at the beginning of the century.

We find ourselves at the end of the century faced with a formidable transformation in the dominant forms of perception perhaps similar to that encountered by those living in the early years of the century. As happened then, speculations about the condition of the house are being presented as speculations about cultural life in general.

In each moment of the twentieth century the house has represented different things, and in each case the polemical use of the home depends on a particular use of the media that has infiltrated the very core of the design. The twentieth-century house is exhibitionistic in character. It is not just that it is designed for publication, designed to photograph well. Rather, it is concerned with new forms of exposure, new forms of display, new forms of transparency. The modern house has been deeply affected by the fact that it is both constructed in the media and infiltrated by the media. Always on exhibition, it has become thoroughly exhibitionist.

Thomas Leeser, Twin House
1991-92

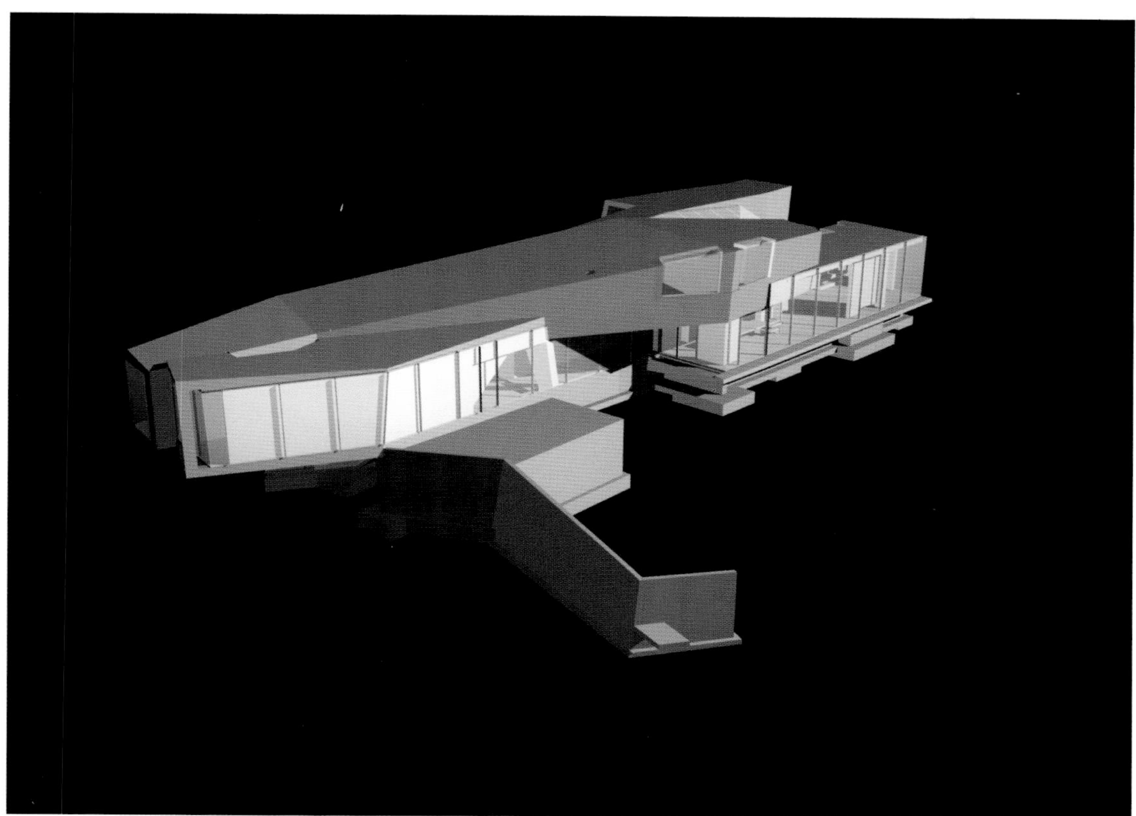

Ben van Berkel, Möbius House,
't Gool, The Netherlands, 1993-97

Sutemi Horiguchi, Okada Residence, Omori, Tokyo, 1933, exterior detail

INTERNATIONALISM VERSUS REGIONALISM

Hajime Yatsuka

One of the most distinguishing characteristics of twentieth-century architecture is the belief that architecture is globally shared beyond a regional understanding.[1] The term "international architecture" directly expresses this concept, and it is complemented by the opposing concept, "regionalism." In politics, "region" is a concept that had been established prior to modernism and precedes the notion of internationalism. When architecture is described in terms of regionalism, however, the order is reversed: internationalism or universalism becomes the prerequisite for understanding this opposing notion.

Of course, the dichotomy of local versus international is not peculiar to the case of modern architecture. The relationship between imperialism and nationalism in the late nineteenth and early twentieth centuries (reduced to the simplest terms) follows a similar pattern. The political and economical internationalism known as imperialism came first, followed by nationalism, with one directly resulting from the existence of the other. Obviously, the development of architectural styles cannot be straightforwardly linked to political events. But because architectural styles are often described as "isms," they carry a certain ideological burden. Often a term or concept is discussed or understood by the introduction of its opposite; contrary to the simple notion of "regional things," the idea of "regionalism" arose due to the appearance of "internationalism."

A dialogue between internationalism and regionalism has been ongoing since the late nineteenth century. Since the Industrial Revolution the primary language of modern architecture has been international, but the formation of this international language preceded what was seemingly a primary factor in its development: technology. In the period shortly before, and continuing after, the formation of this new common language formulated and influenced by machine aesthetics, classicism acted as an inter-European language. Before being pushed into the periphery by the development of internationalism — which is (or at least pretends to be) based on anti-historicism — classicism functioned as a language for modernizing individual countries and regions, a phenomenon one saw more clearly in Northern and Eastern Europe than in Western Europe, where such language had already permeated the region.

[1] For example, the notion of the architect as author of a work was rather alien in Japan before the Meiji Restoration in 1868.

In Japan and the Far East, both classicism and the nineteenth-century European eclectic style — themselves both targets of modernism — became the means of "modernizing," the term for Westernizing. Historically, the rigidness of classicism's "grammar" is also related to a type of rationalism that developed in Europe during the Renaissance. When rational "reforms" derive from a hierarchy imposed from a cultural center upon surrounding countries, then a regional reaction — a romantic nationalism — is aroused.[2] The notion of the nation-state was not an ancient invention, but rather a modern one, stemming primarily from the eighteenth and nineteenth centuries: the alliance of architecture with nationalism, and therefore the complementary relationship between international architecture and its regional counterpart, is thus also a modern product.[3]

We can assume that advocates of the new universalism, like Le Corbusier and Walter Gropius (not to mention more leftist architects like Hannes Meyer and the Russian Constructivists) were sensitive to the politics of this "confrontation" between opposing constructs, because they were extremely conscious about the ideological burden of their own work. As far as they were concerned, the new language of architecture had to be a language of liberation and should not be a tool of imperialistic invasion, as had been the case with classicism.

It is significant that the advocates of "critical regionalism" during the later period of postmodernism have been modernist critics such as Alexander Tzonis and Liane Lefaivre, who first used the phrase, and Kenneth Frampton, who spread it widely. Needless to say, this concept is not a denial of modernism but an expansion of it. The dichotomy continues here as well: at the frontline, "critical" regionalism is distinguished from other forms of regionalism. We can thus assume that the critical regionalists see internationalism as also distinguishing between "critical" and other forms (for instance, the corporate modernism that parallels capitalism).

However, what does "critical" mean if not subjective thinking? At first glance, defining a mode as "critical" seems to provide a standard for an individual practice that could be reduced to certain prescribed methods. In actuality, however, isn't hidden decision-making occurring on a much more basic level? Is it possible to have simultaneously a regionalism that is not "critical" and one that has a "critical" use? This statement suggests that the two essential contrasting terms are no longer "international" and "regional," but are being used in relation to the concepts of critical and a-critical; if so, critical regionalism and critical internationalism are not opposing concepts but instead overlap each other considerably. Therefore, in order to properly examine the various issues surrounding regionalism, internationalism must become the focus.

A new trend in architecture was officially named "The International Style," due to the influential 1932 exhibition, "Modern Architecture International Exhibition" at The Museum of Modern Art in New York, and its accompanying exhibition catalogue; in fact, the exhibition's curators, Henry-Russell Hitchcock and Philip Johnson, invented the term for the occasion. Concepts such as "new architecture" and "rational architecture" (as used in a European context) now fell in the category of art history under the heading of "style." This category shift is clearly expressed in the preface to the exhibition catalogue by the museum's director, Alfred H. Barr, Jr. It reads, in part, "They have proven beyond any reasonable doubt, I believe, that there exists today a modern style as original, as consistent, as logical,

2 For a discussion of this dialectic between classicism and romantic nationalism in Scandinavian countries, see Richard Weston, *Alvar Aalto* (London: Phaidon Press, 1995). For the Russian case, see S.O. Khan-Magomedov, *Alexandr Vesnin and Russian Contructivism* (New York: Rizzoli, 1986), and S.O. Khan-Magomedov, *Pioniere der Sowjetischen Architektur* (Vienna and Berlin: Löcker, 1983). In Japan, the resurrected interest in the Japanese character of design versus Western style — seen in the construction of the new parliament building around 1910 — could be regarded as a parallel of this dialectic.

3 For example, see David Harvey, *The Condition of Postmodernity* (Cambridge: Blackwell, 1989).

4 Alfred H. Barr, Jr., preface to Henry-Russell Hitchcock and Philip Johnson, *The International Style* (New York: W.W. Norton), 1995 edition, 27.

and as widely distributed as any in the past."[4] Thus, the European anti-academic movement was sanctioned in the United States by The Museum of Modern Art, itself an academic organization. However, this official acceptance of categories seemed somewhat problematic even to the parties involved; Hitchcock indicated this in his text "The International Style Twenty Years After" (1951), adding with careful reservation, that "it has been the concept of 'style' itself . . . which has been hardest for architects . . . to accept."[5]

Though the exhibition was posited as the introduction of new American and European architecture, the curators' selection of works was based on their stylistic criteria — it was not a simple presentation of little-known architecture. Giving overwhelming weight to European works, they clearly intended to introduce and give authority to the new "style," which was still quite unknown in the United States. Francesco Dal Co and Manfredo Tafuri have harshly criticized the project, saying Hitchcock and Johnson were searching for a nonexistent unity,[6] and Hitchcock himself acknowledged in "Twenty Years After" that hasty standardizing was no longer necessary. The standard of "International Style" would not have been created without this institutional blessing, an important point to keep in mind when discussing regionalism: if internationalism is considered a prerequisite to regionalism, then the standardization of one would be impossible without that of the other.

Kenneth Frampton's essay "Towards a Critical Regionalism," which generalized the term, is included in *The Anti-Aesthetic*, an anthology edited by Hal Foster. The dichotomy of Foster's postmodernism of resistance and postmodernism of reaction, presented in the introduction, clearly indicates both the book's and Frampton's basic view. According to Foster, "In cultural politics today, a basic opposition exists between a postmodernism which seeks to deconstruct modernism and resist the status quo and a postmodernism which repudiates the former to celebrate the latter."[7] I refer to Frampton in particular because the "reaction" of postmodernism was obvious in the field of architecture more so than in any other field. The indication of a sense of distance was pointed out specifically in the opening of his text: "Today the practice of architecture seems to be increasingly polarized between, on the one hand, a so-called 'high-tech' approach predicated exclusively upon production and, on the other, the provision of a 'compensatory facade' to cover up the harsh realities of this universal system."[8] Thus Frampton positions "critical regionalism" as the "resistance" against these two poles — the technocratic, or corporate modernism that lost its original liberating force almost completely, and what Foster called the "postmodernism of reaction" — that are frequently two sides of the same coin.

That the modernist Frampton had burned the bridge behind him by this call for critical regionalism is best illustrated by his own positioning as *arrière-garde*. It is not only the degeneration of modernism into techocracy, but also the "fragmentation and decline of critical adversary culture" (Andreas Huyssen as quoted by Frampton) that allows architecture to be sustained only by a critical practice, the *arrière-garde*. In contrast to "critical regionalism," "populistic regionalism" is, in his mind, a "simple-minded attempt to revive the hypothetical forms of a lost vernacular" through "the communicative or instrumental sign"; after all, it is "the strong affinity of Populism for the rhetorical techniques and imagery of advertising." This is merely shifting the division of "resistance" and "reaction" made by Foster on the two poles of the postmodern culture in general. It is a superbly modernistic compositional arrangement. It is not by chance that Frampton advo-

5 Henry-Russell Hitchcock, "The International Style Twenty Years After," in *The International Style*, 242-43.

6 Francesco Dal Co and Manfredo Tafuri, *Architettura contemporanea* (Milan: Electa, 1976).

7 Hal Foster, "Postmodernism: A Preface," in Hal Foster, ed., *The Anti-Aesthetic: Essays on Postmodern Culture* (Seattle: Bay Press, 1983), xi-xii.

8 Kenneth Frampton, "Towards a Critical Regionalism: Six Points for an Architecture of Resistance," in *The Anti-Aesthetic*, 17.

Jørn Utzon, Sydney Opera House, 1956. Government Printing Office Collection, State Library of New South Wales

cated the idea of tectonics, which is familiar with modernism's attempt, if not specific to it.

In the case of Frampton — or in the case of Tzonis and Lefaivre, who preached a similar point — most of the people they consider the activists of "critical regionalism" are architects in Western Europe where modernism is practiced, and those in countries embracing the "tradition of the new" (which corresponds to modernism). By no means are they the architects from the developing countries outside this tradition. The architects Frampton uses as examples are Jørn Utzon (Denmark), Mario Botta (Switzerland), and Alvar Aalto (Finland). Similarly, in the first article in which Lefaivre and Tzonis advocated the notion of "critical regionalism," they first cited Greek architects as examples, then, in a reprisal of the argument ten years later, they used William Wurster (United States), Giancarlo de Carlo and Ernesto Nathan Rogers (Italy), and Kenzo Tange (Japan). This is a variation of my earlier proposition that internationalism created regionalism; "critical regionalism" could not be formed unless it had gone through the "baptism" of internationalism. Frampton and the other critics never discussed these architects individually, but instead grouped them as an international frontline. The "regional" issue certainly had nothing to do with an international frontline before the advent of modernism, and the fact that this regionalist front is represented by individual

BBPR (Ludovico Belgiojoso, Enrico Peressutti, and Ernesto Nathan Rogers), Torre Velasca, Milan, 1956-58

William Wurster, Experimental housing, Carquinez Heights, Vallejo, California, 1941. Roger Sturtevant Collection, The City of Oakland, Oakland Museum. Gift of the artist

architects rather than larger self-generating groups is itself characteristic of a modern European practice. Therefore, the enclosure and selection of "regionalism" as a specific expressive practice by adding the prefix "critical" is obviously a political action based on a modern European model. This disposition urges us to inspect how this enclosure — which is still based on a belief in common criteria for universal evaluation of architectural works — could be justifiable. This is best done through individual case studies; here the work of three Japanese architects is examined.

Three Japanese Architects

Fortunately, modern Japanese architecture is now allowed to take part in the international forum. Tzonis once promoted Kenzo Tange, and Frampton considered Tadao Ando as one of the primary architects to embody the concept of critical regionalism. However, not all Japanese modern architectural achievements are recognized by these critics or the broader Western audience. It is extremely difficult to know whether the basis of this recognition is indeed "critical." In a text entitled "Why Critical Regionalism Today?" Tzonis and Lefaivre wrote that "Kenzo Tange's work in the second part of the 1950s, particularly his Kagawa Prefectural Office of 1956, is the work with which Japan enters the 'international forum.'"[9] This statement summarizes a typical reaction of the "international forum" — but what about the work of two other architects, Isoya Yoshida and Sutemi Horiguchi?

Isoya Yoshida, Kineya Villa, Shizuoka, Japan, 1936

9 Liane Lefaivre and Alexander Tzonis, "Why Critical Regionalism Today?" *A+U* (May 1990).

Isoya Yoshida, Sekirekiso Villa, Shizuoka, Japan, 1941, exterior

Yoshida, born in 1894, and Horiguchi, born in 1895, cannot be immediately classified as being of the same generation as Tange, who was born in 1913. Tange's approach, which will be discussed later in this essay, may have been impossible for the preceding generation; but the differences in their reputations within the international forum cannot be ascribed solely to the difference in their ages, nor to their talent.

Horiguchi went to Europe in 1923 and Yoshida in 1924; both were extremely impressed with the European architecture they saw. Yoshida was thoroughly shocked by the early Renaissance architecture in Florence and the Gothic architecture in other countries. He wrote:

> When architecture comes this far, it becomes an issue of more than wisdom and ability. It has something to do with race, family, history, and tradition, and is an issue which won't be understood unless one goes back to the difference in the color of skin or the difference between the lifestyle of a chair versus a tatami mat.

Isoya Yoshida, Sekirekiso Villa, interior

Horiguchi stated that when he saw the capital of the colonnade at the Parthenon, "I could not help but moan" and "was desperately aware that this is not the type of achievement we, from the Far East, would ever be allowed to approach." The profound experience of encountering Western architecture *in situ* led the two architects to reconsider their own regional traditions upon their return to Japan.

However, the two did not simply turn to traditional Japanese architecture without modifying and updating it — that would have been merely a reaction. Yoshida stated his intentions quite clearly: "We cannot rival Western Europe with the present Japanese architecture as it is, because it is no more than an historical inheritance." With this in mind, Yoshida undertook the modernization of one of the historical styles, *sukiya*, which is more of a genre than a style. *Sukiya* is derived from sixteenth-century teahouse construction, and is a style without explicit rules or order. "Among traditional Japanese architecture, *sukiya* is the closest in concept to modern structures, and I thought was the easiest means to modify for the present lifestyle." He chose *sukiya* not because it was in the form of traditional Japanese art — the complete opposite of Western European art — but because it was a convenient medium for modernization in a Japanese context. Though Yoshida chose to go in a different direction from Western European architectural traditions, he was not necessarily giving up on modernization. His idea that native Japanese should build (and live) steeped in an innate sense of their own culture and climate might sound regionalist, but it is a rather modern type of ideology that may arise after an international perspective is gained (as Yoshida did in Europe). Yoshida's claim to want to carry out modernization in a Japanese way was modern in two senses. In his essay "*Sukiya no Kindai*" (Modernity of *Sukiya*), Kazuhiro Ishii, illustrating the striking affinity between the reductive and sophisticated (modern) detailing of Yoshida and Horiguchi, notes that Yoshida never deleted modern devices such as fluorescent lights or air-conditioning vents in the interiors of his modern buildings. Ishii also points out that he mixed the European lifestyle with traditional Japanese facilities: for instance, he positioned Western-style living-room furniture (tables and chairs) in the wooden periphery (*Hiro-en*) of the tatami rooms, and hung a *kakejiku* scroll in a *tokonoma* niche of a room with a carpeted floor. In addition, Yoshida never relied on chance factors such as uneven shapes and sizes or odd colors in his choice of materials, a practice respected in the traditional *sukiya*. Ishii concludes, "One can understand that Yoshida's *sukiya* is genuinely modern."[10]

Horiguchi also returned to *sukiya*, but in his case, he did not abandon modern architecture (in the Western European sense). To use the terminology of critical regionalism, the work was not simply nostalgic. Horiguchi's initial work upon his return to Japan was *Shiin-so*, which was a combination of Dutch expressionist architecture and a *chaya* (Japanese teahouse). However, he soon turned to a more international direction after the completion of the Yoshikawa residence in 1930. In an essay on Horiguchi, Arata Isozaki argues that Horiguchi put this residence at the beginning of a monograph about his work, completely out of chronological order, to suggest that the international style was the starting point of his career.[11] At the same time, Horiguchi did not necessarily subdue his interest in

Sutemi Horiguchi, Wakasa House, Tokyo, 1939

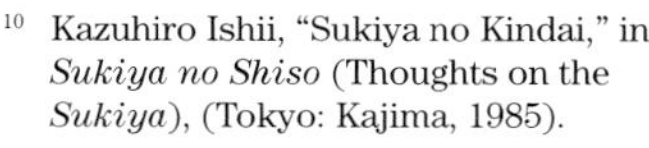

[10] Kazuhiro Ishii, "Sukiya no Kindai," in *Sukiya no Shiso* (Thoughts on the *Sukiya*), (Tokyo: Kajima, 1985).

[11] Arata Isozaki, "Yoshiki no Heizon" (Juxtaposition of the Styles), in *Shinkenchiku* (November 1976).

[12] Arata Isozaki, *Sutemi Horiguchi — Ie to Niwa no Kukan-Kosei* (Tokyo: Kajima, 1978).

[13] Demetri Porphyrios, *Sources of Modern Eclecticism: Studies on Alvar Aalto* (London: Academy Editions, 1982).

Sutemi Horiguchi, Kikkawa Residence, Meguro, Tokyo, 1930

Sutemi Horiguchi, Okada residence, Omori, Tokyo, 1933

sukiya, a fact he makes clear in the title of his monograph, *Ie to Niwa no Kukan-Kosei* (Spatial Composition of the House and Garden): the integration of the house and garden is integral to the essence of the *sukiya*.[12] From then on, Horiguchi's basic concern was how to balance two interests: international-style architecture and traditional Japanese concepts.

Sutemi Horiguchi, Okada residence, Omori, interior

Yoshida's new *sukiya*, as Ishii argued, is an alteration of traditional methods of composition, and is based on a modern aesthetic and methods that could even be called a deconstruction of the authentic *sukiya*. It retains familiar elements of Japanese style, but the use of space and compositional elements is certainly closer to — and even more systematic than — the work of Mies van der Rohe than to traditional Japanese architecture, a fact clearly evident in Ishii's photographic illustrations. In a book entitled *Sources of Modern Eclecticism*,[13] Demetri Porphyrios discusses Alvar Aalto in terms of his regionalism and his use of eclectic modern language; Yoshida's works belong in the same category. Horiguchi's method is different. About the time the international direction was being established at the Kikkawa residence, Horiguchi started to study *sukiya* architecture. Horiguchi did not dare mix up elements as Yoshida had; he approached *sukiya* more as a researcher, trying to evaluate the most authentic parts. This is the opposite attitude from Yoshida's, who felt free to experiment with alterations of traditional forms. To be more specific, the existence of Japanese rooms has never been, even today, deleted from Japanese homes, and so Yoshida tried to bring a modern eclecticism to bear on the Japanese style. In Horiguchi's case, he respected the original forms as much as possible: the treatment of the Japanese-style rooms and Western-style wings in his 1938 Yamakawa residence is one example of his

Sutemi Horiguchi, Okada residence, Omori, interior

juxtaposition of the two traditions, but the Okada residence of 1933 is perhaps most typical. In the Okada residence, Japanese and Western-style wings are separated as though in two different homes; except for the relationship between garden and house, there are no connections. Horiguchi's belief in retaining what is Western as Western and what is Japanese as Japanese is entirely modern in terms of its purism. Just as Western modernists paid respect to the Japanese tradition, Horiguchi tried to bridge the gap between the regional and the international; obviously, with more extensive knowledge of and sympathy for his own tradition.

From this standpoint, the philosophy of Kenzo Tange, the youngest of the three architects discussed here, differs even more. Contrary to Horiguchi's ideology, which was entirely modern and purist, Tange was forthrightly symbolistic and romantic from the beginning. The overwhelming expression of technology in his postwar-era works — especially around the 1960s — seemed to be an inheritance from modernism but had nothing to do with functionalism based on the straightforward aspirations for an egalitarian society. Even before the war, Tange did little to hide his distaste for the work of the International Style architects (his "elders"), likening their work to "hygienic ceramics" lacking in spiritual excitement.

Tange's first success was established by winning first place in two competitions: for the Japan Cultural Center in Bangkok in 1942, and for the Monument of the Great East Asia Co-prosperity Sphere in 1943. These two structures adopted a Japanese idiom modeled after shrines and *shinden-zukuri*, the style of noblemen's palaces, rather than *sukiya*. In an argument about the architectural style of the Great East Asia Co-prosperity Sphere, Horiguchi criticized Tange's use of the Japanese style, saying Tange used it as if "pulling it out of a warehouse"; to Tange, if this "new Japanese style strict as God but dependable, and grand as a giant but solemn," was a new means of defining space, he was willing to adopt it. However, these surface styles were actually grafted onto a Western layout modeled on projects such as Le Corbusier's Mundaneum project (1929) (which was so annoying to more rigorous modernists like Karel Teige and El Lissitzky), and had nothing to

Kenzo Tange, Hiroshima Peace Center Complex (Hiroshima Peace Memorial Museum), Hiroshima, Japan, 1949-55. Photo by Yasuhiro Ishimoto

do with the traditional spatial typology characteristic of Japanese architecture. Tange's aspirations for the new Japanese style were much more metaphysical than tectonic; this enabled him to design the Hiroshima Peace Center Complex in 1949, which was based on the same Corbusian site plan but with completely "modern" idioms.

Tange's style in the postwar period was neither authentically Japanese nor purely modernist. His metaphysics were most typically illustrated by his comment concerning a dispute with Ernesto Nathan Rogers about regionalism at the CIAM 9 conference in Otterlo. Tange criticized the Italian architect's appeal for the introduction of traditional typology, saying "we inherit spirit, not individual idioms." This metaphysical spirituality gave Tange a justification for his free alteration of the traditional (or the regional). His attitude toward this freedom is 180 degrees removed from Horiguchi's purist attitude toward the authentically Japanese style; it is actually much closer to Yoshida's new *sukiya*. If Porphyrios is invoked again, Tange's work could also be considered "Modern Eclecticism." The difference

Kunio Maekawa, Tokyo Metropolitan Festival Hall, Ueno, Tokyo, 1961. Photo by Yoshio Watanabe

lies simply in the fact that Tange looked modernist because of the modern idioms he used during the postwar period, while Yoshida looked traditionalist and regionalist because of the *sukiya* style. In this perspective, Yoshida and Tange would be on opposite ends, with Horiguchi in the middle, though it is somewhat difficult to determine which of the three is further away from the original concept of modernism.

Tange is the only one among these three architects who has received wide recognition in the international community of architects. Though Leonardo Benevolo's *Storia dell'architettura moderna* (The History of Modern Architecture)[14] contains a few references to Japanese modern architecture of the 1930s (including one to Horiguchi), it was a common perception in Western Europe

14 Leonardo Benevolo, *Storia dell'architettura moderna* (The History of Modern Architecture). Translated by H. J. Landry (Cambridge: The MIT Press, 1966).

15 The typical argument for Japanese inferiority regarding modern artistic or cultural issues is usually supported by pointing out the absence of the notion of the subject in Japanese individuals in the case of literature, the absence of the notion of space in the case of architecture, and the absence of the public in the case of social practices such as political ideology and town planning. In these arguments, most of the achievements by Japanese after the Meiji Restoration in 1868 came to be regarded as a second-rate imitation of the foreign import and too feeble to acquire international reputation. See the following argument by Kōjin Karatani as well.

that Tange was the first among Japanese architects to appear in the international forum; this view is also shared by Lefaivre and Tzonis. Kunio Maekawa may have been somewhat of an exception, but Yoshida and Horiguchi did not receive such international recognition; however, neither should they receive only minor treatment in the history of Japanese modern architecture. Is this simply an issue of coexistence, as in any other country where the classification of first- and second-rate architecture results in the latter only being evaluated domestically? The Japanese critics and historians who tend to believe in Japanese peculiarity and who prefer to describe the history of modern architecture (or literature or art) in Japan as a distortion of the essence of modernity *because* of its peculiarity, never dared to cast doubt on the authority of the international forum. We may call this a typically provincial reaction by the Japanese community.[15]

Mamoru Yamada, Electrical Laboratory, Ministry of Public Works, Tokyo, 1929

Junzo Sakakura, Japanese Pavilion at Paris World Exposition, 1937. Photo by Kollar

The Museum of Modern Art's "International Style" exhibition of 1932, as previously discussed, was the first event to give Japanese works authorization in the international architectural community. The installation chosen from Japan for this exhibit was Mamoru Yamada's Electrical Laboratory (1929). Built after he had completed a series of expressionist works, this structure was far below the standard of Yamada's earlier works, and the review from Hitchcock and Johnson was quite unfavorable: in fact, it was not until the 1930s that Japanese architects began to create first-rate work in the International Style. Therefore, one can say that it was simply bad timing that caused Yamada to be treated like a "bad student"

[16] Kōjin Karatani, "Japan as Museum: Okakura Tenshin and Ernest Fenollosa," in Alexandra Munroe, ed., *Japanese Art After 1945: Scream Against the Sky* (New York: Harry N. Abrams, 1994), 33, 34.

despite Japan's enthusiasm for the ideology of the exhibit.

However, until Tange's dramatic debut two decades later, cited by Lefaivre and Tzonis, most 1930s Japanese masterpieces of modern architecture went without international recognition (although there were individual exceptions such as the success of the Japanese Pavilion by Junzo Sakakura at the 1937 Paris World Exposition and Bruno Taut's appraisal of the works of Tetsuro Yoshida); one can assume various causes for this neglect, including miscommunication during the war. The critics who are persistent about Japanese peculiarity might attribute it to inferiority based on differences in blood or heritage, or an inherent inability to grasp the Western concept of architecture (as Yoshida and Horiguchi themselves might have felt). For example, pre-war wooden residential works which were given a concrete-like appearance were cited as evidence of Japanese architects' "limitations." But in actuality, it was not unusual to see plaster applied to bricks to create the appearance of concrete in "true" modernist architecture, as in buildings by Gropius, whose authority was then widely recognized. Even Isozaki, who wrote an outstanding article about Horiguchi's work, discusses the lack of expression of volume in Horiguchi's design of the 1930s, particularly at the Yoshikawa residence; this concept — the expression of volume — was held by Hitchcock and others to be the standard of internationalism. But in the Wakasa residence of 1939, the most mature Western work of Horiguchi, Isozaki suggested that the defect "was overcome." The first year of World War II was an unfortunate and difficult time for the Wakasa residence to appear in the international forum, since communication between nations deteriorated. However, excellent works such as Tokyo Institute of Technology's hydraulic research building (1932) by Yoshiro Taniguchi, the Bancho Collective Housing (1933) and Japan Dental University (1934) by Bunzo Yamaguchi, and Kameki Tsuchiura's own residence (1935), all of which were built before the outbreak of the war, did not receive international attention either. To what can this failure of critical recognition be attributed: the fact that they did not reach some international standard, or that they had not been documented abroad, or because of the intervention of the war?

My hypothesis differs from the above. This group of works, including Horiguchi's, was excluded from the international forum not because the buildings failed to meet the international standard, but rather, because they were much too true to it. Kōjin Karatani, in his article "Japan as Museum: Okakura Tenshini and Ernest Fenollosa," discusses the paradoxical fact that the American aesthete Ernest Fenollosa, who acted as a director of the newly established Tokyo School of Fine Arts in the early Meiji period, felt the need to resist the invasion of Western art. According to Karatani, it was Fenollosa who "discovered" traditional Japanese art: "In this sense, the 'traditionalists' must be viewed as modernists — Westerners *par excellence*." But less than ten years after the school's founding, its leadership was replaced by Japanese Westernizers. Karatani, mentioning the ambivalence with which this Westernization, "which is praised as new and anti-traditionalist in Japan, appears to be mere mimicry in the West, where, conversely, a return to Japanese traditionalism is viewed as cutting edge," suggests that this shift in direction from the traditionalists to the Westernizers was regressive in terms of

Kameki Tsuchiura, Tsuchiura Residence, Tokyo, 1935

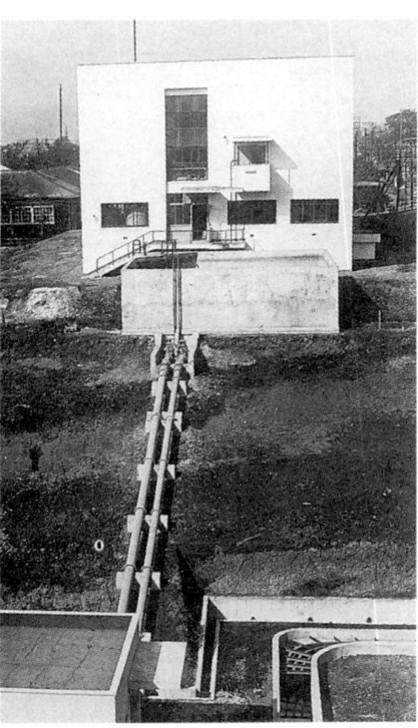

Yoshiro Taniguchi, Hydrodynamics Experimental Laboratory, Institute of Technology, Tokyo, 1932

Bunzo Yamaguchi, Bancho Collective Housing, Tokyo, 1933

Hiroshi Sugimoto, Row House in Sumiyoshi (Azuma House) (architect: Tadao Ando, 1975), 1997

the internationalization of the Japanese art community. He also notes that, "We remain trapped in this same predicament today. In fact, most of the Westernizationists who are currently admired in Japan could not be less valued in the West, while Japanese artists who achieve some recognition abroad are those who have literally returned to traditionalism in some sense; it is this return that makes them appear to be avant-garde."[16]

If we apply this concept to Japanese architecture, Horiguchi and others are "internationalists" who are praised only domestically, while Tange's free use of traditional idioms in modern disguise, which Horiguchi forbade for himself, is recognized internationally (as is the contemporary work of Tadao Ando). The idea of Japan as imitator is a popular one, but since the International Style itself had homogeneity as a prerequisite, similarity is a natural result. If the work of architects in Scandinavia and California such as Aalto and Richard Neutra is not termed imitation, but instead a natural extension of modernism in Europe, and Japanese works such as Horiguchi's are called imitations, we cannot but call the argument

Tadao Ando, Row House in Sumiyoshi (Azuma House), 1975, interior view

Tadao Ando, Row House in Sumiyoshi (Azuma House), section drawing

colonialistic or Eurocentric. More importantly for this discussion, not all Japanese traditionalists/regionalists who turned away from modernist influence to the tradition specified by Karatani were fully recognized; this includes Yoshida and Horiguchi, this time in traditional mode, a stance also highly respected in Japan. If one explains this difference by saying that Tange represents "critical regionalism," as Tzonis and others suggest, then the conclusion can be reached that Yoshida does not fit the definition.

However, Yoshida's work cannot be classified as simply nostalgic and reactionary; a more appropriate interpretation is that, for the advocates of critical regionalism, a new category should not be viewed outside the criteria of modernism and works such as Yoshida's, unlike Tange's, simply didn't look modernist enough to meet this category. In other words, while Tange's method appeared adaptable, no such ability for crossover was discovered in Yoshida's work. For corroboration we could point out the fact that it is only old *sukiya* that is recognized in the West as one of the sources of inspiration for the modern composition of space; the Western audience ignores the presence of contemporary *sukiya*. A plausible reason for this is a tendency to recognize historical references only in their original contexts (an argument Horiguchi might have shared). More essentially, the problem lies in a failure to differentiate between old and new *sukiya*: the elements of *sukiya* are not familiar enough in the West for subtle differences to be appreciated, which is quite significant in the Japanese modern context. That is, the new *sukiya* looked either like an uninventive derivation of the authentic *sukiya* or like a modernized kitsch knockoff of the original.

By comparison, Tange's method must have been far easier to understand in the international context, which led to the interpretation of his work as internationalism/"critical regionalism," Horiguchi's as internationalism with only regional validity, and Yoshida's as nostalgic regionalism. And, as previously discussed, only the first category was recognized and discussed by the international critical community. This is a choice based on one facet of modernism: internationalism is seen as superior to regionalism, a position that requires some historical perspective. This proposition can be examined through an analysis by Slavoj Žižek.

Intermission

Internationalism and regionalism are not narrow concepts relating just to a style of architecture or the classical issues that arose between the first and second generation of modernists. They can be reread in terms of European democracy and nationalism as none other than a discussion of the present political situation in Eastern Europe. From this standpoint, Slavoj Žižek offers an interesting argument. Žižek, a Slovenian, analyzes the issues of nationalism and democracy in present-day Eastern Europe, referring to the prediction made by Jacques Lacan in the 1960s about the intensity of national confrontation; Žižek provides an interesting analogy to a discussion of internationalism and regionalism in architecture.

Lacan, following Marx in his recognition that the breakdown of unique, substantial, national, and genetic unity is the defining characteristic of capitalism, predicted that the pursuit of universality based on capitalism would eventually break down and generate a resurgence of nationalism. Lacan's proposition seems fairly close to the clichéd cultural criticism of conservatives who argue that modern civilization creates people without roots, causing a loss of identification with any specific community, causing in reaction an intense rally of nationalism. Lacan, however, according to Žižek, "has reversed this standpoint from the root." This leads us to the basic question: "Who is the subject of democracy?" For Žižek:

> The Lacanian answer is unequivocal: the subject of democracy is not a human person, "man" in all the richness of his needs, interests, and beliefs. The subject of democracy, like the subject of psychoanalysis, is none other than the Cartesian subject in all its abstraction, the empty punctuality we reach after subtracting all its particular contents.[17]

After abstracting the specific characteristics of the "human" portrait such as race, sex, and religion, the concept of "all people" established "despite" these differences is not a definitive people but rather an operational concept characterized by cruel abstraction.

[17] Slavoj Žižek *Looking Awry: An Introduction to Jacques Lacan Through Popular Culture* (Cambridge: The MIT Press, 1991), 163.

Alvar Aalto, Baker House, Cambridge, Massachusetts, 1947-51 Photo by Ezra Stoller

Alvar Aalto, Baker House (interior). Photo by Ezra Stoller

This is not necessarily an attack on democracy; Žižek merely outlined the components of this concept. In another article, he quotes Winston Churchill's paradoxical statement: "It is true that democracy is the worst among every system. The problem is that any other system is no better than democracy." The essential lesson for our argument here is that a society needs to adopt some kind of social system, and while democracy may not be the best one, there may not be any better.

What Žižek calls "cultural criticism" — which attacks democracy as an abstract concept — is quite similar in logic to the attack on the disciplines of architecture and city planning by the postmodernists. Our interest in Žižek's modernist argument lies in the difference he found between this kind of criticism and Lacan's arguments. We could probably paraphrase Churchill and say that it is true that modernism is the worst of systems, but that no other system is any better. However, Žižek's argument was not extended simply to lead to this conclusion: An examination of the work of Alvar Aalto — the architect considered by many to have brought regionalism into the context of modernism — will perhaps clarify the meaning of Žižek's lesson.

Alvar Aalto and the "Transfiguration" of Internationalism

At the present time, all architectural theories recognize the historical transfiguration of internationalism as occurring during the shift from the first generation of modern architects (such as Le Corbusier, Mies van der Rohe, and Walter Gropius, all born in the mid-1880s) and to the next generation, and Alvar Aalto would be considered the leading architect of the second generation. In his book *Space, Time, and Architecture*, Sigfried Giedion has given this master from Finland the unusual position — which reveals as much about this historian who himself directed the current of modernism — of achieving the "organic humanization" of modernism, which "existed in a hidden form of a functionalist idea." Thus Aalto became an architect who made functionalism more mature. Giedion's perspective can also be discerned in Henry-Russell Hitchcock's 1951 essay, "The International Style Twenty Years After":

> Aalto's Senior House at the Massachusetts Institute of Technology, of 1948, is obviously the most striking illustration of the increased use of curved and oblique forms. Whether most people approve of this prominent building or not, they tend to assume that Aalto was here consciously breaking with the rigidities of the International Style. Actually . . . even this notable post-War structure, though it may be at the extreme limit of the International Style as we understood it twenty years ago, is still in actual opposition to its sanctions only in the expressive irregularity of the plan and a few rather minor details, such as the willful roughness of the brickwork and the excessive clumsiness of some of the membering.[18]

It is interesting to note that Hitchcock, in criticizing the dogmatic standard he himself had set twenty years before, still felt it necessary to judge architectural works by referring to the authority of the International Style. But for what reason? With these observations, it is clear that both Giedion and Hitchcock felt it important to link Aalto with the definition of modern architecture, to defend it and help it survive.

Much has been written about Aalto, primarily because his large body of work is quite diverse and was created over a long period of time, thus providing scholars a variety of themes and topics to discuss. However, when it comes to a comprehensive description of his work, a common ground among critics surfaces; when critics praise Aalto, the tone of their praise is surprisingly similar. He is the rare type of architect whose work is almost never criticized, standing in contrast to the polemical Le Corbusier, who generally received as much criticism as praise. Despite its diversity, Aalto's work is surrounded by a collection of uniformly favorable criticism, with the clichéd categories of "human" and "organic" utilized to redefine and extend the categories of functionalism and rationalism. This is not simply the view of critics of an older generation such as Giedion and Hitchcock; more recent critics such as Paul David Pearson and Göran Schildt strive to avoid looking at Aalto from the view of modernist orthodoxy. Eventually, however, it is by

18 "The International Style Twenty Years After," 259. In the original *International Style* only the Turun Sanomat Building of 1930 was included because the MOMA show preceded those works that signaled Aalto's designation as an architect of the International Style.

19 Paul David Pearson, *Alvar Aalto and the International Style* (New York: Whitney Library of Design), 1978, and Göran Schildt, *Nykyaika* (Helsinki: Octava, 1986).

20 Demetri Porphyrios, *Sources of Modern Eclecticism: Studies on Alvar Aalto* (London: Academy Editions, 1982).

Alvar Aalto, Viipuri Library reading room, Viipuri, Finland, 1927-35. Photo by William P. Bruder

simply extending the categories of functionalism and rationalism — such as "biological functionalism," "Romantic Modernism," or "New Rationalism" — that they justify their (favorable) judgment of Aalto's achievements.[19] When the critics try to avoid this type of argument, their reasoning becomes obscure. Using a term that became popular during a certain period in Eastern Europe (peripheral in terms of modernization, as was Finland), Aalto was, for them, an architect who succeeded in giving a human face to ideology without being tied down by it. I do not necessarily disagree, but would like to ask one question: *how* does an architect become a functionalist and a regionalist at the same time?

I know that this rhetorical question is somewhat ridiculous. If we were able to ask Aalto himself, his answer would undoubtedly have been, "I don't pay attention to such matters." Though he was fairly diligent (especially in his youth) in writing articles about specific issues such as the standardization and mechanization of the building industry, he never argued this kind of broad theoretical concept. In a short article commissioned by the Finnish magazine *Arkkitehtir* for their special issue on "National-International" (1967), he suggested that the local could simply be extended to the national and international, which almost negates the dualism. It is quite unlikely that he would have argued that works such as the Viipuri Library and the Paimio Sanatorium are functionalist and the Villa Mairea is regionalist, but despite the propagated image of an architect not biased by an "ism" there are many "isms" hovering around him. Writers and critics continue to argue about whether or not Aalto was a functionalist or how he did or did not become a regionalist, but no one will argue definitively that Aalto would not have anything to do with such matters, as we have imagined his reaction. Even Demetri Porphyrios, trying to detach Aalto from the movement, said, "the similarity between Aalto and modernism is much less than has usually been supposed; or rather, if it exists, it lies in areas where it was not thought to lie"; after all, he placed the architect in the category of "Modern Eclecticism."[20]

Alvar Aalto, Tuberculosis Sanatorium, Paimio, Finland, 1929-32. Photo by William P. Bruder

There is obviously a trap in the question about functionalism and regionalism asked above. The situation would be far simpler if "functionalism" (or internationalism) and "regionalism" were not connected, or if they had a simple "or" separating them. Even in the case of architects full of contradiction and diversity such as Le Corbusier, if one questions whether or not he was a "functionalist," one can make one's point clear: because of the diversity of his work, the answer may be either affirmative or negative. General wisdom holds that Le Corbusier was the leader of functionalism, but the reaction of Le Corbusier himself was more or less a denial of this claim. However, his refutation does not prove that the general understanding is incorrect, but reveals an argument about the very standards of functionalism. In a certain context, saying that Le Corbusier was not a functionalist — as he himself did — has a polemic meaning, but to generalize from that statement that he did not pay attention to functionalism is clearly an exaggeration, and any argument related to functionalism will thus lose its meaning. In this sense, Le Corbusier consciously became a "functionalist" at a certain point in his career, and at another, he ceased to be one.

Such was not the case with Aalto. Setting aside his early functionalism, Aalto's work was surrounded by thediscourses of others, and it was these discourses (and not his own choice) that made him what he was. The fact that Le Corbusier was a functionalist in some cases and not in others and the fact that certain works by Aalto are more functionalist than others is not the same thing: one reflects a conscious choice while the other does not. Although critics admit that Aalto is an architect who surpasses the "ism," they in fact adopted that "ism" as a category and attempted to identify Aalto in these magnified "isms". In other words, the important thing is to see that they made the critical attempt to see in Aalto's work a redefinition of the concept of modernism — established upon complemen-

Alvar Aalto,Villa Mairea, Noormarkku, Finland, 1937-39. Photo by Ezra Stoller

Alvar Aalto, Villa Mairea, Noormarkku, Finland, 1937-39. Photo by William P. Bruder

tary concepts such as "romanticism" and "regionalism". Why were these the standards that had to be overcome? Why was modernism rejected, then called back repeatedly? This is not simply an issue of superficial labeling. When one argues about Aalto, the fact that critics developed a new view of functionalism and rationalism (a different way of saying modernism) has the same logic as Žižek's analysis of democracy: We have no better choice against which we are to judge Aalto's (or any other architect's) works. We may say that this is not because modernism is the best scale for measurement but rather that it is at the core of the formal logical structure of our argument.

Democracy — along with modernism, functionalism, and internationalism — is a manipulative concept without a subject, a notion one can ignore in discussing individual components of these concepts without attempting to put them in a general context. An activist like Aalto, therefore, could stay away from this issue when he deemed it inconvenient or when he had no interest. The same holds true as long as one is involved in the simple spatial (or aesthetic) experience of a building, not as a critic but as a mere observer. Critics, however, when functioning in their roles as critics, cannot always avoid the issue. According to Žižek, Lacan, describing democracy as vacant rule, found similarity with the subject of psychoanalysis. Might we not then be able to add that it is not necessary for us to call for this kind of formal specificity, as long as one does not try psychoanalysis, nor try to see and judge architectural pieces against social and historical contexts?

According to Žižek, the interest of Lacan's speculation lies in his argument on the subject of democracy, that abstraction might not destroy the "real", contrary to the postmodern argument of the neo-conservatives of "cultural criticism." This abstraction would be accompanied by physical remains which hold back the collapse of the conceptual framework: that is the state as an ethical moment. This insight helps us to extend the proposition we set that internationalism generates regionalism to the complementary relationship of the two. Although it seems that democracy has a global directive, Žižek argues that such "democracy of the entire planet" will never be realized but will remain alive by a connection with the "pathological fact" known as the nation-state. It might sound scandalous to say that regionalism in architecture is "pathological," but if it is viewed from the standpoint of the original intention of internationalism, it is the limit that must eventually be conquered. However, that is not the reality. Following Žižek's claim that the limit of democracy — its irreducible remains — is now the condition of the existence of democracy, we might be able to conclude that the regionalism that is preventing the ideal completion of internationalism is what is making internationalism's existence possible today. Perhaps then we can answer the rhetorical question raised above, "How does a person become a functionalist and a regionalist at the same time?" in the following way: *by pretending to believe it is possible, even if one knows it is not true.*

Translated by Marianne Wada

Hassan Fathy, plan and elevation with Hathor, New Gourna, Egypt, 1948. Photo by Gary Otte. Aga Khan Trust for Culture

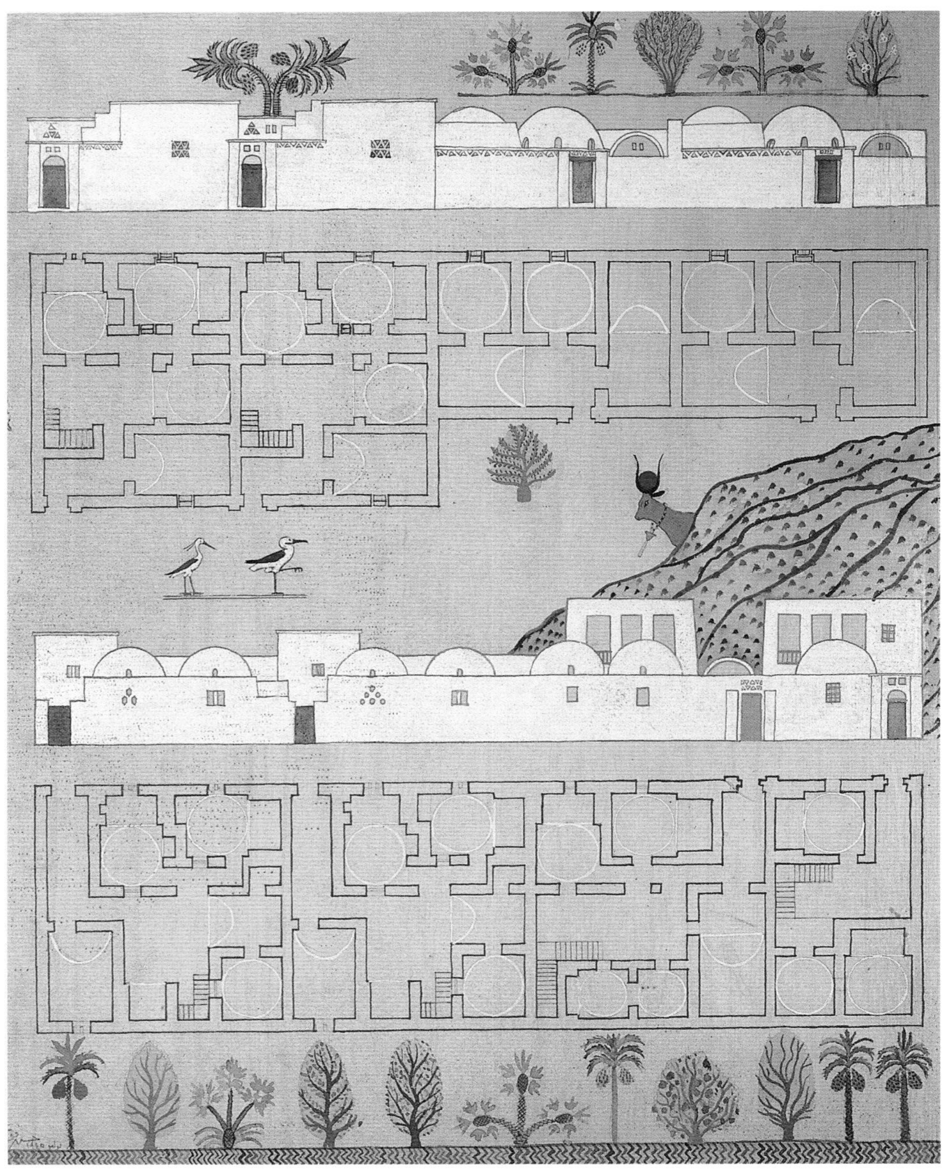

CULTURAL INTERSECTIONS: RE-VISIONING ARCHITECTURE AND THE CITY IN THE TWENTIETH CENTURY

Zeynep Çelik

Homogeneity and Cultural Difference

Architecture and urbanism at the end of the century reveal a hitherto unwitnessed globalization. Cultural boundaries can no longer be neatly drawn and notions such as "purity" and "authenticity" have become obsolete. Echoing Paul Ricoeur's observation that "everywhere throughout the world, one finds the same bad movie, the same slot machines, the same plastic or aluminum atrocities, the same twisting of language by propaganda,"[1] urban forms and architecture have increasingly become universalized. At the end of the century, the suburbs of Boston, Houston, and Paris, the heights of Algiers, the hills of the Bosphorus in Istanbul, and the center of Taipei share the slick, uniform, and interiorized environments of shopping malls, where similar or even identical products are enthusiastically consumed. Steel and glass skyscrapers transform urban landscapes everywhere; they overshadow previous layers of history with their sheer size and signify new directions in the economic structure. This architecture belongs to the era of transnational corporations that "represent neither their home countries nor their host nations but simply their own corporate selves" which began to dominate the world economy from the 1970s on, creating a specific culture and a privileged, transnational class of professionals who live a global lifestyle.[2] Furthermore, boundaries and borders are increasingly being replaced by interface as access to the contemporary city through electronic systems, global information, and capital networks begin to devalue the physical idea of space.[3]

Shopping mall, Algiers. Photo by Zeynep Çelik

If the new transnational class represents one end of the spectrum in homogenizing cities throughout the world, poverty is the equalizer at the other end. Social segregation according to class and ethnicity divides cities into fragments, with the formal characteristic of the residential quarters of low-income groups, for example, displaying striking similarities despite geographic distances. Not only do the squatter settlements around Bombay, Rabat, Brasilia, Caracas,

1 Paul Ricoeur, "Universal Civilization and National Cultures," in *History and Truth*, trans. C. A. Kelbley (Evanston, Il.: Northwestern University Press, 1965), 276-77.

2 Masao Miyoshi, "A Borderless World? From Colonialism to Transnationalism and the Decline of the Nation-State," *Critical Inquiry* 19 (Summer 1993): 739-42.

3 Ackbar Abbas, "Building on Disappearance: Hong Kong Architecture and the City," *Public Culture* 6 (1994): 443.

Algiers, and Paris (the last prominent in the 1960s, now cleared) display similar configurations and architectural and constructional features, but the housing "solutions" aimed to prevent such developments follow the same formulas, creating strikingly similar environments in disparate parts of the globe. The edges of many cities during the last decades of the century consist of sprawls of housing blocks, unanimously inadequate measures against the towering shortage of decent housing, united in their visual anonymity and the sad barrenness of the spaces separating them.

The anonymity that marks the end-of-the-century city is accompanied by an immense pressure for an expression of identity. In the 1990s — torn with ethnic and neonationalist struggles and deep conflicts over cultural, ethnic, and racial differences — this urge may hark back to the artistic and literary productions of the "third world" in the aftermath of the Second World War, when nationalism became a trope for "belonging," "bordering," and "commitment."[4] Nevertheless, the expression of cultural identity now takes on new meanings and is absorbed into the

Andreas Gursky. *Happy Valley, Hong Kong*, 1996. Courtesy of Monika Sprüth Galerie, Cologne

logic of today's global markets. As observed by one cultural critic in specific reference to Benetton advertisements, the global markets now not only acknowledge but also depoliticize cultural differences by presenting them in "categorical rather than relational terms."[5] Although reaching a peak at the end of the century, the two interlocked and seemingly contradictory paradigms of homogeneity and expression of cultural difference in architecture and urbanism run throughout it, shifting in form and meaning within a complex web of social, cultural, political, and

4 Timothy Brennan, "The National Longing for Form," in *Narration and Nation*, ed. Homi Bhabha (London and New York: Routledge, 1990), 47.

5 Henry A. Giroux, "Consuming Social Change: The 'United Colors' of Benetton," *Cultural Critique* (Winter 1993-94): 15.

Sixth Avenue, view to the southwest from West 51st Street, New York City, 1974. Photo by Ezra Stoller

economic entanglements. Modernism — understood according to Marshall Berman's definition as "a struggle to make ourselves at home in a constantly changing world" that "implies an open and expansive way of understanding culture" — constitutes the broad framework for the entire century.[6]

Even at moments when expression of identity emerges as the leading drive, notions such as "purity" and "authenticity" remain obsolete due to the complexities of cultural interchange.[7] Nonetheless, the discourse on architecture and urbanism still pursues the nineteenth-century compulsion to classify, categorize, and frame: empire-building techniques linger, pigeonholing societies and cultures according to familiar hierarchies. It often glosses over the porous nature of present-day borders or capitalizes upon them to emphasize a one-way traffic that ends up reiterating the supremacy of certain cultures over others. The systematic repetition of tired formulas continues to coalesce into a seemingly coherent and authoritative "truth." The division of the world into "first" and "third" (with the clouded "second" disappearing ever faster), "developed" and "underdeveloped," "central" and "peripheral," "Western" and "non-Western," culminates in the contrived debate between (Western) modernism and the traditions of others and is reduced to a paradigm, memorably summarized by Rasheed Araeen as "our Bauhaus, others' mudhouse." Araeen suggests that, as important as it is to understand the construction of the other by the dominant culture, a more interesting question is how this other subverts the assumptions on which it is based.[8] Regardless of where and how it originated, it is essential to understand modernism as a universal phenomenon in the twentieth century and not as something that belongs solely to the "West." To expand on these concepts, a closer look at colonialism is indispensable.

Squatter houses, Paris (Nanterre, Bidonville), 1969

Seoul, Korea. Photo by Seong Kwon

With its powerful nineteenth-century legacies, colonialism has continued to play a crucial role in defining relationships between societies and cultures during our century as well. Cultural production was fundamental in establishing the colonial condition, because, as Edward Said argued, culture enabled the formation of the idea of imperiality, which depended on "the enterprise of empire."[9] Yet cultural formations responded during the arduous process of decolonization, resisting notions of imperiality and subverting the order of the world (if not changing it). Among cultural formations, architecture occupies a prominent position because it bears the potential to express social relations and power structures at certain

6 Marshall Berman, *All That Is Solid Melts into Air: The Experience of Modernity* (New York: Viking Penguin, 1988), 5-6.

7 This notion was articulated as early as 1950 by Aimé Césaire: "Ce n'est pas une société morte que nous voulons faire revivre. Nous laissons cela aux amateurs de l'exotisme." See Aimé Césaire, *Discours sur le colonialisme* (Paris and Dakar: Présence africaine, 1989), 29.

8 Rasheed Araeen, "Our Bauhaus, Others' Mudhouse," *Third Text* 6 (Spring 1989): 3-14.

9 Edward Said, *Culture and Imperialism* (New York: Alfred Knopf, 1993), 11-12.

Thomas Struth. *Beaugrenelle*, Paris, 1979

critical moments in crystallized forms: as physical frame to all human activity and because of its experiential qualities that engage everybody, architecture constitutes an essential part of the human experience. It expresses cultural values and is firmly grounded in material and daily life. Its connection to the everyday world is so substantial that if it can never be divorced from worldly associations; neither can it transcend them.

Colonialism and Cities

The sheer scope of building activity, as well as the innovative, varied, and experimental nature of architectural and urban projects undertaken in the colonies in the twentieth — as well as the nineteenth — century call for a more extensive analysis than the discipline of architectural history has dedicated to the topic so far. The history of modernism cannot be abstracted from the architectural and urban practices in the colonies scattered to all corners of the world, and the study of colonialism cannot be treated separately from that of the *métropole* or treated as a subtext to it. The interlocked nature of the *métropole* and the colony was well understood at the height of the colonial age and underlined by two promi-

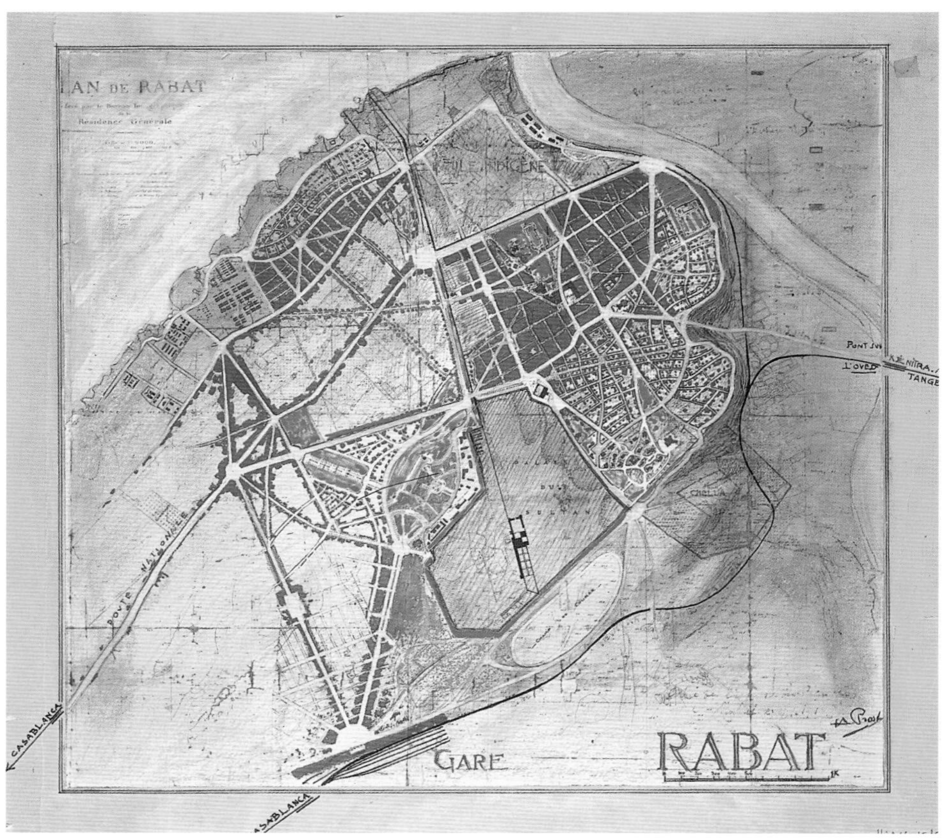

Henri Prost, Plan for Rabat, Morocco, c. 1920, from *L'Oeuvre de Henri Prost* (Paris: Academie d'architecture, 1930).

nent French figures. Louis Hubert Gonzalve Lyautey, the resident general of the French protectorate in Morocco, in a widely-quoted statement called the colonies "the laboratories for modernism," and Albert Sarraut (former governor of Indochina and minister of colonies) explained the phenomenon with a modernist architectural metaphor: "Henceforth, the European edifice rests on colonial *pilotis*."[10]

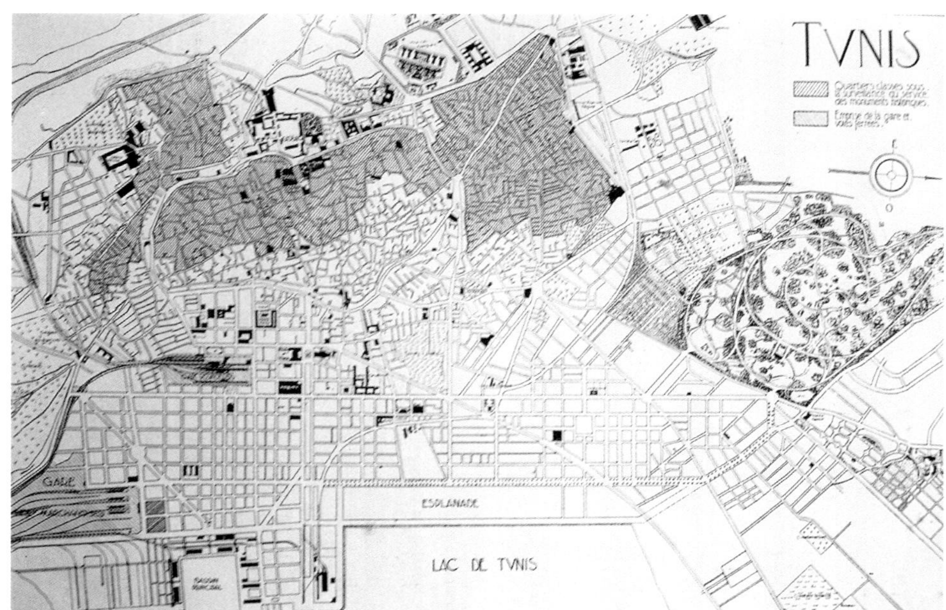

Plan of Tunis, c. 1930. The *medina* is in the north, and the French town, designed by Victor Valensi, in the south

[10] Albert Sarraut, *Grandeur et servitude coloniales* (Paris: Editions du Sagittaire, 1931), 220-21.

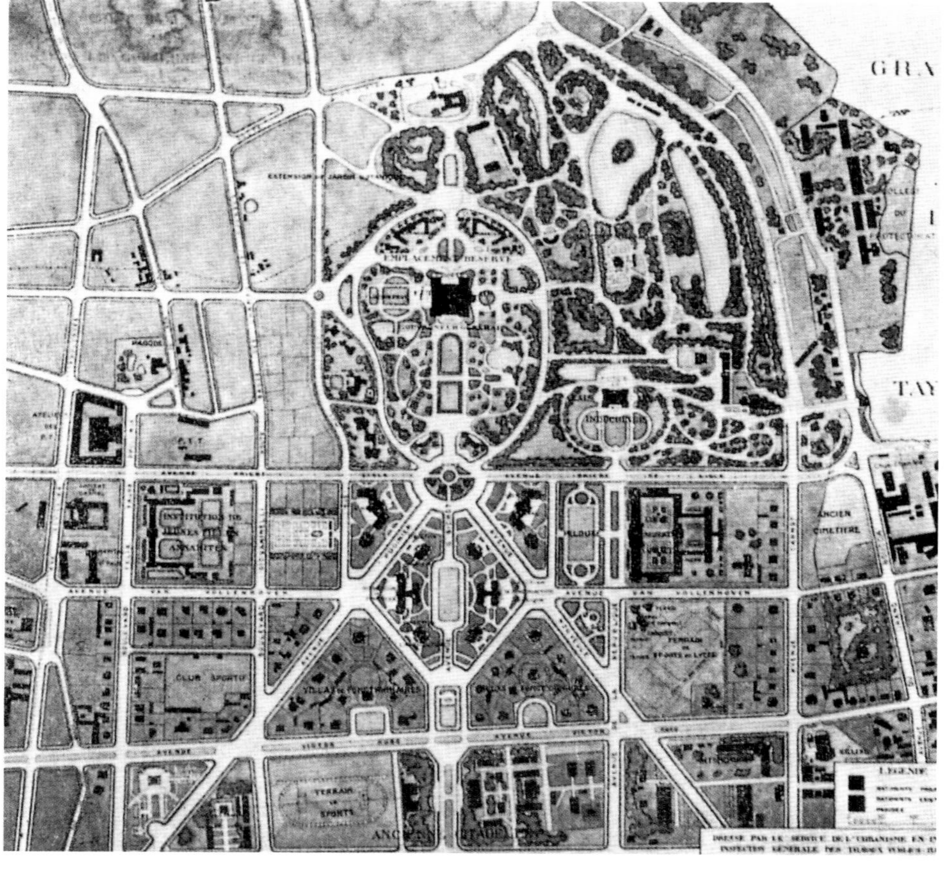

Ernest Hébrard, Plan of Quartier du Gouvernement Général, Hanoi, 1924

Regardless of the shifts in colonial policies adopted by different powers and at different times, the architecture of European quarters in colonized territories relied upon the newly developing concepts of modernism, as well as on nineteenth-century traditions (themselves forming the basis for modernist notions). To refer to a few memorable case studies, in Rabat — called by Lyautey the "Washington, D.C. of Morocco" — Henri Prost created a road network in the 1910s that combined radial and orthogonal avenues; these spatial avenues highlighted the public and monumental structures by framing them with vistas, and the whole system was "aired" by parks and gardens. A decade later in French Indochina, Ernest Hébrard's addition to Hanoi, a monumental administrative center, emulated the diagonal and grid street network and incorporated into it spacious green areas. In 1913 Sir Edwin Lutyens designed the showcase of British colonialism, New Delhi, according to another complex plan of diagonals and grids, and very deliberately utilized grand vistas to highlight the buildings that symbolized the British Empire. In colonial Manila (1906-14), Daniel Burnham was able to realize his

Sir Edwin Lutyens, germinal sketch plan and elevation of Government House, and plan of the capitol complex, New Delhi, 1912. British Architectural Library, RIBA, London

City Beautiful *par excellence*, surpassing in scale and coherence of design any of his projects in the United States. In the Belgian Congo, the city of Goma, built in the 1920s and 1930s, displayed another ambitious design with converging avenues.

The Delhi Town Planning Commission at work, 1913

If the colonial city planners' designs shared similarities, the architecture built in each city was different. In the French colonies the nineteenth-century practice of equating the "conqueror's style" with public buildings as a blatant political statement gave way in the early years of this century to a more flexible attitude reflecting "tolerance" toward local cultures in accordance with new experiments in colonial policies: the move from "assimilation" to "association."[11] This trend resulted in many notable buildings that combined Beaux-Arts principles with decorative programs derived from local architecture and endowed each colonial city with its own image. Landmarks in two French colonial cities — the Hôtel de Ville in Sfax, Tunisia, by Raphaël Guy, clad in neo-Islamic elements, and

Sir Edwin Lutyens, Viceroy's House and Secretariat, aerial view from the west, New Delhi, 1920. Country Life Picture Library

Fez, Morocco
Photo by Philippe Ploquin

the Musée d'histoire Louis Finon in Hanoi by Ernest Hébrard, with Indochinese details, both designed in the 1920s — exhibit this attitude, which can be interpreted as the absorption of the colonies into the cultural repertoire of the empire, albeit in a controlled and tamed manner. The architectural references in Lutyens's New Delhi operate in a similar frame.

Colonial cities came in different shapes and scales but shared one prominent characteristic: a dual structure that clearly delineated the separation of the colonizer from the colonized. During the most intense phase of decolonization struggles, Frantz Fanon described the generic "colonial city" as being composed of two irreconcilable parts:

> The zone where the natives live is not complementary to the zone inhabited by the settlers. The two zones are opposed, but not in the service of a higher unity. Obedient to the rules of pure Aristotelian logic, they both follow the principle of reciprocal exclusivity. No conciliation is possible, for of the two terms, one is superfluous. The settler's town is a strongly built town, all made of stone and steel. It is a brightly lit town; the streets are covered with asphalt, and the garbage cans swallow all the leavings, unseen, unknown and hardly thought about. . . . The settler's town is a well-fed town, an easygoing town; its belly is always full of good things. . . .
>
> The town belonging to the colonized people, or at least the native town, the Negro village, the medina, the reservation, is . . . a world without any spaciousness; men live there on top of each other, and their huts are built one on top of the other. The native town is a hungry town, starved of bread, of meat, of shoes, of light. The native town is a crouching village, a town on its knees, a town wallowing in the mire.[12]

The dichotomy was not an accident, but a deliberate creation. Following nineteenth-century practices, "European" cities were built adjacent to "native" towns in all corners of the world, with long-term consequences that have contributed to the endurance of bipolar cultural and societal formulas even now, at the end of the twentieth century. Guillaume de Tarde, a former secretary general of the Protectorate of Morocco, expressed the need for a revised understanding of the dual-city pattern in his report to the International Congress of Urbanism in the Colonies, held in conjunction with the 1931 Colonial Exposition in Paris:

> Separation should exist, but this should not be a radical separation. The issue is not to establish distance with an attitude of contempt toward the indigenous town . . . , but to the contrary, to maintain a discreet separation of two towns otherwise closely united. . . . In summary, the European town should be sufficiently far from the indigenous town in order not to absorb it, but close enough to it so that it can live off it to some measure.[13]

In Morocco during the 1910s and the 1920s, under the leadership of Marshal Lyautey and his chief architect, Henri Prost, this duality was explained within a philosophy of tolerance as a protective measure to save the architectural and urbanistic heritage of the medinas. Moroccan cities, varying from major settlements such as Rabat, Fez, and Marrakesh, to smaller centers like Tétouan and Meknèz, thus remained untouched by colonial interventions but were subjected to another kind of pressure from the planned new developments outside their bound-

[11] See François Béguin, *Arabisances: décor architectural et tracé urbain en Afrique du Nord, 1830-1850* (Paris: Dunod, 1983).

[12] Frantz Fanon, *The Wretched of the Earth*, trans. Constance Farrington (New York: Grove Press, 1963), 38-39.

[13] Guillaume de Tarde, "L'Urbanisme en Afrique du Nord," in Jean Royer, ed., *L'Urbanisme aux Colonies et dans les pays tropicaux* (Delayance: La Charité-sur-Loire, 1932), v. 1, 29-30.

[14] A considerable literature has developed on French colonial planning in Morocco within the last fifteen years or so. I consider Janet L. Abu-Lughod's *Rabat: Urban Apartheid in Morocco* (Princeton, N.J.: Princeton University Press, 1980), by far the best study on the topic.

[15] "L'Urbanisme à Tunis" in Royer, *L'Urbanisme aux colonies*, v. 1, 54.

[16] Henri Prost, "Rapport Général," ibid., 22. See also Abu-Lughod, *Rabat*, 145.

[17] For an analysis of Le Corbusier's Algiers projects within the framework of colonial policies, see Zeynep Çelik, "Le Corbusier, Orientalism, Colonialism," *Assemblage* 17 (April 1992): 58-77.

Le Corbusier, model of Le plan Obus, Algiers, 1932. Fondation Le Corbusier, Paris

aries.[14] In Tunisia, the municipality of Tunis commissioned architect Victor Valensi in 1920 to devise a *projet d'aménagement, d'embellissement, et d'extension* with a specification to "conserve carefully the medina and especially the zone of the souks" and extend the European city according to modern concepts.[15]

The recommendation that a green zone — a *cordon sanitaire* — be placed whenever possible between the two parts of the city revealed concerns other than "tolerance" behind the physical separation. As an urban design feature, this item became transcribed into the "wish list" of participants in the 1931 congress on colonial urbanism in order to ensure the maintenance of ethnic segregation.[16] Le Corbusier's unrealized Obus projects for Algiers (1931-42) re-interpreted the same notion and took it to an extreme by making the new European city bridge over the intact Casbah, transforming the greenbelt into an air band and reversing the horizontality of the former into a vertical element. The implications of these designs extended the colonial premise farther: Le Corbusier's plans established constant visual supervision over the local population and clearly marked the hierarchical social order onto the urban image, with the dominating located above and the dominated below.[17]

The meticulous order and imperial facade of Lutyens's New Delhi contrasted with the dense and "chaotic" fabric of historic Delhi nearby. The Italian planners working under Mussolini also followed the familiar formula. In Tripoli,

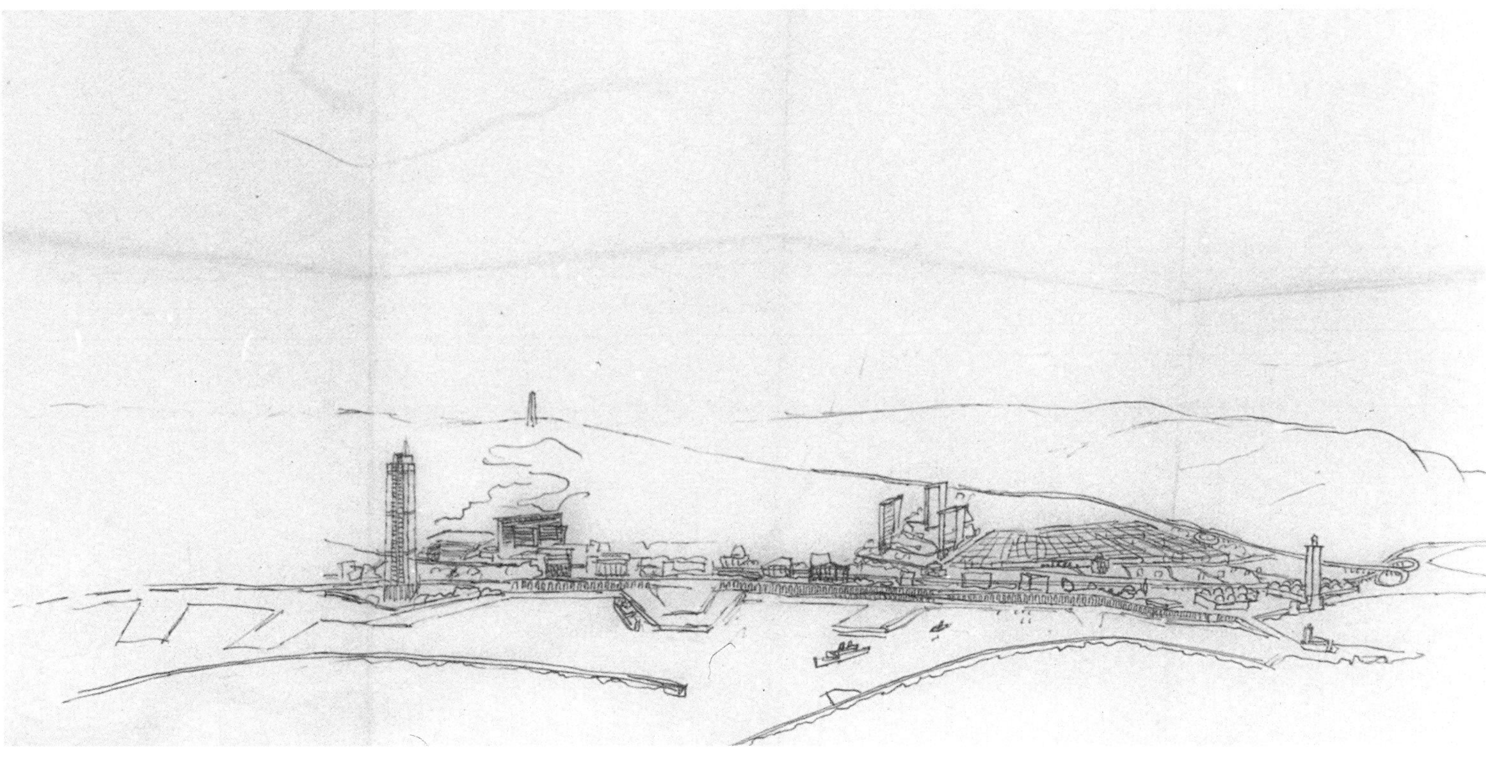

Le Corbusier, sketch of the reurbanized neighborhood of the Marine in perspective, Le plan Obus, Algiers, 1932. Fondation Le Corbusier, Paris

Le Corbusier, sketches of the European and the Arabic city, in *The Radiant City,* 1933. Fondation Le Corbusier, Paris

Libya, for example, a monumental piazza separated the Muslim town from the new Italian quarters while bringing a touch of Venice: two pillars on the waterfront act as the "gate" to the city.[18] In the "functional" plan developed for Addis Ababa, Ethiopia, the officially stated principle was segregation. According to a 1937 report, the first problem to be resolved (rather, "disciplined") in a colonial city was "coexistence of metropolitans and natives . . . so profoundly different in terms of race, religion, and (above all) civilization." Therefore, indigenous markets and living quarters were relegated to the edges of the city (which also contained the industries); the administrative center and European residential and commercial areas were in the center.[19]

The separation of Europeans from the colonized population was camouflaged with a more "scientific" and "technical" tone following the new methodologies developed in urban planning; "zoning" emerged as the key term. In the plans for the extension of Hanoi, for example, the dual structure was presented in

Albert Laprade, new medina, Casablanca (the Habous Quarter), early 1920s. Published in Léandre Vaillat, *Le visage français du Maroc* (Paris, 1931)

terms of residential and commercial "zones" for Europeans and the "indigenous," in addition to industrial, administrative, military, and recreational zones. In French Equatorial Africa, defined as a "new country" whose urbanistic, hygienic, and residential development had to happen "at once" (*d'un seul coup*), Brazzaville had become "unrecognizable" within the short period of three years. Brazzaville was "separated from [the indigenous settlements to the southwest and northeast] in order to radically isolate illness in case of an epidemic." With its "beautiful arteries . . . that connected the important points, the train stations, and the harbors," the city was divided into clear zones: civic center, military and colonial establishments, commercial activities, harbor and warehouses, and residential neighborhoods of the *nouvelle ville*.[20] In this order, the "indigenous villages" were presented as an additional zone. Another striking example of this trend is a generic "Belgian colonial town," designed in 1949 in an ideal and linear configuration along a rail line. The five alternative schemes are divided into European, indigenous, commercial, and industrial zones, with the European and the indigenous quarters divided either by a commercial or an industrial buffer. Two of the schemes are further complicated by the presence of a third group, the *évolués*, who were zoned away from the *non-évolués* by commerce and placed next to the Europeans, though separated from them by the railroad.[21] These are only a few among the myriad examples that illustrate the marriage between the hierarchical order of colonial thinking and the principles of modern planning.

Colonial Discourse and Cultural Identity

The hierarchical order, imposed by the colonial condition and based on ethnic, social, and cultural differences, gave rise to a charged notion of identity. Involving both the colonizer and the colonized, the expression of identity through cultural and artistic means became a major trope of the twentieth century, extending well beyond the colonial era. The phenomenon is not only relevant to the specificities of colonialism, but covers a much broader base stemming from global economic and political power structures. Once again with its roots firmly grounded in the previous century, the imposing presence of "Western" culture acted as the ultimate referent for expressions of identity. Issues surrounding cultural identity were addressed in a complicated reactive web; solutions ranged from adopting the "advanced" imagery of European forms, to finding a synthesis between the local and the "Western," to diametrically opposing the dominating "Western" culture with a search for purity — with a wealth of gradations in between. This dynamic process also redefined European cultural forms.

The colonial discourse that punctuated cultural differences led to the "construction" of architectural "traditions" for colonized territories. The later adoption, interpretation, and transfiguration of these definitions reveal intriguing questions about issues of authenticity in an age that desperately looks for a sense of national identity even as it is engulfed by globalization.[22]

Research and writing on "non-Western" architecture had already coalesced into a significant body of literature in nineteenth-century Europe, as evidenced by the number and scope of publications on "Islamic" architecture. Nevertheless, in the 1920s and 1930s a major turn from monumental to residential forms occurred in architectural discourse. North-African French colonies present a particularly rich case study as their vernacular architecture was the subject of

18 For Tripoli under Mussolini, see Krystyna von Henneberg, "Piazza Castello and the Making of a Fascist Colonial Capital," in *Streets: Critical Perspectives on Public Space*, eds. Zeynep Çelik, Diane Favro, and Richard Ingersoll (Berkeley and Los Angeles: University of California Press, 1994), 135-50.

19 Mia Fuller, "Wherever You Go, There You Are: Fascist Plans for the Colonial City of Addis Ababa and the Colonizing Suburb of EUR '42," *Journal of Contemporary History* 31 (1996): 403-06. Fuller argues that even the terminology revealed the segregation: "natives" lived in "quarters," whereas Italians lived in the "city" or the "center."

20 Ernest Spanner, "L'Urbanisme en Afrique Equatoriale Française," in Royer, *L'Urbanisme aux colonies*, 160.

21 Bruno DeMeulder, *Reformisme, thuis en oversee: Geschiedenis van de Belgische planning in een kolonie* (Ph.D. diss., Katholieke Universiteir te Leuven, 1990), vol. 2.2, fig. 13.5.

22 The classic text for the development of a sense of nationality is Benedict Anderson's *Imagined Communities: Reflections on the Origin and Spread of Nationalism* (London and New York: Verso, 1983; rev. 1991).

scrupulous documentation and analysis. This focus originated in part from European modernist sensibilities that saw the cubical, whitewashed masses and sparse spaces of North African medinas as potential sources of inspiration for a modernist vocabulary. It was also connected to the growing number of construction programs for collective housing in the colonies and the need to find appropriate stylistic and spatial models. In addition, the valorization of vernacular residential fabrics justified the colonial urban policy to leave the old towns intact in a gesture of preservation. Lyautey explained this decision, which contributed to the creation of dual cities: "Yes, in Morocco, and it is to our honor, we conserve. I would go a step further, we rescue. We wish to conserve in Morocco Beauty — and it is not a negligible thing."[23]

Popular books such as Victor Valensi's *L'Habitation tunisienne* (Paris, 1923), Jean Galotti's *Les Jardins et les maisons arabes au Maroc* (Paris, 1926: with sketches by Albert Laprade, one of the leading architects working with Henri Prost under Lyautey), and A. Maitrat de la Motte-Capron's *L'Architecture indigène nord africaine* (Algiers, 1932) presented a wealth of images depicting vernacular buildings, often shown in their urban or landscape settings. Le Corbusier's own interest in vernacular architecture and his frequent incorporation of sketches and photographs of North African buildings in his publications supported his arguments for a modern architecture and urbanism, and thus enhanced the entry of "indigenous" architecture into the discourse of modernism.[24] Furthermore, the creation of temporary quarters — deemed "authentic" — at the world's fairs from the second half of the nineteenth century on, culminating in the extensive Tunisian section of the 1931 Paris Colonial Exhibition (designed by Victor Valensi), played a crucial role in the dissemination of North African vernacular imagery.[25]

When French architects built housing schemes for "indigenous" people, they relied on their own definitions of local architecture. A striking example is the new medina of Casablanca (the Habous Quarter), intended to accommodate the growing Moroccan population of the city. Designed by Albert Laprade and built in the early 1920s, the scheme combined the "customs and scruples" of Moroccans with French considerations for "hygiene"[26] and highlighted the contrast between the street and the courtyards of the houses. Reinterpreting local "traditions," Laprade created "sensible, vibrant walls, charged with poetry"; these white walls defined cubical masses, but their irregularity gave them a "human" touch. However, the project was more than a stylistic exercise, for the architect's ambition was to integrate into his design "values of ambiance" as well as a "whole way of life." Architecture for Laprade was a "living thing" and "should express a sentiment." The spatial and programmatic qualities adhered to these goals: there were pedestrian streets and courtyard houses, markets, neighborhood ovens, public baths, mosques, and Quranic schools in a stylistic integrity that "preserved everything respectable in the tradition" but used modern technology and construction materials.[27]

Similar projects were carried out in other North African colonies. For example, about two decades later, the architecture of the Cité Musulmane el Omrane in Tunis echoed Laprade's whitewashed houses with courtyards and no exterior openings, with the addition of vaulted roofs. The architects (G. Glorieux and L. Glorieux-Monfred) organized the site plan according to a relaxed orthogonal street network that allowed for a certain flexibility in the positioning of individual units and their collective massing. If Cité el Omrane formalized the principles for residential patterns, another Tunisian project dating from the same period — the Mosque and Market in Bizerte — articulated the essence of the community center

23 Quoted in Abu-Lughod, *Rabat*, 143.

24 The most widely disseminated of Le Corbusier's publications is *La Ville radieuse* (Paris: Vincent, Fréal, 1933). Corbusier's interest in non-Western vernacular architecture goes back to the 1910s, to his "*Voyage en Orient.*"

25 Valensi's design mimicked an "organic" settlement, down to patched uses of building materials and irregular plastering. In the words of a contemporary critic, the architect "forced himself to reconstitute something badly built, and he succeeded perfectly." See Anthony Goissaud, "A l'exposition coloniale, le pavillon de la Tunisie," *La Construction moderne* 18 (October 1931): 34-37. For the representation of colonial architecture in the expositions, see Zeynep Çelik, *Displaying the Orient: Architecture of Islam at Nineteenth-Century World's Fairs* (Berkeley and Los Angeles: University of California Press, 1992).

26 Léandre Vaillat, *Le Visage français du Maroc* (Paris: Horizons de France, 1931), 12.

27 Albert Laprade, "Une Ville crée specialement pour les indigènes à Casablanca," in Royer, *L'Urbanisme aux colonies*, 94-99; Vaillat, *Le Visage français du Maroc*, 15-17.

for the Muslim population. Rows of vaulted small shops fronted with colonnades framed the public space, significantly named Place de la France; a mosque attached to the market structures stood out with its shifted angle oriented toward Mecca, its multiple domes, and its square minaret. The cumulative effect in both projects was that of a dense settlement composed of small and simple repetitive units woven together with some irregularity, with simple vaults and domes further uniting the scheme on the roof level. The persistence of this residential pattern in new projects constructed for the indigenous people reinforced the existing sociocultural duality, already nurtured in the colonial cities. A comparison of Cité el Omrane with the Quartier Gambetta housing project — built at the same time, also in Tunis but intended for Europeans — acknowledges the policy to maintain, enhance, and express cultural differences between the colonizer and the colonized: Quartier Gambetta is envisioned as a Corbusian grid of longitudinal apartment blocks separated from each other by ample communal green spaces. [28]

It is curious that during the very same years (the mid-1940s), the distinguished Egyptian architect Hassan Fathy turned to the rural vernacular of buildings in the Egyptian countryside in his own search for "authenticity"; he proposed an architectural vocabulary for the "poor" that echoed the prototypes offered by French architects in their North African colonies. Fathy's drive to return to a past period of purity, decontaminated from the ills of rapid change, was in reaction to the unquestioning subscription to modernity had that resulted in "cultural confusion" and loss of tradition in Egyptian cities and villages.[29] As such, it may be indicative of "the passion with which native intellectuals defend the existence of their national culture," analyzed by Fanon.[30] Fathy was a cosmopolitan architect, with strong intellectual ties to Europe and in close touch with the recent developments in the profession. His designs for the village of New Gourna, then, should be historically contextualized and not read as the isolated experiments of a lone visionary. Fathy's courtyards, private streets, and residential clusters, his aesthetics founded upon simple forms (the square domed unit, the rectangular vaulted unit, and the alcove covered with a half-dome), his public-building types (markets, crafts *khan*, mosque, bath), and even his socially ambitious program had counterparts in the French projects. In New Gourna, Fathy attempted social reform by revitalizing the traditional way of life both in the built environment and in the patterns of production, which were founded on crafts and construction materials (namely brick-making); this approach echoed Laprade's idea of allowing for "a whole way of life" in the new medina of Casablanca. To return to Fanon's analysis of the "native intellectual," in his attempt to express national identity Fathy relied on techniques and language borrowed from European architects. Like Fanon's "native intellectual," Fathy ended up creating a "hallmark which he wishes to be national, but which is strangely reminiscent of exoticism."[31]

Behind the similar forms and programs, the originating concerns and future implications differed. For Fathy, a return to vernacular forms meant endowing contemporary Egypt with a cultural image, a manifest identity in the face of the universalizing power of Western technology: it was an act of resistance. For the French colonists, however, the architecturally emphasized differences of North African cultures enhanced the power of France, not only because it displayed the diversity of its colonial possessions but also because it demonstrated tolerance toward the subjugated culture. Situating Fathy's architecture and that of the French architects building in North Africa in relation to each other shows how deeply colonial productions and those conscientiously created in opposition to them were

[28] For these projects, as well as others built in Tunisia, see the "Tunisie" issue of *L'Architecture d'aujourd'hui*, no. 20 (October 1948). Cité Musulmane el Omrane and Quartier Gambetta are presented next to each other in the pages of *L'Architecture d'aujourd'hui*, emphasizing the spatial and aesthetic differences between the two projects.

[29] Hassan Fathy, *Architecture for the Poor: An Experiment in Rural Egypt* (Chicago and London: University of Chicago Press, 1973), 19-20.

[30] Fanon, *The Wretched of the Earth*, 209.

[31] Ibid., 223.

Jean Pierre Ventre, Mosque and Market, Bizerte, Tunisia, c. 1945

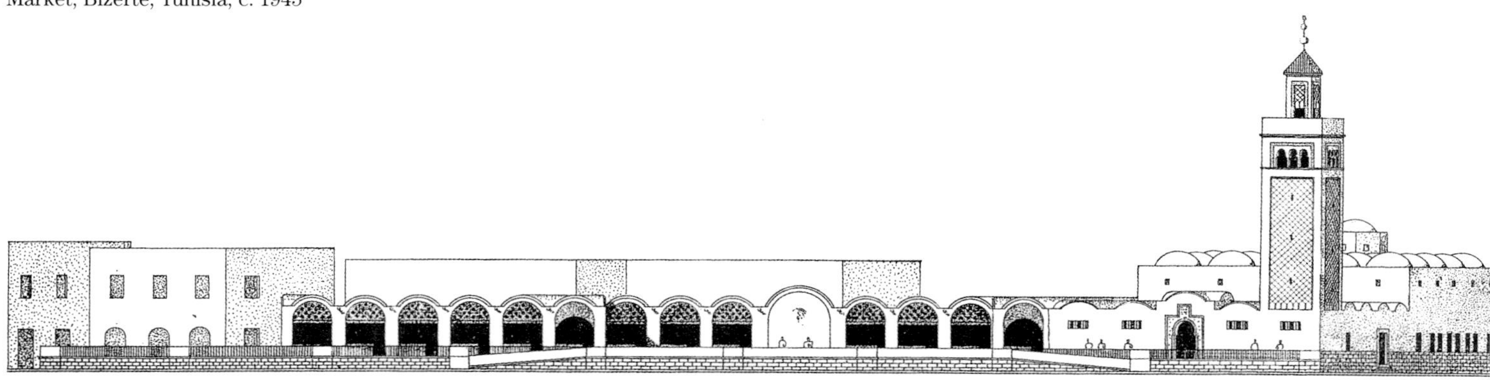

Hassan Fathy, New Gourna, Egypt, 1948, view of village from mosque minaret. Photo by A. Kawati. Aga Khan Trust for Culture

entangled, supporting Masao Miyoshi's recent thesis that a "return to 'authenticity'. . . is a closed route" and that there is no such concept as "authenticity."[32]

The intricate relationship between the colonial definitions and adaptations of North African vernacular and Fathy's vocabulary has been overlooked by architectural historians and critics, who abstracted Fathy as a pioneer in a unique search for authenticity — a position that trivializes the complexity of his thinking and his worldly status among the leading architects of the century. Nevertheless, the extraordinary following of Fathy's architecture found in a wide range of "third world" (and some "first world") countries makes a statement about the more discreet meanings read into the familiar forms and the significance of the search for expression of cultural identity (albeit still caught up in the exercise of "exoticism" Fanon discussed in the early 1960s). It also points to the enduring otherness created by the colonial discourse — appropriated, twisted, and turned by the "third world" architect, and endowed with an oppositional symbolism that expresses self-identity.

The Cross-Cultural Dialogue

The cross-cultural dialogue operated in several other directions. For example, the aesthetics of the North African vernacular corresponded to the vocabulary of modernist architects, an issue well understood by Fathy, who characterized historic Egyptian houses as "light constructions, simple, with the clean lines of the best modern houses."[33] Le Corbusier's earlier architecture, for example, had already displayed an affinity with the Turkish vernacular he had studied: a number of his villas, such the Villa Jeanneret-Perret (1912), Villa Favre-Jacot (1912), and Villa Schwob (1916), were inspired by Ottoman houses in terms of their interior organization around a central hall, their simple spaces, massing, and blank street façades. The North African vernacular surfaced sporadically in his work — to name

Sidi Ibrahim Mosque, near El Ateuf, Algeria. Photo by Mary McLeod

[32] Miyoshi, "From Colonialism to Transnationalism," 747.

[33] Fathy, *Architecture for the Poor*, 20.

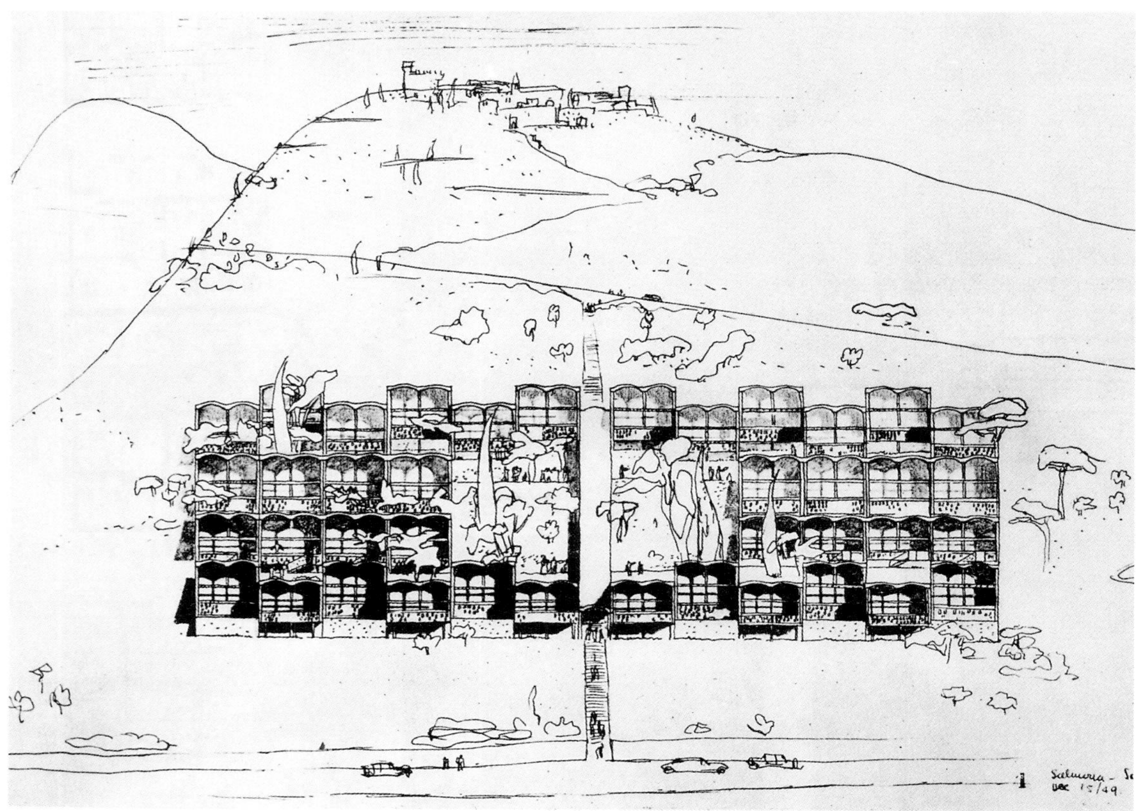

Le Corbusier, elevation of the first study, Roq et Rob housing at Cap-Martin, France, 1949. Fondation Le Corbusier, Paris

a few, in the Weekend House (1935), the Roq and Rob project (1949), and the Maisons Jaoul (1953) — recording its most poignant moment with the Notre-Dame-du-Haut, Ronchamp (1950-54), which echoed the sculptural mass of the Sidi Ibrahim Mosque near El Ateuf in the Algerian countryside.

Although described and admired at length by others, the Algerian casbah (the precolonial al-Jaza'ir) entered the modernist discourse of architecture in Le Corbusier's memorable sentences: "Inscribed in the site, it is irrefutable. It is in consonance with nature."[34] It was "beautiful," "charming," and "adorable," and it "never, no, never must be destroyed." The housing patterns in the casbah had abolished the street but "conquered the view of the sea for every house" by means of roof terraces that "created a roof over the city." The casbah was "an immense stairway, a tribune invaded at night by millions of adorers of nature." Juxtaposing his own housing proposal with the patterns offered by the casbah, Le Corbusier summarized the lessons he had learned: "terraces, suspended gardens, grand bays open to a landscape of dreams conquered by height."[35] Le Corbusier's appreciation of the casbah, then, focused on isolated features that he interpreted in his own designs.

It was "in direct opposition to the arbitrary isolation of [Le Corbusier's] so-called communities of the Unité," to his *tabula rasa* attitude toward urban fabrics, and in order to promote "a hierarchy of human association" and "a direct expression of a way of life" that vernacular patterns were brought back into the discourse of modern architecture; Alison and Peter Smithson introduced these ideas at the 1953 meeting of the Congrès Internationaux d'Architecture Moderne (CIAM) in Aix-en-Provence, while the CIAM group based in Algiers studied an

34 Le Corbusier, "Le Folklore est l'expression fleurie des traditions," *Voici la France de ce mois* 16 (June 1941): 31.

35 Le Corbusier, *La Ville radieuse*, 229, 230, 233.

Le Corbusier, Maisons Jaoul, Neuilly-sur-Seine, 1953. Fondation Le Corbusier, Paris

Le Corbusier, Notre-Dame-du-Haut, Ronchamp, 1950-54. Fondation Le Corbusier, Paris

Le Corbusier, Unité d'Habitation, Marseille-Michelet, France, 1945-52. Photo by Ezra Stoller

extensive squatter settlement to find many principles applicable to modern planning and architecture.[36] The flexibility (and "organic" nature) of the street systems designed by the Smithsons for Hauptstadt Berlin (1958), for example, echoed vernacular patterns, with their elevated placement of pedestrian walkways owing something to the model offered by the casbah. Others who deviated from the rigidity of CIAM's urban-design principles referred to the same models in different ways. Yona Friedman's "mobile architecture" (1959) proposed a flexible arrangement of demountable rectilinear units inserted above ground into a multideck space frame; their clustering strongly recalled the familiar image of the casbah. George Candilis, Alexis Josic, and Shadrach Woods used methodologies and forms learned from North African urban fabrics. They argued, for example, that the cellular scheme they developed for the 1955 "Nid d'Abeille" housing project in Oran (Algeria) allowed for a "more or less new, more or less ingenious plastic arrangement"; in a 1956 scheme for Bagnole-sur-Cèze (France), they maintained a "systematic (additive)" movement from "cell to *plan masse*." They thus understood that North African vernacular house forms and urban patterns had the capacity to absorb cultural differences because of their flexibility, modifiability, and appropriability.[37]

Postcard in the personal collection of Le Corbusier. Fondation Le Corbusier, Paris

The image of the casbah reemerges in many different contexts. Giancarlo de Carlo's student residences at the University of Urbino (1962-66) resemble a small city nestled against the hillside in a fanlike, dense configuration composed of crisp, orthogonal units attached to each other; the communal facilities gathered on the highest point seem almost like a castle dominating the city — another reference to the casbah of Algiers.[38] His Mateotti village in Terni (1974-77), a low-cost housing development outside Rome, is a dense conglomeration of cubical units with narrow passageways and ample roof terraces. The Dutch architect Herman Hertzberger's Centraal Beheer insurance offices reiterate the casbah both inside and outside. His square-planned work platforms (small standardized units) are arranged irregularly within a rectilinear structural grid, creating a labyrinthine interior landscape complete with level changes and tortuous alleyways. The exterior massing that seems incrementally grown reflects the interior organization, and the useable rooftop terraces create a "continuous roof" over the building complex. But it is Moshe Safdie's Habitat at Expo '67 in Montréal that perhaps evokes the strongest reference to the casbah; its prefabricated blocks superimposed in a dynamic configuration and its spacious decks turn the building itself into a "hill," as though composed of additive units.

[36] Groupe CIAM Alger presented an extensive study on a squatter settlement in Algiers, the *bidonville* Mahieddine, drawing many lessons from this spontaneous development for modern planning and architecture.

[37] Bernard Huet, "G. Candilis, A. Josic, S. Woods: Le Marriage de la casbah et du meccano," *L'Architecture d'aujourd'hui* 177 (1975): 44-45.

[38] The inspirations for this configuration are many. However, the image of the Algerian casbah, with its triangular fanlike pattern and its castle that crowns the top of the hill, is a powerful reference.

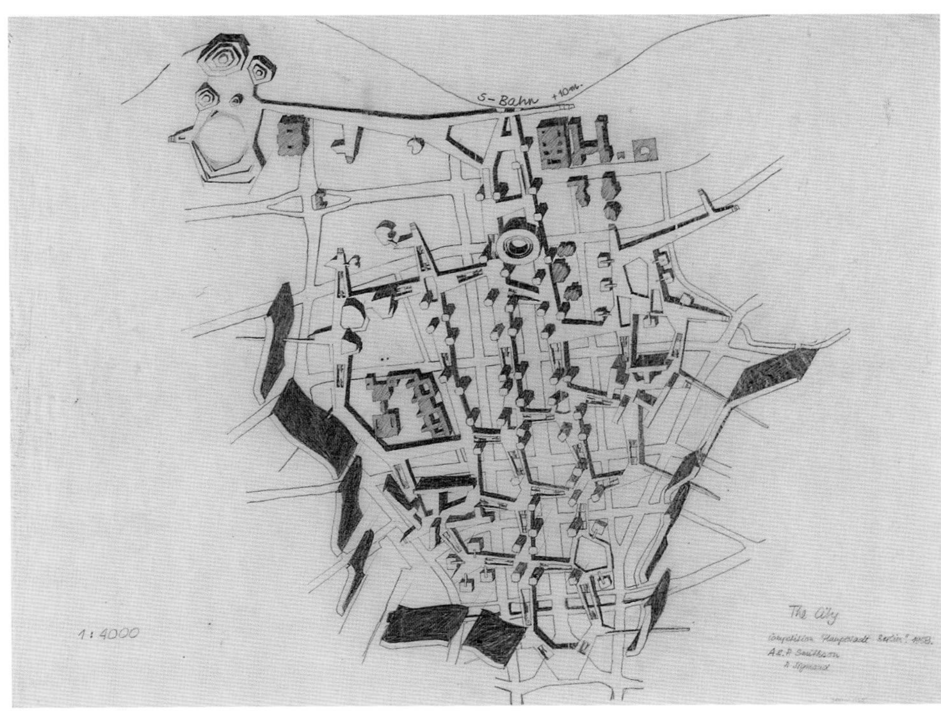

Alison and Peter Smithson, "The City." Sketch of Hauptstadt Berlin plan, 1958. Deutsches Architektur-Museum Archiv, Frankfurt

George Candilis, Alexis Josie, and Shadrach Woods, Nid d'Abeille, Oran, Algeria, 1955. Photo courtesy of Centre Georges Pompidou, Paris

Herman Hertzberger, view into light well, Centraal Beheer Insurance Building, Apeldoorn, The Netherlands, 1972. Photo by Willem Diepraam

Herman Hertzberger, Centraal Beheer Insurance Building, Apeldoorn, The Netherlands, 1972

Moshe Safdie, Habitat at Expo '67, Montréal, 1967.
Photo by Jerry Spearman

Modernism and the New Capitals

While one group of modernist architects was finding inspiration in "non-Western" vernacular forms, modern architecture in its purest "Western" manifestation was being adopted by many "developing" countries because of its symbolic significance: its association with technological advancement and contemporary civilization. This is perhaps most clearly expressed in the creation of new capital cities. The earliest modernist example of a brand-new showcase is Ankara, made the capital of the Republic of Turkey in 1923. The Turkish Republic, declaring a radical departure from the Ottoman Empire upon whose ashes it was built, undertook a series of reforms aimed to bring the country to the level of technological and cultural development achieved in the Western world. These reforms, qualified by one historian as "Westernizing despite the West," extended to urbanism and architecture.[39] With a goal defined as the creation of a "civilized and healthy" city in the "Western style," Ankara's design was entrusted to German planners early in the process, and the master plan drawn in 1927 by Herman Jansen of Berlin was

Christopher Williams. *Super Quadra Sul 308 Bloco 'D' Asa Sul (South wing) 70. 355 BRASILIA-DF. Lucio Costa, Oscar Niemeyer, 1960. January 31, 1997 (Nr.1).* Museum Boymans-van Beuningen, Rotterdam.

put into effect despite pressing economic problems faced by the new state.[40] The image sought for Ankara, with its location in the center of the country carrying symbolic and practical significance, was deliberately very different from that of Istanbul, the capital of the Ottoman Empire for almost five centuries. Istanbul's impressive monumental complexes, strategically situated on the hills of the city and complementing them with their domes and minarets, expressed the image of a once-powerful empire still imbued with religious values in the early twentieth century. In

[39] Tarik Zafer Tunaya, "Devrim Hareketi Içinde Atatürk ve Atatürkçülük," *Siyaset Ilmi Serisi* (Istanbul) 14 (1964): 122, quoted in Inci Aslanoğlu, *Erken Cumhuriyet Dönemi Mimarli˘gi* (Ankara: ODTÜ Mimarlik Fakültesi, 1980), 8-9. Tunaya used this phrase to underline the dilemmas of the reformers who passionately believed in the model set by Western powers, despite the fact that the declaration of the new Turkish state was met with hostility by European powers who wanted to establish exclusive control over the Ottoman Empire defeated in World War I.

[40] Aslanoğlu, *Erken Cumhuriyet Dönemi Mimarli˘gi*, 12.

contrast, Ankara's monumentality would be defined by government, administrative, and educational buildings designed in a rational formalism, representing the essence and dynamism of the young and secular republic and its desperate longing to belong to the modern world.

Similar disassociations from the past surfaced frequently in the design of other capital cities, though much later than in Ankara. Brasilia, designed by Lucia Costa and Oscar Niemeyer in the late 1950s and early 1960s, was situated in the heart of Brazil in response to a desire to integrate the country geopolitically;[41] the city plan also corresponded to the modernization reforms undertaken during the same period under the democratic government of Juscelino Kubitschek. The plan was a grand gesture very much inspired by Le Corbusier's theoretical schemes and the practical dictums of numerous CIAM charters. What mattered was the construction of an image of modernity with large blocks and vast open spaces, with each zone clearly delineated according to function — at the expense of public space.[42] Costa and Niemeyer thus turned away from the historic precedents of Latin urbanism, which organized the life of a city around a central plaza and provided for the needs of the individual as well as social interaction within the urban public spaces. Yet, despite all its shortcomings, the city embodied the hopes of many Brazilians and "in particular, their desire for modernity."[43]

Christopher Williams. *Super Quadra Sul 308 Bloco 'D' Asa Sul (South wing) 70. 355 BRASILIA-DF. Lucio Costa, Oscar Niemeyer, 1960. January 31, 1997 (Nr. 2).* Museum Boymans-van Beuningen, Rotterdam.

This longing for modernity accounts largely for the forms and images of numerous new capitals built for nations that have gained their indepen-

41 Ankara was also chosen to be the capital due to its location in the geographical center of Anatolia.

42 For critical evaluations of Brasilia, see: David G. Epstein, *Brasilia, Plan and Reality: A Study of Planned and Spontaneous Urban Development* (Berkeley and Los Angeles: University of California Press, 1973); Norma Evenson, "Brasilia: 'Yesterday's City of Tomorrow,'" in *World Capitals: Toward Guided Urbanization*, ed. H. Wenthworth Eldredge (Garden City, N.Y.: Anchor Press, 1975); and James Holston, *The Modernist City: An Anthropological Critique of Brasilia* (Chicago: University of Chicago Press, 1989).

43 Berman, *All that Is Solid Melts into Air*, 7.

dence since the 1960s. Islamabad, the capital of Pakistan designed by Doxiadis Associates in the early 1960s, embodied, according to its military ruler General Ayub Khan, "the sum total of the aspirations, the life and the ambitions of the people of the whole of Pakistan."[44] Intended by Doxiadis as a "dynapolis" — a dynamic city with its own impetus of growth provided by a master plan — Islamabad was organized in a rectilinear pattern along a central axis, a ceremonial avenue that culminated at the government complex; the buildings that filled the grid further enhanced the image of modernity. Another example is Abuja, planned in 1975 as Nigeria's new capital. Its geographical location in the center of the country was in accord with another official attempt to unite heretofore disconnected regions physically (by means of an extensive transportation network) and symbolically (by implying peace and harmony among the numerous tribes). Abuja's master plan, prepared by Kenzo Tange, also has a predominant axis with an impressively scaled "mall" that centers on the parliament. The plan may be reminiscent of the City Beautiful plans of the turn of the century, but the imagery is that of the space age defined by impressive frame structures filled in with modular components. Despite the designers' insistence on the "indigenous" roots of their inspiration (based on their study of many Nigerian cities), the scheme projects the aesthetics of a late twentieth-century modernity. Perhaps it was the future-oriented (yet ambivalent) quality of this image that made the project symbolically appropriate to surpass the many schisms in the country.

In these master plans the governmental buildings are situated at the vistas of the principal axes; they dominate the city as visual reflections of the all-mighty state and its control mechanisms. They hence follow in the footsteps of colonial urban designs that also mapped a hierarchical order. However, such schematic metaphors evince conflicts regarding the essence of modernism. In modern regimes, power is not centralized; disciplinary practices are broken into small mechanisms that are disseminated in a different pattern than that of a centralized, singular political authority with its institutions radiating power.[45] Therefore, the contemporary and modern façades of the new capitals are about appearance and aspirations; consideration of their urban design principles exposes other realities.

Even more complex is the choice of Ralph Lerner's project for the Indira Gandhi National Center for Arts in New Delhi. The 1987 competition for the center outlined a complicated and extensive program for a compound to be built on the Central Vista green in the administrative core of New Delhi. The framework was Lutyens's imperial design; the project was to complete it, but the nature of the completion was not obvious. How would a building complex intended to promote all aspects of Indian culture fit into an urban design scheme that represented the colonial past of India? The controversy was voiced by certain critics who challenged the appropriateness of an international competition for a center devoted to Indian art and who argued that it should be open only to Indian architects. However, Prime Minister Rajiv Gandhi insisted and, referring to Mahatma Gandhi's statement about artistic boundaries not being restricted by national boundaries, he accused the critics of myopia.[46]

Lerner, an American architect and an outsider to Indian culture, followed a formalistic approach and almost innocently overlooked India's recent history and the memory of the colonial period. While he explained his project as inspired by Hindu, Moghul, and classical architecture and as a synthesis of the two traditions of planning in New Delhi — the monumental and axial planing of Lutyens

[44] Ayub Khan, quoted in Glenn Stephenson, "Two Newly-Created Capitals: Islamabad and Brasilia," *Town Planning Review* 41 (October 1970): 323. For new capitals, also see Lawrence J. Vale, *Architecture, Power, and National Identity* (New Haven, Conn., and London: Yale University Press, 1992), 128-62.

[45] Partha Chatterjee, "The Disciplines in Colonial Bengal" in *Texts of Power: Emerging Disciplines in Colonial Bengal*, ed. Partha Chattarjee (Minneapolis and London: University of Minnesota Press, 1995), 23.

[46] *Architectural Record* 175, no. 3 (March 1987): 62.

[47] For Lerner's explanation of the project, see J. P. Partenaires, "Concours international pour le Centre National d'Arts Indira Gandhi," *L'Architecture d'aujourd'hui*, no. 249 (February 1987): vi.

[48] Ibid., iv.

Oscar Niemeyer, Congress complex, Brasilia, 1958. Photo by Julius Shulman

and the treatment of the city as an extensive garden[47] — the project largely reflects Lutyens's design and adheres to it both on urban-design principles and architectural style. The references to the local heritage are very much in accord with Lutyens's own incorporation of the "Indian" styles into his classical architecture, thereby making Lerner's addition a continuation of the imperial style — with perhaps a touch of the "western fashions and stylistic preoccupation" of the 1980s.[48] In this case, then, unlike those of the other capitals discussed above, it is not the apparent modernity of the proposal that appealed to the jury, but rather its straightforward continuity with colonial monumentality.

In contrast to Lerner's scheme, the second-prize winner, Indian architect Gautam Bhatia, opted for an oppositional design that answered back to Lutyens's open and ceremonial vistas, to his architectural rendering of power

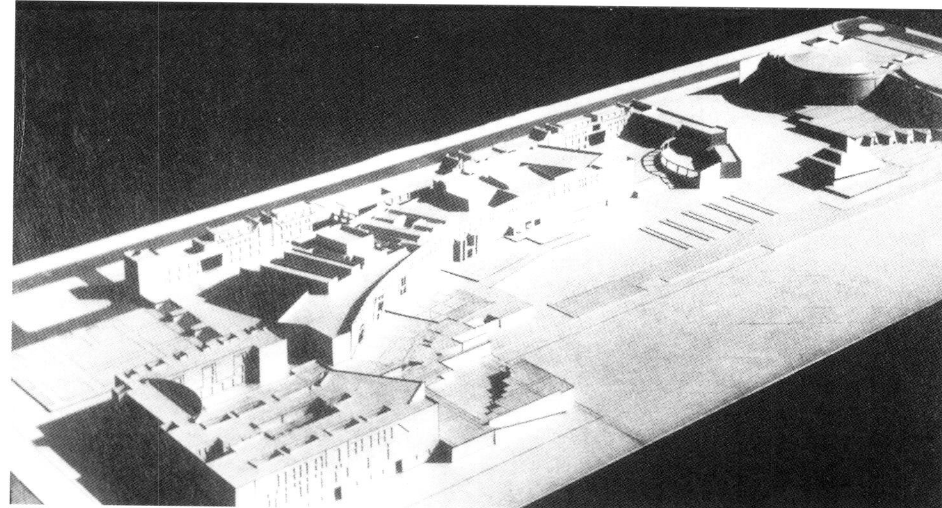

Gautam Bhatia, model for the Indira Gandhi National Center for Arts

relationships and hierarchies. Bhatia proposed an asymmetrical *parti* for the organization of the site, a metaphor that saw "Rajpath [the main avenue that the site faces] as a river, with the city taking the form of a journey along the river." He pursued the symbolism by developing the project as a "ghat" (a bathing place by a river, an important component of Indian life and religion) that faced onto the "Rajpath River."[49] Anchoring himself in the historic heritage of India and following the standards set by the sophisticated and by now truly mature experiments of Indian architects, he proposed an architecture that turned inward, that compartmentalized the program into smaller units, and that privileged modesty over monumentality.[50] At the same time, with this intervention he disrupted the order imposed on the city by Lutyens.

The unanimous choice of Lerner's scheme over Bhatia's opens up a web of questions related to end-of-the-century issues of cultural identity as represented through architecture.[51] Is the colonial past so overwhelming that it imposes a

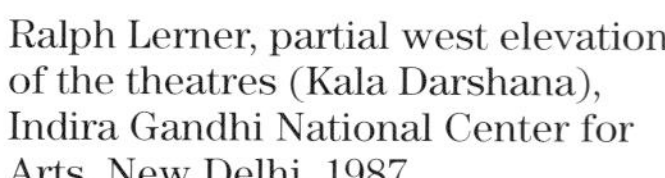

Ralph Lerner, partial west elevation of the theatres (Kala Darshana), Indira Gandhi National Center for Arts, New Delhi, 1987

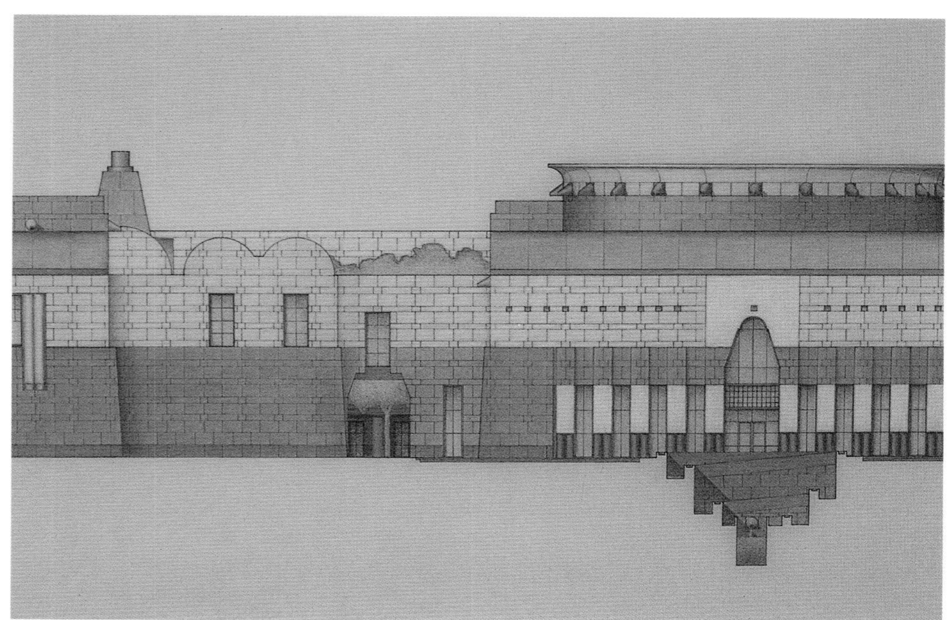

continuity on its cultural and artistic products? Do the forms of this past overshadow those of modernism, with its potential for neutrality and its future-oriented symbolism? Or can it be argued that four decades after independence, cultural products of colonialism can be forcefully appropriated into the rich and multilayered history of contemporary India and that they can be reshaped to reflect its new image? Is there a charged reciprocity between Lutyens's appropriation of Indian motifs and the preference for a scheme that reappropriated Lutyens's forms? Is this another way of talking back and metaphorically claiming the power that previously belonged to the colonizer?

First and Third Worlds at the End of the Century

While spatial globalization dominates the world at the end of the century, its slippery fragmentation and chaos defy clear definitions, categorizations, and boundaries. In the words of Arif Dirlik,

> Third Worlds have appeared in the First World and First Worlds in the Third. New diasporas have relocated the Self there and the Other here, and consequently borders and boundaries have been confounded. And the flow of culture has been at once homogenizing and heterogenizing; some groups share in a common global culture regardless of localization even as they are alienated from the culture of their hinterlands while others are driven back into cultural legacies long thought to be residual to take refuge in cultural havens that are as far apart from one another as they were at the origins of modernity — even though they may be watching the same TV shows.[52]

Therefore, in urban centers as diverse as Paris, Berlin, Los Angeles, New York, Istanbul, Cairo, Lagos, and Singapore, the "first" and the "third" worlds coexist, with the seeming contradictions redefining the essence of urban culture and disturbing the notions of identity and belonging. There are, nevertheless, historic differences between "third"-world cities with their "first"-world enclaves and "first"-world cities with their "third"-world enclaves. The "contamination" of the first world happened only recently, whereas it has been going on for quite some time in the third.

In the nineteenth century, colonialism caused ruptures in colonized cities, whereas other "non-Western" centers (such as Istanbul and Cairo) were submitted to similar transformation and fragmentation by their own administrative cadres who followed European norms to "modernize." Therefore, despite their dramatic scope, the enclaves of the "first" world in "third"-world cities have not been culturally as traumatic as the transformations to the cities of the "first" world during the last decades of the twentieth century. While slick skyscrapers — corporate headquarters that replicate their counterparts anywhere else in the world — dot the hills of Istanbul, to take one example, the city has a history of absorbing "modern" insertions since the earlier part of the last century. Sociocultural norms and daily life patterns, too, share a past of fracturing that led to the coexistence of seemingly contradictory worlds. Chanel and Max Mara boutiques — with their distinct windows and select clientele that transform the previous patterns of daily life on these streets — are not exotic novelties in the urban fabric, for they follow the course set by nineteenth-century stores such as Maison Baker, Paris-Londres, and Bon Marché, thus alluding to the continuity of the economic power structure. In

[49] Ibid., vi.

[50] The list of Indian architects who synthesized local and historic forms with modern principles in most impressive experiments is long. Among the best known are Balkrishna Doshi, Charles Correa, and Raj Rewal.

[51] Obviously, the make-up of the jury had a great deal to do with the choice. Nevertheless, I suspect that because the issues were so important, so obvious, and so publicized, personal preferences may have been left in the background. The jury consisted of James Stirling (U.K.), Fumihiko Maki (Japan), Olufemi Majekodunmi (Nigeria), A. P. Kavinde (India), B. Doshi (India), Srimati Pupul Jayakar (India), and Kapila Vatsyayan (India).

[52] Arif Dirlik, "The Postcolonial Aura: Third World Criticism in the Age of Global Capitalism," *Critical Inquiry* 20, no. 2 (Winter 1994): 352-53.

this context, then, the coexistence of the "first" and "third" worlds is not a new phenomenon, but is permeated with its own past.

"Western" cities have been more profoundly affected by recent changes, coming to terms with the consequences of the colonial era as national identities are challenged and reformulated. Analyzing the transformations brought to French culture by its sizable immigrant population, Michel de Certeau sees immigrants as "pioneers of a civilization founded on the mixing of cultures" and elaborates on their role to redefine familiar landmarks and enforce new codes. Operating within "systems of translations," not only do immigrants adapt to their settings, but they also transform them according to their own needs and goals.[53] These transformations are profound, because the public realm is defined not only by its formal and architectural attributes, but also by the manner in which it is used; by the patterns of movement, the sounds (languages, music), the smells, and the signs that pervade it with life. A back street in the Belleville quarter of northeastern Paris, for example, has not been physically altered, but its "image" undergoes a major transformation when an Algerian wedding ceremony occupies it, as the male members of the party crowd onto the street and the chanting of the women emanates from the windows of a nondescript nineteenth-century apartment building. In addition to engraving a new referential layer onto Parisian public space by the customs and rituals of an immigrant culture, this sociocultural pattern also shifts its customary use by overlaying it with a gender-defined one. Urban life thus becomes an "urban frontier," reformulating the public space with new rites and behavior.[54]

Uniformity or Hypercomplexity?

The universalization that dominates urban centers in the twentieth century marks the end of an era: local and "pure" cultural identities as the evocation of difference by the juxtaposition of cultures now gives way to a dispersed heterogeneity. Borders, fragments, cultures, and hybrids interpenetrate and redefine the urban space everywhere. However, as Henri Lefebvre points out in his analysis of "social space," this is not a simple juxtaposition that leads to the disappearance of the "local" space: "the worldwide does not abolish the local." The combinations, superpositions, and even collisions in question do not lead to the absorption of the local, but to the creation of "innumerable places" within the urban space, resulting in a hypercomplexity that is crisscrossed by a myriad of currents. The analysis of urban space thus becomes further complicated as a result of such interpenetrations and superpositions that subject each fragment to a host of social relationships.[55]

A much-publicized building complex is already acknowledged as a signifier of end-of-the-century architecture. The Petronas Twin Towers in Kuala Lumpur, Malaysia (1997), present a curious and extreme case study and help to reveal the multiplicity of forces that lead to a hypercomplexity, with the local and the universal interpenetrating in a most visible (if reductive) formula. Designed by Cesar Pelli and Associates for the headquarters of the Petroliam Nasional Berhad (Petronas), the eighty-eight-story towers have been hailed as the world's tallest skyscrapers. They were commissioned with a clear agenda to make a worldwide statement about Malaysia's goal to become a fully industrialized nation by the year 2020 according to Prime Minister Mahathir Mohamad's economic program, "Vision 2020."

53 Michel de Certeau, "Idéologie et diversité culturelle," in *Actes du colloque: diversité culturelle, société industrielle, état national* (Paris: Editions L'Harmattan, 1984), 132. See also Winifred Woodhull, "Exile," *Yale French Studies* 82 (1993): 11. The translation of the quotation is Woodhull's.

54 Barbara Kirshenblatt-Gimblett, "The Future of Folklore Studies in America: The Urban Frontier," *Folklore Forum* 16 (1983): 180.

55 Henri Lefebvre, *The Production of Space*, trans. Donald Nicholson-Smith [Oxford, U.K., and Cambridge, Mass.: Blackwell, 1991 (French ed. 1974)], 86-88.

Cesar Pelli and Associates, Petronas Twin Towers near completion, Kuala Lumpur, Malaysia, 1997. Photo by J. Apicella

The towers utilize a complicated technology: the vertical loads are supported by a central concrete core and concrete columns on the periphery; the semicircular and triangular floor extensions that cantilever beyond the perimeter columns are carried by prefabricated steel trusses; and a two-story steel skybridge joins the two towers. The technological sophistication is reflected on the exterior: the towers are completely clad with horizontal rows of glass and stainless steel.[56] Yet a technological statement was not sufficient for the image sought for twenty-first-century Malaysia. As emphasized by the administrative cadres of Petronas, the architecture had to be "Malaysian." In the words of Cesar Pelli, "The new towers should not look as if they could have been built in America or Europe, but as somehow belonging to Malaysia. The most important objective, therefore, was to design towers with their own character, belonging to the place."[57]

Two "Malaysian" sources — one Buddhist, the other Islamic — inspired the design. The tapered and faceted outline of the towers was derived from Kek Lok Si, the country's (and Southeast Asia's) largest Buddhist temple, hence a most obvious local monument. Pelli also equated "Malaysian" with what he called "Islamic geometric traditions," thus lumping the entire world of Islam and its long history into the prosaic formula that geometric patterns are much more important in "Islamic countries" than in the West and that "they are perceived and appreciated by everyone in their society." Arguing that he and his team worked hard not to create a "cultural pastiche," Pelli maintained the resulting design responded to "the sense of form and patterning that I could perceive in traditional Malaysian buildings and objects." Utilizing what the architects identified as the most important geometric forms underlying "Islamic designs," the architectural *parti* became two interlocking squares that were rotated in horizontal levels and filled in with small circular elements. The "Islamic" nature of the building was underlined further by characteristic "colors, patterns, traditions, and crafts"; the geometric patterns of the lobby floors, the wooden screens on the lobby windows accentuated, according to one report, "the complex's imaginatively Malaysian character."[58] Furthermore, a flavor of Chinese culture was interjected by a steel skybridge inspired by Chinese philosopher Lao Tse, who, Pelli claims, "taught us that the reality of a hollow object is in the void and not in the walls that define it." The rationale for the placement of a conference room, executive dining room, and mosque in this "portal to the sky" remains obscure.[59]

The corporate image presented by the Petronas Twin Towers is in accord with the customary representation of a transnational business and thus reflects its prominent position in the world market. At the same time, the emphasis put on technology expresses the construction of a national image and makes a statement about the level of development and modernity aimed by the government; it recalls the modernist imagery sought after in the building of new capitals. Nevertheless, a sense of locality (which is another level of belonging) is also required by the clients. In today's configuration of power and culture this does not conflict with the mentality of transnational corporations that function in a "color-blind" manner, seamlessly reducing notions of difference to a simple kit of selected symbols — in the case of the Petronas towers, a tapered silhouette and geometric patterns.

The choice of the architect for the towers indicates the continuing authority of the technically advanced Western world. As a senior architect at Cesar Pelli and Associates puts it with self-confidence, tall buildings are considered the specialty of large American firms that have developed a reputation to "design them

[56] The structure is designed by the Thornton-Tomasetti Engineers of New York City, in collaboration with the Malaysian engineering firm of Ranhill Bersekutu. For a technical exposé, see *Architecture* 85, no. 9 (September 1996): 160-61.

[57] Quoted in "A Monumental Achievement for Malaysia: Petronas Towers, 'The Tallest of 'em all'," *Islamic Horizons* (July-August 1996): 22.

[58] Philip Langdon, "Asia Bound," *Progressive Architecture* 76, no. 3 (March 1995): 47.

[59] "A Monumental Achievement for Malaysia: Petronas Towers," 22.

[60] Langdon, "Asia Bound," 45.

[61] Larry Self, chief operating officer and executive director of European and Middle Eastern operations, HOK, St. Louis, Missouri, "The Impact of the Mega Firm," presented at the *Progressive Architecture* forum "New Directions in Architectural Practice," Washington, D.C., 23 September 1995.

[62] Arjun Appadurai, *Modernity at Large*, (Minneapolis and London: University of Minnesota Press, 1996) (especially the chapter titled "Here and Now," 1-23).

Catherine Opie, *Untitled #4*, 1997, from the Mini-malls series. The Museum of Contemporary Art, Los Angeles. Purchased with funds provided by The Citibank Private Bank Emerging Artist Award, 1997

efficiently and with an artistic intention." Another American architect who works in China adds that "in China, it is assumed that if you're an American firm, you're qualified to do all kinds of work."[60]

This reputation provides American architects with opportunities not available in the United States during the last decade of the twentieth century and invests them with a great deal of authority and power to give architectural and aesthetic expression to cultural and national identities elsewhere — a pattern reminiscent of the colonial era. Like colonial architects, but often with less patience to study the culture and architecture of the place they are designing for ("time is money"), they rely on stereotypical and quick formulas about cultures and architectural forms unfamiliar to them and use them to adorn corporate high-technology structures.

Colonial structures thus survive (albeit in renewed forms), and the superordinates and the subordinates remain unchanged even if building activity has shifted to the East. The global organization of the profession reflects this condition. Recent computer technologies have totally transformed the professional scene, giving much greater fluidity to architectural ideas and their efficient dissemination — and contributing further to the inequity between the "developed" and the "developing" worlds. Consider the recent scheme by a major American firm, Hellmuth, Obata & Kassabaum (HOK), to establish a centralized production office in India for all their East Asian operations, with the ability to keep the workshops open for twenty-four hours (in shifts) to handle the office's European work as well. At a forum organized by *Progressive Architecture*, a spokesman for HOK presented the plan diplomatically, emphasizing the office's high regard for the training of architects in India, while leaving out another primary factor in the decision: salary levels.[61]

In summary, the end of the century is marked by a break with the past. Highly affected by new developments in media and the recent patterns of displacement, the notions of national space and identity are ruptured and modernity is re-written by a globalization that is vernacular. Nevertheless, the divide with the past is not absolute and globalization is not equal to homogenization.[62] The continuity manifests itself in several realms. The former power relationships still survive, although their centralized mechanisms are now dispersed and sometimes even intangible. Large American architectural firms thus dominate the international construction market and furthermore, empowered with new technologies, can employ “third world” architects on low salaries. The search for cultural identity continues as well. In some instances, it is absorbed by the globalized market structure — as in the case of the Petronas Towers; in others, it redefines space and urban image by appropriation and hybridity — as in the transformation of Paris by its new immigrant populations.

The Institut du Monde Arabe (1987), one of the most celebrated buildings of the late twentieth century, stands in its prominent location in Paris as the embodiment of the leading themes in cultural intersections today, as well as their links to the past. Rightly considered one of the highlights of the recent Parisian *grands projets*, Jean Nouvel’s design has been hailed by critics as a particularly sensitive response to the site, context, materials, and modernism at large. The Insitut du Monde Arabe is also an intriguing visual symbol of Islam in the heart of Europe. The building’s main concept is duality: its modern facade overlooking the Seine is juxtaposed with its back that represents Arab culture by means of stylized *mushrabiyyas*. The front and the back are separated from each other by a narrow, dead-end “street” that ends up in a courtyard — in obvious reference to two spatial “signs” that defined Islam to the West for a long time. Nevertheless, all visual references to Arab culture are appropriated by a powerfully expressed high technology which corrects and incorporates them into the architectural repertory of the late twentieth century, while underlining their otherness.

The Institut du Monde Arabe’s global and corporate imagery absorbs and tames cultural difference, but maintains much of the past associations, thereby calling for further reflection on Miyoshi’s argument that this is “an age of . . . intensified colonialism, even though it is under an unfamiliar guise.”[63]

[63] Miyoshi, “From Colonialism to Transnationalism,” 720.

Jean Nouvel, interior view of the Institut du Monde Arabe, Paris, 1987. Photo by Scott Frances

Hugh Ferriss, *Chicago Tribune Tower, 1930*. Avery Architectural and Fine Arts Library, Columbia University, New York. Architects Raymond Hood and John Mead Howells, 1923-25

URBAN ARCHITECTURE AND THE CRISIS OF THE MODERN METROPOLIS

Jean-Louis Cohen

Urban space has served throughout the twentieth century not only as horizon, or backdrop, but as raw material for the theory and practice of architecture. The city has thus, in accordance with its changing forms, conditioned both the *logos* and the *praxis* of architects. Principal theater of transformations in the culture of architecture, confronted by brutal changes and the decline of old neighborhoods, the city has offered a field of observation and theoretical reflection to architects, while at the same time resiliently opposing their transformative projects. The articles and books that make up the theoretical corpus of contemporary architecture have constructed a dense discursive space to account for the continuities and transformations of the city. Otto Wagner, Raymond Unwin, Le Corbusier, Eliel Saarinen, Ludwig Hilberseimer, Robert Venturi, Aldo Rossi, Rem Koolhaas, and many others have founded their professional strategies on the observation of urban transformations.

If one considers the totality of this critical production, it seems difficult today to summarize twentieth-century debate as only between the supporters of a continuing pre-industrial or Haussmannized city and those of the "functional" city, for whom the dogmas of the *Congrès internationaux d'architecture moderne* (CIAM) can be taken as emblematic.[1] It is equally necessary to remember, despite over-simplified assumptions, that the history of cities and the urban projects of architects do not advance at a regular and synchronized pace across the century. On the contrary, the specificities of each national scene are offset and tangled, rendering illusory all attempts to account for the "progress" of modern urbanism, and complicating any all-embracing historical project.[2]

The exigencies of the times imposed rigorous frameworks upon the most radical projects of the twentieth century. The nineteenth century's campaigns of modernization, on the other hand, continued almost uninterrupted until 1940.[3] The widening of streets that began in the European urban centers in 1848 continued long past World War I, while the principles of regulation of peripheral growth, developed since 1875, were not critically examined until the 1930s. However, it is hazardous to stretch the cycle of Haussmannian processes until 1950, as some have suggested.[4] The figures of modern urban architecture have evolved within a constant dialectic between the long duration of urban projects and an ever-changing set of conceptual inductions.

1 Among more recent discourse, see Olivier Mongin, *Vers la troisième ville* (Paris: Hachette, 1995).

2 Among the most notable of these attempts: Leonardo Benevolo, *History of Modern Architecture*, trans. H.J. Landry (Cambridge, Mass.: MIT Press, 1966), and Paolo Sica, *Storia dell'urbanistica* (Rome: Laterza, 1978). For a more recent argument, see Benedetto Gravagnuolo, *La progettazione urbana in Europa, 1750 - 1960: storia e teorie* (Rome: Laterza, 1991).

3 On the nineteenth century, see Walter Kiess, *Urbanismus im Industriezeitalter: von der Klassizistischen Stadt zur Garden City* (Berlin: Ernst & Sohn, 1991).

4 On the extended "Haussmannian cycle," see Maurice Agulhon, *La ville de l'age industriel*, t. 4 of *Histoire de la France urbaine*, ed. Georges Duby (Paris: Seuil, 1984).

The Mastering of Density

The first question that reformers and designers have to face in a century characterized by unprecedented urban growth is the control of urban areas. Far from being an issue of politics, economy, and land regulation, the establishment of a balance between built space and natural (open) space has been a primary concern of architects since the end of the nineteenth century. The control of the edges of the city, from the beginning a crucial question for the proponents of garden cities, has since become a theme of major projects, inspiring the most contradictory theories.

Control of metropolitan congestion, specifically in central districts, also became a fundamental goal of planners in New York, Berlin, and Paris at the beginning of the twentieth century. This game between growth regulation and the shaping of a density that asserts itself as an uncontrollable phenomenon involved opposing principles whose concrete manifestations were often far removed from their point of conception. In fact, the circulation of ideas and forms was almost immediate, as frequent contacts between professional organizations and publications allowed for rapid exchanges.[5]

The twentieth century has been characterized, then, by unprecedented urban growth and by the creation of a network of cities expanding beyond national borders to conquer entire continents. In general, architects have sidestepped the new techniques employed by city planners, despite their recurrent efforts in each generation to claim the territory. Projects for remodeling urban

Otto Wagner, Project for Karlsplatz, Vienna, 1909. Museen der Stadt Wien

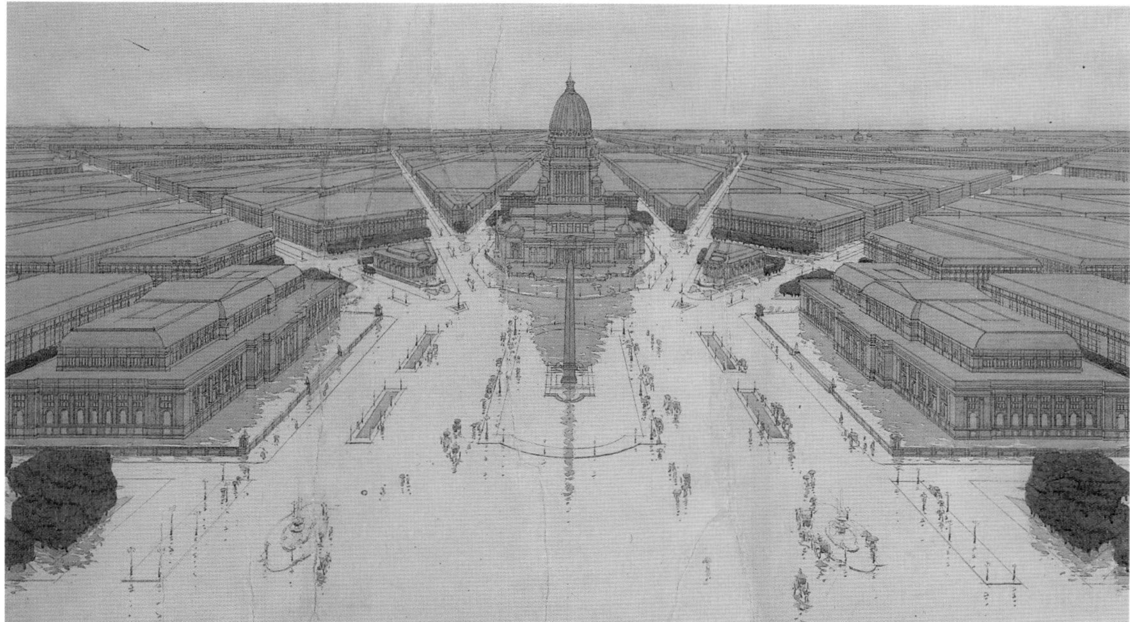

Daniel H. Burnham and Edward H. Bennett, Chicago, Illinois, partnership 1903-1912, Chicago. View, Looking West of the Proposed Civic Center Plaza, plate 132 from Plan of Chicago, 1909, delineated by Jules Guérin (American, 1866-1946). On permanent loan to The Art Institute of Chicago from the City of Chicago, 28.148.1966

centers and for accommodating urban growth were prevalent in the years before World War II, as evidenced by the multiplication of large city plans intended to impress the public as well as to address urban problems.

Several master plans designed at that time suggest a continuous and dense expansion of large cities that no human nor natural boundary seemed able to stop. This is the case in Otto Wagner's 1911 project, which intended to transform Vienna into a *unbegrentze Groszstadt*, a "metropolis without limits," whose monotonous and systematic grid seems to expand without effort to the borders of the Austro-Hungarian monarchy.[6] More complex is the 1909 proposal by Daniel Burnham and Edward Bennett (informed by an undeniable sense of advertising) for the reorganization of Chicago. It entailed both the monumental redesign of the center (to increase a sense of urban identity) and a new network of ring roads and parkways, the whole requiring the irrigation of the prairie far beyond the existing city at that time.[7]

The idea of the garden city, formulated in 1898, which derives from the observation by Ebenezer Howard of "this *Urbs in horto* that is Chicago," led to the elaboration of an alternative to the continuous city, the extraordinary semantic success of which illustrates its historical pertinency.[8] Within a decade, all the great Western countries and Russia were diffusing Howard's doctrine, and the first practical experiments were undertaken. Raymond Unwin and Barry Parker built the garden suburb of Hampstead and the garden city of Letchworth, north of London. The squares and angular streets of these complexes are the result of a hybrid between picturesque composition inspired by Camillo Sitte's book *Der Städtebau nach seinen künstlerischen Grundsätzen* and by the vernacular architecture of England and Normandy.[9] The issues of American "new urbanism" of the 1980s are derived directly from these tendencies.[10]

The experimental and reforming dimension of the garden city, more restrained in American projects due to employers' initiatives in the case of

5 On the urbanism movement, see the comparative study by Anthony Sutcliffe, *Towards the Planned City: Germany, Britain, the United States, and France 1780 - 1914* (Oxford, U.K.: Blackwell, 1981).

6 Otto Wagner, *Die Groszstadt, eine Studie über diese* (Vienna: A. Schroll, 1911). The project was published in *The Architectural Record* of 1912; cf. "The Development of a Great City," *Oppositions*, no. 17 (Summer 1979): 99-116.

7 Daniel H. Burnham and Edward H. Bennett, *Plan of Chicago*, ed. Charles Moore (1909; reprint, New York: Princeton Architectural Press, 1993).

8 The manifesto of the garden-city movement is Ebenezer Howard's *To-morrow: A Peaceful Path to Real Reform* (London: S. Sonnenschein, 1898). On Howard, see Robert Beevers, *The Garden City Utopia: A Critical Biography of Ebenezer Howard* (New York: St. Martin's Press, 1988). On the fate of the garden-city principle, see Stephen Ward, ed., *The Garden City: Past, Present, and Future* (London/New York: E & FN Spon, 1992).

9 Raymond Unwin, *Town Planning in Practice* (London: George Allen & Unwin), 1909.

10 Andres Duany and Elizabeth Plater-Zyberk, *Towns and Town-Making Principles*, ed. Alex Krieger (New York: Rizzoli, 1991).

Ridge Avenue, Letchworth, England, c. 1912. First Garden City Heritage Museum

Aurora, and due to philanthropy in the case of Forest Hills Gardens, was primary in German housing complexes such as Stockfeld in Strasbourg and especially the Dresden-Hellerau project.[11] In the master plan of Richard Riemerschmid, the houses and the *Festhaus* of Heinrich Tessenow were directed at the reform of the individual as much as the city.[12] In France, the Paris-Jardins development, built in Draveil in 1911 by Jean Walter, was much more prosaic in its goals and strictly limited to the welfare of the members of the founding cooperative. In Russia, the City-gardens Society originated several projects, one of which, the Prozorovskoe suburb, was on the Moscow-Kazan railway (1912); in Helsinki, Eliel Saarinen's 1918 master plan combined a large use of garden-cities with a monumental redefinition of the center.

As early as 1915, the concept of the garden-city reached a major turning point when the American Graham R. Taylor suggested the creation of "satellite-cities."[13] These truly autonomous entities, somewhat distant from the urban center. Raymond Unwin and Charles Purdom led innovation on this theme, proposing the ideal scheme as a large city surrounded by a double ring, with garden cities nearby and satellite cities on a further orbit. The New York Town Planning Conference confirmed such a scheme, and a particular interpretation of it was executed in Germany by Ernst May. Directing the urban extension of Frankfurt am Main between 1925 and 1930, May proposed an ambitious program founded on the *Trabantenprinzip* (satellite principle), which he toned down by merely conceiving extensions, physically separated from the existing urban fabric but by no means autonomous. It was only in his proposal for the extension of Moscow that he would fully draw the conclusions of the process.[14]

The Rational Reorganization of the Metropolis

To stabilize or redefine the boundaries of the metropolis it was not sufficient to regulate its development; it was also necessary to address problems of concentration and congestion. An overall reorganization of urban activities may resolve certain conflicts paralyzing the development of industry and services, but may do little for promoting hygienist principles. It was in Germany that the discussion about the *Groszstadt* was the most intense, mobilizing not only architects such as August Endell, who documented the beauties of the metropolis, but also sociologists such as Georg Simmel, who questioned new forms of the "life of the intellect" in the big city.[15]

In *Die Architektur der Groszstadt*, the Berlin architectural critic Karl Scheffler stated in 1913 that the metropolis, which he believed must balance the needs of the family economy with those of the collective, "must respond perfectly to modern exigencies as well as to be a crystallization point of the interest oriented towards an international economy." Scheffler suggested that the urban center be a "city logically organized," surrounded by specialized districts.[16] These reforms were mentioned again in Peter Behrens's reflections on the future of Berlin's center and inspired Le Corbusier, who was very attentive before 1914 to German *Städtebau*, when he proposed his *Plan Voisin* ten years later.[17]

11 Hans Kampffmeyer, *Die Gartenstadtbewegung* (Leipzig: B.G. Teubner, 1909).

12 Marco De Michelis, *Heinrich Tessenow, 1876 - 1950: das architektonische Gesamtwerk* (Stuttgart: DVA, 1991).

13 Graham R. Taylor, *Satellite Cities: A Study of Industrial Suburbs* (New York/London: D. Appleton & Co., 1915). Charles B. Purdom, *The Building of Satellite Towns* (London: M. Dent & Sons, 1925).

14 Justus Buekschmitt, *Ernst May* (Stuttgart: Alexander Koch, 1963); Marco De Michelis and Ernesto Pasini, *La città sovietica 1925-1937* (Venice: Marsilio, 1976).

15 See the anthology assembled by Massimo Cacciari, *Metropolis: Saggi sulla grande città di Sombart, Endell, Scheffler Simmel* (Rome: Officina Edizioni, 1973).

16 Karl Scheffler, *Die Architektur der Groszstadt* (Berlin: Bruno Cassirer Verlag, 1913).

17 Francesco Passanti, "Le Corbusier et le gratte-ciel: aux origines du plan Voisin," in Jean-Louis Cohen and Hubert Damisch, eds., *Américanisme et modernité: l'idéal américain dans l'architecture* (Paris: Flammarion/École des Hautes Études en Sciences Sociales, 1993), 171-189.

18 Franco Mancuso, *Le Vicende della zoning* (Milan: Il Saggiatore, 1978).

19 Le Corbusier, *La Charte d'Athènes* (Paris: Plon, 1943).

As early as 1875 in Germany, the subdivision of cities into "zones" (a word borrowed from the military) became common practice, codified by rules and manuals. At the beginning of the twentieth century, this zoning process was exported to the United States, where it was subjected to multiple improvements, thanks to the architect Georges Burdett Ford, who had begun using the principle approach, in Europe before 1914 . Against the theme of City Beautiful, Ford proposed a new the Scientific City, based on the control of ground use and traffic flow. From then on the term "zoning" it was seen as a technique of American origin when European urbanists re-adopted it to regulate the business centers of industrial cities and the new suburbs.[18]

Initially conceived as a simple technique of management and arbitration, allowing a kind of "moralization" of land speculation, zoning came into use in Germany, the United States, and in some experimental areas (such as the French Protectorate in Morocco) by urbanists nonetheless conservative in regard to architectural forms. However, it gained a kind of magical practice status when the promoters of architectural modernity took hold of it during the 1930s: when constructing the idea of the "functional city" during their meeting in Athens in 1933, the members of CIAM transformed zoning into an act of faith. With the "*Charte d'Athènes*," published by Le Corbusier in 1942 to diffuse into a slightly distorted form the ideas of the congress, the subdivision of urban space into rigorously autonomous "functions" became both a reductive *credo* and the foundation of an aesthetic that extended the notion of the "free plan" to an urban scale.[19]

The emblematic projects designed during the 1920s reinforced this point of view, because they were inseparable from the idea of a complete specialization of metropolitan centers. The development of services and the presence of office workers now characterized the city centers, from which industry tended to be excluded. The *Cité des affaires* (business district) that Le Corbusier placed at the center of his *Plan Voisin* and the *Hochhausstadt* that Ludwig Hilberseimer assigned

Ludwig Karl Hilberseimer, *Hochhausstadt* (Highrise City), east-west street, 1924. The Art Institute of Chicago. Gift of George E. Danforth, 1983.991

Richard Neutra, Rush City Reformed, late 1920s. Department of Special Collections, University Research Library, UCLA

to Berlin were two expressions of these transformations, designed for specific cities. But projects not explicitly located, such as Rush City Reformed, which Richard Neutra, designed inspired by his experience of Chicago, and The Metropolis of Tomorrow, which Hugh Ferriss conceived with New York in mind, validate the hypothesis of a rigorous division of metropolitan space, allowing for the creation of large, autonomous architectural ensembles.

The Urban Face of the Social Reform

Invested by capitalist strategies, urban space became at the same time a fundamental tool for the labor movement and the forces of reform. Control of public administration was one of the stakes in the conflict between the industrial or merchant groups and forces seeking an alternative social project. The launching of sector-based politics was a consequence of the pressure applied to the bourgeois élite, and it was manifested in particular in the field of housing.

The programs of reform intended to answer the housing crisis, a constant element of life in large urban areas, led to the definition of new types of housing districts inhabited by the political clientele of Social Democracy. These districts were far from conforming to a single type. The Austrian Social Democrats, undisputed masters of the Viennese metropolis (which after 1918 was the oversized head of a shrunken state), built strings of dense collective housing. One example of local building typologies, the Viennese *Höfe*, used the resources of monumental architecture to show the vigilant presence of the working class in the capital.[20]

The urban practice of the German Social Democrats during the Weimar Republic was of another nature, even though its financial revenue came from a similar source, taxing the income of real-estate owners. It fully adopted garden-city theories and undertook a radical decentralization of the large cities. The *Siedlungen* built by Ernst May's team in Frankfurt between 1925 and 1930, and those proposed during the same period by Martin Wagner for Berlin, based on Bruno

[20] Manfredo Tafuri, "Das Rote Wien: politica e forma della residenza nella Vienna socialista 1919-1933," in *Vienna rossa: la politica residenziale nella Vienna socialista, 1919-1933* (Milan: Electa, 1980), 7-148.

Hugh Ferriss, Empire State Building, as projected in 1929. Shreve, Lamb & Harmon, Architects. Avery Architectural and Fine Arts Library, Columbia University, New York

Ernst May, Siedlung Römerstadt, Frankfurt, Germany, 1930. Institut für Stadtgeschichte, Frankfurt

Bruno Taut and Martin Wagner, Berlin Siedlung, Berlin, 1925-31. Siftung Archiv der Akademie der Künste, Berlin

Taut's plans, set around the urban core a belt of autonomous complexes in which modern urban compositions would be built. The involvement of the cooperatives, born from the utopian projects of the years 1918-1920 and the introduction of a Taylorist model of rationalization of construction, led to the birth of an economical type of production that privileged the series.

The socialists were not isolated in this politic; Christian-social municipalities launched similar programs. Some architects developed their ideas in both frameworks, as is the case with Fritz Schumacher, who applied his concept of *soziale Stadtbaukunst*, or social urban art, equally to Christian Democratic Cologne and Social Democratic Hamburg. His vision of the large city was in each case based on complexes that combined housing and public buildings in organic units articulated around gardens. Through a diversity based on topographical specificities as well as on the design of original urban figures, each district of the city acquired an irreducible architectural and landscape-inspired identity.[21]

Fritz Schumacher, Elementary School at Dulsberg, Hamburg, 1919-20. Photo by Jean-Louis Cohen

Fritz Schumacher, Stadtpark, Hamburg, 1911-30. Photo by Jean-Louis Cohen

Schumacher's work converged in many ways with the schemes of Dutch municipalities following the 1901 *Woningwet* prescribing public financing of housing. Both municipalities and cooperatives launched projects which shared the same reforming outlook but with divergent architectural expressions. Only the parallel research into rationalization of construction components allows us to compare the idiosyncratic housing complexes of Michel de Klerk in Amsterdam with the serial complexes of Jacobus Johannes Pieter Oud in Rotterdam.[22]

In the Paris region, the policies followed by the Social-Democrat leader Henri Sellier were broadly based on Dutch and German experiences. At the head of the *Office Public d'Habitations de la Seine*, Sellier wove a spider web around Paris. Between the picturesque layouts of the first housing complexes built in the early 1920s in Suresnes, Lilas, or Genevilliers, and the more complex and rational urban areas of Châtenay-Malabry or Plessis-Robinson, and even more the prefabricated towers of La Muette in Drancy, the Office's production evolved architectural and urban solutions increasingly marked by functionalism.[23]

Efforts similar to those of European suburbs appeared on the peripheries of American cities, where cooperatives and labor unions were more influential than municipalities. The housing and landscape designs found in the projects of Henry Wright and Clarence Stein at Sunnyside Gardens in Queens and the garden city built in Radburn, New Jersey, from 1927 on prefigure New Deal programs of the 1930s.[24]

[21] Hartmut Frank, ed., *Fritz Schumacher: Reformkultur und Moderne* (Stuttgart: Gerd Hatje, 1994).

[22] Helen Searing, "With Red Flags Flying: Politics and Architecture in Amsterdam," in *Art and Architecture in the Service of Politics*, eds. Henry A. Millon and Linda Nochlin (Cambridge, Mass.: MIT Press, 1978), 230-70.

[23] Thierry Roze, Les cités-jardins de la Région Ile-de-France," *Les Cahiers de l'AURIF* 51 (May 1978).

[24] Richard Plunz, *A History of Housing in New York City: Dwelling Types and Social Change in the American Metropolis* (New York: Columbia University Press, 1990).

Michel de Klerk, Third block for Eigen Haard housing, Amsterdam, 1917-20. Nederlands Architectuur Institut, Rotterdam

Jacobus Johannes Pieter Oud, Blijdorp Housing Estate, Rotterdam, c. 1931. Nederlands Architectuur Institut, Rotterdam

When it took power in 1917, the revolutionary fraction of the Russian Social Democrats did not at first have policies very different from those of European reformers. Soviet citizens, organized by the Bolsheviks and the cooperatives, relied upon the principles of the garden city when they built their new districts. The housing projects of Alexander Gegello on Traktornaya street in Leningrad (1925) and Alexei Meshkov on Usachev street in Moscow (1926) were very similar to contemporary projects in the West. In the second half of the 1920s, supporters of "left wing" culture introduced new programs intended to transform everyday life. The research of the Stroikom (Building Committee) of the Russian Republic, inspired by the positions of the Constructivists, led to the building of several prototypes for communal houses, combining very small housing units with generous, shared service facilities. The hypothesis of the utopian collectivization of domestic life thus appeared in the communal house built by Moisei Ginzburg and Ignati Milinis for the Narkomfin (1928-29) and the student residence at the Institute of Textiles constructed by Ivan Nikolaev (1929-1930).[25]

Clarence Stein, Sunnyside Gardens, c. 1935. Division of Rare Manuscript Collections, Cornell University Library

[25] Anatole Kopp, *Town and Revolution: Soviet Architecture and City Planning, 1917-1935*, trans. Thomas E. Burton (New York: Braziller, 1970).

[26] Annick Brauman and Maurice Culot, eds., *Maisons du Peuple: Belgique, Allemagne, Autriche, France, Grande-Bretagne, Italie, Pays-Bas, Suisse* (Brussels: Archives d'architecture moderne, 1984).

[27] Alexei Gan, *Konstrukivizm* (Tver: Tverkoe Idz-vo, 2ia Tipografia, 1922).

The location of public buildings in all European districts of the 1920s must be noted. A dense network of schools and sports facilities testified to the intensification of municipalities' politics and to the formulation of new architectural principles. The new policies go along with the claim of a new relationship to light and outdoor space. Buildings designed in response to labor movement commissions also multiplied.[26] Derived precisely from this program, the "workers clubs" designed in Moscow by Konstantin Melnikov or Ivan Golosov created with their provocative shapes new landmarks that asserted the presence of organized labor in the city. They responded, to a certain extent, to the plan formulated by Lenin in 1918 for "monumental propaganda" in order to make the urban space "speak." The Monument for the Third International by Vladimir Tatlin, the kiosks of Alexander Rodchenko, and the Lenin Tribune of El Lissitzky all responded to this desire for new centralities reflecting the dynamic of the Revolution, and derived from the *tektonika* allowing for the manifestation of political movement evoked by the Constructivist theorist Alexei Gan.[27]

Moisei Ginzburg and Ignati Milinis, Narkomfin Communal House, Moscow, 1928-29. Photo by Jean-Louis Cohen

Konstantin Melnikov, Rusakov Workers' Club, Moscow, 1930. Collection Centre Canadien d'Architecture/Canadian Centre for Architecture, Montréal

Ilya Golosov, Zuev Workers Club, Moscow, 1929. Photo by Paul Randall Jacobson

Vladimir Tatlin and his assistants building the model of the Monument to the Third International, 1920. Collection Centre Canadien d'Architecture/ Canadian Centre for Architecture, Montréal

left: Alexander Rodchenko, Project for a Street Kiosk, Moscow, 1919. Rodchenko-Stepanova Archive, Moscow

right: El Lissitzky, Design for Lenin's Tribune, 1924. Collection Centre Canadien d'Architecture/ Canadian Centre for Architecture, Montréal

Towards the Dissolution of the City

At the end of the 1920s, the extreme outlook of the Russian avant-garde was the very negation of the urban phenomenon. The Constructivists were far from alone in their attempt to end the hegemony of the big city. Thought on decentralization came to a turning point right after the end of World War I, thanks to parallel initiatives which appeared in the fields of architecture and industrial policies. In his 1920s essay on the "dissolution" of cities, the Berlin architect Bruno Taut imagined a massive exodus leading the inhabitants of the metropolis toward a more rustic life.[28] These new communities would re-establish a close connection with nature in villages scattered far away from the large urban centers. At the same time, Henry Ford, pioneer of industrial decentralization, tried to convince the United States Senate to let him buy the Muscle Shoals hydro-electric dam and build a linear city along seventy-five miles of the Tennessee River valley. Ford combined a "return to industry in the village" with his vision of a territory accessible in its entirety by the automobile.[29]

As popular as Lenin in the new Russia, where Ford's tractors were copied and his books translated, Ford inspired the thoughts of radical town planners at a time when the future shape of the socialist city was being discussed. The architects of the Constructivist avant-garde saw in the city the very expression of capitalism and rejected it entirely, suggesting two alternative types. The first was proposed by the political leader Nikolai Miliutin, who diagrammed for Nizhni Novgorod and Magnetogorsk linear cities running parallel to the factory assembly lines.[30] Even more extreme was the suggestion made by the sociologist Nikolai Okhitovich, a member of the Constructivist group, who proposed getting rid of the city completely and spreading dwellings and equipment evenly over the land. For

[28] Bruno Taut, *Die Auflösung der Städte, oder Die Erde, eine gute Wohnung* (Hagen: Folkwang Verlag, 1920).

[29] Henry Ford, *Today and Tomorrow* (Garden City, New York: Garden City Pub. Co., 1926).

[30] Nikolai Miliutin, *Sotsgorod: The Problem of Building Socialist Cities*, trans. Arthur Sprague (Cambridge, Mass.: MIT Press, 1974).

Margaret Bourke-White, Magnitogorsk, Russia, 1930. Margaret Bourke-White Papers. Syracuse University Library, Department of Special Collections, Syracuse, New York

him, de-urbanization was "a centrifuge process, a movement of rejection," heralded by Ford's experiments. The widely spread territorial systems of the "desurbanists," such as the linear networks proposed for Magnitogorsk, were based on extensive use of the automobile, which definitely condemned them given the Soviet Union's obvious failure to make cars widely available.

It was Frank Lloyd Wright who made the most convincing interpretation of Ford's idea. In 1932, he formulated the principle of a complete fusion of city and countryside, illustrated by the model of Broadacre City, presented in New

31 Wright's ideas on the question are discussed in three books: *The Disappearing City* (New York: W.F. Payson, 1932); *When Democracy Builds* (Chicago: University of Chicago Press, 1945); and *The Living City* (New York: Horizon Press, 1958).

York in 1935.[31] Responding in a way to Le Corbusier's *La ville radieuse* conceived in 1930, Broadacre City combined Ford's decentralizing ideas with a memory of Thomas Jefferson's agrarian grid and with Daniel Burnham's advertising campaign for his master plan for Chicago. This vision of an "organic capitalism" combined the spread of the automobile, electrification, and standardized production, whereas garden-city developments were based on the railroad. It is therefore legitimate to see, using Patrick Geddes's words, a "neotechnic" project concurrent with Ebenezer Howard's "paleotechnic" one.

Frank Lloyd Wright, model of Broadacre City, 1934-35. Frank Lloyd Wright Foundation, Scottsdale, Arizona. Photo by Skot Weidmann

Le Corbusier, model of the *Plan Voisin* for Paris, designed in 1925, from Pierre Chenal's film, *L'architecture d'aujourd'hui*, 1931

Against the gigantism of the large American metropolis, Broadacre City was a hymn to the "*Little* farms, *little* homes for industry, *little* factories, *little* schools," all centered on the family, its home, and its lot. The 1935 model represented two square miles, consisting less of a fragment of the whole project than of a condensed version of various landscapes and imagined situations. The full range of single-family houses is there, classified according to the number of cars rather than the size of the family, from the House on the Mesa of 1931 (prototype of the luxurious house) to more modest dwellings.

Frank Lloyd Wright, House on the Mesa, Denver, Colorado, 1931. Frank Lloyd Wright Foundation, Scottsdale, Arizona

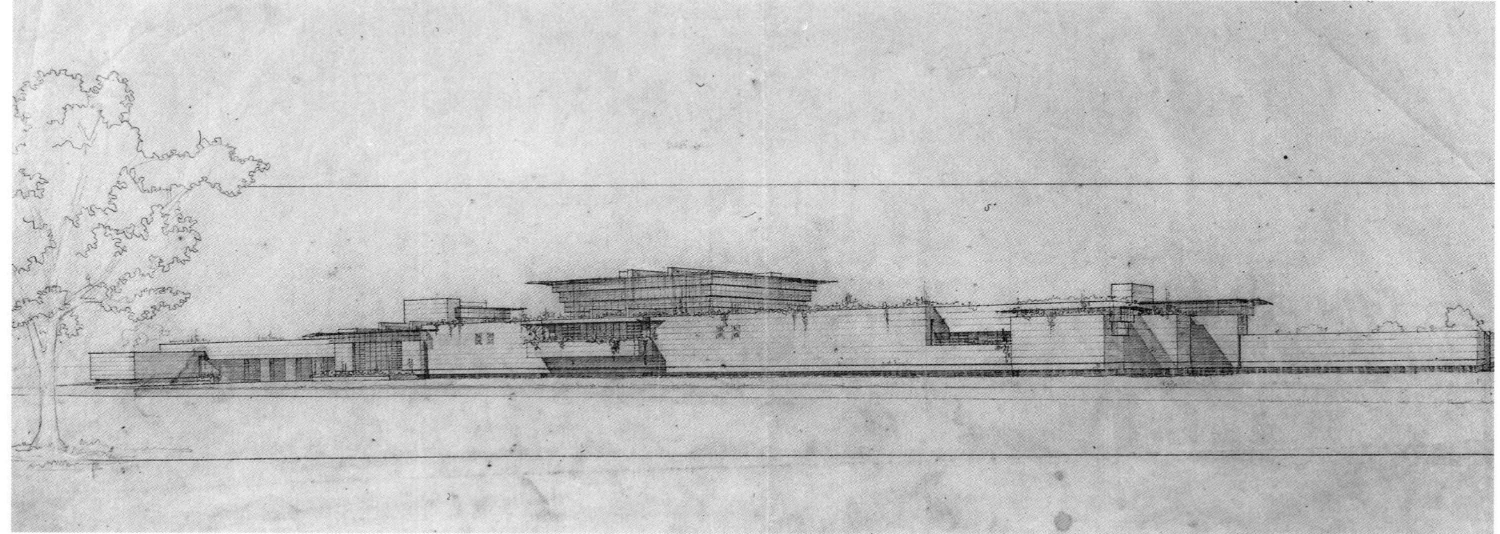

In this continuous entity, intended to replace both cities and countryside, the schools, administrative buildings and places of production (factories) were decentralized. Wright saw in the Roadside Market, which was to replace isolated shops, "the most attractive, educative and entertaining modern typology that one can find in Broadacres," a lucid anticipation of the shopping mall of the 1950s. Following the pattern of his 1935 project, Wright would try to develop a complex of "Usonian" houses, but in practice was never able to go beyond the stage of isolated commissions.

The influence of his project did not reach Europe until after World War II. However, during the period between the world wars, some old-world architects worked with similar hypotheses. Thus, the notion of *Stadtlandschaft*, or "city-landscape," elaborated by Fritz Schumacher for Cologne in the early 1920s, tended to combine rural landscape with urban expansion according to a system denser than the one proposed for Broadacre City. In the 1940s, the research of the Rhinelandarchitect Rudolf Schwarz, relying on Miliutin's ideas, imagined the transformation of Lorraine industrial areas into a continuum of industrial villages located in the countryside.[32] But it is obviously with the growth of American suburbs and, even more, with the shaping of the "urbanized countryside" in northern Italy and The Netherlands of the 1980s that Wright's prophecy would be largely validated.

From Catastrophe to Urban Project

Cities do not escape great catastrophes, whether natural, like earthquakes, or man-made. Punctuated by the greatest campaigns of voluntary destruction that humanity has ever experienced, the twentieth century has witnessed the rebirth of an architecture fed by the ruins of cities. Just as large catastrophes of the past have provided an impetus for renewal, as exemplified by the response to the massive fires of London in 1666, Lisbon in 1772, and Chicago in 1871, the great modern dramas of the first half of the twentieth century propelled the modernization of cities.

Rebuilding following the two world wars provided the opportunity for methodological planning and full-scale experimentations in urban form, particularly in Germany, France, The Netherlands, and Russia. The experiments and proposals were characterized by their grand scale and by the unprecedented speed of their implementation. The destruction of World War I was localized, affecting mainly northeastern France, Belgium, Prussia, and the Balkans. It nonetheless hastened the focus on urbanism, as it offered the possibility to completely transform the structure of cities.[33] Thus, the projects of Georges Burdett Ford for Reims and Ernest Hébrard for Salonique, both cities having been burned during the war, were major events in the consolidation of zoning and large urban composition techniques.

In a similar way, the earthquake and subsequent fire in San Francisco in 1906 led to a partial implementation of Daniel Burnham's master-plan directives, while the Tokyo earthquake of 1923 allowed the establishment of a modern expansion plan for the Japanese capital. But the scale of problems changed with World War II, which caused the most massive destruction that humanity has ever seen.[34] This time, ruins littered Europe, and the devastation spread as far as parts of Asia and North Africa. For architects who had never stopped criticizing the insalubrity and irrationality of existing cities, it was an unhoped-for opportunity.

32 On these projects, see: Jean-Louis Cohen and Harmut Frank, "Architettura dell'occupazione: Francia e Germania 1940-1950," *Casabella*, no. 567 (April 1990), 40-58.

33 For the manuals exploring these circumstances, see: Donat Alfred Agache, Jean-Marcel Auburtin, and Édouard Redont, *Comment reconstruire nos cités détruites: notions d'urbanisme s'applicant aux villes, bourgs et villages* (Paris: Armand Colin, 1915); and Louis van der Swaelmen, *Préliminaires d'art civique: mis en relation avec le "cas clinique" de la Belgique* (Leyden: A. W. Sijthoff, 1916).

34 Marlene P. Hiller, Eberhard Jäckel, and Jürgen Rohwer, eds., *Städte im Zweiten Weltkrieg, ein internationaler Vergleich* (Essen: Klartext Verlag, 1991).

Even before the surrender of the Axis powers, projects were begun on all sides of the conflict. The Nazis intended to leave their imprint on conquered cities such as Warsaw, and to modernize the destroyed ones, while Allied forces made plans for the renewal of a liberated Europe. The fantasy of the total "liberation" of land, cherished by the Modern Movement, was able to project itself onto a *tabula rasa* miraculously cleared out by bombs, announcing the reign of clarity and regularity.

Generously financed by the United States, reconstruction allowed town planners to test most of the hypotheses formulated since 1900 about the structure of cities.[35] Proposals for the complete reorganization of the metropolis on a regional scale were nonetheless doomed to failure, whether the project was conceived by the group MARS for London (1942) or by Hans Scharoun's group for Berlin (1946). The actual reconstruction of London was based on Patrick Abercrombie's master plan, which preserved existing communities within a flexible structure that privileged neighborhoods rather than large new building complexes. In Berlin, the division of the city led to divergent strategies, illustrated by the

Stalinallee (Karl-Marx-Allee), Berlin, 1951-57. Landesbildstelle Berlin

opposition between the large continuous blocks of the Stalinallee, built in the East by Hermann Henselmann (1951-57), and the informal organization of the Hansaviertel, built in the West for the Interbau exhibition in 1957.

Pluralism also characterized the French situation. Projects of an advanced functionalism, such as the one Le Corbusier designed for Saint-Dié, were rejected. Instead, the debate was represented on one hand by the rebuilding of Le Havre, where Auguste Perret drew an ample orthogonal grid upon which reinforced concrete buildings defined a classically inspired order, and on the other by the

35 Max Bill, *Wiederaufbau: Dokumente über Zerstörungen, Planungen, Konstruktionen* (Erlenbach-Zürich: Verlag für Architektur, 1945); Werner Durth and Niels Gutschow, *Träume in Trümmern: Planung zum Wiederaufbau zerstörter Städte im Westen Deutschland 1940-1950*, 2 vols. (Braunschweig-Wiesbaden: Vieweg & Sohn, 1988).

Auguste Perret, Reconstruction of Le Havre, France, 1945-54, view of Avenue Foch. Photo by Jean-Louis Cohen

reconstruction of Sotteville, where Marcel Lods reduced urban complexity to the juxtaposition of parallel prefabricated slabs. Between these two poles, André Lurçat in Maubeuge and Louis Arretche in Saint-Malo strove to add a modern interpretation to the historical fabric of these cities. At first, it might seem that the Soviet model can be compared to the French, because both proceeded from the direct intervention of a centralized state. In reality, the approach was different. Soviet town planners favored large radial avenues, and introduced in their buildings the signs of traditional architecture found in Russian cities, echoing the newly rediscovered nationalist accents favored by the regime after 1942.

Just before reconstruction was completed in North Africa, a wave of earthquakes precipitated the selection of projects in which late modern themes were used. Thus, Jean Bossu brought together a Corbusian poetic with a certain sensitivity to Mediterranean space in the reconstruction of the Algerian city of Orléansville, destroyed in 1957, while the plan of Agadir, destroyed in 1960, was conceived by Pierre Mas as a theorem of functionalist urbanism. Kenzo Tange's 1963 master plan for the Macedonian capital of Skopje used megastructures, then at the center of discussion. More recent earthquakes have led to very different types of policies: architectural innovation and a sense of urban continuity prevailed in Naples, hit in 1986, and infrastructure problems were privileged in Kobe after the earthquake in 1995. As to more recent wartime destruction still to be rebuilt, reconstruction campaigns are underway in Beirut according to a bombastic and mercantile master plan, and plans are still in gestation for Sarajevo. One indication of the delays that can be encountered in reconstruction is the situation in Berlin. Only after the reunification of Germany of 1991, half a century after the capitulation of the Reich, did it become conceivable to complete the rebuilding of the city. The new Berlin now witnesses a third generation of projects that attempt to knit together the disparate spaces left by the Cold War.

The Hansaviertel, Berlin,
photographed in 1930.
Landesbildstelle Berlin

The Hansaviertel, Berlin, 1962.
Landesbildstelle Berlin

The Law of Mass Production

After the reconstruction period came a postwar period of massive expansion which tended to popularize the systems conceived by radical architects in the 1920s. When "big industry [took] over building," as Le Corbusier eagerly wished, the deception became apparent quickly, because the rationalization of components and mass production are usually synonymous with anonymity and social marginalization. This modernization process was realized in two distinct types of residential districts, both derived from the paradigms of the first decade of the twentieth century.

The standard modernist district is defined by vertical and longitudinal buildings (towers and slabs), based on the principles of Le Corbusier as well as the German *Zeilenbau*. At first established on an experimental level, after 1950 these types were used in conservative compositional strategies. Academicism gets on well with the aesthetic of mass production, and especially with the contempt that large

Ludwig Mies van der Rohe with Ludwig Hilberseimer, Lafayette Park, Detroit,1955-63. Photo by Wayne Andrews

master plans have for topography. Once again, there is a convergence between the French and Soviet state-controlled political models during this period. However, when the housing was intended for a middle class that accepted the forms elaborated by the modern aesthetic, building complexes that elsewhere would be synonymous with exclusion became symbols of social status. Such is the case in the Lafayette Park housing complex built in Detroit by Ludwig Hilberseimer and Ludwig Mies van der Rohe (1955-63) and the flats designed by Jean Dubuisson in the Maine-Montparnasse complex in Paris (1968).

A kind of dual development occurred in the large cities of developed countries, with the modernization of urban centers taking place simultaneously with the development of "planned communities" in the suburbs. The

[36] Jane Jacobs, *The Death and Life of Great American Cities* (New York: Random House, 1961).

Levittown, New York, 1949. Photo by Arthur Green

creation of new housing complexes on the outskirts required the migration of the central districts' inhabitants, thus forcing the redesign of the central districts for other social groups or activities. In the outer districts, or in the cities that escaped bombing, urban renovation from 1950 on had effects similar to those of the reconstruction projects. In the slum clearance of American cities or in the Parisian "*îlots insalubres*," urban interventions that ignored existing populations and the historical characteristics of the urban fabric resulted either in a population exodus or in the production of cruelly repetitive housing complexes that scar the landscape. In certain cases, a similar type of architecture was used indifferently in the centers as well as in the vertical "*grands ensembles*" of the suburbs, because industrialization, considered the only efficient method of reducing housing construction costs, required large production quantities. Although the social and cultural risks of these projects were criticized as early as the 1960s,[36] they continued to be used for a long time, due to bureaucratic inertia and the corruption of city officials.

The horizontal districts abandoned little by little the principles of the Unwinian garden city from which they derived. Mass-produced housing also became the subject of industrial politics, especially in the United States, where the GI Bill following World War II opened a huge market for the prefabricated, detached single-family houses of Levitt and others. In the new residential suburbs, a monotonous repetition as fatal as that of the vertical districts was established, reflecting the cultural homogenization of the television era. These suburbs generally required the use of cars for daily commuting; the consequences of this phenomenon were felt intensely in the urban centers, which were crisscrossed by stacks of freeways that brought workers to their offices.

Whether vertical or horizontal, these urban components had such brutal and powerful effects that the preservation of the historical districts of cities ceased to be a political priority. From the technical ability to create whole new districts, the illusion of creating complete new towns was born. No longer the

Andreas Gursky, *Montparnasse*, Paris, 1993. Courtesy of the Tate Gallery, London

colonial towns of the beginning of the century (although the premise of urban "creation" is similar to one of conquest or domination), these new towns find urban complexity reduced to a few social functions — most often geared to production or to political centrality.

Tony Garnier, La cité industrielle: les services publiques, 1917. Musée des Beaux-Arts, Lyon

The Creation of New Cities

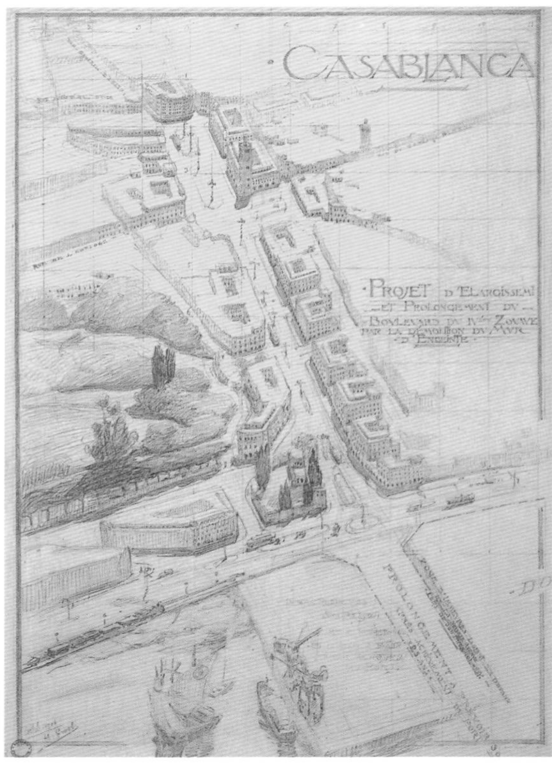

Henri Prost, Project for the avenue des Ive Zouaves, Casablanca, 1914. Academie d'architecture, Paris

The creation of new cities is more characteristic of twentieth-century urban strategies than it was in earlier times.[37] This is so because the hypothesis of a radical rupture between the morphology of existing cities and those of new districts took on the strength of a postulate. For the first time, the idea was put forward that the structure of new cities should not have anything in common with that of historical urban areas.[38] In any case, theoretical projects designed by several young architects were oriented in that direction.

Proposed first in 1901, the "*Cité industrielle*" (Industrial City) of the Lyon architect Tony Garnier was a city with socialist tendencies, made autonomous by hydroelectric power. Private ownership of land was banned, and large public buildings were designed for secular purposes. The overall composition favored collective spaces, and at the same time was influenced by the geographic thoughts of Paul Vidal de la Blache as well as the program outlined by Émile Zola in his Fourierist-inspired novel *Travail*, serialized in 1900. The city found its definitive form in an architecturally more radical version designed in 1916-1917.[39] The "*Cité Mondiale*," designed by the French architect Ernest Hébrard in 1913, in collaboration with the Danish sculptor Hendrik Christian Andersen, was constructed with the help of American financing on a vacant site and followed Daniel Burnham's layout for Chicago.[40]

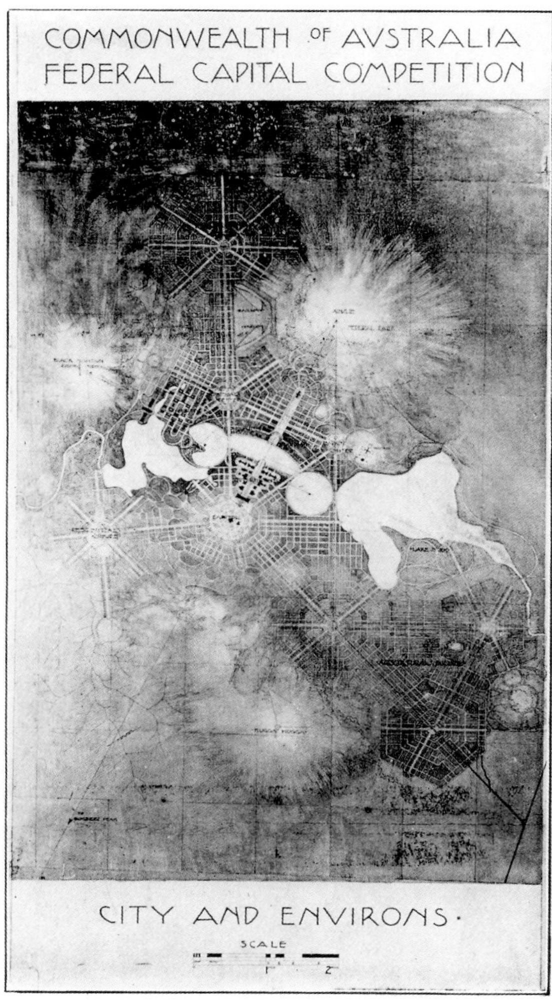

Walter Burley Griffin, Competitive design for the federal capital city of the Commonwealth of Australia, Canberra; plan, 1912. Design no. 18, First Premiated Design. The Art Institute of Chicago

In reality, most new cities actually built were based on the existing urban core or were inserted in existing territorial networks in order to reinforce the power centers. This was the case for New Delhi, a monumental project that symbolized the control of the British *Raj*. There, Edwin Lutyens's master plan imposed a new urban entity on a site that had known many other cities since the Muslim conquest.[41] Another colonial capital, but a center of economic rather than political power, the Moroccan harbor of Casablanca was created on the fringe of a modest historical urban core. There, Henri Prost's 1914 master plan overlayed a network of public avenues, organized according to a precise hierarchy, onto a labyrinth of speculative housing developments.[42] Cases such as the Australian capital of Canberra were exceptional. In 1911, the master plan for the whole urban composition was the subject of an international competition; it was won by Walter Burley Griffin, a former assistant to Frank Lloyd Wright.

Built in the Palestine of the British mandate to Patrick Geddes's master plan, the design of Tel Aviv takes the form of a flexible Mediterranean garden-city and the real face of a European *Siedlung*, because the architects involved used a language of architectural modernism developed in Austria and Germany.[43] Other works by exiled Germans and Swiss included the industrial cities built in the Urals within the framework of Soviet five-year plans. These abandoned picturesque layouts in favor of functionalist compositions. At Magnitogorsk, Novokuznetsk, and Orsk, where the central collective spaces were left fallow for a long time, the teams of Ernst May, Hannes Meyer, and Hans Schmidt developed projects for collective housing neighborhoods, thus continuing the research done in Germany during the Weimar Republic.[44]

After World War II, two new capitals marked the eruption onto the world architectural stage of nations which had been oppressed or considered culturally dependent upon Europe. At the request of Jawaharlal Nehru, and after some serious initial studies by Alfred Mayer, Le Corbusier designed the Punjab capital of Chandigarh. The sectors forming the master plan derived from a subtle observation of the local lifestyle and were coupled with a system of differentiated roads, theorized in 1945 under the name of "7V." Le Corbusier's invention was

37 It is upon this differentiation that Lavedan's classical history is founded: Pierre Lavedan, *Histoire de l'urbanisme*, 3 vols. (Paris: H. Laurens, 1926-1952). See also Convegno internazionale di storia urbanista, *La città di fondazione*, eds. Roberta Martinelli and Lucia Nuti (Venice: Marsilio, 1978).

38 Bruno Fortier, *L'amour des villes* (Paris: Institut français d'architecture, Liège: Pierre Mardaga, 1995).

39 Tony Garnier, *Une cité industrielle: étude pour la construction des villes* (Paris: A. Vincent & Fréal, 1918).

40 Giuliano Gresleri and Dario Matteoni, *La città à mondiale: Andersen, Hébrard, Otlet, Le Corbusier* (Venice: Marsilio, 1982).

41 Robert Grant Irving, *Indian Summer: Lutyens, Baker, and Imperial Delhi* (New Haven: Yale University Press, 1981).

42 Jean-Louis Cohen and Monique Eleb, *L'Expérience Casablanca* (Paris: Hazan, 1998).

43 Volker M. Welter, Biopolis — Patrick Beddes, Edinburgh and the City of Life (Ph.D. diss., Edinburgh, 1996); Michael Levin, *White City: International Style Architecture in Israel, a Portrait of an Era* (Tel Aviv: The Tel Aviv Museum, 1984).

44 Stephen Kotkin, *Magnetic Mountain: Stalinism as a Civilization* (Berkeley: University of California Press, 1995).

Le Corbusier, Secretariat Chandigarh, India, 1958. Fondation Le Corbusier, Paris

focused on the Capitol, containing the major public buildings, such as the Parliament, the High Court, and the Secretariat, while Pierre Jeanneret, Jane Drew and Maxwell Fry designed the housing. The Capitol was endowed with the serenity of an acropolis.[45]

A similar architectural leap could be seen in Brasilia, the creation of which was proclaimed by Brazilian President Juscelino Kubitschek in 1956, in response to wishes formulated as early as the beginning of the nineteenth century. Lucio Costa's "pilot plan" opposes the politico-administrative center, characterized

Oscar Niemeyer, Brasilia, 1959.
Photo by Julius Shulman

by Oscar Niemeyer's lyrical architectural compositions, and the housing *Superquadras*, functionalist complexes made livable by climate and vegetation.[46] Established on a large site, Brasilia was based on the quasi-exclusive use of the automobile. The population explosion has nonetheless fundamentally transformed the founders' vision, and the planned city today is only the center of an otherwise large, shapeless urban area. The success of the Brasilia and Chandigarh projects is due to the fact that the population of these two cities benefits, directly or indirectly, from government employees' salaries, which guarantee a standard of living higher than the national average.

The period following World War II was also marked by the construction of new towns in Europe.[47] The programs launched in Sweden (Vällingby) and in Finland (Tapiola) led to the creation of urban areas adapted to the suburban landscape. But the most determined policy was the one enacted by successive administrations in Great Britain to accomplish the goals of the New Town Act of 1946. This law, promulgated by the Labor government, reasserted the conclusion of the Barlow report (1937). The construction of ten towns was begun between 1945

45 Norma Evenson, *Chandigarh* (Berkeley: University of Calfornia Press, 1966).

46 Norma Evenson, *Two Brazilian Capitals: Architecture and Urbanism in Rio de Janeiro and Brasilia* (New Haven: Yale University Press, 1973).

47 Ervin Y. Galantay, *New Towns: Antiquity to the Present* (New York: George Braziller, 1975).

and 1951, among them Harlow, Stevenage, Crawley, Basildon, and Bracknell, forming autonomous communities which combined in a relatively balanced way housing and industry. Surrounded by a greenbelt, they were meant to house an optimal population of 30,000 to 40,000 inhabitants. The 1960s saw another wave of new towns, such as Runcorn, Cumbernauld, and Milton Keynes, in which the automobile was increasingly important. By the end of the 1970s, the thirty-two built towns had a population of 2.2 million inhabitants, or 3.9 % of the national population.

The British type of new town was the model for the "*Schéma directeur d'aménagement et d'urbanisme de la région parisienne*" (zoning and urban plan for the Parisian area, 1965), which ended a decade of stalling by promising to "break with the radio-concentrism of infrastructures by creating new regional lines of development" and to "break with the monocentrism of urban areas" by creating new towns, organized along two axes parallel to the Seine valley. The demographic projections of fourteen million inhabitants by the year 2000 have not

Town Centre, Cumbernauld, Scotland. Photo by Stewart Shaw

been fulfilled, but the construction of the new cities (Cergy-Pontoise, Saint-Quentin, Marne-la-Vallée, Évry, and Melun-Sénart) was begun with an unusual energy and efficiency.

As opposed to the Franco-British image of the new city, carefully planned and controlled by state organizations hosting a plethora of technical teams, new millennial cities are emerging. Thus, the Chinese neo-capitalist town of Shenzen, founded in 1980 at the edge of Hong Kong, announces a type of horizontal city based on the private financing of infrastructures and on a kind of general *laissez-faire*. The confrontation between vertical high-rise complexes and horizontal developments, and the rapidity with which these breathtaking programs are executed, reveal the limitations of traditional techniques for the control of urban space.

The Specialized City and the Skyscraper

A direct result of capitalist development, increasing specialization of city districts is a fact, and the situation is exacerbated by zoning laws. Dividing the city into zones of differentiated uses and densities directly affects the size of a metropolis, since progress and modernity are identified with the vertical-city type. Thus, the New York zoning code, developed in 1916 to control the damaging effects of high-rise construction on the real estate value of adjacent properties, led to a new type of specialized district in which the relationship between the width of streets and the height of buildings, established in the eighteenth century, lost its pertinence. Vertical structures, initially conceived in North America, were disseminated rapidly to Europe, where they were carefully analyzed before 1914,[48] then spread far beyond the Old World. High-rise buildings were subject to infinite variations from the 1920s on. Inserted into the economic structure of the large city, the skyscraper — initially designed for office space only — experienced typological transformations from the beginning, as evidenced by the early differentiation between New York high-rises and the U-shaped buildings of Chicago.[49]

In the 1920s the vertical city was often conceived in a purely graphic way, and became a pretext for fantastic projects. At the same time, the "culture of congestion"[50] was also conceived in a more structural way, as the articulation between skyscraper and infrastructure was taken seriously. Thus, Le Corbusier's "*Plan Voisin*" for Paris was linked to the idea of a large freeway running through Paris, while the project Raymond Hood designed for New York in 1929, under the title "Manhattan 1950," was based on the intensification of the network of bridges and thoroughfares crossing the island. This figure of the skyscraper, seen not as an isolated gesture but as a functional urban structure, can be found also in the more prosaic urban developments built since the 1960s, from La Défense, located west of Paris, with its road network; to Shinjuku, a district connected to one of Tokyo's main railway stations; and Hong Kong, where Kowloon's hotels are built on the harbor.

The spread of the vertical-city type questioned the identity and individuality of cities as such. When Hugh Ferriss designed his "Metropolis of Tomorrow" in 1929, he set out to differentiate three centers: science, arts, and business. A similar set of problems presented itself in the remodeling of Moscow's urban skyline after 1945: combining in this case with conflicting desires to take into consideration both the topographic features (the hills) and the historical character of the area (the network of steeples and spires of the old Russian capital). Specialized in their function, Moscow's "high-rise buildings" participate not in the reinforcement of the presence of a business center, but in the inscription of a network of modern verticals in the continuity of national history. Combining eclectic exterior decoration with the steel skeleton essential for this type of construction, they are

48 Jean-Louis Cohen, *Scenes of the World to Come: European Architecture and the American Challenge, 1893-1960* (Paris: Flammarion, 1995).

49 Carol Willis, *Form Follows Finance: Skyscrapers and Skylines in New York and Chicago* (New York: Princeton Architectural Press, 1995).

50 Rem Koolhaas, *Delirious New York: A Retroactive Manifesto for Manhattan* (New York: Oxford University Press, 1978).

Hugh Ferriss, Study for Maximum Mass Permitted by the 1916 New York Zoning Law, Stages 1 - 4, 1922. Cooper-Hewitt, National Design Museum, Smithsonian Institution, Art Resource, New York; Gift of Mrs. Hugh Ferriss, 1969-137-4

Alfred Stieglitz, Rockefeller Center seen from the Shelton Hotel, 1935. Collection Centre Canadien d'Architecture/Canadian Centre for Architecture, Montréal

Ludwig Mies van der Rohe, Philip Johnson and Kahn & Jacobs. Seagram Building, New York, 1958. Photo by Ezra Stoller

Gordon Bunshaft/Skidmore, Owings & Merrill. Lever House Corporate Headquarters, New York City, 1952. Photo by Ezra Stoller

Andreas Gursky, Hong Kong Shanghai Bank, 1994. Architect: Norman Foster, 1986. Courtesy of Monika Sprüth Galerie, Köln

closer to pre-1914 New York buildings than to the new style of skyscrapers that Mies van der Rohe and Gordon Bunshaft designed in the early 1950s.

Since then, American architectural research has been oriented toward the aesthetic improvement of the steel-and-glass tower. European contributions remained modest, with the exception of the astonishing dialogue started in 1957 about Milan's skies, ignited by the Pirelli Tower of Gio Ponti and Pier Luigi Nervi and the Torre Velasca of Ludovico Belgiojoso, Enrico Peressutti, and Ernesto Nathan Rogers: on one side, an attempt to find a reinforced concrete alternative to steel towers; on the other, a desire for poetic dialogue between Milan's urban palazzos and high-rise construction. In the 1970s, characterized by a race for new heights, postmodern skyscrapers sadly explored the endless register of historical citations, but a new line of research derived from a radical questioning of the conventional structure of buildings, with a central service core. Developing Jean Prouvé's 1970 idea for a tower in La Défense, Norman Foster built for the Hong Kong Shanghai Bank (1986) a high-rise with a hollow core and suspended floors, a large vertical megastructure that shakes commonly accepted dogma about the skyscraper's shape.

Centrality and Identity: the CIAM Crisis

Reinvigorated by state politics, functionalist architecture was already criticized by some of its authors in the first years of the postwar period. Very early on, the radical architects who gathered at the *Congrès internationaux d'architecture moderne* (CIAM) felt a kind of dismay when faced with the dead-end situation created by the Athens Charter regarding the identity and specificity of cities.[51] The eighth CIAM, which met in Hoddesdon, England, in 1951, provided the opportunity for a discussion on the notion of *core*, a term that Le Corbusier cleverly translated into "*coeur*" (heart), a much richer concept than "*centre civique*" (civic center). The question now was to consider the central functions of cities from a perspective of integration rather than dissociation by reintroducing a symbolic dimension, which had been absent from the movement's doctrines.[52] The challenge was also to try to bring social realities closer to the principles constituted in the *Siedlung* or Saint-Dié master plans.

The debate opened in 1943 with Jose Luis Sert, Fernand Léger, and Sigfried Giedion's "Nine Points on Monumentality." The authors explained that "the people want the buildings that represent their social and community life to give more than functional fulfillment," and "their aspiration to monumentality, joy, pride, and excitement to be satisfied." But at the same time, the group still felt that it was essential to build these monuments in order to create "vast open spaces in the now decaying areas of our cities."[53] Giedion saw in the "core" the promise of a human scale instead of the tyranny of the machine.[54]

In the 1950s, a diversity of strategies, cultures and personal experiences confronted the CIAM members. Nathan Ernesto Rogers presented his thesis on the "*preesistenze ambientali*," bringing to the attention of his colleagues important elements of the urban site and its reference to history. In a similar way, an acute attention to urban identities and scales, such as that of the neighborhood, were found in the ideas of the young critics who became the founders of Team 10 in 1954, an action that contributed to the death of the CIAM in 1959. Aldo Van Eyck,

[51] See the texts assembled in Joan Ockman, ed., *Architecture Culture, 1943-1968: A Documentary Anthology* (New York: Columbia University Press/Rizzoli, 1993).

[52] See *Gli ultimi CIAM, Rassegna*, no. 52 (December 1992).

[53] Giedion published the text in his *Architecture, You and Me: The Diary of a Development* (Cambridge, Mass.: Harvard University Press, 1958).

[54] International Congresses for Modern Architecture, *The Heart of the City: Towards the Humanization of Urban Life*, eds. Jacqueline Tyrwhitt, Jose Luis Sert and Ernesto N. Rogers (New York: Pellegrini and Cudahy, 1952).

Jacob Bakema, and Alison and Peter Smithson expressed their interest in the specificity of relationships established at the level of the building or of the urban neighborhood. They imagined new ways to organize dwellings and town plans that allowed for some complexity, as opposed to the crystalline simplicity of the principles put forward by the CIAM since Athens.[55]

The critique produced by Team 10 had a very specific goal: to suggest new design processes that would facilitate human relationships and make urban space more fluid. In certain ways, this approach was similar to that proposed by the critics and urbanists most resistant to modern themes. The "culturalists"— namely Lewis Mumford in the United States and Gaston Bardet in France (the first being inspired by socialist ideas and the second by an unusual Christian humanism, but both holding to Patrick Geddes's lessons), proposed using social organization as the founding element of urban projects instead of trying to force social organization to conform to preconceived solutions.[56] By the 1960s, the disastrous social impact of urban renovations forced municipal planners and architects to look more closely at their practices, while Marxist critics such as Henri Lefebvre were able to renew a worn-out discourse by injecting utopian visions back into discussions of the city.[57]

Researching the Spaces of Civility

In the period bracketed by Burnham's City Beautiful (which culminated in the master plan for Chicago) and the devastating construction of the Bucharest culture palace, the question of public buildings and spaces never ceased to be discussed among twentieth-century architects. It is perhaps in this arena of civic architecture that the result of their collective reflection is most fragile, although the hypotheses are numerous, from the "people's square" studied by Léon Jaussely in 1901 to the "Assembly Rooms" of Tony Garnier's "*Cité industrielle*," often deriving from a nostalgia for the places of ancient democracy.

This failure probably has two different causes. The first relates to the obsessive importance given by totalitarian regimes to the politics of space and spectacle. The reorganization projects designed for Berlin, Rome, and Moscow transformed the centers of these capitals into parade grounds, where the orderly masses of a well-officered population were put on display, thus discrediting later efforts to conceive large places for civic gatherings.[58]

Another cause of this collective inability to conceive of places for civic life may be found in the modernists' urban-design principles, which were based on the rejection of traditional urban forms such as streets and squares, and their inability to conceive, except on rare occasions, spaces that the community would be able to care for.

This crisis of representation is amplified by the dilution of political life produced by the development of mass media; the popular gathering has been replaced by television events. It has become difficult, even impossible, to represent or symbolize a social link that is being undermined in its reality as well as in its political transcription. Thus, despite the supposed magic of the terminology, no plaza, no piazza, and no forum has been able to provide in a positive way a place for the meetings which have marked history at the end of the twentieth century, although urban space has never ceased to be the stage for conflicts and revolutions.

55 Alison Smithson, ed., *Team 10 Primer* (London: Studio Vista, 1968) and *Team 10 Meetings: 1953-1984* (New York: Rizzoli, 1991).

56 Lewis Mumford, *The Culture of Cities* (New York: Harcourt, Brace and Co., 1938) and *The City in History* (New York: Harcourt, Brace & World, 1961); Gaston Bardet, *Le Nouvel urbanisme* (Paris: Vincent & Fréal, 1948).

57 Henri Lefebvre, *The Production of Space*, trans. Donald Nicholson-Smith (Oxford; Cambridge, Mass.: Blackwell, 1991).

58 Dawn Ades, Tim Benton, et al, eds., *Art and Power: Europe under the Dictators, 1930-1945* (London: Hayward Gallery, 1995).

The forces which contributed to the collapse of the communist states in Eastern Europe and Russia took the street as a stage and the commemorative monuments of the old regimes as targets, but we are obliged to realize that this rejection has been stronger than the adherence to places accepted as the cradle of democracy.

If civic spaces are still in crisis, the street, repeatedly condemned to death between the 1920s and the 1950s, has experienced a spectacular resurrection.[59] After suffering through a campaign of criticism, during which its integrative function was in danger of being reduced to the level of circulation machine, the street is again a place for the convergence of practices and for the cohabitation of architectures. Following general criticism of functionalist urbanism, and thanks to the ideas of the Team 10 generation, the street reappeared in urban projects of the 1970s and became the subject of new strategies, reinforced by the return of commercial activities to the urban center. The reformulation of the street made it a place for consumption rather than a place for civic interaction. The example of City Walk, created in the 1980s at Universal City, is revealing, because here the street is reduced to a simulacrum of urbanity in the middle of a large parking lot, condensing into one location fragments of the urban identity of Los Angeles.

The Urban Paradigm in Architectural Culture

Since 1900, a vast number of projects for theoretical towns have been designed by architects; so many that the capacity to conceive *ex nihilo* a future town might seem a prerequisite for becoming a contemporary public professional. The discourse of the modern movement was constructed in the first half of the twentieth century in opposition to the existing city, judged obsolete in terms of technical as well as aesthetic and social adequacy. At the same time, many architects have tried to establish a dense corpus of observations of the real city. It is this corpus which has allowed for the emergence of the critical processes of the second half of the century. Through the analysis of past and present cities architects and planners can invent fruitful design processes.[60] During the Athens CIAM in 1933, Fernand Léger exhorted the architects: "put your maps in your pocket, go out in the street!"[61] He warned against the ecstasy of total control in creating an urban space one wouldn't dare live in. (Le Corbusier himself was lucid about the "illusion of the plans" designed by him.) With the exception of rare moments such as the reconstruction period, the most radical of the moderns had to renounce their belief that architecture with its mere geometries could resolve problems that far surpass architecture in complexity.

Willingly or not, the moderns had to return to the position of Patrick Geddes, who never ceased to oppose the long series of utopias, judged "consolatory and even inspirational," to what he called "Eu-topia". In his own projects for Dunfermline in Scotland, Tel Aviv, and India, he made a point of "defining the lines of development of the legitimate Eu-topia, specific to each studied city: reality quite different from the vague U-topia which it is impossible to concretely realize anywhere."[62] According to Geddes, it is not by negating the real character of a place that one can build the city of the future. Against such negation he argued for a strategy of careful modification.

The tension between theoretical projects, often loaded with critical intentions, and subtle interpretation of specific contexts remains one of the most

[59] Stanford Anderson, ed., *On Streets* (Cambridge, Mass.: MIT Press, 1978); Zeynep Çelik, Diane Favro and Richard Ingersoll, eds., *Streets: Critical Perspectives on Public Space* (Berkeley: University of California Press, 1994).

[60] Anthony Vidler has thus seen the city as a third "typology," inspired after the typologies of the imitation of nature and of the machine: "The Third Typology," *Oppositions*, no. 7 (Winter 1976): 1-4.

[61] Fernand Léger, "Discours aux architectes," *Tekhnika Khronika* no. 44-46, Oct.-Nov., 1933, 1159-1162.

[62] Patrick Geddes, *Civics as Applied Sociology* (London, 1904), reprinted in *The Ideal City*, ed. Helen E. Meller (Leicester: Leicester University Press, 1979).

fecund contradictions of twentieth-century architecture. Most historical narratives have highlighted the question of the "success" of the master plan, condemning the "obscure forces" that have prevented the realization of architects' noble projects. The chronicle of actualized projects reveals, however, that plans merely define the balance between prospective visions and the inertia of reality. In an unbalanced equilibrium between the desire for new space and the pressure of tradition, architectural projects reveal the changing forms of the alliance between architects, technicians, and politicians.

The notion of "urban architecture" illustrates in its fluctuations the transformation of thought processes with regard to the city. The expression was used initially in 1926 by Pierre Lavedan, who, following Raymond Unwin, sought to build a history of town-planning that addressed the modifications of buildings in their relationship to the city.[63] On the other hand, when Aldo Rossi and the Italian architects of the 1960s resurrected the term, they loaded it with a specific intentionality. If they defined architecture as "urban," it was less by its location within a city than by its ability to create a continuous space to support collective practices and identities, as opposed to the homogeneous and isotropic space of the functional city. The energy invested by Rossi and Carlo Aymonino in their typological and morphological study of the city of Padua, and the earlier studies of Saverio Muratori on the "*operante storia*" of Venice and Rome,[64] simultaneously nurtured the restoration projects of historical districts and design processes meant to produce urbanity. The territorial goals suggested at the same time by Vittorio Gregotti were the result of another process, which acknowledged the new relationship between cities and regional landscape and the spatial importance of transportation infrastructure, but using as well a way of thinking inherited from the field of geography. Reflecting on the condition of architectural projects in existing cities during the 1980s, Gregotti proposed the notion of "modification," thus meeting certain aspects of Geddes's philosophy.[65]

Given the impossibility of modernizing the city with grand master plans, moving gradually from a regional scale to that of the district, the history of town planning finally forced planners to formulate the hypothesis of a city transformed by partial projects that would eventually combine into networks of public interventions. The Parisian *grands travaux* (large-scale projects) of the Mitterrand era may not be included in this type of strategy, because they do not belong to an overall urban policy. They are thus different from the policies used during the 1980s by the *Internationalen Bauausstellung* in Berlin, which gathered in one coordinated program isolated projects to "repair" the city, and different as well from the contemporary urban strategies of Barcelona, which are focused on a network of interventions on buildings, public spaces, and street infrastructure.[66] In both these cases, it is the site-specific project that leads to overall reflection about the city, and not the opposite.

A fundamental step toward the discovery of the real space of the city was accomplished by Kevin Lynch in the laboratory of urban analysis shared by MIT and Harvard; Lynch's analysis tries to make intelligible the mechanisms of perception and orientation.[67] Robert Venturi, in his book, *Complexity and Contradiction in Architecture* (1966), asserted that it is by observing the everyday urban landscape, "vulgar and disdained, that we can draw the complex and contradictory order that is valid and vital for our architecture as an urbanistic whole."[68] In *Learning from Las Vegas*, Venturi and his team examined "a new type of urban form

[63] Pierre Lavedan, *Qu'est-ce que l'urbanisme? Introduction à l'histoire de l'urbanisme* (Paris: H. Laurens, 1926).

[64] Aldo Rossi and Carlo Aymonino, *La città di Padova, saggio di analisi urbana* (Rome: Instituto Poligrafico della Stato, 1960); *Studi per una operante storia di Roma* (Rome: Consiglio Nazionale delle Ricerche, 1963).

[65] Vittorio Gregotti, *Il territorio dell'architettura* (Milan: Feltrinelli, 1966); " Modificazione," *Casabella*, no. 498-499 (January/Feburary 1984), 2-7.

[66] Internationalen Bauausstellung Berlin 1987, *Idee, Prozess, Ergebnis: die Reparatur und Rekonstruktion der Stadt* (Berlin: Frölich & Kaufmann, 1984); Oriol Bohigas, Peter Buchanan and Vittorio Magnago Lampugnani, *Barcelona: City and Architecture 1980-1992* (New York: Rizzoli, 1991).

[67] Kevin Lynch, *The Image of the City* (Cambridge, Mass.: MIT Press, 1960); also with Donald Appleyard and John R. Myer, *The View from the Road* (Cambridge, Mass.: MIT Press, 1964).

[68] Robert Venturi, *Complexity and Contradiction in Architecture* (New York: Museum of Modern Art, 1966), 102-03.

The Strip, Las Vegas, 1978. Photo by Venturi, Scott Brown, and Associates

emerging in America and Europe, radically different from that we have known; one we have been ill-equipped to deal with and that, from ignorance, we define today as urban sprawl."[69] With provocative eclecticism, Venturi analyzed the new relationships established between buildings, signs, and transportation systems, while the practices exemplified by the Las Vegas Strip shape the suburban spaces of most developed countries. In direct continuity with this process, Rem Koolhaas has focused on the unprecedented scales of projects and urban spaces of Atlanta, Seoul, and China's Pearl River delta.[70]

After all, Venturi and Koolhaas belong to the same tradition, the one inaugurated by Le Corbusier in *Vers une architecture*, when in 1923 he invited his readers to open their eyes which do not see. How to look at the city is our subject here; it is, in a way, similar to the method of Erich Mendelsohn, who showed his German readers Manhattan or Detroit.[71] As a place of spatial and visual inquiry, the city in the twentieth century has not been merely a playground for the iconoclastic enterprises of modern architecture. It has been also the very source of significant aesthetic strategies. One may think of the city in the twentieth century not only as the site of changing forms of modernization and of resistance to it, but also as a transformatory apparatus subverting architectural thought.

Translated by David Leclerc

[69] Robert Venturi, Denise Scott Brown, and Steven Izenour, *Learning from Las Vegas: The Forgotten Symbolism of Architectural Form* (Cambridge, Mass.: MIT Press, 1972), ix.

[70] Office of Metropolitan Architecture, Rem Koolhaas, and Bruce Mau, *S, M, L, XL*, ed. Jennifer Sigler (New York: Monacelli Press, 1995).

[71] Erich Mendelsohn, *Amerika: Bilderbuch eines Architekten* (Berlin: Rudolf Mosse, 1926).

Clorindo Testa, Santiago Sánchez Elia, Federico Peralta Ramos, and Alfredo Agostini, Bank of London and South America headquarters, Buenos Aires, 1960-66. Photo by Julius Shulman

LATIN AMERICA: THE PLACES OF THE "OTHER"

Jorge Francisco Liernur

Per speculum in aenigmate, says St. Paul. We see everything in reverse. When we think we are giving, we receive, etc. Then (a dear anguished soul tells me) we are in heaven and God suffers on earth.—Léon Bloy, 1904, quoted by Jorge Luis Borges in "The Mirror of the Enigmas"[1]

Antecedents

After centuries of isolation under Spanish rule, followed by several decades of convulsive independence struggles, Latin America became fully incorporated into the world economy in the second half of the nineteenth century. Every part of this gigantic territory was explored, measured, and described by merchants, intellectuals, artists, clerics, scientists, and adventurers from the North Atlantic countries. A multitude of enthusiasts avidly followed the footsteps of Darwin and Humboldt in what can be considered a second discovery.

In the wake of these first steps came the second conquest, the exploitation of the continent, and with it the urgency to create the physical conditions for this exploitation: transportation systems, encampments, and services of all kinds. To construct these encampments — certainly not only in Latin America but also in Asia and Africa — conditions were required that by mid-century foreshadowed modernist European programs. All these works were to last a short time and to be constructed in the briefest time possible. For this reason the lightest possible prefabricated construction systems were needed. No desire for meaning lay behind these anonymous constructions, usually erected on wooden pylons in the middle of plains or jungles. Furthermore, the characteristically hot climate of the tropical and subtropical regions stimulated openness and a virtual elimination of the barriers between interior and exterior. In all, these constructions were only repetitions, through industrialized construction, of the ideal model of the Caribbean Hut as observed by Gottfried Semper at the Crystal Palace in London of 1851 and later published as the basis of his tectonic theory.

Many of the new settlements in Brazil employed systems prefabricated in other countries, such as that of the Belgian *Societe des Forges d'Assieu*, which from 1885 on produced the Danly system, consisting of cast iron elements

1 Borges, "The Mirror of the Enigmas" in *Other Inquisitions, 1937-1952* (Austin: University of Texas Press, 1964), p.127.

from which all types of structures could be realized, from water tanks to hotels.[2] In Argentina and Chile another method was also widely used: anonymous, prefabricated construction using both domestic and imported materials. This system, consisting of a kind of wooden balloon-frame, the exterior covered with sheets of grooved zinc, the interior with wood, determined the appearance of a large part of Valparaiso in Chile and of the coastal cities of Argentina.[3] In Buenos Aires, builders joined this industrialized, light, and modern technique with classical composition.

Latin America's second conquest was, like the first, implacable. And just as industrialization vanquished mankind with ferocity and technical intelligence, it also attacked cities and territories with the same force, giving rise to inconceivable objects which foreshadowed, in their ugliness, a new beauty. Exceedingly rapid growth demanded the expansion of the cities. No unsuitable site constituted an obstacle capable of resisting the powerful combination of capital and technology. Characterized by high rocky hills, or by deep irregular valleys, enclosed by mountains or sea, São Paulo and Rio de Janeiro, the principal modern Brazilian cities, exploded on land with very strong natural resistance to growth. These cities had to make use of all available technological resources. In Rio the ferocity was literal. In order to expand, tunnels were dug, and when this was not enough, hills were dynamited and their rubble used to create new topographies and a new vision of the landscape.[4] When in São Paulo it was noticed that the space of its original plan would be insufficient to contain the growth that the coffee plantation expansion demanded, the city began to construct its traffic system in a kind of continuous plan, crossing over crests and valleys and making lavish use of overpasses.[5]

Languages for the New World

At the end of the nineteenth century, modernization swept through almost all the countries in the region, with a concomitant change in the characteristics of their societies. The population grew, and in several cases, such as Argentina, Brazil, Uruguay and Chile, large contingents of immigrants from Europe and Asia added to that growth. The urban sector grew considerably in relation to the rural sector. Demands for greater civil rights, for participation in government, and for social equality led to social conflict and a surge in popular organizations. As such movements did everywhere, these transformations stimulated the numerous expressions of cultural modernism.

For the most part, and in contrast to what occurred in Asia or more frequently in Africa, the Latin American countries conserved — with some exceptions — their political independence. In this way, despite the relative stability of some domination patterns, the economic and financial ties with one or other external power were variable.

The search for a "new art" or in our case, for a "new style" is strongly tied to these conditions. The expansion of the bourgeoisie in some North Atlantic cities at the end of the nineteenth century gave rise to a search for differentiation with respect to the older metropolises. This will strongly stimulated movements questioning academic traditions. This occurred in the case of Glasgow with respect to London, of Darmstadt with respect to Berlin, of Brussels with respect to Paris, of Chicago or Los Angeles with respect to New York.[6]

2 See Geraldo Gomez da Silva, *Arquitettura do ferro no Brasil* (Sao Paulo, 1987).

3 See my "La ciudad efimera" in Jorge Liernur and Graciela Silvestri, *El umbral de la metropolis* (Buenos Aires: Editorial Sudamericana, 1993).

4 See Maurício de A. Abreu, *Evolução urbana de Rio do Janeiro* (Rio de Janeiro: Iplanrio, 1987).

5 See Francisco Prestes Maia, *Estudo de um plano de avenidas para a cidada de São Paulo* (São Paulo: Melhoramentos, 1930), Suely Robles Reis de Queiroz, *São Paulo* (Madrid: MAPFRE,1992), and Benedito Lima de Toledo, *São Paulo, trâês cidades em um século* (São Paulo: Livraria Duas Cidades, 1981).

The equivalent metropolis for Latin American cities was Madrid, a city and cultural tradition separated from them by almost a century, by fierce battles and by elaborate disdain. Spain was backwardness, the clergy, impotence.

But what were the academic traditions that had to be questioned? The first waves of the "new styles" only superficially affected a few cultural camps, which were nevertheless committed to their legitimation. The second wave was different. The combination of cubism, monumentalism, exoticism and massive

Andres Kalnay, Munich Brewery, Buenos Aires, 1927. Photo by Jorge Francisco Liernur

production which has been identified with the 1925 "*Exposition des arts décoratifs*" in Paris had valuable manifestations in several Latin American countries, with various degrees of autonomy.

Andres Kalnay, for example, was an immigrant who arrived in Buenos Aires from Hungary in 1920, after having practiced architecture in Budapest and Vienna. Kalnay made use of classical compositions. One of his most important works is the Munich Brewery in Buenos Aires (1927). Symmetrical in design and elongated in volume, the building is full of small sculptures, bas-reliefs and stained-glass windows, among which the curved balconies and the pavilion with a double-curved cupola adorning the main staircase are particularly noteworthy. The insistent unison of diverse elements that characterize this work recall certain manifestations of Czech Cubism. Kalnay appears to have been strongly influenced by the theories of the artist as *Zeitgeist* spokesman so common in his homeland. Thus, he thought that architecture should respond to the technical possibilities of the time, but that it should also avoid mechanical repetition of the solutions. The brewery is entirely built of prefabricated parts *in situ*, but at the same time in its size and in its compositional order it tries to reproduce the harmonies that, its creator thought, ruled the world.

The goal of creating a new language that would simultaneously represent independence, a break with classicism, the vindication of pre-Hispanic traditions, and an "overcoming" of naturalism, was shared by many. In Mexico the creation of such a language was official policy. In Peru the new/old pre-Hispanic language was systematized by Jose Piquieras Cotolí. The deepest and most vigorous attempt to transform this new language into modern expression was the "constructivism" of the Uruguayan Joaquin Torres Garcia, whose work became highly influential.[7]

Modernisms and Avant-Gardes

In Latin America, one of the characteristics that Raymond Williams attributed to avant-gardes — that of being constituted by immigrants coming from peripheral zones — can be better applied to a type of hybrid architecture that can only with difficulty be identified with the concept of the avant-garde defined by Peter Bürger. While for Williams avant-gardes "represent sharp and even violent ruptures with the inherited practical traditions,"[8] this does not help us to identify the differences between the groups that we have referred to and those that took part in earlier, more radical, movements. For Bürger,

> What they have in common [the latter] although they differ in some aspects, consists in not rejecting a determined artistic direction but rather the art of their time in its totality and thus verifying a rupture with tradition. Their extreme manifestations are directed particularly against art as an institution and its formation within the bosom of the bourgeoisie.[9]

The application of this definition to the history of architecture of the region not only clearly separates both groups but also brings to it elements that differentiate between the avant-garde and what we can call an enlightened modernism. In contrast to the first, which proposes a total rejection of art, the second can be characterized by its acceptance of a break with artistic canons of the past as a condition for the renovation of art itself.

6 See Klaus-Jürgen Sembach, *Modernismo* (Cologne, 1991).

7 See Mari Carmen Ramirez, *El Taller Torres-Garcia: The School of the South and its Legacy* (Austin, University of Texas Press, 1992).

8 Williams, *Culture and Society* 1780-1950 (London: Chatto and Windus, 1958).

9 Burger, *Theory of the Avant-Garde* (Minneapolis: University of Minnesota Press, 1984).

10 See Merlin H. Forster, *Vanguardism in Latin American Literature: An Annotated Bibliographical Guide* (New York: Greenwood, 1990); Jorge Schwartz, *Vanguarda e cosmopolitismo na década de 20* (São Paulo: Editora Perspectiva, 1983); Ana Maria de Moraes Belluzzo, *Modernidade: vanguardias artísticas na América Latina* (São Paulo: UNESP, 1990); and Vicky Unruh, *Latin American Vanguards: The Art of Contentious Encounters* (Berkeley: University of California Press, 1995).

11 See Rafael López Rangel, *La modernidad arquitectónica méxicana: antecedentes y vanguardias, 1900-1940* (Mexico City: Universidad Autónoma Metropolitana, 1989); Diane Davis, *Urban Leviathan: Mexico City in the Twentieth Century* (Philadelphia: Temple University Press, 1994); Enrique Yañez, *Dal funcionalismo al post-racionalismo* (Mexico City, 1990); Enrique De Anda Alanis, *La Arquitectura de la Revolución Mexicana* (Mexico City: Universidad Autónoma Metropolitana, 1990).

12 See Ida Rodríguez Prampolini, *Juan O'Gorman, Arquitecto y Pintor* (Mexico City: Universidad Nacional Autónoma de México, 1982).

In the large cities of the south of the continent, it has not been immigrant groups but rather the bourgeoisie itself, and in particular the *jeunesse doré* of the oligarchies, who have made up the groups proposing the "purifying bath" of modernism. Only in exceptional cases, individual and of short duration, did the avant-garde utopias have relevant expressions.[10]

Revolutionary Mexico, at least up to the government of General Lázaro Cárdenas, is the only country where avant-garde utopias reached an important degree of expansion, of relationship to political power, and thus with fruition.[11] The greatest influence on this avant-garde was in the so-called "Conversations of 33." These "Conversations" on modern architecture were sponsored by the Society of Mexican Architects. In this debate the radical positions of three young men played a prominent role: Juan O'Gorman, Juan Legorreta and Alvaro Aburto. The three shared the idea that modernism should not be discussed only in stylistic or artistic terms but should also include a discussion of completely new building practices (exposed brick and reinforced concrete) as well as new educational systems. This renovation should be based on the search for massive, immediate, solutions for the needs of the Mexican people, for whom artistic preoccupations were irrelevant.

Of the architecture achieved under these premises, the most noteworthy are the Balbuena and San Jacinto "colonias" built by Legorreta and the Diego Rivera and Frida Kahlo house by Juan O'Gorman. Legorreta's houses are constructed according to rigorous procedures which single out the rationality of a series of construction processes yet at the same time respond to traditional cultural rules. O'Gorman used the artists' house as a site for experiment: the exposed concrete and the open floor levels designed without any specific purpose, the electric bathroom fixtures, and the elimination of any showy and vulgar details.[12] The evident similarity with the Ozenfant studio serves only as a signpost, for it is

Juan Legorrata, Workers' houses in Balbuena, Mexico, 1932

Juan O'Gorman, Casa Kahlo and Rivera, Mexico City, 1929. Instituto Nacional de Bellas Artes

Juan O'Gorman, Casa Kahlo and Rivera, Mexico City, 1929. Instituto Nacional de Bellas Artes

Le Corbusier, Ozenfant studio, Paris, 1922. Fondation Le Corbusier

Juan O'Gorman, National Library, Ciudad Universitaria, Mexico City, 1952-53. Photo by Jorge Francisco Liernur

much more important to note the differences: the eloquent cactus fence, the lively "Mexican" colors, the absence (almost rejection) of regularity in the facades.

In the series of schools these characteristics were employed to the point of exasperation. It suffices to observe that in the case of Tres Guerras, the radical indifference with which the unit — in which O'Gorman concentrates his past experiences — is directed toward its context, revealing it as a true "factory of industrial knowledge."

Le Corbusier

If there has been a tendency to undervalue the mutually fruitful interchange with masters such as Richard Neutra, Alvar Aalto, Walter Gropius, Frank Lloyd Wright and Mies van der Rohe, it is nevertheless true that the impact of Le Corbusier on the architecture of Latin America remains unsurpassed.[13] Le Corbusier visited the region for the first time in 1929. During

[13] See Fernando Perez Oyarzún (ed.), *Le Corbusier y Sud America* (Santiago de Chile: Ediciones Arq, 1991).

Juan O'Gorman, secondary school on the calle Tres Guerras, Mexico City

Le Corbusier, Maison Errázuris, 1930. Fondation Le Corbusier

the major part of this four-month trip, he was in Buenos Aires, although he also visited Montevideo, Asunción, Sao Paulo, and Rio de Janeiro.

In Paris, before his departure, he had prepared a project for a house. In South America, he planned a hotel in Mar de Plata and a museum in Buenos Aires, a city for which he also executed sketches for a group of "Savoie villas" and a "little skyscraper." He signed two contracts: one for an apartment project for which he produced only a few sketches, and another for a house that Matias Errazuris commissioned in Chile, on the Pacific coast. It is this last case that Le Corbusier made the fullest use of regionalism — specifically in materials.

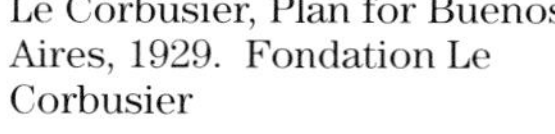

Le Corbusier, Plan for Buenos Aires, 1929. Fondation Le Corbusier

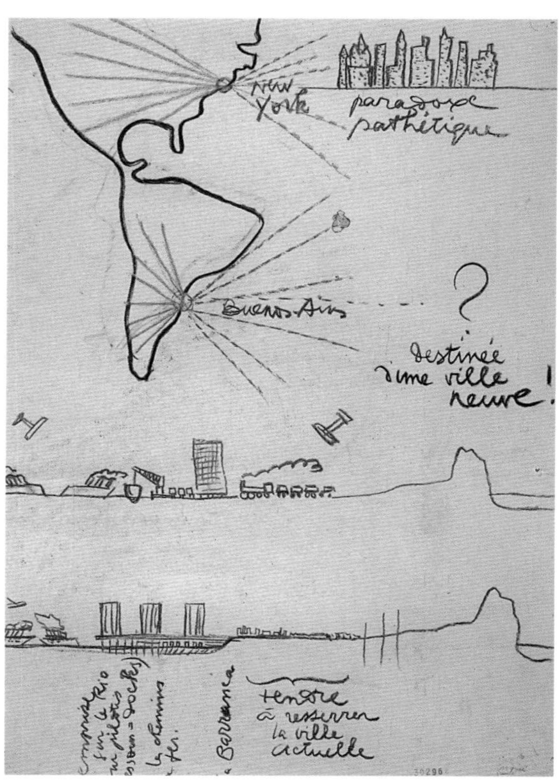

Without a doubt the most important result of the trip was the sketches for various cities, especially those for Buenos Aires and Rio de Janeiro.[14] In the former, he took the first step toward the transformation of the plan of the contemporary city into the Ville Radieuse. The impact on Le Corbusier of the landscape is apparent: the horizontal infinity of the plain upon which he bases, magnificently, "La cité des affaires." In Rio, the opposite occurs: it is the verticals of the hills of the Bahia de Guanabara which inspire the horizontal "infinity" of the building that extends along the coast. The role of landscape in his poetics experienced a definitive change between Buenos Aires and Rio.

Several years later, he was invited by the government of Brazil to give lectures and to consult on the project of the University City in Rio de Janeiro and on the project for the Ministry of Education. Le Corbusier approached the city repeatedly, searching for an undifferentiated or neutral structure that would support the plurality of its functions, on the other, considering it as a civic monument or *axis mundi*. If the scheme of the Ville Radieuse responded to the first focus, the second was developed in projects such as that of the Mundaneum.[15] Conceived as a true acropolis for Rio, the University City was the peak of this monumental form of understanding the city.

In collaboration with two young Argentines, Jorge Ferrari Hardoy and Juan Kurchan, who worked for almost a year in his atelier, he was in 1937 able to further develop his proposals for Buenos Aires. A few important innovations were introduced in the plan, such as a proposal for structural transformation of the central zones, the maintenance of the coastal parks, and the realization of a grouping of "centers" (governmental, business, municipal, Pan-American, etc.).

Le Corbusier, Plan for Rio de Janeiro, 1936. Fondation Le Corbusier

Paradoxically, or perhaps as an expression of the profound changes that resulted from the Second World War, it was not in any of the countries with which contact had been cultivated where Le Corbusier finally received a real commission on the scale he had been seeking since his first trip. Instead it was Dr. Eduardo Zuleta Angel, ambassador of Colombia to the United Nations, who proposed that Le Corbusier begin thinking about a plan for Bogota. In 1947, Le Corbusier came to the city for the first time, returning in 1949, 1950, and 1951. He articulated a plan by means of a restructuring of the transportation system, the consolidation of pre-existing functional areas and respect for the traditional center.

Through Lucio Costa and Oscar Niemeyer, Le Corbusier maintained close relations with Brazil. In the mid-1960s he was invited to carry out a new project in that country, the French embassy in Brasilia, an attempt at articulation between the cylinder and the square of great importance in his work. But it was in Argentina where, despite his many disappointments, he succeeded in having one of his projects carried out: a house for Dr. Pedro Currutchet, consisting of one block for a consultation room and another for living quarters.[16] Both blocks come together in a different manner with the adjoining house, one referring to its "traditional" neighbor and another to its "modern" neighbor. Designed at the moment of maximum activity around the plans for Buenos Aires, the small building was intended to demonstrate the capacity of mediation between both poles.

14 See Marcello Fagiolo, *Le Corbusier 1930: i progetti per Algerie e L'America Latina* (Milan, 1973).

15 See Rogerio de Castro Oliveira, "Dos Proyectos, una ciudad universitaria; las modernidades electivas de Le Corbusier y Lucio Costa" in Pérez Oyarzún, *Le Corbusier Y Sud America*.

16 See Alejandro Lapunzina *Le Corbusier's Maison Currutchet* (Princeton: Princeton Architectural Press, 1997).

Le Corbusier, Currutchet House, La Plata, Argentina, 1949. Fondation Le Corbusier

The "Appearance" of Latin America

In the 1940s and 1950s Latin American architecture won international recognition. The Biennials of São Paulo convoked the cream of international architecture at the beginning of the 1950s. In 1954, as a consequence of one of these Biennials, *Architectural Review* began to question the legitimacy of this approach. The questioning escalated until the construction of Brasilia signaled simultaneously the realization of the dreams of the first Congrès internationaux d'architecture moderne (CIAM) and became the universal symbol of their "failure." After Brasilia, Latin American architecture began to revert to the peripheral position it had occupied before the Ministry of Education in Rio.

It should be noted that these two landmarks are both in Brazil. For most people, to think of Latin American architecture of this period is to think of Brazilian architecture. But it is insufficient, because in representing "Latin American architecture" one also has to include at least one other myth: that of the "Mexican School." Brazil, Mexico. Is it by chance that the leading roles in this story are taken by the two principal Latin American allies of the United States during the Second World War? Is it by chance that "neutral" Argentina plays almost no role at all?

The immediate postwar years were full of promises. Of peace, democracy, independence. But also of projects. Projects for the reconstruction of devastated territories, projects for new independent countries, projects for the

Oscar Niemeyer, Congress complex, Brasilia, 1959. Photo by Julius Shulman

Lucio Costa, Oscar Niemeyer, Carlos Leo, Alfonso Eduardo Reidy, Jorge Moreira, and Ernani Vasconcellos, Ministry of Education and Public Health, Rio de Janeiro, 1937-42

definition of a new international bureaucracy. The United Nations seemed to many the natural agency for organizing and distributing financial and human resources. A special team was organized within the organization dedicated to projects in "developing" countries, and the leaders of CIAM sought its leadership. They were able to obtain roles both in planning and in the construction of the new buildings themselves. Latin American countries was especially influential, because they were the most numerous regional block, united by language and traditions. Good relations with Latin America were thus a possible passport to important future commissions.

But let us return to the Ministry of Education in Rio. The Ministry was the first office building in the form of the vertical slab that would later become canonical. It was also the first in which theories about solar power were applied and developed on a large scale. And even more: the Ministry realized the dream of collective creation and solidarity among many architects, and not only architects, but also landscape designers, engineers, sculptors, and painters. The Ministry announced its own work in two themes linked to representation and taboo for modernism: the articulation of local tradition and of the relationship between modern load-bearing structures and tectonic perception. Regarding the former, the architects were not embarrassed to apply decorated tiles on the walls of buildings in the Portuguese tradition. With regard to the latter, they of sized the diameter of the highest pylons to visual requirements.

The "Brazilian School," especially in the architecture of Costa and Niemeyer, consciously internalized these problems of representation. Moreover, these were the questions in which they were most interested. How to express the festive character of a dance hall? How to articulate a modern church situated in an exuberant landscape? How to be modern in such an ancient country? These questions were profound considerations in their work.

Educated in the academic tradition, Costa did not follow illusions of reproducibility, solutions that he know to be impossible and for which perhaps he had no passion. On the contrary, his search was for a new architecture, or, as he called it, a new plateau for the discipline. Niemeyer's solution was not without cynicism.[17] A country like Brazil, populated by millions of poor and illiterate people could not, should not, orient itself toward architectural thinking based on technological metaphors. As a communist, Niemeyer was convinced that only a true revolution could begin to provide the means for a true transformation. This would perhaps be the moment to think of the austerity and technical extremism proposed by the hard-line sector of European modernism. Meanwhile it was only possible to perceive with sensitivity, and express, the spirit of the Brazilian people: their way of feeling music and rhythm, their passion for the splendors of nature, their beautiful bodies, their happiness.

How can one accept involvement in the economic orbit of the United States, yet maintain the rhetoric of independence and revolution? How can one be modern and Mexican? In the aftermath of the second World War circumstances led Mexico to abandon its posture of pretended autonomy, nationalistic radicalism, and agrarian populism. The buildings that brought fame to the so-called "Mexican School" of architecture, especially the National Preparatory School, the housing projects of the Conjunto Miguel Aleman, and above all the University City, were mostly gigantic official commissions distributed among a handful of professionals linked to the government.

[17] See Niemeyer, *Oscar Niemeyer, architetto* (Florence: Istituto dé Cultura di Palazzo Grassi, 1980) and Stamo Papadaki, *The Work of Oscar Niemeyer* (New York: Reinhold, 1950).

Mario Pani, Unidad Habitacional
Miguel Aleman, Mexico City, 1949.
Compañía Mexicana Aerofoto

The works of Felix Candela are opposed to this "Mexican school." His is a search without a past, and without geography. His shell-like forms do not even touch the ground, but almost seem to fly. The most noteworthy of his buildings is the Church of the Miraculous Virgin (1953).

In Venezuela, unlike Brazil and Mexico, there was not a cultural politics that produced a national and modern movement at the same time. There was instead one exceptional figure, who was able to bypass the authoritarianism, the corrupt bureaucracy, the mediocrity, and the ignorance of the various regimes under which he worked. The history of modern Venezuelan architecture virtually coincides with the biography of Carlos Raul Villanueva. His University City of Caracas (1950-59) shines with power, surprise, and emotion.

In Argentina, the "Austral" group included Antonio Bonet, a Spaniard driven from his country by the Civil War, and Juan Kurchan and Jorge Ferrari Hardoy, fresh from having collaborated with Le Corbusier on his plan for

Félix Candela, Church of the Miraculous Virgin, Mexico City, 1953. Photo by Juan Guzmán

Buenos Aires. They experimented both technically and formally, but in each case their theoretical grounding lay in Surrealism. Of all their varied projects, however, the best known is probably the chair known as the "Butterfly," the "Hardoy," or (after the initials of its creators) the "BKF." With its combination of artisanal technique (raw leather) and industrial rounded profile, it achieves a balance between the pampas and the city that is as Argentine as the tango.

In the Schools of Art of Havana the sound of the boom in Latin American architecture reached a level of complete dissonance. If in 1954 *Architectural Review* had judged and condemned primitivism, baroque-ism and the lack of discipline of Latin American architecture, in the Art Schools all these positions were

Carlos Raúl Villanueva, Plaza Cubierta, University City, Caracas, Venezuela, 1950-59. Photo by Jorge Francisco Liernur

Antonio Bonet, Vera Barros,
Lopez Chas, Ateliers, Buenos Aires,
(showing "Butterfly" chair) 1938

expressed in an extremely provocative manner. Craftsman-like and not industrialized, representative in an explicit manner of carnal sensuality, totally distant from any rationalism, the works of Garatti, Gottardi and especially Ricardo Porro were a kind of retroactive proclamation of Latin Americanism taken to an absurd extreme. On one hand they were disquieting because they were produced by the surprisingly triumphant political expression of "otherness" with respect to the consecrated canons of Western progress. But on the other hand, this very "otherness" was condemned by a revolution that did not want to be seen as an island but as a new model, of universal validity.

The Others of the Others

Were the works and the architects that we are now going to examine left behind or did they position themselves outside the paradigmatic space of the boom? Their presence was disconcerting. They were not very "Latin American," too international to satisfy the desire for "difference" that the universal tendency toward homogenization generated. Perhaps in a few cases their work did not contain enough novelty, but neither was it as inferior as that of many of their colleagues in the region or even as that of many established architects in Europe or the United States. Their architecture was not strident and their affiliations were pluralist.

Think, for example, of the strong although today under-recognized influence of Auguste Perret. He visited the south of the region in 1937, but his ideas had a much wider reach. In Colombia his influence is most evident in the mature work of Bruno Violi.[18] Violi was born in 1909 in Italy, and moved to Colombia in 1940. He had studied in Milan, and worked in other European countries. In the early 1950s he developed possibilities of continuity in the classical principles of regularity, recognition, and articulation of structural elements as a language. The extraordinary results of this search can be seen in the El Tiempo building and in the Synagogue of the Adat Israel community, both in Bogota.

The Faculty of Engineering building in Montevideo is one of the most magnificent works of Latin American architecture. Its author was Julio Vilamajó, educated in Montevideo and during a long stay in Europe in the 1920s. The building was conceived at the end of the 1940s and built slowly in the years that followed. Its strength lies in the exceptional union of a neoplastic composition and the subtle influence of academic traditions. The building does not constitute an indifferent abstraction: its location at the point of the coastal landscape of the city, surrounded by a park, led to control of numerous visual parameters and with them, a changing relationship to its surroundings. With its bridge-like structure, and the combination of vertical volumes with horizontal brickwork, it can be seen as a type of Bauhaus on an American scale. Built with exposed concrete and in this differing from the school of Weimar, the structure plays a dominant role, uniting the major and minor rhythms that make up the complete volume.

If Corbusian plasticism constituted a path of formal expression, it was Richard Neutra who proposed a dialogue about environmental and cultural problems. Already established in the United States, with good ties to official circles, in Latin America Neutra broadened reflections on the influence of climactic conditions that had already been stimulated by his experiences in California. This process

[18] See Hans Rother, *Bruno Violi* (Bogota, 1986).

Julio Vilamajó, Faculty of Engineering, Montevideo, Uruguay, 1945-53. Photo by Jorge Francisco Liernur

Richard Neutra, Industrial Arts Urban Schools, Puerto Rico, 1944. Department of Special Collections, University Research Library, UCLA

began with his work in Puerto Rico, during the war-time recession in construction in the rest of the United States. He designed primarily residences and academic buildings. Later he began to systematize his observations and to promote discussion in the rest of the continent, exercising a powerful influence.[19]

In Neutra, modern compositional principles (structural lightness, absence of interior/exterior barriers, flat roofs, pylons, etc.) reached an explicit formulation in the context of warm climates. These ideas, born in the tropical camps of the nineteenth century, thus returned, renewed and transformed, to their place of origin, in which they disseminated themselves until becoming exhausted.

Amancio Williams was a controversial and strange personality with an extraordinary sensibility: messianism and lack of any sense of reality on one hand, sharpness and clarity on the other.[20] Williams was the son of a noted musician and came from a family of the traditional upper class. As a product of these and other factors his production had an improbable and extreme rigor. Most of his ideas were developed as pure research, continuing logical premises that he never for a moment abandoned. His work possesses two characteristics that distinguish it: mostly it was not built and, perhaps in part because of this, it constitutes in each case a premise of absolute exactitude.

Amancio Williams, House on the Stream, Mar del Plata, Argentina, 1943-45

Let us refer to two examples. One is his skyscraper, conceived in 1948. Williams's obsession was to produce an architecture that would respond exactly to the conditions of modernity. At the center of his preoccupations was the tectonic question: lightness should be sought because it was the logical consequence of the new materials, but lightness was also a metropolitan condition. His problem was how to build the paradox of a skyscraper without weight.

If construction principles of his skyscraper had to wait many years to be incarnated in Norman Foster's Hong Kong and Shanghai Bank, the House on

19 Neutra, *Architecture of Social Concern in Regions of Mild Climate* (São Paulo: Gerth Todtmann, 1948).

20 Williams, *Amancio Williams* (Buenos Aires: C. Williams, 1990). See also Jorge Silvetti (ed.), *Amancio Williams* (Cambridge, Massachusetts, 1987).

Amancio Williams, suspended skyscraper, 1948

the Stream for his father was actually built. Situated in the middle of a beautiful forest, it was supported on a bridge structure over a small stream. The curvature of the bridge is employed as an ascent and descent toward the rooms inscribed in a perfect parallelpied. The curvature replicates exactly the profile of the land.

Cities: From Expansion to Explosion

The modern city came about, in Latin America, on territory already conceived in a modern manner, onto which were applied on a massive scale ideas of order, rationality and equality. This fact should suffice to differentiate Latin American experiences of urban transformation from those elsewhere. European extensions were ruptures, while those in Latin America appeared as simple continuity. Precisely because it was not novel, the protagonists of such expansion were not great persons of culture but rather civil or military surveyor and anonymous engineers.

The transformation, the opposition to the homogenous square (plaza), came about in opposition to that ancient "barbarian" method. The square was a form of representation of the past that had to be overcome by modernization, although with the force of its simplicity and inertia, it remained in fact the easiest and most utilized instrument of urban expansion, even as all the voices of Progress took it on as an arch-enemy that had to be destroyed.

The expression of these desires was in plans. As is obvious the first ones most frequently affected the capitals. Good examples are the Paseo de la Reforma in Mexico City and the Avenida de Mayo in Buenos Aires. The Paseo de la Reforma consisted of an extensive boulevard that went from the old quarter of the city to Maximilian's Palace, situated in a park which was then on the outskirts; the avenue built in Buenos Aires joined the buildings of the National Congress and the Governor's mansion, creating an urban environment of Haussmannian ambitions.

Early in the century, the Anglo-Saxon idea of urban garden districts had a certain influence, especially in Bogota, Santiago de Chile, Buenos Aires, and in Puerto Rico.

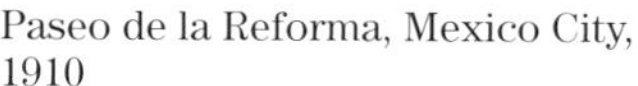

Paseo de la Reforma, Mexico City, 1910

Paseo de la Reforma, Mexico City, c. 1955. Photo by Juan Guzmán

The City Block for Buenos Aires that Vladimiro Acosta designed in the early 1930s united the Plaza-square, the cruciform Corbusian skyscraper, and the ideas of Hilberseimer about the vertical city. But Mexico was the country that had the best conditions to imagine advanced experiences of urban engineering. Carlos Contreras published the first modern attempt at planning in Latin America, reflecting discussions that were taking place in CIAM.[21]

In Jose Luis Sert's projects for Chimbote, Cidade dos Motores, Bogota, and Havana, among others, a series of new problems began to arise that brought together this research with the preoccupations of the young architects of Team X.[22] In these works we can see the themes of high density at low heights, of open interior spaces, of urban enclosures, of the interrelation of functions. Sert sought to fuse the universal principles of the first CIAM with both Mediterranean influences and the Anglo-Saxon influences — especially that of Olmstead — that he had absorbed during his long stay in the United States.

Even if the plans of Corbusier and Sert were only partially realized, the ideas that modernist urbanism had planted nevertheless had their apotheosis in Latin America, in the construction of Brasilia.[23] The inauguration of the city in 1960 was the culmination of a history that goes back to 1891, when in the new constitution of the recently created republic a clause was included stipulating the necessity to relocate the capital from Rio de Janeiro to a new seat.[24] A 1958 competition under the direction of Oscar Niemeyer was won by Lucio Costa.

Lucio Costa, Plan for city of Brasilia, 1957. Departamento de Patrimônio Histórico e Artístico/ Governo de Distrito Federal

Costa gave the Pilot Plan the elemental form of a Latin cross, with its shortest bar slightly curved, which makes the form of the city read as that of an airplane. Since then, the project has received much criticism, for the naivete of making the plan a symbol, and such an obvious one; for its monumental scale; and for the rigidity of a form that does not permit future growth. Nevertheless, these criticisms can be considered more as aspects of sixties anti-CIAM rhetoric than as true faults.[25] The "symbol" of the cross/airplane has two advantages. The first is its response to Latin American political instability: its most significant segments — the point of the cross and its head — were sufficiently small to guarantee their rapid construction during the presidential term of the person who had led the initiative, Juscelino Kubitschek; the second is the necessity to fix an image — that could only be symbolic — of the city both for Brazilians and for the world. The "monumental" dimensions attempted to overcome the municipalism towards which the dominant sector of CIAM tended. Brasilia was envisioned to house 500,000 inhabitants, but its plan was only the center of a system of satellite cities intended to absorb probable future expansions.[26] Observed fully functioning in the final years of the century, it should not be forgotten that it is still young, scarcely four decades in existence.

The urban explosion of Latin America in the second half of the twentieth century is well known. This explosion has provoked two opposing reactions that elsewhere I have called the "contaminated city" and the "white city."[27]

21 Contreras, "La planificación de la ciudad de Mexico, 1918-1938" in *16 Congreso Internacional de Planificación y de la Habitación* (Mexico City, 1938).

22 See Anahi Ballent, *America Latina en los CIAM* (Buenos Aires, 1996) and Knud Basltlund, *José Luis Sert: Architecture, City Planning and Urban Design* (New York: 1967).

23 See Alberto Xavier, *Bibliografia sobre Brasilia y arquitectura moderna brasileira* (1973).

24 See Alexander Fils, *Brasilia: Moderne Architektur in Brasilien* (Dusseldorf, 1988).

25 James Holston, *The Modernist City: an Anthropological Critique of Brasilia* (Chicago: University of Chicago Press, 1989).

26 Costa's position can be found in *Lucio Costa: Registro de uma vivencia* (Rio, 1997).

27 Liernur, *America Latina; Architettura gli ultimi Vent'anni* (Milan: Electa, 1990).

28 See Claire Pailler (ed.), *Les Ameriques et l'europe: Voyage, emigration, exile* (Toulouse: Université de Toulouse-Le Mirail, 1985).

Brasilia, Aerial view, 1986. Companhia de Desenvocvimento do Planalto/Governo do Distrito Federal

The "contaminated city" is a form linked to the expansion and presence of democracy. Caracas, Mexico, Bogota, or Rio, the majority, are cities of this type because obviously the "white city" only exists as an exception. "Contaminated" cities are those in which the poor cannot be banished to the outskirts, its privileged sectors resign themselves to find modes of living within/among/over them. In this manner the cities become medievalized: in the middle of chaos, the order of castles and monasteries is imposed in the modern version of precincts and neighborhoods, shopping centers or office towers.

Coming and Going in the Town

In Latin America there is a sector of architecture whose pertinence is difficult to classify geographically. Nobody would doubt the classification of the Seagram Building as North American, but the house built by Gio Ponti in Caracas is Italian. The church of Riola in Italy is by the Finn, Alvar Aalto, but is the Ministry of Finance in Paris by the Chilean, Borja Huidobro? Migrant architects are not a modern phenomenon. Nevertheless it is certain that the communications explosion and the global marketplace have overcome wars and economic crises, converting mobility into a characteristic of this century. In Latin America the centrifugal forces appear equivalent to the centripetal ones. Here exile is a two-way tradition.

The region succeeded in distancing itself from full participation in the two wars that shook the rest of the world in this century, and this made it a refuge for the persecuted or for those who sought simply peace or opportunities to work.[28]

Alvar Aalto, Riola Church and Parish Center, near Bologna, 1978. Photo by William P. Bruder

Before traveling to England, Gropius tried to obtain commissions in Argentina, which he finally received in the 1970s in the form of a project for the embassy of the then German Federal Republic which was never built.[29] Mies had better luck because he worked on two projects for the Bacardi firm, one in Havana and the other in Mexico, and he actually built the second. But neither the first nor the last director of the Bauhaus established a relationship with the subcontinent such as that of the second, Hannes Meyer.[30] His experience in Mexico was a profound but tragically sterile experience. In spite of the great recognition that he received from the group of "Socialist Architects," with their close ties to the power structure, he never succeeded, during his ten-year stay, in making his proposals concrete. He developed various projects, organized urban studies, participated in the Taller de Grafica Popular, but at the beginning of the 1950s he returned, frustrated once more, to Switzerland to die.

There was interest in Italian modernism in Latin America before the Second World War. It was after the war, however, that Italian influence reached its peak. The early 1960s saw the expansion of large Italian corporations, among them, with a special role for our theme, Olivetti. Olivetti was not only a launching pad for Italian design, but it also introduced to Buenos Aires the ephemeral but also very important impact of Gae Aulenti's work, and the

Lina Bo Bardi, Museu de Arte de São Paulo, 1968. Photo by Luiz Hossaka.

Lina Bo Bardi, "Study for an exhibition - toys for children," 1968. Instituto Lina Bo e P.M. Bardi

monument of industrial architecture represented by the factory designed down to the smallest details by Marco Sanuzzo.

Venezuela also experienced immigration from Italy during and after the war. Its most renowned product is the house built by Ponti in Caracas. This is a radical work, an extreme manifestation of total design, of the unstoppable force of inventing everything new that so profoundly characterized a sector of Italian culture of the 1950s. But it is as if Ponti had realized that this total freedom, or at least the sensation of possessing it, could only be realized in a landscape like these hills at the border of the Guaire river. Even with all his formal caprices, his infinite palette of colors and materials, his planters, his furniture, his odd light fixtures and dishes, the house is ultimately a humble act of admiration toward the communal space.

The Italian roots of the modern Brazilian experience are especially evident in São Paulo. Filippo Tommaso Marinetti was one of the references taken into account by the "modernists" who scandalized the inhabitants of the city in 1922. But after the war the scene was dominated by the "Francophile" Carioca group, and only a few figures such as Rino Levi were linked with the Italian experience. Lina Bo Bardi had a doubly lateral entrance: in the first place because she was the young wife of the great collector and critic of the modern Fascist architects Pietro Maria Bardi. But Lina Bo's trajectory was an ascent toward "Brazilianization." Being of foreign origin she was more than anyone a lover and a student of the most exotic Afro-Brazilian traditions — especially Bahian — and among the first to defend and revindicate the ethical and aesthetic world of the poor.

If the contributions of foreigners in Latin America were important, those, in turn, of Latin Americans in other countries were no less so. During Le Corbusier's lifetime his small studio on the Rue de Sèvres functioned as a magnet for the majority of the young architects of the world — Latin Americans were no exception.

[29] See Reginald Isaacs, *Gropius: An Illustrated Biography of the Creator of the Bauhaus* (Boston: Little, Brown, 1991).

[30] See A. Gorelik and Jorge Liernur, *La sombra de la Vanguardia: Hannes Meyer en Mexico* (Buenos Aires, 1990).

The situation was somewhat different in the United States. There there were two opposing impulses: on the one hand that the "Latinization" of North American culture; on the other the tendency for architects who have come from Iberian countries to become "globalized."

The first of these impulses is evident in the border zones with a strong Hispanic presence: Southern California, Texas, Miami. The most relevant exponents of this group have been Carlos Jiménez,[31] Arquitectónica, Jorge Rigau and Teofilo Victoria. But the figure that expresses this tendency most eloquently is Ricardo Legorreta. His work has often been presented as a continuation of that of Luis Barragán. If this comparison was relevant in his early works, such as the IBM Factory in Guadalajara, it is difficult to recognize in his later works, in which the use of large blank walls and the application of "Mexican" colors on rough textures are the only features that remain of this relationship. Of increasing influence and presence, the architecture of Legorreta shows, in relation to that of the master of "silence," a tremendous change in scale. In his works in Texas or California (and

Ricardo Legorreta, IBM Factory, Guadalajara, Mexico, 1975. Photo by Julius Shulman

[31] See Jiménez, *Carlos Jiménez* (Barcelona: G. Gili, 1991).

Arquitectónica, The Atlantis, Miami, Florida, 1980-82. Photo by Norman McGrath

Ricardo Legorreta, Camino Real Cancún Hotel, 1975. Photo by Julius Shulman

Rafael Viñoly, Tokyo International Forum, 1996.

also in the Mexican hotels for foreign tourists) the lack of alteration of the elemental components as a consequence of this shift induces a recognition of the "Mexican."

In the 1970s the projects and theories formulated by a group of young Argentines won international renown. Mario Gandelsonas, Diana Agrest,[32] Jorge Silvetti, and Rodolfo Machado played a major role alongside figures such as Peter Eisenman and Michael Graves in the great wave of renovation of architecture that Charles Jencks baptized with the effective but narrow name of Postmodernism. Emilio Ambasz plays an important role in this movement, not only through his "discovery" of Barragán, but also through the strength of his original ecological projects and his brilliant furniture designs.

While all of these architects have successfully continued their careers, the Latin American figures that have attracted the most international attention in recent years have been Cesar Pelli and Rafael Viñoly. While they are very different — Pelli cautious, Viñoly expansive — two common characteristics are especially notable in their production. The first is that both pay attention to the pragmatic conditions imposed by the profession on the construction of a theoretical armature. The second is their increasingly intense activity outside of the United States, particularly in Asia. Pelli's Petronas Towers in Kuala Lumpur and Viñoly's Tokyo Forum are truly monuments of the end of the millennium.[33]

Recent Years

After the boom years of the 1960s, interest in Latin American architecture almost disappeared from international debate. But then a new phase of external evaluation began, a re-evaluation that produced new, homogenizing interpretations that did not always coincide with reality.

The heart of this new reading, its paradigm, was determined by the figure of Luis Barragán. The site of this consecration was The Museum of Modern Art in New York.[34] How was it that Barragán could win an international reputation through the New York museum, followed by numerous publications (almost all very similar to the magnificent catalogue by Emilio Ambasz) that would give him a prominent place in architectural libraries throughout the world? His was an architecture that exalted silence in the face of urban noise; the use of minimal elements and simple techniques in the face of the sophistication of High Tech; a certain surreal magic, images of a wild and arid land. This Barragán was the perfect figure of the "other" that could demonstrate the total breakdown of the old myths of the city and the machine. He became an architectonic incarnation of the "magic realism" popularized by the literary boom of the 1970s, a complete expression of maximum cultural relativism.

On the Latin American side, this external reading was joined to a strong ideological base. As is well known, the Cuban Revolution had a strong impact on the intellectuals of the region. The most influential beliefs that this experience and its later expressions — especially the epic of Che Guevara — instilled have been: 1) the idea of the "people" as a pure and motivating subject of History; 2) the belief that local problems originated in dependence on dominant external powers; 3) moralism sustained by economic, social, and cultural programs.

[32] See *Agrest and Gandelsonas: Works* (New York: Princeton Architectural Press, 1995); Agrest, *Architecture from Without* (Cambridge: MIT Press, 1991); and Gandelsonas, *The Urban Text* (Cambridge: MIT Press, 1991).

[33] See Pelli, *Cesar Pelli: Selected and Current Works* (Mulgrave: Images Publishing Group, 1993).

[34] Emilio Ambasz, *The Architecture of Luis Barragán* (New York: The Museum of Modern Art, 1976).

[35] See German Tellez, *Rogelio Salmona* (Bogota: Facultad de Arquitetura, Universidad de los Andes, 1992).

Luis Barragán, Barragán House, Tacubaya, Mexico City, 1947. Photo by Alberto Moreno

These concepts were easily interlaced with the principles that emerged from pastoral socialism and the post Vatican II church, and had their extreme expression in so-called "revolutionary Christianity." From these positions there began to emerge a critical reading of the evolution of modern architecture in Latin America, a reading that attributed the "evils" of modernism to its status as an imported ideology. This reading constructed a Luis Barragan capable of resisting the attacks of internationalism by drawing on two resources: popular tradition, and his own, very strong, religious ethics.

It was necessary to discuss the construction of this paradigm because of its centrality to the historiography and criticism of the 1980s. It almost always ignored contradictions in persons and processes, eliminating the qualitative differences between protagonists while at the same time clearly delineating the camps of good and evil, the former defined as the "national" and "popular" interests and the latter those who did nothing but express external domination.

If we break away from this reductive structure, events are of course more complex. Let us look at another key figure of the period: Rogelio Salmona.[35] Born in Paris in 1929, Salmona came with his parents to Colombia at the beginning of the thirties. He studied at the Lycée Française of Bogota, and in 1948, without finishing his architectural studies, he returned to France, where he lived until 1958. Having traveled throughout Europe, having studied art history, having worked in and been dismissed from the studio of Le Corbusier, Salmona decided to jump into the Colombian scene in a more Colombian manner than anyone. The historic times of the avant-garde had disappeared, but Salmona behaved like other illustrious modernists of earlier ages, breaking with canonical standards. Basically, he worked in accordance with the line of an "organic" modernism that had been spearheaded in Latin America by the works of Bruno Zevi. This tendency also incorporated elements of Wrightian origin and of English pragmatism. None of these

Rogelio Salmona, Torres del Parque, Bogota, Colombia, 1964-70

facts diminish the value of Salmona's work. On the contrary, it expressed a strong creative personality. He emphasized walls rather than independent structures, rejected orthogonality, and made artisanal use of brick masonry. It was above all in the Torres del Parque (Park Towers) in Bogota (1964-70) where Salmona's creative force was used to the greatest effect. Strongly questioned at the time of its construction for its height and its density, the grouping combined with the Plaza de Toros and with a magnificent adjacent park to generate a high-quality urban ring. The towers were configured into escalating spirals that simultaneously established relationships with the cylindrical plaza, with the detailed texture of the surrounding housing, and with the wooded surroundings of the mountains against which they stand out.

Eladio Dieste in Uruguay was also highly influential. Dieste is an engineer. He adheres to a code of conduct inspired by the Christian traditions of modesty, austerity, and solidarity. For these reasons he turned to brick as an easily fabricated material that was also easy to use, even by relatively unskilled workers. His great knowledge and experience allowed him to develop a technique of vaulting that was applied as much to horizontal as to vertical planes, in order to cover large spaces and to resolve spires and towers. His most celebrated work is the church at Atlantida (1959), a small work generated by warped planes constructed with different joints of bricks that accent the magnificent light.

The work of Pedro Ramírez Vásquez in Mexico runs from the stupendous Museum of Anthropology to the mastodonic Palace of the Legislative Assembly. His office has produced an enormous quantity of buildings both for the state and for corporations, and his firm has distinguished itself by its organizational capacity. The Museum remains without doubt his best work, for its simplicity and the exceptional spatial quality of its resolution, united around the monumental totem/umbrella/fountain that shades the principal patio.

The ideologization of "regional roots" was not the only mandate that has guided recent architecture in Latin America. Many Latin American architects have been able to follow their own, personal understanding of the possibilities and the limits of the discipline.

In what pigeonhole, for example, could we place the architecture of the group Amereida headed by Alberto Cruz in Valparaiso? For more than thirty years it has been made up of poets, artists, and architects who have rejected the canons. They reject the determining role of the individual and affirm collective creation, they reject geometry, they reject industrialized materials, they reject any commercial motive whatsoever. Certainly, in their very name there is an explicit search for local expression but, note well: the chosen name is Amereida, not Latin-Amereida. Theirs is a continental reference, a search for poetic sublimation of contents that sustain the condition of being American. The Open City, built in a zone of immense dunes, the architecture of which has surprised many as deconstructivist before the fact, has no formal relation with tradition or the past. Its plazas, monuments, and "hostelries" made with leftover tin, plastics, or wood recall the huts of the most miserable barrios. Changing and ephemeral, the constructions are at the same time a rejection and a sublimated expression of the metropolitan condition.

And to what "ism" can the architecture of Clorindo Testa be ascribed? There is no doubt that, as a citizen of a globalized planet and not a

Eladio Dieste, Church at Atlantida, Uruguay, 1959. Photo by Vicente del Amo Hernández

Eladio Dieste, Church at Atlantida, interior. Photo by Vicente del Amo Hernández

Pedro Ramírez Vásquez, National Museum of Anthropology, Mexico City, 1964. Photo by Julius Shulman

Alberto Cruz (Amereida), Escuela de Valparaiso, Chile, 1970

prophet, Testa is sensitive to what he perceives in this world. Moreover, it could be said that these perceptions are the very material with which Testa works: without a doubt, the complete work of Le Corbusier, certain works or traits of the Japanese Metabolists, vernacular houses of Middle Eastern towns, "postmodern" caprices, the always living forms of boats, memories of Naples, leaves and flowers, all is admissible for his omnivorous imagination. But his works are "Testian" and inimitable. His building for the Bank of London and South America, conceived and built in the 1960s, is another of the great architectonic monuments of Latin America. It is a monument to creativity and frustration: on one hand the culminating point of a long study of interior space, on the other informed by the values of structure and construction that his colleagues would introduce as followers of Perret.

In Brazil, the feeling post-boom is one of devastation. An exception is the work of Paulo Mendez da Rocha, who continues to work out of the austere tradition in which he began in the 1950s as a disciple of the school of Villanova Artigas. His sculpture museum in Sao Paulo reaches a very high level of abstraction and purity.

The variety in Latin American architecture today is not in fact a Latin American phenomenon, but rather the expression of a worldwide crisis of architecture in the era of late modernism. Nevertheless, there are also those with serious intentions of building a theoretical corpus on which praxis can be founded, and in some case the results are relevant.

The work of Juan Borchers, for instance, is one such example.[36] Borchers comes from the School of Valparaiso, and to his experiences in Chile he added profound contacts with Spanish culture, working and studying at length in that country. His early death interrupted one of the most committed and intense searches for a rational, harmonic system of handling architectural forms. Borchers produced an enormous quantity of writings, drawings, and projects, some published but most still in unpublished notes. His project is in some ways comparable to that of John Hejduk. The Electric Cooperative of Chillan, one of his few completed works, is a condensation of very high formal tensions. Each of the architectural themes integrated in it is explored in its variables and relationships with an extreme level of concentration. These forms are still implosive, at the precise instant before their explosion.

Again, the Beginning

During the last decade of the century the region has been affected by the great technical, cultural, and political transformations that have characterized these years. The fall of the Berlin Wall has removed the rationale for the cruel, corrupt, and inefficient military dictatorships that maintained the status quo during the 1970s and the beginning of the 1980s. Almost everywhere there are new democratic regimes, and a liberalization of debates. The general process of globalization has contributed to a theoretical openness and has introduced new techniques of organization and production to the profession of architecture, alongside a tendency toward concentration and therefore to an increase in the volume of undertakings.

The country in which these changes have been maturing with the greatest speed is Chile. It would be an error to assume that this speed is economic

[36] Juan Borchers, *Institucíon arquitectónica* (Santiago:Editorial Andrés Bello, 1968).

Clorindo Testa, Santiago Sánchez Elia, Federico Peralta Ramos, and Alfredo Agostini, Bank of London and South America headquarters, Buenos Aires, 1960-66. Photo by Julius Shulman

only. Certainly Chile's is the most consolidated economy of the region, that in which the transformations began earliest, under the Pinochet dictatorship. Moreover, it could be risky to presume that the best recent architecture in Chile has been produced, in response to these transformations. These works are the product of intense theoretical activity that has its principal base in the schools of architecture of the Catholic University, activity that for many of its protagonists goes back to the 1970s.

In Mexico as well, a new generation has begun to forge a path in expressed contrast with "Barraganism" and with the "monumentalism" of preceding expressions. This does not mean that the work of Enrique Norten or Alberto Calach does not possess traits determined by its relationship to the society to which they belong. In general terms, young architects are trying to respond to the demands and characteristics of one of the most gigantic metropolises of the planet. It is not strange then that their architecture rejects forced primitivism and prefers to employ the most current urban technological resources: iron, glass, synthetic materials, industrialized finishes, prefabricated parts. But beyond their technology, works like Norten's Televisa strive to constitute organisms on the scale of the new urban peripheries, with their absence of attributes, with their highways and their indifferent perception.[37]

The panorama of architectural culture at the end of the century in Latin America does not permit the encouragement of solid speculations about growth and maturity. This culture is passing through its own crisis beyond that of the more general crisis of international architecture. If the demands are gigantic, fortunately the sources from which resources can be extracted are equally gigantic. Nevertheless this operation, no matter how obvious and simple it seems, depends on a no less enormous force of will, allowing for the confrontation of concrete problems instead of those of the imagination, to lucidly revise the antiquated institutions of the profession, to build new structures of thought and analysis, to develop regional ties that will improve the economy of operations, and to establish links between culture and social forces. Although there are not enough reasons for optimism, perhaps this time we can start again by building testimonies of culture over the rubble of barbarism.

[37] See Miguel Adria, *México 90's: A Contemporary Architecture* (Barcelona: G. Gilli, 1996).

TEN Arquitectos (Enrique Norten), Televisa Mixed Use Building, Mexico City, 1995

Craig Hodgetts and Ming Fung, Towell (Temporary) Library at the University of California, Los Angeles, 1992

BIBLIOGRAPHY

Compiled by Dana Hutt

Adalid, Mario Melgar, ed. *6 Años de Arquitectura en México 1988-1994.* Mexico City: Ediciones del Equilibrista, S.A. de C.V., y Turner Libros, S.A. and Universidad Nacional Autónoma de México, 1994.

Adam, Peter. *Eileen Gray: Architect/Designer.* New York: Harry N. Abrams, 1987.

Adjmi, Morris, and Giovanni Bertolotto, eds. *Aldo Rossi: Drawings and Paintings.* New York: Princeton Architectural Press, 1993.

Adolf Loos, 1870-1933: Raumplan, Wohnungsbau. Exh. cat. Berlin: Ausstellung der Akademie der Künste, 1983.

Adrià, Miquel. *Mexico 90's: A Contemporary Architecture.* Translated by Graham Thomson. México: Ediciones G. Gili, S.A. de C.V., 1996.

Agrest, Diane. *Architecture from Without: Theoretical Framings for a Critical Practice.* Cambridge, Massachusetts: The MIT Press, 1991.

Agrest, Diane, Patricia Conway, and Leslie Kanes Weisman, eds. *The Sex of Architecture.* New York: Harry N. Abrams, 1996.

Alanis, Enrique X. de Anda, coordinator. *Luis Barràgan: Clasico del Silencio.* Translated by Brian J. Mallet. Bogotá, Colombia: Escala, 1989.

Albrecht, Donald, ed. *World War II and the American Dream: How Wartime Building Changed a Nation.* Exh. cat. Washington, D.C.: National Building Museum, and Cambridge, Massachusetts: The MIT Press, 1995. Essays by Peter S. Reed, Robert Friedel, Margaret Crawford, Greg Hise, Joel Davidson, and Michael Sorkin.

Alexander, Christopher. *Notes on the Synthesis of Form.* Cambridge, Massachusetts: Harvard University Press, 1964.

——. *The Timeless Way of Building.* New York: Oxford University Press, 1979.

Alofsin, Anthony. *Frank Lloyd Wright - The Lost Years, 1910-1922: A Study of Influence.* Chicago: University of Chicago Press, 1993.

Ambasz, Emilio. *The Architecture of Luis Barragan.* New York: The Museum of Modern Art, 1976.

Anderson, Martin. *The Federal Bulldozer: A Critical Analysis of Urban Renewal, 1949-1962.* Cambridge, Massachusetts: The MIT Press, 1964.

Antonio Sant'Elia: l'architettura disegnata. Venice: Marsilio, 1991.

Antonowa, Irina, and Jörn Merkert, eds. *Berlin - Moskau 1900-1950.* Exh. cat. Berlin: Berlinische Galerie, and Munich: Prestel, 1995.

Apollonio, Umbro, ed. *Futurist Manifestos.* Translated by Robert Brain, R.W. Flint, J.C. Higgitt, and Caroline Tisdall. New York: Viking Press, 1973.

Appelbaum, Stanley, ed. *The New York World's Fair 1939/1940 in 155 Photographs by Richard Wurts and Others.* New York: Dover Publications, 1977.

Arata Isozaki: Architecture 1960-1990. Exh. cat. Los Angeles: The Museum of Contemporary Art, Los Angeles, and New York: Rizzoli, 1991. Essays by David B. Stewart and Hajime Yatsuka.

Archaeology of the Future City. Exh. cat. Tokyo: Museum of Contemporary Art, 1996.

Archigram. Exh. cat. Paris: Editions du Centre Georges Pompidou, 1994.

Architectural Drawings of the Russian Avant-Garde. Exh. cat. New York: The Museum of Modern Art, 1990. Essay by Catherine Cooke.

Architecture for the Future. Paris: Éditions Pierre Terrail, 1996.

The Architecture of Frank Gehry. Exh. cat. Minneapolis, Minnesota: Walker Art Center, and New York: Rizzoli, 1986. Essays by Rosemarie Haag Bletter, Coosje van Bruggen, Mildred Friedman, Joseph Giovannini, Thomas S. Hines, and Pilar Viladas.

Arnell, Peter, and Ted Bickford, eds. *James Stirling: Buildings and Projects.* New York: Rizzoli International Publications, 1984. Introduction by Colin Rowe.

Art Into Life: Russian Constructivism 1914-1932. Exh. cat. Seattle, Washington: The Henry Art Gallery, University of Washington, and New York: Rizzoli International Publications, 1990. Essays by Jaroslav Andel, Stephen Bann, Hal Foster, Selim O. Khan-Magomedov, Christina Lodder, Anatole Senkevitch, Jr., and Anatolii Strigalev.

The Avant Garde in Russia, 1910-1930: New Perspectives. Exh. cat. Los Angeles: Los Angeles County Museum of Art, and Cambridge, Massachusetts: The MIT Press, 1980.

Avantgarde 1900-1923: Russisch-sowjetische Architektur. Exh. cat. Stuttgart: Deutsche Verlags-Anstalt, 1991.

Bachelard, Gaston. *The Poetics of Space.* Translated by Maria Jolas. New York: Orion Press, 1964.

Baer, Steve. *Dome Cookbook.* Corrales, New Mexico: Lama Foundation, 1969.

——. *Sunspots: Collected Facts and Solar Fiction*. Albuquerque, New Mexico: Zomeworks Corporation, 1975.

Banerjee, Tridib, and Michael Southworth, eds. *City Sense and City Design: Writings and Projects of Kevin Lynch*. Cambridge, Massachusetts: The MIT Press, 1991.

Banham, Reyner. *A Concrete Atlantis: U.S. Industrial Buildings and European Modern Architecture, 1900-1925*. Cambridge, Massachusetts: The MIT Press, 1986.

——. *Los Angeles: The Architecture of Four Ecologies*. New York: Harper & Row, 1971.

——. *Megastructure: Urban Futures of the Recent Past*. London: Thames and Hudson, 1976.

——. *Theory and Design in the First Machine Age*. London: Architectural Press, 1960.

Bayón, Damián, and Paolo Gasparini. *The Changing Shape of Latin American Architecture: Conversations with Ten Leading Architects*. Translated by Galen D. Greaser. Barcelona: Editorial Blume, 1977; Chichester, New York, Brisbane, and Toronto: John Wiley & Sons, 1979.

Beard, Richard R. *Walt Disney's EPCOT: Creating the New World of Tomorrow*. New York: Harry N. Abrams, 1982.

Beevers, Robert. *The Garden City Utopia: A Critical Biography of Ebenezer Howard*. New York: St. Martin's Press, 1988.

Benevolo, Leonardo. *History of Modern Architecture* (Storia dell'architettura moderna). Translated by H. J. Landry. Cambridge, Massachusetts: The MIT Press, 1971.

Benson, Timothy O. *Expressionist Utopias: Paradise, Metropolis, Architectural Fantasy*. Exh. cat. Los Angeles: Los Angeles County Museum of Art, 1993. Essays by Timothy O. Benson, David Frisby, Reinhold Heller, Anton Kaes, and Iain Boyd Whyte.

Berman, Marshall. *All That is Solid Melts into Air: The Experience of Modernity*. New York: Viking Penguin, 1988.

Betsky, Aaron. *Queer Space: Architecture and Same-Sex Desire*. New York: William Morrow & Co., 1997.

——. *Violated Perfection: Architecture and the Fragmentation of the Modern*. New York: Rizzoli, 1990.

Bettinoti, Massimo, ed. *Kenzo Tange, 1946-1996: Architecture and Urban Design*. Milan: Electa, 1996.

Bhatt, Vikram, and Peter Scriver. *After the Masters*. Ahmedabad: Mapin Pub. Pvt. Ltd., 1990.

Birrell, James. *Walter Burley Griffin*. St. Lucia, Australia: University of Queensland Press, 1964.

Bishop, Jeff. *Milton Keynes - The Best of Both Worlds? Public and Professional Views of a New City*. Bristol, England: School for Advanced Urban Studies, 1986.

Blake, Peter. *Form Follows Fiasco: Why Modern Architecture Hasn't Worked*. Boston: Little, Brown, 1977.

——. *God's Own Junkyard: The Planned Deterioration of America's Landscape*. New York: Holt, Rinehart and Winston, 1964.

Blaser, Werner. *Mies van der Rohe: The Art of Structure*. London: Thames and Hudson, 1965.

Blueprints for Modern Living: History and Legacy of the Case Study Houses. Exh. cat. Los Angeles: The Museum of Contemporary Art, Los Angeles, and Cambridge, Massachusetts: The MIT Press, 1989. Essays by Esther McCoy, Thomas S. Hines, Helen Searing, Kevin Starr, Reyner Banham, and Dolores Hayden.

Boardman, Philip. *The Worlds of Patrick Geddes, Biologist, Town Planner, Re-educator, Peace-warrior*. London, Henley, and Boston: Routledge and Kegan Paul, 1978.

Bognár, Botond, ed. *The New Japanese Architecture*. New York: Rizzoli, 1990. Essays by Hajime Yatsuka and Lynn Breslin.

Botey, Josep Ma. *Oscar Niemeyer: Works and Projects*. Barcelona: Editorial Gustavo Gili, S.A., 1996.

Bown, Matthew Cullerne, and Brandon Taylor, eds. *Art of the Soviets: Painting, Sculpture and Architecture in a One-Party State, 1917-1992*. Manchester and New York: Manchester University Press, 1993.

Boyd-Whyte, Iain, ed. *The Crystal Chain Letters. Architectural Fantasies by Bruno Taut and His Circle*. Cambridge, Massachusetts: The MIT Press, 1985.

Boyer, Christine M. *CyperCities: Visual Perception in the Age of Electonic Communication*. New York: Princeton Architectural Press, 1996.

——. *Dreaming the Rational City: The Myth of American City Planning*. Cambridge, Massachusetts: The MIT Press, 1983.

Brooks, H. Allen. *Le Corbusier's Formative Years: Charles-Edouard Jeanneret at La Chaux-de-Fonds*. Chicago: The University of Chicago Press, 1997.

Brownlee, David B., and David G. DeLong. *Louis I. Kahn: In the Realm of Architecture*. Exh. cat. Los Angeles: The Museum of Contemporary Art, Los Angeles, and New York: Rizzoli International Publications, Inc., 1991. Introduction by Vincent Scully.

Bruno Taut 1880-1938. Exh. cat. Berlin: Akademie der Künste, 1980. Essays by Kurt Junghanns, Franziska Bollerey, Kristiana Hartmann, Rosemarie Haag Bletter, Heinrich H. Waechter, Barbara Kreis, Yoshio Dohi, Heinrich Taut, Tokuguen Mihara, and Inci Aslanoğlu.

Bucci, Federico. *Albert Kahn: Architect of Ford*. New York: Princeton Architectural Press, 1993.

Buchanan, Peter. *Renzo Piano Building Workshop: Complete Works*. London: Phaidon Press, 1995.

Buddensieg, Tilmann, ed. *Berlin: 1900-1933: Architecture and Design*. Exh. cat. New York: Cooper-Hewitt Museum, 1987. Essays by Tilmann Buddensieg, Fritz Neumeyer, Angela Schönberger, and Michael Esser.

Bullrich, Francisco. *New Directions in Latin American Architecture*. New York: George Braziller, 1969.

Burnham, Daniel H. *The Final Official Report of the Director of Works of the World's Columbian Exposition*. Two vols. New York: Garland Publishing, 1989. Introduction by Joan E. Draper and preface by Thomas Hines.

Burnham, Daniel H., and Edward H. Bennett. *Plan of Chicago*. New York: Princeton Architectural Press, 1993.

Cahoone, Lawrence E. *From Modernism to Postmodernism: An Anthology*. Cambridge, Massachusetts: Blackwell Publishers Ltd., 1996.

Cantacuzino, Sherban, ed. *Architecture in Continuity: Building in the Islamic World Today; The Aga Khan Award for Architecture*. New York: Aperture, 1985.

Caramel, Luciano, and Alberto Longatti. *Antonia Sant'Elia: The Complete Works*. New York: Rizzoli, 1987.

Caro, Robert A. *The Power Broker: Robert Moses and the Fall of New York*. New York: Alfred A. Knopf, 1974.

Carrieri, Raffaele. *Futurism*. Translated by Leslie van Rensselaer White. Milan: Edizioni del Milione, 1963.

Çelik, Zeynep. *The Remaking of Istanbul. Portrait of an Ottoman City in the Nineteenth Century*. Seattle: University of Washington, 1986.

Çelik, Zeynep, Diane Favro, and Richard Ingersoll, eds. *Streets: Critical Perspectives on Public Space*. Berkeley and Los Angeles: University of California Press, 1994.

Chambless, Edgar. *Roadtown*. New York: Roadtown Press, 1910.

Charles Correa. London: Thames and Hudson, 1996. Essay by Kenneth Frampton.

Clavel, Pierre, John Forester, and William W. Goldsmith, eds. *Urban and Regional Planning in an Age of Austerity*. New York: Pergamon Press, 1980.

Clough, Rosa Trillo. *Futurism: The Story of a Modern Art Movement*. New York: Philosophical Library, 1961.

Cohen, Jean-Louis. *Le Corbusier and the Mystique of the USSR: Theories and Projects for Moscow, 1928-1936*. Princeton, New Jersey: Princeton University Press, 1992.

——. *Scenes of the World to Come: European Architecture and the American Challenge, 1893-1960*. Exh. cat. Montréal: Centre Canadien d'Architecture/Canadian Centre for Architecture, and Paris: Flammarion, 1995.

Cohen, Jean-Louis, and Hubert Damisch, eds. *Américanisme et Modernité, l'ideal américain dans L'Architecture*. Paris: Flammarion and École des Hautes Études en Sciences Sociales, 1993.

Colenbrander, Bernard, ed. *Style: Standard and Signature in Dutch Architecture of the Nineteenth and Twentieth Centuries*. Rotterdam: Nai Publishers, 1993. Essays by Bernard Colenbrander and Aart Oxenaar.

Collins, George R., and Christiane Crasermann Collins. *Camillo Sitte: The Birth of Modern City Planning*. New York: Rizzoli, 1986.

Collins, Peter. *Changing Ideals in Modern Architecture 1750-1950*. London: Faber and Faber, 1965.

——. *Concrete: The Vision of a New Architecture: A Study of Auguste Perret and His Precursors*. London: Faber and Faber, 1959.

Colomina, Beatriz. *Privacy and Publicity: Modern Architecture as Mass Media*. Cambridge, Massachusetts: The MIT Press, 1994.

——, ed. *Sexuality & Space*. New York: Princeton Architectural Press, 1992.

Colquhoun, Alan. *Modernity and the Classical Tradition: Architectural Essays 1980-1987*. Cambridge, Massachusetts: The MIT Press, 1989.

Concepts of the Bauhaus. Exh. cat. Cambridge, Massachusetts: Busch-Reisinger Museum, Harvard University, 1971.

Condit, Carl W. *American Building Art: The Twentieth Century*. New York: Oxford University Press, 1961.

Conrads, Ulrich, ed. *Programs and Manifestoes on 20th-Century Architecture*. Translated by Michael Bullock. Cambridge, Massachusetts: The MIT Press, 1970.

Conrads, Ulrich, and Hans G. Sperlich. *Fantastic Architecture*. Translated, edited, and expanded by Christiane Crasemann Collins and George R. Collins. London: Architectural Press, 1963.

Constant, Caroline, and Wilfried Wang, eds. *Eileen Gray: An Architecture for All Senses*. Frankfurt: Deutsches Architektur-Museum, 1996. Essays by Caroline Constant, Volker Fischer, Eileen Gray and Jean Badovici, Stefan Hecker Kitsios and Christian F. Müller, Stephan von der Schulenburg, Suzanne Tise, and Sarah Whiting.

Cooke, Catherine. *Chernikhov Fantasy and Construction: Iakov Chernikhov's Approach to Architectural Design*. London: Architectural Design, 1984.

——, ed. *Russian Avant-Garde Art and Architecture*. London: Academy Editions and Architectural Design, 1983.

Coop Himmelb(l)au: Construire le ciel. Exh. cat. Paris: Centre Georges Pompidou, 1993.

Correa, Charles. *The New Landscape: Urbanisation in the Third World*. Bombay: Butterworth Architecture, 1989.

Creese, Walter L., ed. *The Legacy of Raymond Unwin: A Human Pattern for Planning*. Cambridge, Massachusetts: The MIT Press, 1967.

Curtis, William J.R. *Balkrishna Doshi: An Architecture for India*. New York: Rizzoli International, Inc., 1988.

——. *Le Corbusier: Ideas and Forms*. Oxford: Phaidon Press, and New York: Rizzoli, 1986.

——. *Modern Architecture Since 1900*. Third ed. London: Phaidon Press Limited, 1996.

Dahinden, Justus. *Urban Structures for the Future*.Translated by Gerald Onn. New York: Praeger Publishers, 1972.

Dal Co, Francesco. *Figures of Architecture and Thought: German Architectural Culture 1880-1920*. New York: Rizzoli, 1990.

——. *Tadao Ando: Complete Works*. London: Phaidon Press, 1995.

Dal Co, Francesco, and Giuseppe Mazzariol. *Carlo Scarpa: The Complete Works*. Milan: Electa, and New York: Rizzoli International Publications, 1985.

Dawn of a New Day: The New York World's Fair, 1939/40. Exh. cat. Flushing, New York: Queens Museum, and New York: New York University Press, 1980.

De Long, David G., Helen Searing, and Robert A.M. Stern. *American Architecture: Innovation and Tradition*. New York: The Temple Hoyne Buell Center for the Study of American Architecture, Columbia University and Rizzoli, 1986.

De Wit, Wim, ed. *Louis Sullivan: The Function of Ornament*. Exh. cat. St. Louis: The Saint Louis Art Museum, and New York: W.W. Norton, 1986. Essays by David van Zanten, William Jordy, Wim de Wit, and Rochelle Berger Elstein.

Dearstyne, Howard. Inside the Bauhaus. New York: Rizzoli, 1986.

Dickerman, Leah, ed. *Building the Collective: Soviet Graphic Design 1917 - 1937, Selections from the Merrill C. Berman Collection*. New York: Princeton Architectural Press, 1996.

Diller, Elizabeth, and Ricardo Scofidio. *Flesh: Architectural Probes*. New York: Princeton Architectural Press, 1994. Essay by Georges Teyssot.

Doordan, Dennis P. *Building Modern Italy: Italian Architecture, 1914-1936*. New York: Princeton Architectural Press, 1988.

Drawings of the Russian Avant-Garde. Essay by Catherine Cooke. New York: The Museum of Modern Art, 1990.

Drew, Philip. *Sydney Opera House: Jorn Utzon*. London: Phaidon Press, 1995.

Drexler, Arthur. *Architecture of Japan*. New York: The Museum of Modern Art, 1955.

Droste, Magdalena. *Bauhaus.1919-1933*. Berlin: Bauhaus-Archiv Museum für Gestaltung, 1990.

Edwin Lutyens. London: Academy Editions, and New York: St. Martin's Press, 1986.

Eladio Dieste: la estructura ceramica. Bogota, Colombia: Escala, 1987.

Elliott, David, ed. *Photography in Russia, 1840-1940*. Exh. cat. Oxford, England: Museum of Modern Art, and Berlin: Ars Nicolai, 1992.

Emanuel, Muriel, ed. *Contemporary Architects*. Third ed. New York: St. James Press, 1994.

Erich Mendelsohn: Complete Works of the Architect: Sketches, Designs, Buildings. Translated by Antje Fritsch. New York: Princeton Architectural Press, 1992.

Escher, Frank, ed. *John Lautner, Architect*. London: Artemis, 1994.

Etlin, Richard A. *Modernism in Italian Architecture, 1890-1940*. Cambridge, Massachusetts: The MIT Press, 1991.

Ewen, Stuart. *All Consuming Images: The Politics of Style in Contemporary Culture*. New York: Basic Books, 1988.

Experimental Tradition: Twenty-Five Years of American Architecture Competitions, 1960-1985, Essays on Competitions in Architecture. Exh. cat. New York: National Academy of Design, 1988. Essays by Barry Bergdoll, Sarah Bradford Landau, Hélène Lipstadt, Mary McLeod, and Helen Searing.

Fathy, Hassan. *Architecture for the Poor: An Experiment in Rural Egypt*. Chicago and London: The University of Chicago Press, 1973.

Ferriss, Hugh. *The Metropolis of Tomorrow* (New York: Ives Washburn, 1929). Princeton: Princeton Architectural Press, 1986.

Fiedler, Jeannine, ed. *Photography at the Bauhaus*. Cambridge, Massachusetts: The MIT Press, 1990.

Fishman, Robert. *Urban Utopias in the Twentieth Century: Ebenezer Howard, Frank Lloyd Wright and Le Corbusier*. New York: Basic Books, 1977.

Five Architects: Eisenman, Graves, Gwathmey, Hejduk, Meier. New York: Oxford University Press, 1975

Ford, Edward R. *The Details of Modern Architecture*. Two vols. Cambridge, Massachusetts: The MIT Press, 1990, 1996.

Ford, James, and Katherine Morrow Ford. *Design of Modern Interiors*. New York: Architectural Book Publishing, 1942.

Foster, Hal, ed. *The Anti-Aesthetic: Essays on Postmodern Culture*. Port Townsend, Washington: Bay Press, 1983.

Frampton, Kenneth. *Modern Architecture, A Critical History*. Third ed. London: Thames and Hudson, 1992.

——. *Studies in Tectonic Culture: The Poetics of Construction in Nineteenth and Twentieth Century Architecture*. Cambridge, Massachusetts: The MIT Press, 1995.

Franck, Karen A., and Lynda H. Schneekloth, eds. *Ordering Space: Types in Architecture and Design*. New York: Van Nostrand Reinhold, 1994.

Frank Lloyd Wright: The Phoenix Papers. Tempe, Arizona: Herberger Center for Design Excellence, College of Architecture and Environmental Design, Arizona State University, 1994.

Frederick, Christine. *Household Engineering: Scientific Management in the Home*. Chicago: American School of Home Economics, 1919.

——. *The New Housekeeping: Efficiency Studies in Home Management*. Garden City, New York: Doubleday, Page & Company, 1913.

Fuller, R. Buckminster. *Ideas and Integrities: A Spontaneous Autobiographical Disclosure*. Edited by Robert W. Marks. Englewood Cliffs, N.J.: Prentice-Hall, 1963.

Gargiani, Roberto. *Auguste Perret 1874-1954: La théorie et l'+uvre*. Milan: Gallimard/Electa, 1994.

Garnier, Tony. *Une cité industrielle: Etude pour la construction des villes*. New York: Princeton Architectural Press, 1989.

Garofalo, Francesco, and Luca Veresani. *Adalberto Libera*. New York: Princeton Architectural Press, 1992.

Geddes, Patrick, Sir. *Cities in Evolution: An Introduction to the Town Planning Movement and to the Study of Civics*. London: Williams & Norgate, 1915.

——. *City Development, A Study of Parks, Gardens and Culture-Institutes*. Edinburgh: The Saint George Press, 1904.

Genauer, Emily. *Modern Interiors Today and Tomorrow: A Critical Analysis of Trends in Contemporary Decoration as Seen at the Paris Exposition of Arts and Techniques and Reflected at the New York World's Fair*. New York: Illustrated Editions Company, 1939.

Geretsegger, Heinz, Max Peintner, and Walter Pichler. *Otto Wagner 1841-1918: The Expanding City, The Beginning of Modern Architecture*. New York: Rizzoli, 1979.

Gerosa, Pier Giorgio. *Mario Chiattone: un itinerario architettonico fra Milano e Lugano*. Milan: Electa, c. 1985.

Ghirardo, Diane. *Architecture After Modernism*. London: Thames and Hudson, 1996.

——. *Building New Communities: New Deal America and Fascist Italy*. Princeton, New Jersey: Princeton University Press, 1989.

——, ed. *Out of Site: A Social Criticism of Architecture*. Seattle: Bay Press, 1991.

Giedion, Sigfried. *Architecture, You and Me: The Diary of a Development*. Cambridge, Massachusetts: Harvard University Press, 1958.

——. *Mechanization Takes Command: A Contribution to Anonymous History*. New York; Oxford University Press, 1948.

——. *Space, Time and Architecture: The Growth of a New Tradition*. Fifth ed. Cambridge, Massachusetts: Harvard University Press, 1967.

Gilbreth, Frank B. *Motion Study, A Method for Increasing the Efficiency of the Workman*. New York: D. Van Nostrand Company, 1911.

Ginzburg, Moisei. *Style and Epoch*. Cambridge, Massachusetts: The MIT Press, 1982.

Gio Ponti 1891-1979 from the Human Scale to the Post-Modernism. Exh. cat. Tokyo: The Seibu Museum of Art, 1986.

Giuseppe Terragni. Milan: Electa, 1996.

Glaeser, Ludwig. *The Work of Frei Otto*. New York: The Museum of Modern Art, 1972.

Goodman, Robert. *After the Planners*. New York: Simon and Schuster, 1972.

Goodwin, Philip L. *Brazil Builds; Architecture New and Old, 1652-1942*. New York: The Museum of Modern Art, 1943.

Gössell, Peter, and Gabriele Leuthäuser. *Architecture in the Twentieth Century*. Cologne: Benedikt Taschen, 1991.

Grassi, Giorgio. *La costruzione logica dell'architettura*. Padova, Marsilio, 1967.

Gresleri, Giuliano, Dario Matteoni. *La Citta à mondiale: Andersen, Hébrard, Otlet, Le Corbusier.* Venice: Marsilio, 1982.

Gropius, Walter. *Scope of Total Architecture.* New York: Collier Books, 1962.

A Guide to Archigram 1961-74. Exh. cat. Vienna: Kunsthalle Wien, and London: Academy Editions, 1994.

Günther, Sonja. *Lilly Reich 1885-1947: Innenarchitektin, Designerin, Ausstellungsgestalterin.* Stuttgart: Deutsche Verlags-Anstalt, 1988.

Habermas, Jürgen. *The Structural Transformation of the Public Sphere: An Inquiry into a Category of Bourgeois Society.* Translated by Thomas Burger. Cambridge, Massachusetts: The MIT Press, 1989.

Hales, Peter B. *Silver Cities: The Photography of American Urbanization, 1839-1915.* Philadelphia: Temple University Press, 1984.

Hall, Peter. *Cities of Tomorrow: An Intellectual History of Urban Planning and Design in the Twentieth Century.* Oxford, England: Blackwell Publishers, 1988.

Harris, Neil, Wim de Wit, James Gilbert, and Robert W. Rydell. *Grand Illusions: Chicago's World's Fair of 1893.* Exh. cat. Chicago: Chicago Historical Society, 1993.

Harvey, David. *The Condition of Postmodernity: An Enquiry into the Origins of Cultural Change.* Oxford and Cambridge: Blackwell, 1989.

Hauptstadt Berlin: Internationaler städtebaulicher Ideenwettbewerb 1957/58. Exh. cat. Berlin: Berlinische Galerie, and Berlin: Gebr. Mann Verlag, 1990. Essays by Carola Hein, Dorothea Tscheschner, and Hartmut Frank.

Hayden, Dolores. *The Grand Domestic Revolution: A History of Feminist Designs for American Homes, Neighborhoods, and Cities.* Cambridge, Massachusetts: The MIT Press, 1981.

Helmer, Stephen D. *Hitler's Berlin: The Speer Plans for Reshaping the Central City.* Ann Arbor, Michigan: UMI Research Press, 1985.

Herbert, Gilbert. *The Dream of the Factory-Made House.* Cambridge, Massachusetts: The MIT Press, 1984.

Herzog, Thomas, Gernot Minke, and Hans Eggers. *Pneumatic Structures: A Handbook of Inflatable Architecture.* New York: Oxford University Press, 1976.

Heyer, Paul. *Mexican Architecture: The Work of Abraham Zabludovsky and Teodoro González de León.* New York: Walker and Company, 1978.

Hines, Thomas S. *Burnham of Chicago: Architect and Planner.* Chicago and London: The University of Chicago Press, 1979.

——. *Richard Neutra and the Search for Modern Architecture; A Biography and History.* New York: Oxford University Press, 1982.

Hitchcock, Henry-Russell. *Architecture: Nineteenth and Twentieth Centuries.* Harmondsworth, Middlesex, England: Penguin Books, 1958.

——. *Latin American Architecture Since 1945.* Exh. cat. New York: The Museum of Modern Art, 1955.

Hitchcock, Henry-Russell, and Philip Johnson. *The International Style: Architecture Since 1922.* New York: W.W. Norton & Company, 1932.

Hodgetts + Fung: Scenarios and Spaces. New York: Rizzoli International Publications, 1997. Introduction by Kurt W. Forster.

Hollier, Denis. *Against Architecture: The Writings of Georges Bataille.* Translated by Betsy Wing. Cambridge, Massachusetts: The MIT Press, 1989.

Holston, James. *The Modernist City: An Anthopological Critique of Brasilia.* Chicago: The University of Chicago Press, 1989.

Howard, Ebenezer. *Garden Cities of To-morrow.* Cambridge, Massachusetts: The MIT Press, 1965. Introductory essay by Lewis Mumford.

Hudson, Hugh D. *Blueprints and Blood: The Stalinization of Soviet Architecture, 1917-1937.* Princeton, New Jersey: Princeton University Press, 1994.

Hulten, Karl Gunnar Pontus. *Futurism & Futurisms.* New York: Abbeville Press, 1986.

Hussey, Christopher. *The Life of Sir Edwin Lutyens.* London: Antique Collector's Club, 1984.

Huxtable, Ada Louise. *The Tall Building Artistically Reconsidered: The Search for a Skyscraper Style.* New York: Pantheon Books, 1984.

Huyssen, Andreas. *After the Great Divide: Modernism, Mass Culture, Postmodernism.* Bloomington: Indiana University Press, 1986.

Interbau Berlin 1957: Internationale Bauausstellung im Berliner Hansaviertel. Berlin-Grunewald: Graphische Gesellschaft Grunewald, 1957.

Irving, Robert Grant. *Indian Summer: Lutyens, Baker and Imperial Delhi.* New Haven: Yale University Press, 1981.

Jackson, J.B. *Discovering the Vernacular Landscape.* New Haven: Yale University Press, 1984.

——. *The Necessity for Ruins and Other Topics.* Amherst: University of Massachusetts Press, 1980.

Jackson, Kenneth. *Crabgrass Frontier: The Suburbanization of the United States.* New York: Oxford University Press, 1985.

Jacobs, Jane. *The Death and Life of Great American Cities.* New York: Random House, 1961.

Jacobus, John. *Twentieth-Century Architecture: The Middle Years 1940-65.* New York: Frederick A. Praeger, Publishers, 1966.

James, Cary. *Frank Lloyd Wright's Imperial Hotel.* Rutland, Vermont, and Tokyo: Charles E.Tuttle Company, 1968; New York: Dover Publications, Inc., 1988.

Jencks, Charles A. *The Language of Post-Modern Architecture.* New York: Rizzoli, 1977.

——. *Modern Movements in Architecture.* Garden City, New York: Anchor Press, 1973.

Joedicke, Jürgen. *Architecture Since 1945: Sources and Directions.* Translated by J.C. Palmes. New York: Frederick A. Praeger, Publishers, 1969.

——. *A History of Modern Architecture.* Translated by James C. Palmes. London: Architectural Press, 1961.

——, ed. *Documents of Modern Architecture 1: CIAM '59 in Otterlo.* Stuttgart: Karl Krämer Verlag, 1961.

Johnson, Philip, and Mark Wigley. *Deconstructivist Architecture.* Exh. cat. New York: The Museum of Modern Art, 1988.

Jones, Peter Blundell. *Hans Scharoun.* London: Phaidon Press, 1995.

Jordy, William H. *American Buildings and Their Architects: The Impact of European Modernism in the Mid-Twentieth Century.* New York: Oxford University Press, 1986.

Kalia, Ravi. *Chandigarh: In Seach of an Identity.* Carbondale and Edwardsville: Southern Illinois University Press, 1987.

Kamran Diba: Buildings and Projects. Stuttgart: Verlag Gerd Hatje, 1981.

Kaufmann, Edgar, Jr. *Introduction to Modern Design: What is Modern Interior Design?* Reprint ed. New York: Published for the Museum of Modern Art by Arno Press, 1967.

Kelley, Barbara M. *Expanding the American Dream: Building and Rebuilding Levittown.* Albany, New York: State University of New York Press, 1993.

Kenzo Tange: 40 ans d'urbanisme et d'architecture. Tokyo: Process Architecture Pub. Co., 1987.

Kepes, Gyorgy. *Structure in Art and in Science.* New York: George Braziller, 1965.

Khan, Hasan-Uddin. *Charles Correa.* Singapore: Concept Media Pte Ltd., and New York: Aperture, 1987. Essays by Sherban Cantacuzino and Charles Correa.

——. *Contemporary Asian Architects.* Cologne: Taschen, 1995.

Khan-Magomedov, Selim O. *Pioneers of Soviet Architecture: The Search for New Solutions in the 1920s and 1930s.* Translated by Alexander Lieven. New York: Rizzoli International Publications, Inc., 1987.

——. *Rodchenko: The Complete Work.* London: Thames and Hudson, 1986.

Kleihues, Josef P., and Heinrich Klotz, eds. *International Building Exhibition Berlin 1987: Examples of a New Architecture.* Translated by Ian Robeson. New York: Rizzoli, 1986.

Klotz, Heinrich. *The History of Postmodern Architecture.* Translated by Radka Donnell. Cambridge, Massachusetts: The MIT Press, 1988.

——. *20th Century Architecture: Drawings, Models, Furniture from the Exhibition of the Deutschen Architekturmuseums Frankfurt am Main.* New York: Rizzoli, 1989.

——, ed. *Vision der Moderne: Das Prinzip Konstruktion.* Exh. cat. Frankfurt: Deutsches Architekturmuseum Frankfurt a.M., 1986. Essays by Heinrich Klotz, Julius Posener, Michael Müller, Hans-Peter Schwarz, Andrea Gleiniger-Neumann, Volker Fischer, and Peter Blake.

Koolhaas, Rem. *Delirious New York: A Retroactive Manifesto for Manhattan.* New York: Oxford University Press, 1978.

Kostof, Spiro. *The City Assembled: The Elements of Urban Form Through History.* London: Thames and Hudson, 1992.

——. *The City Shaped: Urban Patterns and Meanings Through History.* London: Thames and Hudson, 1991.

——, ed. *The Architect: Chapters in the History of the Profession.* New York: Oxford University Press, 1977.

Krier, Leon, ed. *Albert Speer Architecture, 1932-1942.* Bruxelles: Archives d'architecture moderne, 1985.

——. *Leon Krier: Architecture and Urban Design, 1967-1992.* London: Academy Editions, 1992.

Krier, Rob. *Urban Space.* Translated by Christine Czechowski and George Black. New York: Rizzoli International Publications, 1979. Foreword by Colin Rowe.

Kruft, Hanno-Walter. *A History of Architectural Theory from Vitruvius to the Present.* Translated by Ronald Taylor, Elsie Callander, and Antony Wood. London: Zwemmer, 1994.

Kultermann, Udo. *New Japanese Architecture.* New York: Frederick A. Praeger, 1960.

——, ed. *Kenzo Tange 1946-1969: Architecture and Urban Design.* New York and London: Praeger Publishers, 1970.

Kunio Maekawa: Sources of Modern Japanese Architecture. Tokyo: Process Architecture Co., and New York: Van Nostrand Reinhold, 1984.

Küper, Marijke, and Ida van Zijl, eds. *Gerrit Th. Rietveld, 1888-1964: The Complete Works.* Utrecht: Centraal Museum, 1992.

Kurokawa, Kisho. *Each One a Hero: The Philosophy of Symbiosis.* Tokyo: Kodansha International, 1997.

La Arquitectura Mexicana del Siglo XX. Coordinated by Fernando González Gortázar. México, D.F.: Dirección General de Publicaciones del Consejo Nacional Para La Cultura y Las Artes, 1994.

La Città di Padova: Saggio di analisi urbana (Carlo Aymonino, Manilo Brusatin, Gianni Fabbri, Mauro Lena, Pasquale Lovero, and Aldo Rossi). Rome: Officina, 1970.

La ville: art et architecture en Europe 1870-1993. Exh. cat. Paris: Centre Georges Pompidou, 1994.

Lancaster, Robert. *Letchworth Garden City: Britain in Old Photographs.* Phoenix Mill, England: Alan Sutton Publishing Limited, 1995.

Landau, Sarah, and Carl W. Condit. *Rise of the New York Skyscraper, 1865-1913.* New Haven: Yale University Press, 1996.

Lane, Barbara Miller. *Architecture and Politics in Germany, 1918-1945.* Cambridge, Massachusetts: Harvard University Press, 1968.

Larson, Magali Sarfatti. *Behind the Postmodern Facade: Architectural Change in Late Twentieth-Century America.* Berkeley and Los Angeles: University of California Press, 1993.

L'art de l'ingénieur: constructeur, entrepreneur, inventeur. Exh. cat. Paris: Centre Georges Pompidou, 1997.

Le Corbusier: Architect of the Century. Exh. cat. London: Arts Council of Great Britain in collaboration with the Fondation Le Corbusier, Paris, 1987. Essays by William Curtis, Colin Rowe, Kenneth Frampton, Adrian Forty, Tim Benton, Christopher Green, Charlotte Benton, Sunand Prasad, and Judi Loach.

Le Corbusier. *The City of Tomorrow and Its Planning.* Translated by Frederick Etchells. New York: Payson & Clarke Ltd., n.d. [1929]; New York: Dover Publications, Inc., 1987.

——. *Precisions: On the Present State of Architecture and City Planning.* Cambridge, Massachusetts, and London: The MIT Press, 1991.

——. *The Radiant City: Elements of a Doctrine of Urbanism to be Used as the Basis of Our Machine-Age Civilization.* New York: Orion Press, 1967.

——. *Towards a New Architecture.* Translated by Frederick Etchells. New York: Praeger Publishers, 1960.

Leach, Neil, ed. *Rethinking Architecture: A Reader in Cultural Theory.* London: Routledge, 1997.

Lefebvre, Henri. *The Production of Space* (original French ed., 1974). Translated by Donald Nicholson-Smith. Oxford, England, and Cambridge, Massachusetts: Blackwell, 1991.

Lesnikowski, Wojciech. *The New French Architecture.* New York: Rizzoli, 1990.

Levin, Michael. *White City: International Style Architecture in Israel.* Exh. cat. Tel Aviv: The Tel Aviv Museum, 1984; special edition, 1994.

Levine, Neil. *The Architecture of Frank Lloyd Wright.* Princeton, New Jersey: Princeton University Press, 1996.

Liernur, Jorge Francisco. *America latina: Architettura, gli ultimi vent'anni.* Milan: Electa, 1990.

——. *Amerique latine, architecture 1965-1990.* Paris: Editions du Moniteur, 1990.

Lina Bo Bardi. Milan: Charta, and São Paulo: Instituto Lina Bo Bardi e P.M. Bardi, 1994.

Lissitzky, El. *Russia: An Architecture for World Revolution.* Translated by Eric Dluhosch. Cambridge, Massachusetts: The MIT Press, 1970.

L'oeuvre de Henri Prost; architecture et urbanism. Paris: Academie d'architecture, 1960.

Lozano, Eduardo E. *Community Design and the Culture of Cities: The Crossroad and the Wall.* Cambridge, England: Cambridge University Press, 1990.

Lucan, Jacques, ed. *OMA-Rem Koolhaas: Architecture 1970-1990.* New York: Princeton Architectural Press, 1991.

Lupton, Ellen, and J. Abbott Miller. *The Bathroom, the Kitchen, and the Aesthetics of Waste: A Process of Elimination.* Cambridge, Massachusetts: The MIT List Visual Arts Center, and New York: Princeton Architectural Press, 1992.

Lustenberger, Kurt. *Adolf Loos.* Zurich: Artemis Verlags-AG, 1994.

Lutyens, the Work of the English Architect Sir Edwin Lutyens. Exh. cat. London: Hayward Gallery and Arts Council of Great Britain, 1981. Essays by Colin Amery, Mary Lutyens, Jane Brown, John Cornforth, Gavin Stamp, and John Summerson.

Lynch, Kevin. *The Image of the City.* Cambridge, Massachusetts: Technology Press, 1960.

Macfadyen, Dugald. *Sir Ebenezer Howard and the Town Planning Movement.* Manchester, England: Manchester University Press, 1977.

Macrae-Gibson, Gavin. *The Secret Life of Buildings: An American Mythology for Modern Architecture.* Cambridge, Massachusetts: The MIT Press, 1985.

Mallgrave, Harry Francis, ed. *Otto Wagner: Reflections on the Raiment of Modernity.* Santa Monica: The Getty Center for the History of Art and the Humanities, 1993.

March, Lionel, and Judith Sheine, eds. *RM Schindler: Composition and Construction.* London: Academy Group, and Berlin: Ernst & Sohn, 1993. Essays by Harry Francis Mallgrave, August J. Sarnitz, Barbara Giella, Lionel March, Kathryn Smith, Elizabeth Moule, Stefanos Polyzoides, Judith Sheine, David Gebhard, and Esther McCoy.

Marciano, Ada Francesca. *Giuseppe Terragni: Opera Completa, 1925-1943.* Rome: Officina, 1987.

Marder, Tod A., ed. *The Critical Edge: Controversy in Recent American Architecture.* New Brunswick, New Jersey: Jane Voorhees Zimmerli Art Museum, Rutgers State University of New Jersey; and Cambridge, Massachusetts: The MIT Press, 1985.

Marks, Robert W. *The Dymaxion World of Buckminster Fuller.* New York: Reinhold Pub. Corp., 1960.

Marling, Karal Ann. *Designing Disney's Theme Parks: The Architecture of Reassurance.* Exh. cat. Montréal: Centre Canadien d'Architecture/ Canadian Centre for Architecture, and Paris: Flammarion, 1997.

Martin Wagner 1885-1957; Wohnungsbau und Weltstadtplanung: Die Rationalisierung des Glucks. Berlin: Akademie der Kunste, 1985.

McCoy, Esther. *Five California Architects.* New York: Reinhold, 1960.

——. *Richard Neutra.* New York: George Braziller, 1960.

McQuaid, Matilda. *Lilly Reich: Designer and Architect.* Exh. cat. New York: The Museum of Modern Art, 1996. Essays by Matilda McQuaid and Magdalena Droste.

Merkle, Judith A. *Management and Ideology: The Legacy of the International Scientific Management Movement.* Berkeley and Los Angeles: University of California Press, 1980.

Meyer, Esther da Costa. *The Work of Antonio Sant'Elia: Retreat into the Future.* New Haven: Yale University Press, 1995.

Miller, Mervyn. *Letchworth: The First Garden City.* Chichester, Sussex, England: Phillimore, 1989.

Mindlin, Henrique E. *Modern Architecture in Brazil.* New York: Reinhold Publishing Corporation, 1956.

Moos, Stanislaus von. *Le Corbusier, Elements of a Synthesis.* Cambridge, Massachusetts: The MIT Press, 1979.

Morphosis: Buildings and Projects 1989-1992. New York: Rizzoli, 1994.

Mumford, Lewis. *Art and Technics.* New York: Columbia University Press, 1952.

——. *The City in History: Its Origins and Transformations, and Its Prospects.* New York: Harcourt, Brace & World, 1961.

——. *The Highway and the City.* New York: Harcourt, Brace & World, 1963.

Mutlow, John V., ed. *Ricardo Legorreta Architects.* New York: Rizzoli, 1997.

Naylor, Gillian. *The Bauhaus Reassessed: Sources and Design Theory.* New York: E.P. Dutton, 1985.

Nelson, George. *Tomorrow's House: How to Plan Your Post-War Home Now.* New York: Simon & Schuster, 1945.

Nerdinger, Winfried, ed. *Bauhaus-Moderne im Nationalsozialismus Zwischen Anbiederung und Verfolgung.* Munich: Prestel-Verlag, 1993.

Nervi, Pier Luigi. *The Works of Pier Luigi Nervi.* Translated by Ernest Priefert. New York: F.A. Praeger, 1957. Preface by Pier Luigi Nervi, introduction by Ernesto N. Rogers, and explanatory notes to illustrations by Jurgen Jöedicke.

Neuhart, John, Marilyn Neuhart, and Ray Eames. *Eames Design: The Work of the Office of Charles and Ray Eames.* New York: Harry N. Abrams, Inc., 1989.

Neumann, Dietrich, ed. *Film Architecture: Set Designs from Metropolis to Blade Runner.* Exh. cat. Providence, Rhode Island: David Winton Bell Gallery, Brown University, and Munich: Prestel, 1995. Essays by Donald Albrecht, Anton Kaes, Dietrich Neumann, Anthony Vidler, and Michael Webb.

Neumann, Eckhard, ed. *Bauhaus and Bauhaus People: Personal Opinions and Recollections of Former Bauhaus Members and Their Contemporaries.* Translated by Eva Richter and Alba Lorman. New York: Van Nostrand Reinhold, 1970.

Neumeyer, Fritz. *The Artless Word: Mies van der Rohe on the Building Art.* Translated by Mark Jarzombek. Cambridge, Massachusetts: The MIT Press, 1991.

Newman, Oscar. *CIAM '59 in Otterlo, Group for the Research of Social and Visual Inter-relationships.* London: Alec Tiranti, 1961.

Noelle, Louise. *Luis Barragán: Búsqueda y Creatividad.* Mexico: Universidad Nacional Autónoma de México, D.F., 1996.

Noever, Peter. *Die Frankfurter Küche von Margarete Schütte-Lihotzky.* Berlin: Ernst & Sohn, 1992.

——, ed. *Margarete Schütte-Lihotzky: Soziale Architektur Zeitzeugin eines Jahrhunderts.* Exh. cat. Vienna: MAK - Österreichisches Museum für angewandte Kunst, Wien, and Böhlau, 1996. Essays by Renate Allmayer-Beck, Susanne Baumgartner-Haindl, Marion Lindner-Gross, and Christine Zwingl.

——, ed. *Tyrannei des Schönen: Architektur der Stalin-Zeit.* Exh. cat. Vienna: MAK - Österreichisches Museum für angewandte Kunst, Wien, 1994.

Ockman, Joan, compiler, with Edward Eigen. *Architecture Culture 1943-68: A Documentary Anthology.* New York: Columbia University Graduate School of Architecture, Planning and Preservation, and New York: Rizzoli, 1993.

Oscar Niemeyer. Milan: Arnoldo Mondadori Editore, 1975.

Overy, Paul, Lenneke Büller, Frank den Oudsten, and Bertus Mulder. *The Rietveld Schröder House.* Cambridge, Massachusetts: The MIT Press, 1988.

Pearson, Paul David. *Alvar Aalto and the International Style.* New York: Whitney Library of Design, 1978.

Pehnt, Wolfgang. *Expressionist Architecture.* London: Thames and Hudson, 1973.

Pevsner, Nikolaus, Sir. *An Outline of European Architecture.* Harmondsworth, Middlesex, England, and New York: Penguin Books, 1945.

——. *Pioneers of Modern Design, from William Morris to Walter Gropius.* Rev. ed. London: Harmondsworth, Middlesex, England, 1966.

Pfeiffer, Bruce Brooks, ed. *Frank Lloyd Wright Collected Writings.* 5 vols. New York: Rizzoli; Scottsdale, Arizona: Frank Lloyd Wright Foundation, 1992-1995. Introduction by Kenneth Frampton.

Phillips, Lisa. *Frederick Kiesler.* Exh. cat. New York: Whitney Museum of American Art, and New York: W.W. Norton & Company, 1989. Essays by Dieter Bogner, Cynthia Goodman, Barbara Lesák, Jeanne T. Newlin, and Lisa Phillips.

Pommer, Richard, and Christian F. Otto. *Weissenhof 1927 and the Modern Movement in Architecture.* Chicago: The University of Chicago Press, 1991.

Pommer, Richard, David Spaeth, and Kevin Harrington. *In the Shadow of Mies: Ludwig Hilberseimer, Architect, Educator and Urban Planner.* Chicago: The Art Institute of Chicago, and New York: Rizzoli International Publications, 1988.

Porphyrios, Demetri. *Sources of Modern Eclecticism: Studies on Alvar Aalto.* London: Academy Editions, and New York: St. Martin's Press, 1982.

Posener, Julius. *Hans Poelzig: Reflections on His Life and Work.* Translated by Christine Charlesworth. New York: Architectural History Foundation, and Cambridge, Massachusetts: The MIT Press, 1992.

Puppi, Lionello. *Oscar Niemeyer.* Rome: Officina Edizioni, 1996.

Quantrill, Malcolm. *Alvar Aalto: A Critical Study.* New York: New Amsterdam Books, 1983.

——. *Finnish Architecture and the Modernist Tradition.* London and New York: E & FN Spon, 1995.

Raymond, Antonin. *An Autobiography.* Rutland, Vermont: C.E. Tuttle, 1973.

Remembering the Future: The New York World's Fair From 1939 to 1964. Exh cat. Flushing: New York: The Queens Museum, and New York: Rizzoli, 1989. Essays by Rosemarie Haag Bletter, Morris Dickstein, Helen A. Harrison, Marc H. Miller, Sheldon J. Reaven, Robert Rosenblum, and Ileen Sheppard.

Rétrospective Kurokawa Kisho: Penser la symbiose - De l'âge de la machine à l'âge de la vie. Exh. cat. Paris: Maison de la culture du Japon à Paris, 1998.

Richard Meier Architect 1964/1984. New York: Rizzoli International Publications, 1984.

Richard Rogers + Architects. London: Academy Editions, and New York: St. Martin's Press, 1985.

Richardson, Margaret. *Sketches by Edwin Lutyens.* London: Academy Editions, 1994.

Riley, Terence. *The International Style: Exhibition 15 and The Museum of Modern Art.* Exh. cat. New York: Columbia University Graduate School of Architecture, and New York: Rizzoli International Publications, 1992. Foreword by Philip Johnson and preface by Bernard Tschumi.

——. *Light Construction.* Exh. cat. New York: The Museum of Modern Art, 1995.

Riley, Terence, and Peter Reed, eds. *Frank Lloyd Wright Architect.* Exh. cat. New York: The Museum of Modern Art, 1994. Essays by Anthony Alofsin, William Cronon, Kenneth Frampton, Terence Riley, and Gwendolyn Wright.

Risse, Heike. *Frühe Moderne in Frankfurt am Main 1920-33.* Frankfurt am Main: Societats-Verlag, 1984.

Rob Krier. Architectural Monographs No. 30. London: Academy Editions, 1993.

Rob. Mallet-Stevens: architecture, mobilier, décoration - ouvrage collectif. Paris: Action Artistique de Paris, 1986.

Robbins, Bruce, ed. *The Phantom Public Sphere.* Minneapolis: University of Minnesota Press, 1993.

Robbins, David, ed. *The Independent Group: Postwar Britain and the Aesthetics of Plenty.* Exh. cat. Cambridge, Massachusetts: The MIT Press, 1990. Essays by Lawrence Alloway, Theo Crosby, Barry Curtis, Diane Kirkpatrick, David Mellor, David Robbins, Denise Scott Brown, Alison and Peter Smithson, and David Thistlewood.

Roberts, Jennifer Davis. *Norman Bel Geddes: An Exhibition of Theatrical and Industrial Designs.* Exh cat. Austin, Texas: Michener Galleries, Humanities Research Center, The University of Texas at Austin, 1979.

Roca, Miguel Angel. *The Architecture of Latin America.* London: Academy Editions, 1995.

Rosa, Joseph. *A Constructed View: The Architectural Photography of Julius Shulman.* New York: Rizzoli, 1994. Essay by Esther McCoy.

Ross, Michael Franklin. *Beyond Metabolism: The New Japanese Architecture.* New York: Architectural Record Books, 1978.

Rossi, Aldo. *L'architettura della città.* Padua: Marsilio Editori, 1966. English ed., *The Architecture of the City.* Translated by Diane Ghirardo and Joan Ockman. Cambridge, Massachusetts: The MIT Press, 1982.

Rowe, Colin. *The Mathematics of the Ideal Villa and Other Essays.* Cambridge, Massachusetts: The MIT Press, 1976.

Rowe, Colin, and Fred Koetter. *Collage City.* Cambridge, Massachusetts: The MIT Press, 1978.

Rowe, Peter G. *Modernity and Housing.* Cambridge, Massachusetts: The MIT Press, 1995.

Rudofsky, Bernard. *Architecture without Architects, a Short Introduction to Non-Pedigreed Architecture.* New York: Doubleday, 1964.

Russian Modernism: The Collections of the Getty Research Institute for the History of Art and the Humanities, 1. Santa Monica, California: The Getty Research Institute for the History of Art and the Humanities, 1997.

Ryabushin, Alexander. *Landmarks of Soviet Architecture, 1917-1991.* New York: Rizzoli, 1992.

Saarinen, Aline B., ed. *Eero Saarinen on His Work: A Selection of Buildings Dating from 1947 to 1967 with Statements by the Architect.* Rev. ed. New Haven and London: Yale University Press, 1968.

Saliga, Pauline, and Mary Woolever, eds. *The Architecture of Bruce Goff, 1904-1982: Design for the Continuous Present.* Exh. cat. Chicago: The Art Institute of Chicago, and Munich and New York: Prestel. Essays by Jack Golden, David G. DeLong, Sidney K. Robinson, Timothy Samuelson, Philip B. Welch, and Joe D. Price.

Saito, Yutaka, supervisor; Naomi Miwa, ed. *Felix Candela.* Tokyo: TOTO Shuppan, 1995.

Saito, Yutaka, supervisor. *Luis Barragan.* Tokyo: TOTO Shuppan, 1992.

Sanders, Joel, ed. *Stud: Architectures of Masculinity.* New York: Princeton Architectural Press, 1996.

Sasaki, Hiroshi, ed. *Jacob Tchernykhov and his Architectural Fantasies.* Tokyo: Process Architecture Pub. Co., 1981.

Saunders, William S. *Modern Architecture: Photographs by Ezra Stoller.* New York: Harry N. Abrams, 1990.

Schulze, Franz. *Mies van der Rohe: A Critical Biography.* Chicago and London: The University of Chicago Press, 1985.

Schumacher, Thomas L. *The Danteum: A Study in the Architecture of Literature.* Princeton, New Jersey: Princeton Architectural Press, 1985.

——. *Surface and Symbol: Giuseppe Terragni and the Architecture of Italian Rationalism.* New York: Princeton Architectural Press, 1991.

Schwartz, Frederic, ed. *Mother's House: The Evolution of Vanna Venturi's House in Chestnut Hill.* New York: Rizzoli, 1992. Preface by Aldo Rossi. Essays by Vincent Scully and Robert Venturi.

Segre, Roberto. *América Latina Fim de Milênio: Raízes e Perspectivas de Sua Arquitetura.* Translated by Luis Eduardo de Lima Brandïo. São Paulo: Studio Nobel, 1991.

Scully, Vincent. *American Architecture and Urbanism.* New York: Praeger Publishers, 1969.

Segre, Roberto. *Arquitectura y urbanismo modernos; capitalismo y socialismo.* Havana: Editorial Arte y Literatura, 1988.

——, ed. *Latin America in Its Architecture.* Translated by Edith Grossman. New York: Holmes & Meier Publishers, Inc., 1981.

Sert, José Luis. *Can Our Cities Survive?* Cambridge, Massachusetts: Harvard University Press, and London: Oxford University Press, 1947.

Sharp, Dennis. *Modern Architecture and Expressionism.* London: Longmans, 1966.

——. *A Visual History of Twentieth-Century Architecture.* Greenwich, Connecticut: New York Graphic Society, 1972.

Sherwood, Roger, ed. *Apartment Footprints 2.* Los Angeles: School of Architecture, University of Southern Architecture, 1990.

Shkapich, Kim. *John Hejduk - Mask of Medusa: Works, 1947-1983.* New York: Rizzoli International Publications, 1985.

Silvetti, Jorge, ed. *Amancio Williams.* Exh. cat. Cambridge, Massachusetts: Harvard University Graduate School of Design, and New York: Rizzoli, 1987.

6th International Architecture Exhibition - Sensing the Future: The Architect as Seismograph. Exh. cat. Venice: La Biennale di Venezia, 1996.

Slessor, Catherine. *Eco-tech: Sustainable Architecture and High Technology.* New York: Thames and Hudson, 1997.

S,M,L,XL: Office for Metropolitan Architecture, Rem Koolhaas, and Bruce Mau. New York: The Monacelli Press, 1995.

Smith, Elizabeth A. T. *Urban Revisions: Current Projects for the Public Realm.* Exh. cat. Los Angeles: The Museum of Contemporary Art, Los Angeles, and Cambridge, Massachusetts: The MIT Press, 1994. Essays by Mike Davis, M. Patricia Fernandez-Kelly, Richard Sennett, Elizabeth A.T. Smith, and Gwendolyn Wright.

Smithson, Alison, ed. *Team 10 Primer.* Cambridge, Massachusetts: The MIT Press, 1968.

Smithson, Alison and Peter. *Ordinariness and Light: Urban Theories 1952-1960 and Their Application in a Building Project 1963-1970.* London: Faber and Faber, 1970.

——. *Without Rhetoric: An Architectural Aesthetic, 1955-1972.* Cambridge, Massachusetts: The MIT Press, 1974.

Snyder, Robert, ed. *Buckminster Fuller: An Autobiographical Monologue/Scenario.*New York: St. Martin's Press, 1980.

Soja, Edward. *Postmodern Geographies: The Reassertion of Space in Critical Social Theory.* London and New York: Verso, 1989.

Soleri, Paolo. *Visionary Cities: The Arcology of Paolo Soleri.* New York: Praeger Publishers, 1970.

Sorkin, Michael, ed. *Variations on a Theme Park: The New American City and the End of Public Space.* New York: Hill and Wang, 1992.

Starr, S. Frederick. *Melnikov: Solo Architect in a Mass Society.* Princeton, New Jersey: Princeton University Press, 1978.

Steele, James. *Hassan Fathy.* London: Academy Editions, and New York: St. Martin's Press, 1988. Introduction by A. Wahed El Wakil.

——, ed. *Architecture for a Changing World.* Exh. cat. Seville, Spain: Fundación Internacional de Síntesis Arquitectónica, and Geneva, Switzerland: The Aga Khan Trust for Culture, 1995.

Stein, Clarence S. *Toward New Towns for America.* Liverpool: University Press of Liverpool, and Chicago: Public Administration Service, 1951. Introduction by Lewis Mumford.

Stern, Robert A.M. *New Directions in American Architecture.* New York: George Braziller, 1969.

Stern, Robert A.M., Thomas Mellins, and David Fishman. *New York 1960: Architecture and Urbanism between the Second World War and the Bicentennial.* New York: The Monacelli Press, 1995.

Stewart, David B. *The Making of a Modern Japanese Architecture: 1868 to the Present.* Tokyo and New York: Kodansha International, 1987.

Sussman, Elizabeth, ed. *On the Passage of a Few People Through a Rather Brief Moment in Time: The Situationist International 1957-1972.* Exh. cat. Boston: The Institute of Contemporary Art, and Cambridge, Massachusetts: The MIT Press, 1989. Essays by Mark Francis, Peter Wollen, Troels Andersen, Mirella Bandini, Thomas Y. Levin, and Greil Marcus.

Sutcliffe, Anthony. *Towards the Planned City: Germany, Britain, the United States and France 1780-1914.* New York: St. Martin's Press, 1981.

——, ed. *Metropolis, 1890-1940.* Chicago: University of Chicago Press, 1984.

——, ed. *The Rise of Modern Urban Planning, 1800-1914*. London: Mansell, 1980.

Tafuri, Manfredo. *Progetto e Utopia: Architettura e sviluppo capitalistico*. Rome: Bari, 1973.

——. *The Sphere and the Labyrinth: Avant-Gardes and Architecture from Piranesi to the 1970s*. Translated by Pellegrino d'Acierno and Robert Connolly. Cambridge, Massachusetts: The MIT Press, 1987.

Tafuri, Manfredo, and Francesco Dal Co. *Modern Architecture*. Translated by Robert Erich Wolf. New York: Harry N. Abrams, Inc., 1979.

Tarkhanov, Alexei, and Sergei Kavtaradze. *Architecture of the Stalin Era*. New York: Rizzoli International Publications, Inc., 1992.

Taut, Bruno. *Houses and People of Japan*. Second ed. Tokyo: Sanseido Co., 1958.

Taylor, Frederick Winslow. *The Principles of Scientific Management*. London and New York: Harper & Brothers, 1911.

Tegethoff, Wolf. *Mies van der Rohe: The Villas and Country Houses*. Exh. cat. New York: The Museum of Modern Art, 1985.

Timms, Edward, and David Kelley, eds. *Unreal City: Urban Experience in Modern European Literature and Art*. London: Manchester University Press, 1985.

Toca, Antonio, ed. *Nueva Arquitectura en América Latina: Presente y Futuro*. Mexico, Naucalpan: Ediciones G. Gili, 1990.

Tony Garnier: L'Oeuvre complète. Exh. cat. Paris: Centre Georges Pompidou, 1990. Essays by Bruno Henri Vayssière, Alain Charre, Anthony Vidler, Pierre Pinon, Oliver Cinqualbre, Pierre Vaisse, and Alain Guiheux.

Torre, Susana, ed. *Women in American Architecture: A Historic and Contemporary Perspective*. New York: Whitney Library of Design, 1977.

Torroja Miret, Eduardo. *The Structures of Eduardo Torroja; an Autobiography of Engineering Accomplishment*. New York: F.W. Dodge Corp., 1958. Foreword by Mario Salvadori.

Tournikiotis, Panayotis. *Adolf Loos*. New York: Princeton Architectural Press, 1994.

Toyo Ito. London: Academy Editions, 1995.

Treib, Marc. *An Everyday Modernism: The Houses of William Wurster*. Exh. cat. San Francisco: San Francisco Museum of Modern Art, and Berkeley and Los Angeles: University of California Press, 1995. Essays by David Gebhard, Daniel Gregory, Greg Hise, Dorothée Imbert, Alan R. Michelson, Richard C. Peters and Caitlin Lempres, Marc Treib, and Gwendolyn Wright.

Troy, Nancy J. *The De Stijl Environment*. Cambridge, Massachusetts: The MIT Press, 1983.

Turner, J.F. *Housing by People: Towards Autonomy in Building Environments*. London: Marion Boyars, 1976.

Tzonis, Alexander, and Liane Lefaivre. *Architecture in Europe Since 1968: Memory and Invention*. New York: Rizzoli, 1992.

Underwood, David. *Oscar Niemeyer and Brazilian Free-form Modernism*. New York: G. Braziller, 1994.

——. *Oscar Niemeyer and the Architecture of Brazil*. New York: Rizzoli, 1994.

Unwin, Raymond. *Nothing Gained by Overcrowding! How the Garden City Type of Development May Benefit Both Owner and Occupier*. Third ed. London: Garden Cities and Town Planning Association, 1912.

Vale, Lawrence J. *Architecture, Power, and National Identity*. New Haven: Yale University Press, 1992.

Van der Ryn, Sim, and Peter Calthorpe. *Sustainable Communities: A New Design Synthesis for Cities, Suburbs and Towns*. San Francisco: Sierra Club Books, 1986.

Ven, Cornelius van de. *Space in Architecture: The Evolution of a New Idea in the Theory of the Modern Movements*. Assen/Maastricht: Van Gorcum, 1987.

Venturi, Robert. *Complexity and Contradiction in Architecture*. New York: The Museum of Modern Art, 1966.

Venturi, Robert, Denise Scott Brown, and Steven Izenour. *Learning from Las Vegas*. Cambridge, Massachusetts: The MIT Press, 1972.

Vidler, Anthony. *The Architectural Uncanny: Essays in the Modern Unhomely*. Cambridge, Massachusetts: The MIT Press, 1992.

Visionary Drawings of Architecture and Planning: 20th Century through the 1960s. Exh. cat. Compiled by George R. Collins. Cambridge, Massachusetts, and London: The MIT Press, 1979.

Wachsmann, Konrad. *The Turning Point in Building: Structure and Design*. Translated by Thomas E. Burton. New York: Reinhold Pub. Corp., 1961.

Walden, Russell, ed. *The Open Hand: Essays on Le Corbusier*. Cambridge, Massachusetts: The MIT Press, 1977.

Ward, Stephen V., ed. *The Garden City: Past, Present and Future*. London and New York: E & FN Spon, 1992.

Weisman, Leslie Kanes. *Discrimination By Design: A Feminist Critique of the Man-made Environment*. Urbana: University of Illinois Press, 1992.

Welsh, John. *Modern House*. London: Phaidon Press, 1995.

Weltge, Sigrid Wortmann. *Women's Work: Textile Art from the Bauhaus*. San Francisco: Chronicle Books, 1993.

Weston, Richard. *Alvar Aalto*. London: Phaidon Press, 1995.

——. *Villa Mairea: Alvar Aalto*. London: Phaidon Press, 1992.

Whitford, Frank, ed. *The Bauhaus: Masters and Students by Themselves*. Woodstock, New York: The Overlook Press, 1993.

Wiebenson, Dora. *Tony Garnier: The Cité Industrielle*. New York: George Braziller, 1969.

Willis, Carol. *Form Follows Finance: Skyscrapers and Skylines in New York and Chicago*. New York: Princeton Architectural Press, 1995.

Wilson, Elizabeth. *The Sphinx in the City: Urban Life, the Control of Disorder, and Women*. Berkeley and Los Angeles: University of California Press, 1992.

Wingler, Hans M. *The Bauhaus*. Cologne: Verlag Gebr. Rasch & Co., Bramsche and M DuMont Schaubert, 1962; Cambridge, Massachusetts: The MIT Press, 1993.

Wodehouse, Lawrence. *The Roots of International Style Architecture*. West Cornwall, Connecticut: Locust Hill Press, 1991.

Woods, Shadrach. *Candilis Josic Woods: Building for People*. New York: Frederick A. Praeger, Publishers, 1968. Introduction by Jürgen Joedicke.

The Work of Charles and Ray Eames: A Legacy of Invention. Exh. cat. Washington, D.C.: Library of Congress, and New York: Harry N. Abrams, 1997. Essays by Donald Albrecht, Beatriz Colomina, Joseph Giovannini, Alan Lightman, Hélène Lipstadt, and Philip and Phylis Morrison.

Wrede, Stuart. *The Architecture of Erik Gunnar Asplund*. Cambridge, Massachusetts: The MIT Press, 1980.

Wrede, Stuart, and W.H. Adams, eds. *Denatured Visions: Landscape and Culture in the Twentieth Century*. Exh. cat. New York: The Museum of Modern Art , 1991.

Wright, Frank Lloyd. *The Living City*. New York: Horizon Press, 1958.

Wright, Gwendolyn. *Building the Dream: A Social History of Housing in America*. New York: Pantheon Books, 1981.

Zabalbeascoa, Anatxu. *The House of the Architect*. New York: Rizzoli, 1995.

Zabel, Craig, and Susan Scott Munshower, eds. *American Public Architecture: European Roots and Native Expressions*. University Park, Pennsylvania: Pennsylvania State University, 1989.

Zevi, Bruno. *Saper vedere l'architettura; saggi sull'interpretazione spaziale dell'architettura*. Turin: G. Einaudi, 1948 (*Architecture as Space; How to Look at Architecture*. Translated by Milton Gendel. New York: Horizon Press, rev. ed., 1974.)

——. *Storia dell'architettura moderna*. Second ed. Torino: Einaudi, 1953.

Zukowsky, John, ed. *Chicago Architecture and Design 1923-1993: Reconfiguration of an American Metropolis*. Exh. cat. Munich: Prestel-Verlag, and Chicago: The Art Institute of Chicago, 1993. Essays by Mark J. Bouman, David Brodherson, Robert Bruegmann, Dennis P. Doordan, Neil Harris, Victor Margolin, Ross Miller, Deborah Fulton Rau, Sidney K. Robinson, Pauline Saliga, Franz Schulze, R. Stephen Sennott, Stanley Tigerman, Carol Willis, Wim de Wit, and John Zukowsky.

_____. *Chicago Architecture 1872-1922: Birth of a Metropolis*. Exh. cat. Munich: Prestel-Verlag, and Chicago: The Art Institute of Chicago, 1987. Essays by Robert Bruegmann, Sally Chappell, Meredith L. Clausen, Joan E. Draper, Roula M. Geraniotis, Elaine Harrington, Neil Harris, Heinrich Klotz, Gerald R. Larson, Henri Loyrette, Ross Miller, Martha Pollak, Thomas J. Schlereth, Stanley Tigerman, David Van Zanten, Lauren S. Weingarden, C.W. Westfall, Richard Guy Wilson, and John Zukowsky.

——. *The Many Faces of Modern Architecture: Building in Germany Between the World Wars*. Munich and New York: Prestel, 1994. Essays by Kennie Ann Laney-Lupton, Wojciech Lesnikowski, and John Zukowsky.

INDEX

PHOTO CREDITS

All images courtesy of the artist, architect, or institution named in the accompanying captions unless otherwise indicated below.

Property of the Casa-Museo Luis Barragán, p. 8, 311 (photo credit Alberto Moreno); © Julius Shulman, pp. 10, 72, 87, 88 top, 126, 139, 155, 219, 261, 276, 289, 306, 308, 315 top, 317; Rollin R. LaFrance, p. 24; © The Architectural Archives of the University of Pennsylvania, p. 30; © 1997 The Museum of Modern Art, New York, pp. 32, 44 bottom; Gottscho, p. 33; Studio Thomas Struth, Düsseldorf, pp. 36, 195; 1997 © Massachusetts Institute of Technology. All images produced as part of the project UNBUILT at Department of Architecture, Massachusetts Institute of Technology. The project is co-led by Takehiko Nagakura and Kent Larson with the funding of TAKENAKA Corporation of Tokyo, rendering by Andrzej Zarzycki, model by Mark Sich and Dan Brick, pp. 43, 146; © Pedro E. Guerrero, pp. 50 bottom, 140 bottom; Copyright Fondation Le Corbusier, pp. 51, 66 top, 105, 114, 115, 130, 132 top, 201 all, 202 top, 212, 208, 209, 210, 250 top, 260, 284 top, 286 all, 287, 288; © Grant Mudford, p. 53; Copyright © 1998 Frank Lloyd Wright Foundation, Scottsdale, AZ, pp. 56 bottom, 94 bottom, 153 bottom, 249, 250 bottom; © 1997 Board of Trustees, National Gallery of Art, Washington, p. 59 top; © August Sander Archiv/SK Stiftung Kultur, VG Bild-Kunst, Bonn 1997, p. 62 top; Copyright 1960 Allegra Fuller Snyder. Courtesy, Buckminster Fuller Institute, Santa Barbara, p. 64; Aga Khan Trust for Culture, pp. 66 bottom (© Rena Gunay), 70 bottom (© C. Avedissian), 71 (© Kamkan Adle); Richard Bryant/ Arcaid, p. 67, 206 bottom (© A. Kawatli); Courtesy Steven Holl Architects, p. 68; Ezra Stoller © Esto, pp. 69, 74, 183 both, 187, 193, 211, 266, 267; Courtesy of Kenzo Tange Associates Urbanists-Architects, pp. 70 top, 80, 81, 94 top and 96 (94 and 96 photo credit Osamu Murai), 176 (photo credit Yasuhiro Ishimoto); Courtesy of Renzo Piano Building Workshop, photo credit Michel Denance, p. 76 top; Courtesy of Kazuo Shinohara Office, photo credit Masao Arai, p. 76 bottom; Courtesy of Nicholas Grimshaw & Partners, photo credit © Peter Cook/VIEW, p. 77; © Paul Warchol, p. 78; © Disney Enterprises, Inc., p. 83; Courtesy of Enric Miralles Arquitectos, p. 88 bottom; Courtesy of Kikutake Architects, photo credit Yukio Futagawa, p. 89; © Scott Frances/Esto, pp. 90 top, 227; Courtesy of Toyo Ito & Associates, photo credit Tomio Ohashi, p. 90 bottom; Photograph © 1989 The Metropolitan Museum of Art, p. 92; Courtesy of Richard Rogers Partnership, photo Richard Bryant, p. 95; Courtesy of Pei Cobb Freed & Partners, photo credit Paul Warchol, p. 98; © Jeff Goldberg/Esto, pp. 100, 121; Courtesy of The Academy of Motion Picture Arts and Sciences, p. 107; © Tim Street-Porter/Esto, p. 120; Courtesy of Herman Miller, Inc., p. 124; © Hans Werlemann, Courtesy of Office for Metropolitan Architecture, p. 129; Courtesy of School of Architecture, Princeton University, pp. 131, 132 bottom, 133 bottom, 134, 136, 138, 140 top and center, 141 all, 144, 149, 151, 152, 153 top, 157; Dana Hutt, p. 133 top; Courtesy of Office for Metropolitan Architecture, p. 135; Josef Hoflehner, courtesy of Coop Himmelb(l)au, p. 150 top; Courtesy of the Marian Goodman Gallery, New York, p. 161; Courtesy of Diller + Scofidio, pp. 162, 163; Courtesy of Thomas Leeser, p. 164; Courtesy of van berkel & bos architectuurbureau bv, p. 165; Courtesy of Kunio Maekawa Associates, Architects & Engineers, © Yosio Watanabe, p. 177; Courtesy of Sakakura Associates, Architects & Engineers, photo par Kollar, p. 178 bottom; Courtesy of Hajime Yatsuka, p. 179 both right; Tadao Ando Architect & Associates, p. 181 both; UPI/Corbis-Bettmann, pp. 194 top, 257 top; Copyright Mary Lutyens, p. 198 top; Country Life Picture Library, p. 198 bottom; Philippe Ploquin, Moroccan National Tourist Office, p. 199; © Jerry Spearman, collection of Moshe Safdie and Associates, p. 215; Ralph Lerner Architect, p. 220 bottom; J. Apicella/ Cesar Pelli & Associates Inc., p. 223; Fotostudio Otto, p. 230; © 1997, The Art Institute of Chicago, All Rights Reserved, pp. 231, 259; © Wayne Andrews/Esto, p. 256; Studio Basset, Caluire (Lyon), p. 258 top; © Stewart Shaw, p. 262; Venturi, Scott-Brown and Associates, p. 273; Jorge Francisco Liernur, pp. 279, 281, 284 bottom, 285, 290, 294, 295, 297, 298 bottom, 299, 300, 312, 315 bottom; Courtesy of Margara Pani, photo credit Campañia Mexicana Aereofoto S.A., p. 292; Courtesy of Louise Noelle Mereles, photo credit Juan Guzmán, pp. 293, 301; Courtesy of Wladimir Teixeira de Souza Rosa, pp. 302, 303; William P. Bruder, 304 top; Luis Hossaka, p. 304 bottom; © Norman McGrath, p. 307; © Rafael Viñoly Architects, p. 309; Vicente del Amo Hernández, p. 314 all; Courtesy of TEN Arquitectos, p. 319; © Hodgetts + Fung, p. 320.